Learn Java
with JBuilder 6

JOHN ZUKOWSKI

Apress™

Learn Java with JBuilder 6

Copyright © 2002 by John Zukowski

ISBN (pbk): 1-893115-98-4

Printed and bound in the United States of America 12345678910

Trademarked names may appear in this book. Rather than use a trademark symbol with every occurrence of a trademarked name, we use the names only in an editorial fashion and to the benefit of the trademark owner, with no intention of infringement of the trademark.

Technical Reviewer: Rob Castaneda

Editorial Directors: Dan Appleman, Peter Blackburn, Gary Cornell, Jason Gilmore, Karen Watterson, John Zukowski

Managing Editor and Project Manager: Grace Wong

Copy Editor: Nicole LeClerc

Production Editor: Kari Brooks

Compositor: Impressions Book and Journal Services, Inc.

Indexer: Nancy A. Guenther

Cover Designer: Tom Debolski

Marketing Manager: Stephanie Rodriguez

Distributed to the book trade in the United States by Springer-Verlag New York, Inc., 175 Fifth Avenue, New York, NY, 10010

and outside the United States by Springer-Verlag GmbH & Co. KG, Tiergartenstr. 17, 69112 Heidelberg, Germany.

In the United States, phone 1-800-SPRINGER, email orders@springer-ny.com, or visit http://www.springer-ny.com.

Outside the United States, fax +49 6221 345229, email orders@springer.de, or visit http://www.springer.de.

For information on translations, please contact Apress directly at 901 Grayson Street, Suite 204, Berkeley, CA 94710.

Phone 510-549-5930, fax: 510-549-5939, email info@apress.com, or visit http://www.apress.com.

Contents at a Glance

Contents

Skill 17 Working with Menus *453*

Skill 18 Creating a JToolBar *471*

Skill 19 Internationalization *487*

Skill 20 Customizing JBuilder *513*

Skill 21 Debugging Multithreaded Programs *537*

About the Technical Reviewer

Rob Castaneda is a senior architect and instructor at CustomWare Asia Pacific, where he provides clients with architecture consulting and training in Java, J2EE, CORBA, and XML-based application and integration servers throughout Australia, Asia, and the United States. Rob previously held various positions at Borland, most recently as a Java software engineer. Rob has contributed to and reviewed various technical books and articles.

Acknowledgments

THANKS GO OUT TO EVERYONE at Borland for continuing to create such a great tool. I'd also like to thank everyone at Apress for putting up with me in getting this book out, especially Grace Wong, Nicole LeClerc, Kari Brooks, and Stephanie Rodriguez. Special thanks go out to Rob Castaneda of CustomWare Asia Pacific, my technical reviewer, for finding missing steps and invalid explanations in my text. Through everyone's hard work, the end result is all the better. Any remaining problems are my own fault, not theirs. Hopefully, there won't be many found.

For putting up with my wife during her root canal I'd like to thank Doctor Ayotte. Congratulations to the Patriots for finally winning the big one. For actually showing up when they said they would to move my DSL line, thanks go out to ADS Communications (http://www.adscomm.com/). Congrats to Java Jill for leaving the realm of the evil empire and coming back to the good side. Good luck with BEA. For Michele and the gang at The Red Cross, sorry for putting you off. Now that the book is done I should be back. And thanks to Bernice and Mike at Mail Boxes Etc. for all their help.

As always, thanks to my wife Lisa and our pup Jaeger. Sometimes I wonder why Lisa puts up with the long hours. Thanks for the support and encouragement. We both know Jaeger just hangs around for the free food, walks, and cookies. ☺

Introduction

SUN PROVIDES A SERIES of free tools with the Java Software Development Kit (SDK) to create Java programs. All of these tools are command-line driven. Add in your own text editor and you have a series of standalone programs to help you write, compile, package, and run your Java programs. If you are accustomed to developing within a visual programming environment such as Borland's Delphi or Microsoft's Visual Basic, using the SDK is like returning to the dark ages. It certainly gets the job done, but there has to be a better way.

Borland's JBuilder is that better way. It is a fully integrated development environment (IDE) where you can edit, compile, test, and debug your programs for rapid application development. JBuilder creates 100% Pure Java solutions and is written in Java itself. It supports features such as inner classes, Java archives (JAR files), Java Database Connectivity (JDBC), the Java Foundation Classes (JFC), and Enterprise JavaBeans.

JBuilder also supports JavaBeans technology. JavaBeans is the component architecture of Java. With it, you no longer create monolithic applications; you have only to worry about creating the ever-smaller pieces. Then, all you have to do is connect the beans to create your working programs. JBuilder is the tool to use to both create the JavaBeans components and connect the JavaBeans.

With Borland's JBuilder, you can create Java programs fast, whether by hand, with the help of the many wizards, or by pointing and clicking. With the help of this book, you'll get up to speed with JBuilder even faster.

Who This Book Is For

Whether you have beginning or expert computer skills, if you're looking for a hands-on way to learn about JBuilder—to prepare for a job interview, to create an applet or application, to learn about JavaBeans, or just for the fun of it—this book is for you. It's a learn-by-doing book that requires only enough computer know-how to be able to point, click, and type. You don't have to be a developer or programmer, although it certainly doesn't hurt.

After you've completed this book, you'll be able to do the following:

- Install and configure JBuilder 6

- Understand Java syntax

- Use JBuilder wizards

- Create graphical Java programs

- Build and connect JavaBeans by hand and automatically

- Work with multithreaded programs

- Use the JBuilder debugger

All exercises include step-by-step instructions. As JBuilder 6 runs on Windows, Linux, Solaris, and Macintosh platforms, you should be able to make your way through all the examples on all these platforms. Plenty of illustrations and tips accompany the instructions.

How This Book Is Organized

This book is divided into three parts. Each builds on the skills and knowledge developed in the earlier sections.

Part One: Starting Out

In Part One, you'll learn about the basics of Java programming in general while you explore some specific pieces of the JBuilder tool. You'll be introduced to Java applets and applications, Java syntax, and the applet life cycle. You'll then learn about creating graphical programs, and you'll finish up working with files.

Part Two: Digging into JavaBeans

In Part Two, you'll learn about JavaBeans: what they are, how they work, and how to create your own beans. You'll also learn about connecting, creating, and customizing beans.

Part Three: Advanced Skills

In Part Three, you'll learn about working with menus and toolbars, internationalization, and customizing JBuilder to your liking. You'll be introduced to the JBuilder debugger and end the book with a look at features on versioning, UML visualization, refactoring, testing, and EJB design.

Online JBuilder Support

There are many available sources of online support for JBuilder.

- There is an online FAQ/forum for JBuilder at jGuru
  (`http://www.jguru.com/faq/JBuilder`).

- There is a mailing list on Yahoo! Groups for JBuilder questions at
  `http://groups.yahoo.com/group/jbuilder-dev/`.

- JBuilder's home at Borland is `http://www.borland.com/jbuilder/`. They
  offer newsgroups (`http://www.borland.com/newsgroups/#jbuilder`) and
  other community-related resources (`http://community.borland.com/java/`).

- You can get a third-party look at the latest news from Borland from
  Dr. Bob's JBuilder Machine at `http://www.drbob42.com/JBuilder/`.

Conventions Used in This Book

This book uses the following typographical conventions:

- Monospace font (`foo.gif`, for example) is used for program code and the
  names of files, directories, paths, methods, classes, properties, objects,
  keywords, parameters, and URLs.

- Italic is used for variable file or directory names; that is, the portions of
  instructions that you modify and still have the instructions work, such as
  installdir, meaning the name of *your* installation directory.

- Bold is used for entries that must be typed exactly as shown
  (**SimpleBeanInfo**), form field settings (Set the title to **Objective**), and
  portions of lines that must be entered as is (prompt> **appletviewer
  MyApplet.html**). Also, in source code listings, some lines are highlighted
  in bold. This is just to focus your attention to those lines, as directed by
  the text.

Special information is set off from the regular text as Notes, Tips, and Warnings:

NOTE *Notes contain information that needs to be emphasized.*

TIP *Tips help clarify the text and make you productive with JBuilder quickly.*

WARNING *Warnings point out potential trouble spots.*

About the CD

On the CD accompanying this book you'll find the book's source, the JBuilder product, and some additional tools.

You can find the book's source in the BookSource subdirectory. It is both in the BookSource.jar file and spread out across subdirectories, one per project. The class files are present, too, in case you just want to run the examples.

The CD includes a 30-day trial of the JBuilder Enterprise Edition for Windows, Linux, Solaris, and Mac OS X. Once the 30-day trial period expires, the tool reverts to the free Personal Edition of the tool. You must go to http://www.borland.com/jbuilder/keys/jb6_ent_steps.html to get a license key before you can use the tool. Skill 1 explains how to install the tool and get the license key.

You'll find two supplemental tools on the CD. The first is a free program called jbWheel that adds mouse wheel support to JBuilder. The second is a trial edition of Optimizeit Suite. To get a 14-day license for this, you'll need to visit http://www.optimizeit.com/learnjava.html. Optimizeit is useful for optimizing program performance during development.

Enjoy.

Part One

Starting Out

Exploring JBuilder

- Introducing JBuilder

- Installing JBuilder

- Getting a registration key

- Working in the JBuilder environment

- Creating and running a Java applet

- Understanding the source

- Introducing the basics of object-oriented programming

Introducing JBuilder

JBuilder is Borland Software Corporation's visual Java development environment. With the award-winning JBuilder product, you can quickly and easily build Java programs on your computer for delivery on any Java-enabled hardware platform. In fact, JBuilder itself is written in Java and works on Microsoft Windows 98/2000/NT4, Linux, Solaris, and Mac OS X systems.

Instead of using the independent command-line tools provided with Sun Microsystems' Java 2 Software Development Kit (SDK, aka Java Development Kit or JDK), JBuilder provides a tightly integrated, rapid application development (RAD) environment. With the many wizards and the rich Object Gallery, JBuilder can help you create applets for inclusion on your Web pages, standalone Java applications, and servlets for integration into your Web server.

JBuilder is also built to take full advantage of JavaBeans technology. Beans enable you to use small, reusable software components to create full-blown applications quickly and easily. Instead of having to build programs from scratch, with JavaBeans components you can easily integrate pieces from disparate sources to create fully functional programs with minimal effort. With JBuilder, this support is seamless.

In addition, JBuilder easily integrates with databases. With a rich set of Java Database Connectivity (JDBC) components, you can connect to any JDBC- or ODBC-compliant data source. The programs you create can scale from your desktop PC to an enterprise-wide database server.

> **NOTE** *While you can create JDBC-enabled programs from the Personal Edition of JBuilder, you won't get tight integration unless you're using at least the Professional Edition. Essentially, the capabilities are there but you have to code everything by hand.*

All of this leads to at least one conclusion: JBuilder enables you to streamline the development process, so you, the programmer, can be much more efficient. With all that said, let's install the tool and start working smarter.

> **NOTE** *If you already have JBuilder installed, skip over the next two sections and jump right to the "Working in the JBuilder Environment" section.*

Installing JBuilder

Installing JBuilder is fairly straightforward. Essentially you just stick the book's companion CD in your CD-ROM drive and off it goes for Windows, Linux, Solaris, and Mac OS. As long as the installation launcher automatically starts, it's easy. If the launcher doesn't start, you'll need to click `install_windows.exe`, `install_linux`, or `install_solaris` from the CD's root directory, depending upon which platform you're using. After the autostart or you launch the application yourself, you'll see a window similar to the one shown in Figure 1-1.

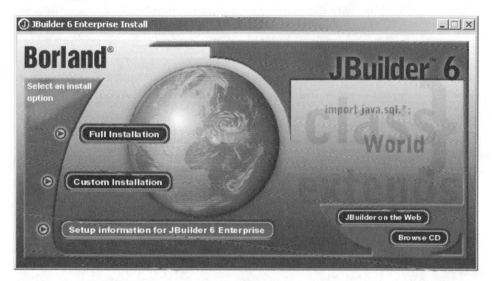

Figure 1-1. The JBuilder 6 Enterprise Install window. Select Custom Installation to install JBuilder 6 without the Borland Application Server.

NOTE *The installation instructions in this section are specifically for Windows 98/2000/NT 4.0. However, by just changing the destination directory name, the instructions will work for Linux, Solaris, or Mac, too, with minor changes. The same rule applies for all directory references in this book. Just don't use spaces in your directory (or file) names and everything will be okay on all platforms.*

Before you start, you need to make sure your system meets JBuilder's system requirements. You should have available at least 250MB of disk space (less if you don't mind lopping off some features, 500MB if you also want the Borland Application Server installed), 128MB of memory (256MB is preferred), SVGA graphics (800×600, 256 colors), and one of the many operating system variants JBuilder supports. Officially, JBuilder works under Windows XP, 2000, and NT 4.0. It should work under Windows Me and 98, but for some reason Borland doesn't advertise support of this, probably because the operating systems aren't meant as a serious development environment. For Solaris, Solaris 7 or Solaris 8 will do. For Linux, Red Hat 6.2 or 7.1 with GNOME or KDE work best and on the Mac front you need Mac OS X release 10.1 or later.

Assuming you have the right configuration, you can install the product. Select Custom Installation to start the installation process. The next window you'll see is shown in Figure 1-2. Running your mouse over either of the selected components brings up component information in the bottom area. To just install JBuilder 6, uncheck the second option, the AppServer, and click Install.

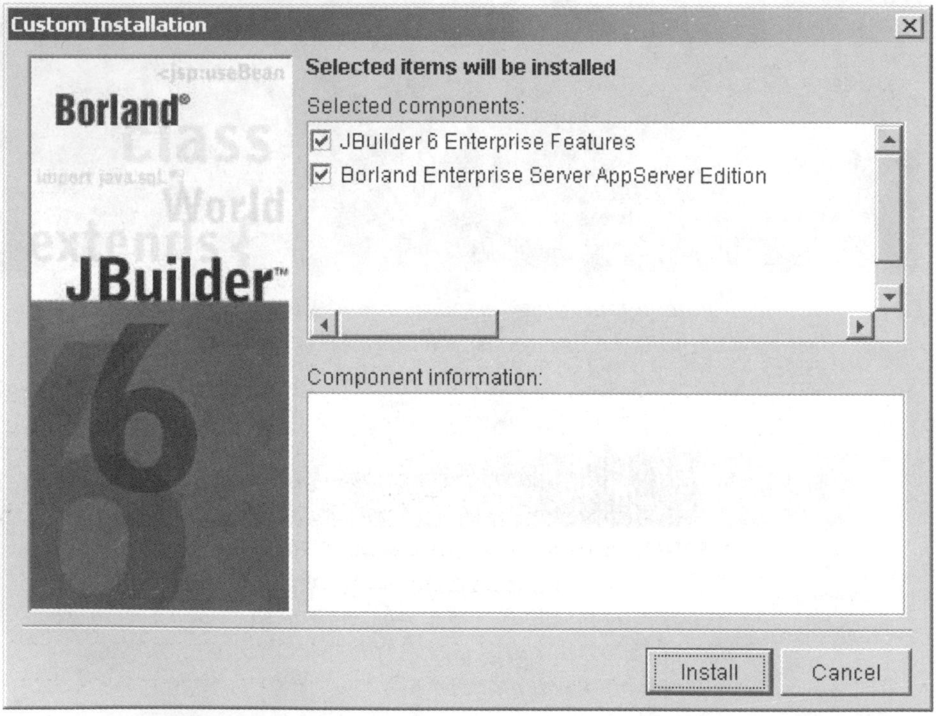

Figure 1-2. The JBuilder 6 Enterprise Install window. Uncheck the AppServer and click Install to start.

NOTE *Feel free to install the Borland Application Server if you have the disk space; however, it won't be used in this book.*

After you click the Install button, you'll be prompted for the language to use within the program (menus and error messages). Assuming you want an English installation, just click OK, though you can select Deutsch, Español, or Français if you'd prefer working with the tool in German, Spanish, or French instead (see Figure 1-3).

Figure 1-3. The JBuilder 6 Language Prompt window. Select a language and then click OK.

The next screen from the installer, shown in Figure 1-4, is just informational. Feel free to read it and then click Next.

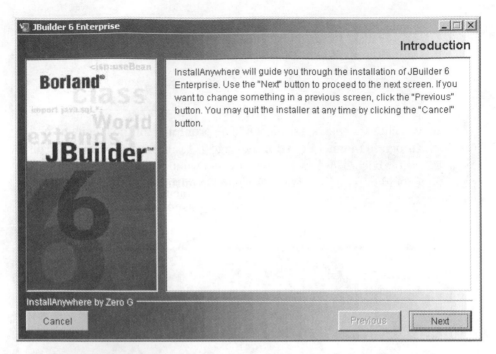

Figure 1-4. The JBuilder 6 Introduction window. Read it before clicking Next.

After you get past the Introduction window, you're prompted to read the license agreement shown in Figure 1-5. Essentially, it states that the Enterprise Edition on the CD is a trial version and the Enterprise features will become disabled after a 30-day trial period. Afterward, the edition reverts to the free (Personal) version downloadable from the Web. Some features won't work after the trial period and you shouldn't use the program for high-risk activities "as in the operation of nuclear facilities, aircraft navigation or communication systems, air traffic control," and so on. Assuming you agree to the license, select "I accept the terms of the License Agreement" and click the Next button. If you don't agree, please just return this book (assuming the bookstore you bought it from will accept it with the CD seal broken).

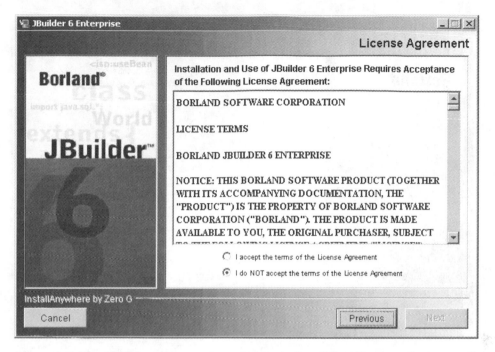

Figure 1-5. The JBuilder 6 License Agreement window. Select "I accept the terms of the License Agreement" and click the Next button.

Next you're prompted to choose how much of the tool you want to install (see Figure 1-6). Assuming you want all the documentation and samples copied to your hard drive, leave Full Install selected and click Next.

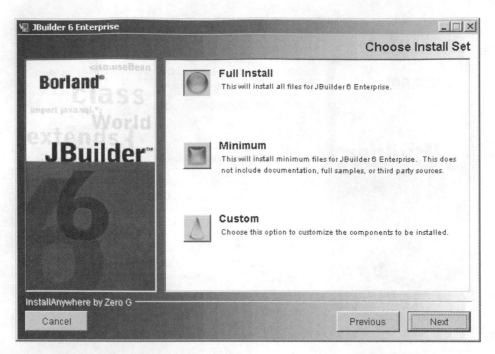

Figure 1-6. The JBuilder 6 Choose Install Set window. Select Full Install and click Next.

You'll get a quick configuring window before you are prompted for an installation directory (shown in Figure 1-7). If you have enough space on the default device, just click Next. Otherwise, change the location and then click Next.

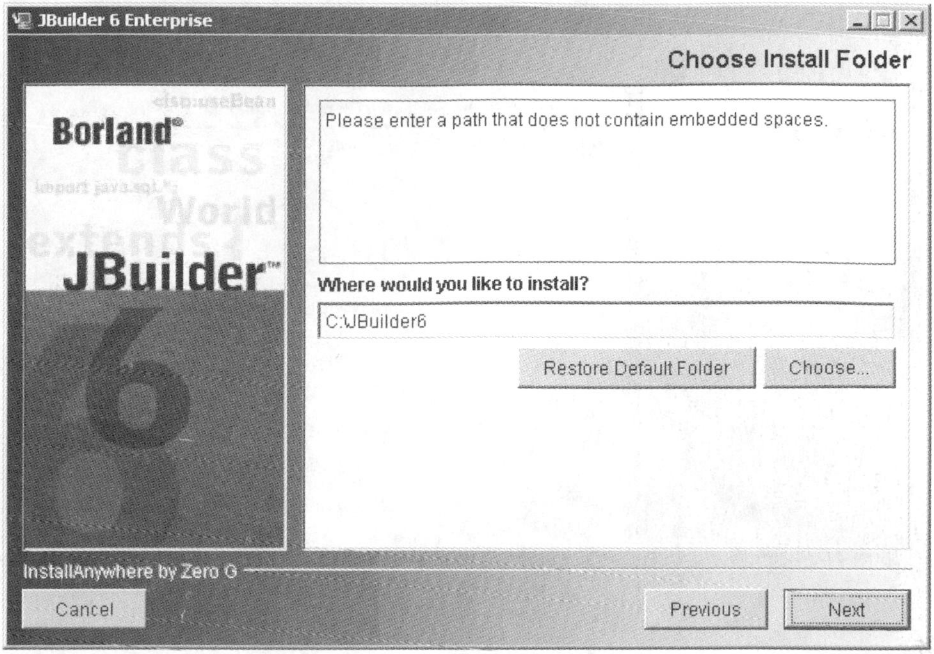

Figure 1-7. The JBuilder 6 Choose Install Folder window. Leave the default directory and click Next.

As one last task before the actual installation, you're offered the chance to review what you've just done. After you've looked through the features to be installed in Figure 1-8, click Install.

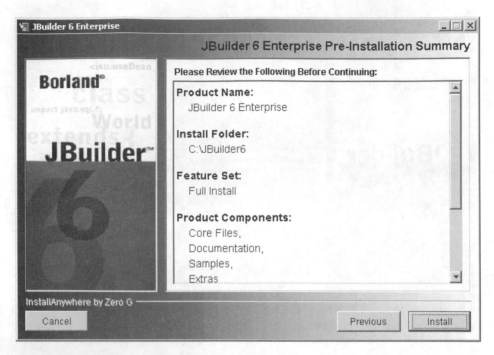

Figure 1-8. The JBuilder 6 Pre-Installation Summary window. Review the options and click Install.

After another configuring JBuilder window you'll see the window in Figure 1-9. You can watch the setup progress bar increase until it reaches 100 percent full, which indicates the software is installed. You'll get another configuring JBuilder window before you see the screen in Figure 1-10 that tells you the installation is complete. Click Done to wrap up the tool installation.

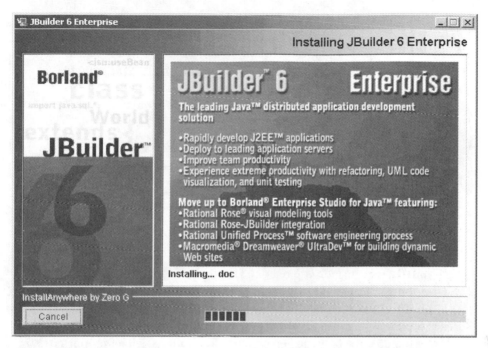

Figure 1-9. The JBuilder 6 Installing window. Watch the progress bar fill as everything is installed.

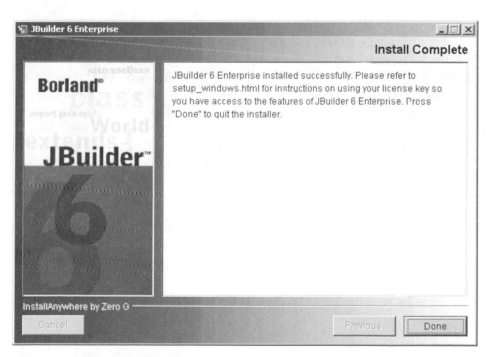

Figure 1-10. The JBuilder 6 Install Complete window. Click Done to wrap up the JBuilder 6 tool installation.

NOTE *Figure 1-10 mentions looking at an HTML setup file for your platform. You can easily view this file by selecting the Setup Information for JBuilder 6 Enterprise Trial option shown in Figure 1-1. If you don't select the button, you'll need to locate the file on your hard drive or in the installation directory.*

Once the JBuilder installation is complete, you can close the initial installation screen (see Figure 1-1).

Getting a Registration Key

Before you can use the tool, you need to visit the JBuilder Web site to get a registration key. Just go directly to
`http://www.borland.com/jbuilder/keys/jb6_ent_steps.html` to obtain a key. Borland will allow you to get a 30-day license for the Enterprise features of the product. After 30 days, only the Personal Edition options will be supported. No program created during the 30 days will stop working, but you may not be able to use the wizards and other parts of JBuilder that helped you create programs after 30 days.

Getting a key is a three-step process. Step 1 is to become a Borland Community member. If you're already a member, you don't have to sign up again—you just have to log in. Click the Step 1 link and the Borland Community Login window will appear, as shown in Figure 1-11. Existing members can log in and move on to Step 2. New members need to click the New User button to fill in their registration information. New users must provide a valid e-mail address to receive their activation key (and later the licensing key to use JBuilder). To get that key, find an unused user ID, fill in the identifying information form, fill in a profile of areas of interest, receive an activation key through e-mail, and activate your membership with the link provided in the e-mail.

```
Borland Community - Login - Microsoft Internet Explorer          _ □ ×
 File   Edit   View   Favorites   Tools   Help
   ←        →        ⊗       ↻       ⌂          ⬡          ⬛
  Back    Forward    Stop    Refresh   Home      History      Print

                   Cookies Required.                          ▲

  Please enter your
            Login [                              ]
            Name
         or Email [                              ]
          Address
             and [                              ]
         Password
        Character [Western (American/European) (ISO8859_1) ▼]
              Set
         Encoding
           you use
                    Save my login information in this browser for [90 ]
                    days
                    (Enter 0 to set the cookie for this browser session
                    only)
                  [ Login ][ Reset ]   [ Forgot My Password! ]   [ New User ]
                                                              ▼
 ◄                                                          ►
 🖹 Done                                          🔒  🌐 Internet
```

Figure 1-11. The Borland Community Login window. Log in or click New User if you aren't a user yet.

NOTE   *Depending on your love of receiving commercial e-mail, you can choose among a handful of options to receive e-mail from Borland. If you uncheck the options but are warned that your chosen user ID is unavailable, remember to uncheck the options again when you submit the form each subsequent time until you find an unused ID.*

Once you log in, you're automatically taken to a survey, as shown in Figure 1-12. This survey is Step 2. Fill in the survey and click Submit.

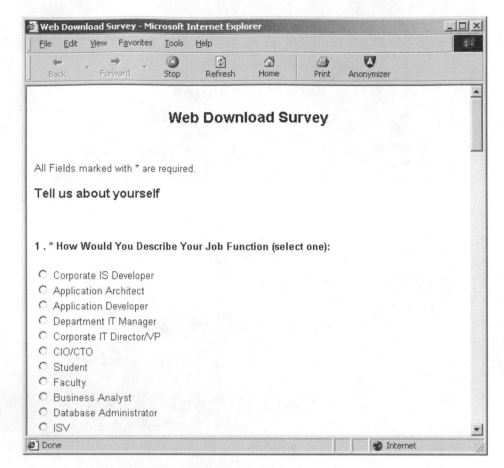

Figure 1-12. The JBuilder 6 Web Download Survey window. Fill in the survey and click Submit.

After you click Submit, you'll need to verify your e-mail address (see Figure 1-13). Assuming your e-mail address is still correct (since you just entered it and received your user verification e-mail), just select Submit a second time. Your registration key will arrive shortly in your e-mail inbox.

Figure 1-13. The JBuilder 6 Email Verification form. Make sure your e-mail address is correct and then click Submit.

The first time you start up JBuilder, you'll be prompted to enter the registration information you just received by e-mail. From the Windows Start menu, select Programs ➤ JBuilder 6 Enterprise ➤ JBuilder 6 Enterprise to access the window shown in Figure 1-14.

17

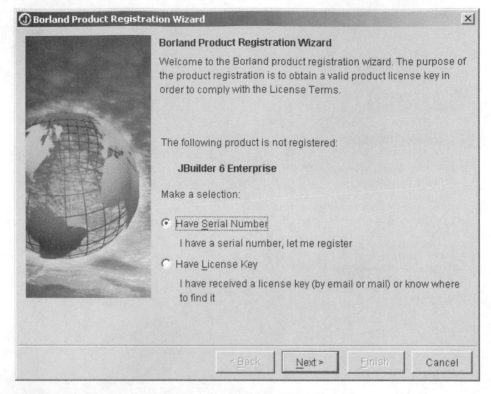

Figure 1-14. The Borland Product Registration Wizard window

To enter the licensing information, you must fill in another form. Select the Have License Key option and click Next to move on to the Product Registration Wizard shown in Figure 1-15. What you received in the e-mail from Borland was a license key, so you'll need to select the "Paste license key text" option. Next, in your e-mail program, select and copy the content between the `-----BEGIN BLOCK-----` and `-----END BLOCK-----` sections to the clipboard. Clicking the Clipboard Paste button will then copy the contents into the input field in the wizard.

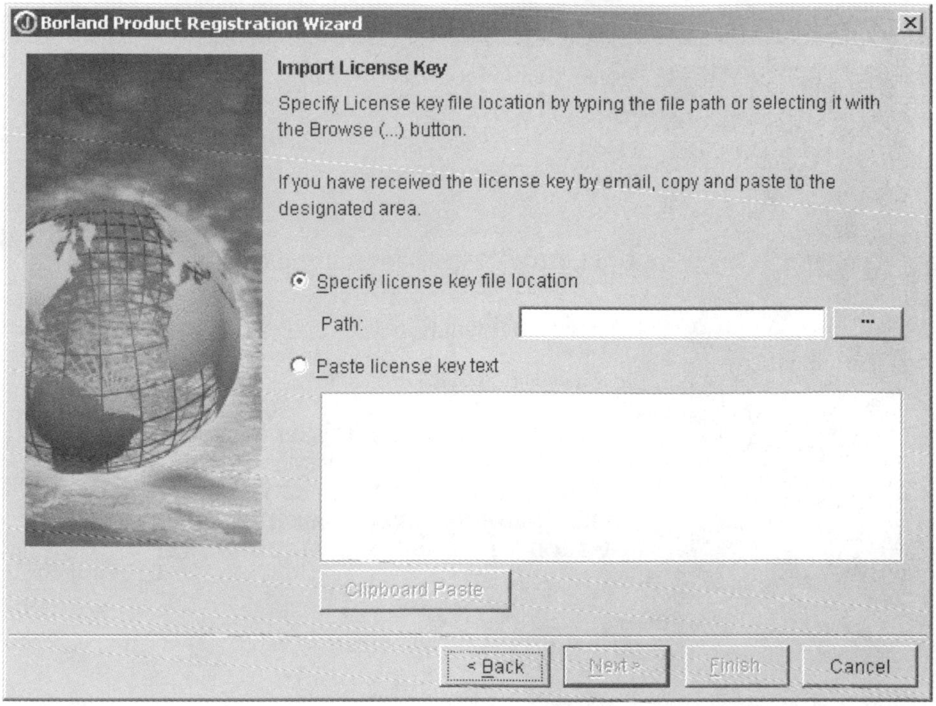

Figure 1-15. The Borland Product Registration Wizard. Enter the license key you received by e-mail.

After you've entered the license key, click Next. You'll see yet another License Terms screen, as shown in Figure 1-16. Select the "I ACCEPT THE LICENSE TERMS" option and click Next to move on.

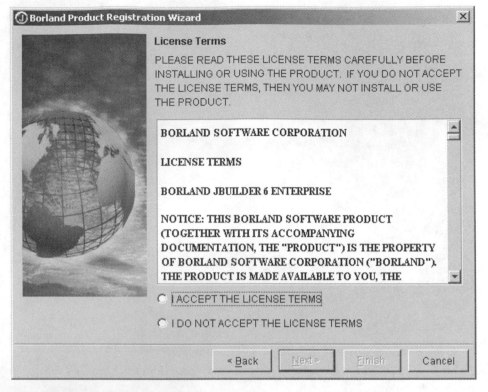

Figure 1-16. Another License Terms window to read. Select "I ACCEPT THE LICENSE TERMS" and click Next.

On the final screen, shown in Figure 1-17, just click Finish to indicate your successful registration.

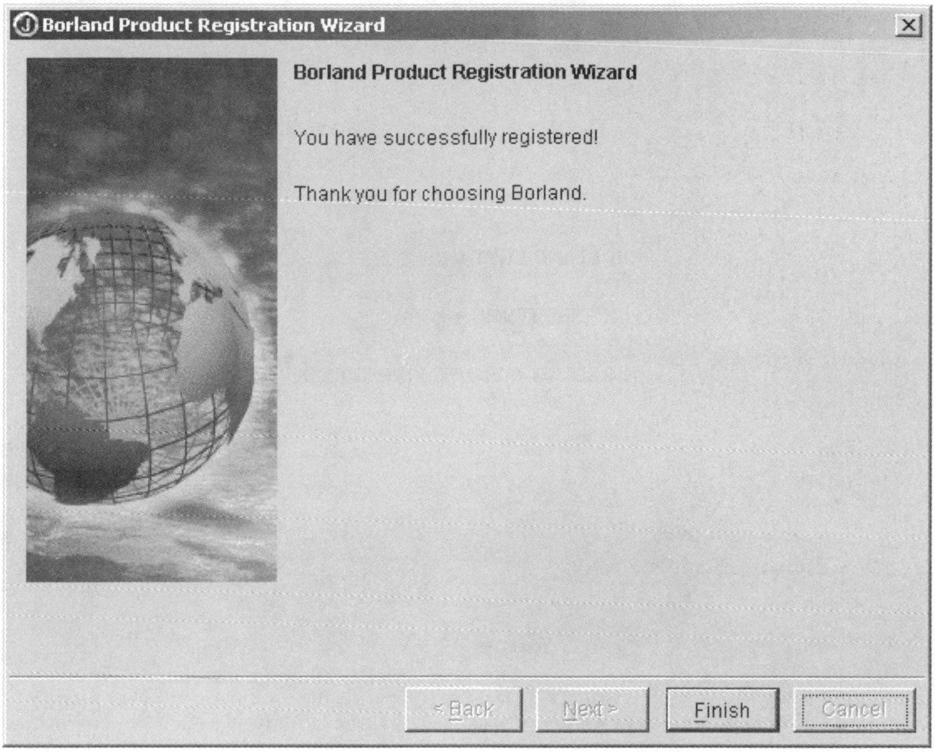

Figure 1-17. The final Borland Product Registration Wizard window. Click Finish to indicate you're done.

JBuilder will automatically start up at this point, and you'll see that you have 29 days to use the Enterprise Edition (see Figure 1-18).

Figure 1-18. JBuilder 6 start-up window with 29 day usage

Working in the JBuilder Environment

With JBuilder's license key properly installed, you'll be presented with its *integrated development environment (IDE)*. The IDE is where you build and test your Java programs (see Figure 1-19). You also get a Tip of the Day window, which shows tool usage tips. Feel free to hide the Tip of the Day window permanently by deselecting the "Show 'tip of the day' after launching" option and clicking Close. Leave the option selected if you want the tip each time you start JBuilder.

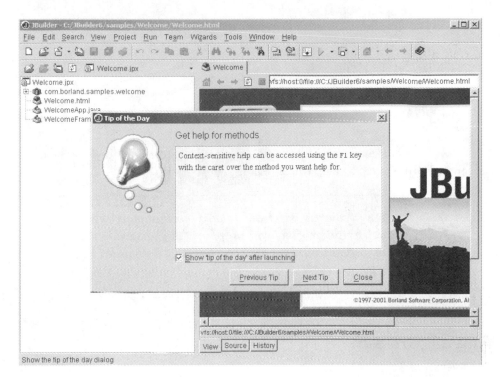

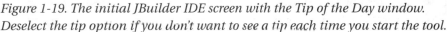

Figure 1-19. The initial JBuilder IDE screen with the Tip of the Day window. Deselect the tip option if you don't want to see a tip each time you start the tool.

Before jumping in and developing your Java programs, you should become familiar with the development environment. Until you're comfortable with the environment, you will spend development time thinking "How do I . . . ?" instead of immediately seeing the results you're after.

The JBuilder IDE is divided into multiple areas, each with a number of different parts. The top area consists of a menu bar, and the bottom area contains your main workspace—the AppBrowser.

The Toolbar

Immediately below the menu bar, across the entire window, is the JBuilder toolbar (see Figure 1-20). It consists of 25 buttons that provide access to main development tasks. If you don't see some of the buttons, go to the menu and select View ➤ Toolbars. You can then enable (or hide) any of the seven subareas on the toolbar: File, Editing, Search, Build, Run/Debug, Navigation, and Help. All the buttons provide quick access to menu bar commands. If the command is not valid at a certain time, the toolbar button is disabled/grayed out.

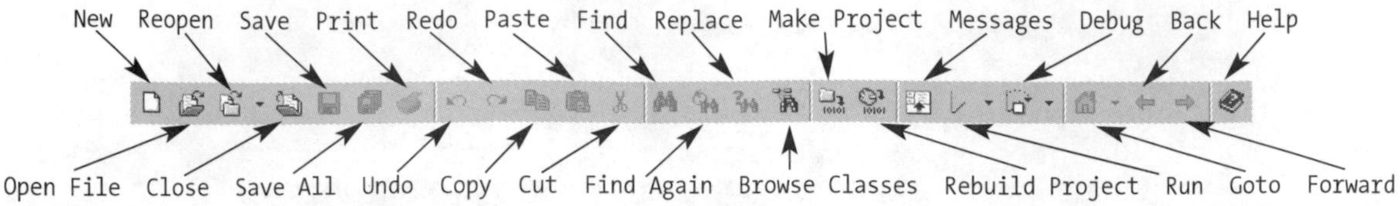

New Reopen Save Print Redo Paste Find Replace Make Project Messages Debug Back Help

Open File Close Save All Undo Copy Cut Find Again Browse Classes Rebuild Project Run Goto Forward

Figure 1-20. The JBuilder toolbar

If you ever forget which button is which, you can hover your mouse cursor over the button and a tool tip will appear that describes it.

 **TIP** *A* tool tip *is a cream-colored box that pops up with a description of an item's purpose. It appears when the mouse cursor hovers (rests) over an area designated with a defined tip.*

The AppBrowser

The AppBrowser, your main working area, is located below the toolbar. It consists of many different areas, some of which change depending upon the state of the tool. Figure 1-21 points out the different areas when the tool is in Source mode. Figure 1-22 shows the tool in Design mode.

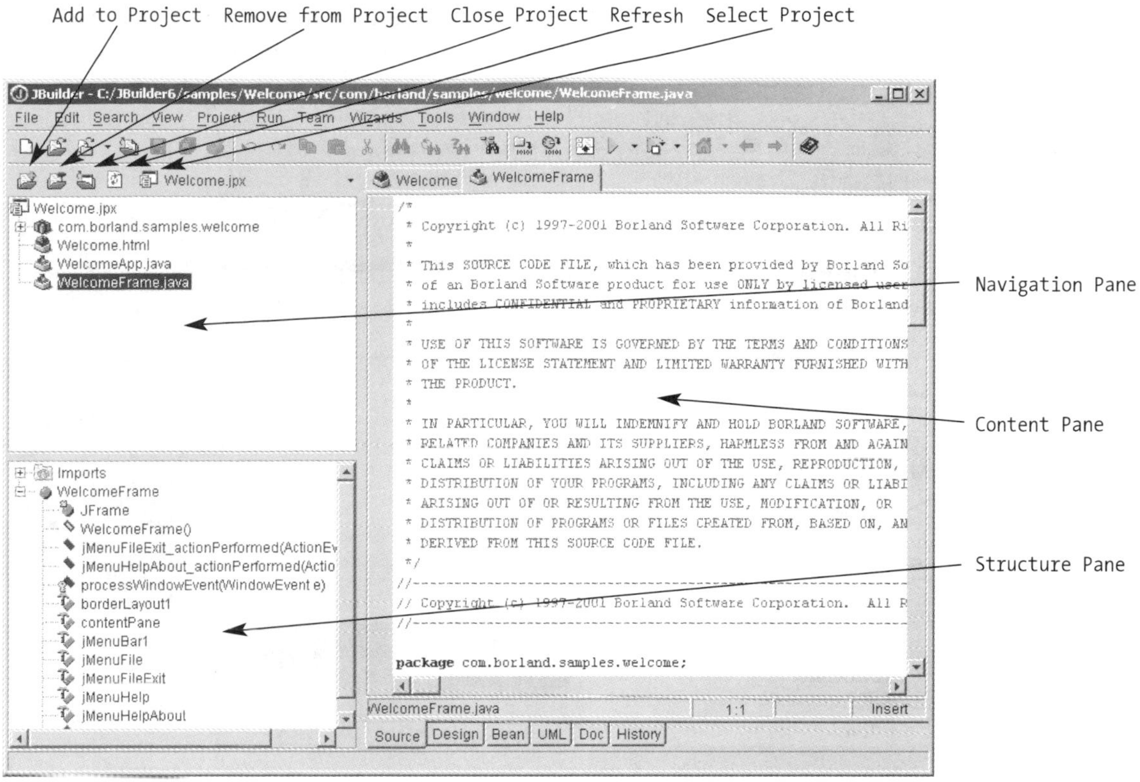
Add to Project
Remove from Project
Close Project
Refresh
Select Project
Navigation Pane
Content Pane
Structure Pane

Figure 1-21. The JBuilder AppBrowser in Source mode

Table 1-2. Subset of Component Tree Icons

Icon	Description
	Layout manager
🗀	Grouping folder
💖	Object being designed
🔲	Generic component

Play around with all the different pieces of the environment to get comfortable in your new home. Once you think you know where everything is, you can move on to create some code.

> **NOTE** *If you notice that the cursor isn't properly drawing the IDE background, close down JBuilder and uncomment the* vmparam -Dsun.java2d.noddraw *line in the* jdk.config *file in* \JBuilder6\bin. *When you restart JBuilder, your screen-drawing glitch should be corrected. I had this drawing problem under Windows 2000 but not under Windows 98. After I uncommented the line, everything worked fine.*

Creating a Java Program

You're going to create a simple example in JBuilder now, without using all the bells and whistles available. The example you create will be an applet. An *applet* is a Java program that runs within a Web page. The applet will display the phrase "Good Morning, JBuilder."

>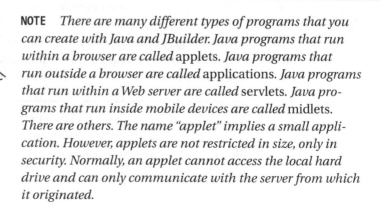
> **NOTE** *There are many different types of programs that you can create with Java and JBuilder. Java programs that run within a browser are called* applets. *Java programs that run outside a browser are called* applications. *Java programs that run within a Web server are called* servlets. *Java programs that run inside mobile devices are called* midlets. *There are others. The name "applet" implies a small application. However, applets are not restricted in size, only in security. Normally, an applet cannot access the local hard drive and can only communicate with the server from which it originated.*

To get started, close anything that's open by using the File ➤ Close Projects menu option. Select All and OK on the window that appears.

Before you create your first applet, you need to create your first *project*. JBuilder works with a project metaphor to keep related things together. If you ever do anything dealing with files, you need to work in a JBuilder project. For an applet, there are two necessary pieces: the applet source file and the applet loader, which makes it possible to view the applet with a browser.

To create a project, select File ➤ New Project. This brings up the Project Wizard, as shown in Figure 1-23.

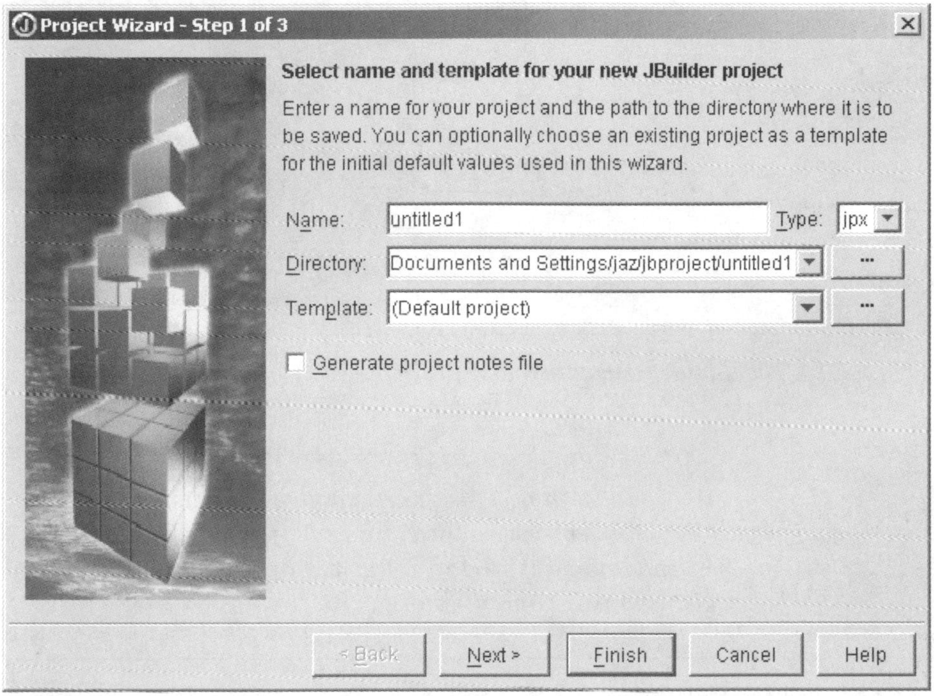

*Figure 1-23. The JBuilder Project Wizard. Name the project **skill1** and click Finish.*

In the Name field, type in **skill1** and click Finish. This creates the file skill1.jpx in the default project directory and opens up the project in the AppBrowser window, as shown in Figure 1-24.

Figure 1-24. The JBuilder IDE with a new project

> **NOTE** *JBuilder project filenames automatically end in* `.jpx`. *Earlier JBuilder versions used* `.jpr` *as the filename extension. The default project directory is the* `jbprojects` *directory under your user home directory.*

Now that you've created a project, you can begin work on your first applet. Select File ➤ New to bring up the Object Gallery. Select the Web tab and the Applet icon to bring up the Applet Wizard screen shown in Figure 1-25. Accept all the default settings by clicking Finish.

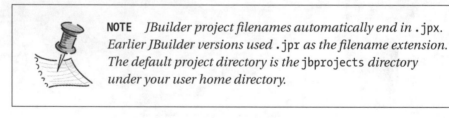

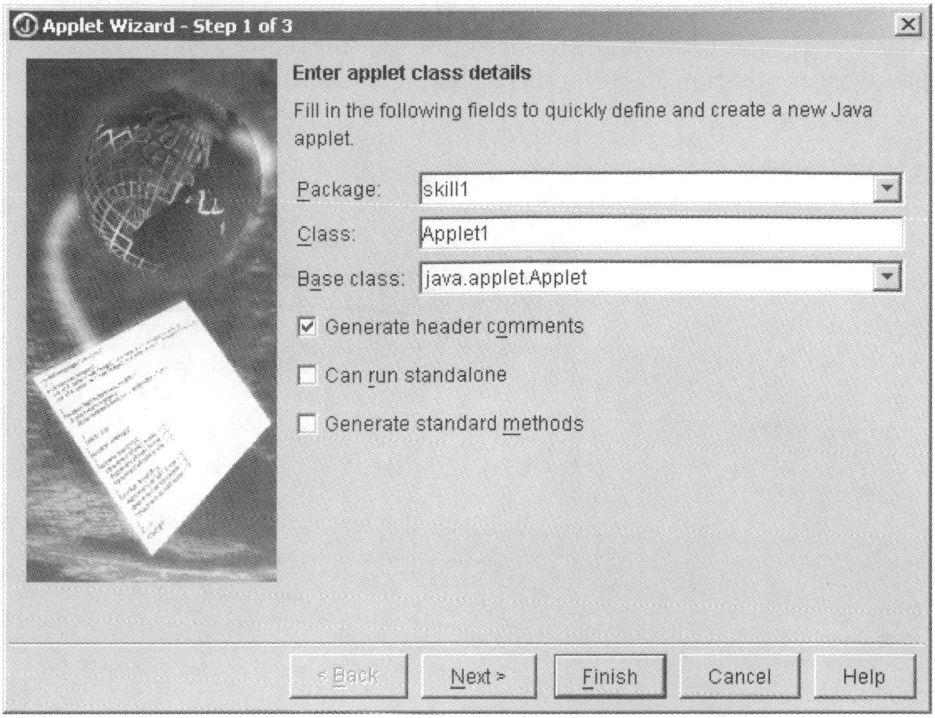

Figure 1-25. The JBuilder Applet Wizard. Just click Finish to accept the default settings.

In the Content pane for Applet1.java, replace the source code with the following:

```
package skill1;
import java.awt.Graphics;
public class Applet1 extends java.applet.Applet {
  public void paint(Graphics g) {
    g.drawString("Good Morning, JBuilder", 40, 50);
  }
}
```

This is your Java program, and soon you'll understand what each line means. To save it to a disk, select File ≻ Save Applet1.java. Before you can run the applet, you need to compile it by selecting Project ≻ Make Applet1.java (or clicking the Make Project icon). If there are no typos, you'll see the message "Build succeeded" in the status message area at the bottom of the IDE. Otherwise, you'll receive a message something like "Build completed with 1 error" and the Message pane will appear. You can then highlight each error and correct it before recompiling. Figure 1-26 shows what would happen with the , 50 missing in the drawString() line. Once you correct the error, save the source again and recompile. Once the program has been successfully compiled, it's time to move on.

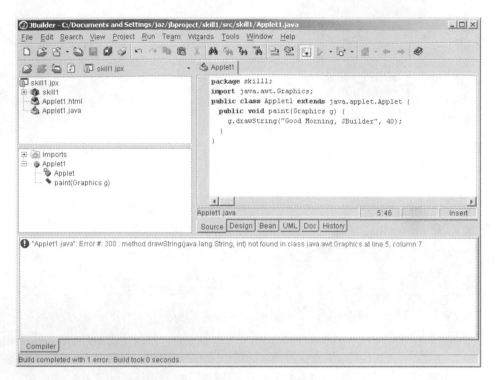

Figure 1-26. Compilation error for missing parameter in the drawString() *call*

Running the Applet

Because Java applets run within a Web browser, you need to have a file to load the applet into the browser. The Applet Wizard actually created this for you. If you double-click the Applet1.html file in the Navigation pane and select the Source tab in the Content pane, you'll see the generated source. It will be explained shortly.

```
<html>
<head>
<title>
HTML Test Page
</title>
</head>
```

```
<body>
skill1.Applet1 will appear below in a Java enabled browser.<br>
<applet
  codebase = "."
  code     = "skill1.Applet1.class"
  name     = "TestApplet"
  width    = "400"
  height   = "300"
  hspace   = "0"
  vspace   = "0"
  align    = "middle"
>
</applet>
</body>
</html>
```

Because you have the applet loader file already created for you, you can just run your applet. Select Run ➢ Run Project to load the applet into the applet viewer program that comes with JBuilder. This will bring up the window shown in Figure 1-27.

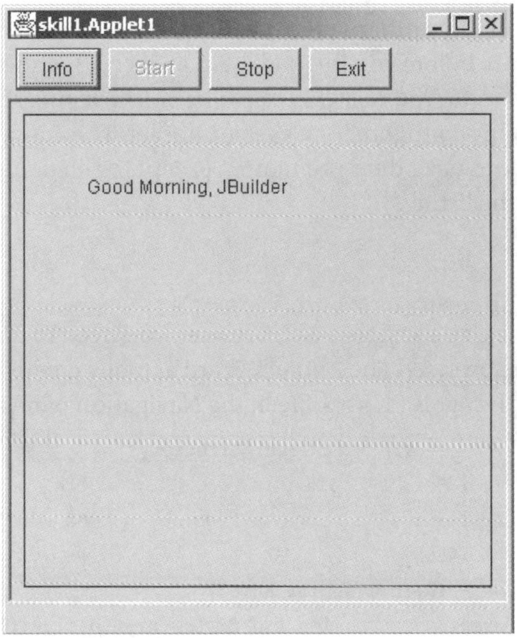

Figure 1-27. Running the applet

> **NOTE** *The program that JBuilder uses to test applets is some-times called* appletviewer *because that is the command-line tool that comes with Sun's JDK. This is not a full-fledged browser—it only understands the* <APPLET> *tag within the* .html *file. If you want to display text or images within the Web pages,* appletviewer *will not display them. However, a normal browser such as Internet Explorer, Opera, or Netscape Navigator will.*

The <APPLET> HTML Tag

Applets are incorporated into Web pages with the help of the <APPLET> tag. In the simplest case, you only have to specify the class name and the size required by the applet within the Web page:

```
<applet code=Applet1 width=300 height=100>
</applet>
```

When you used the Applet Wizard, many of the additional options were auto-matically set for you. Any other options with special circumstances that require you to do extra work before you include them aren't part of the Applet Wizard. The complete syntax for the <APPLET> tag follows. The listing shows everything that you can possibly configure for a specific applet. The actual order and capital-ization of the options used does not matter, except for filenames. Table 1-3 provides a key to the listing.

```
<APPLET
    [ALIGN=LEFT|RIGHT|TOP|TEXTTOP|MIDDLE|ABSMIDDLE|BASELINE|BOTTOM|ABSBOTTOM\
    [ALT=Alternate Text - (none)]
    [ARCHIVE=filename.zip|filename.jar|comma-separated list of the two - (none)]
    CODE=AppletName[.class] | OBJECT=SerializedApplet.ser
    [CODEBASE=Applet Directory - (current directory)]
    HEIGHT=Applet Pixel Height
    [HSPACE=Extra Pixel Space to Left and Right of Applet - (0)]
    [MAYSCRIPT=TRUE | FALSE]
    [NAME=Applet Name - (Actual Applet Name)]
    [VSPACE=Extra Pixel Space for Top and Bottom of Applet - (0)]
    WIDTH=Applet Pixel Width
  >
```

```
[<PARAM NAME=Parameter1 Value=Value1]
[<PARAM NAME=Parameter2 Value=Value2]
...
[<PARAM NAME=ParameterN Value=ValueN]
[Alternate anything for when no Java available or disabled.]
</APPLET>
```

Table 1-3. Option Configuration Key

Element	Description
[...]	Square brackets signal that something is optional.
|	A list of choices separated by a separator signifies only one of the choices is to be used.
[ALIGN=**LEFT**	Default values/choices are bold.
[ALT=*Alternate Text*	Italics are used for user-specified values.
(...)	Entries within regular parentheses are assumed values when nothing is entered and a list of choices isn't available.

So, with all those options, what does it mean? Well, you normally just include the CODE, WIDTH, and HEIGHT options and ignore the rest. If you use the Applet Wizard, though, you don't have to worry about any of this, unless you want to package your classes into an archive.

Keyboard Navigation

To become really productive in the source code editor, you need to learn the keyboard mappings for various shortcuts. By default, the mappings follow the Common User Access (CUA) guidelines. However, you can also change the shortcuts by selecting Tools ➢ Editor Options. Other mappings are available for Brief, Emacs, Macintosh, Codewarrior, and Visual Studio for those transitioning to JBuilder from those environments or those who just prefer those mappings. At any time, you can get a list of the specific key mappings by selecting Help ➢ Keyboard Mappings. Table 1-4 lists some of the common keyboard shortcuts as well as some of the not-so-common ones you might like to know about.

Table 1-4. Common Keyboard Shortcuts

Shortcut	Action
F1	Display context-sensitive help
Ctrl-S	Save current element
Ctrl-Shift-A	Save all files in project
Ctrl-F4	Close current element
Ctrl-Shift-F4	Close all files in project
F9	Run project
Ctrl-F9	Make project
Ctrl-Shift-F9	Make current element
Ctrl-[0-9]	Go to bookmark
Ctrl-Shift-[0-9]	Set bookmark
Ctrl-N	Open Object Gallery (think N for "New")
Ctrl-Shift-N	Next message in Message pane
Tab	Indent highlighted block
Shift-Tab	Unindent highlighted block
Ctrl-], Ctrl-[, Alt-], Alt-[	Find matching brace
Ctrl-/	Turn current line into a // comment or from a // comment back into source

Understanding the Source

Now that you have something up and running, let's take a look at exactly what this means by examining each line of the source code.

The first line of your program tells the compiler that the program belongs to a *package,* in this case skill1. Packages are logical ways of grouping related classes. If you leave off the package line, the applet will go into the "unnamed" package. If another class exists in the unnamed package with the same name, the compiler will overwrite the class and replace it with yours. It's a good idea to place all your code in packages so as to avoid the potential for name collisions.

```
package skill1;
```

The next line has you import a class called `Graphics` from the `java.awt` package.

```
import java.awt.Graphics;
```

Not only can you use packages for your classes, but others can also use packages for theirs. When you need to use classes, you have to "import" them to tell the compiler where to find them. In this case, the `Graphics` class is part of the Abstract Window Toolkit (AWT) package. The AWT package includes classes that have to do with drawing and how things appear on the screen. If you come from the C/C++ world, you can think of a package as a class library and an `import` statement as a #include statement. They don't map directly, but they are similar. Instead of recreating everything from scratch, you can create more complex Java programs by reusing the prebuilt Java packages. In fact, much of this book discusses how to reuse the predefined packages within JBuilder.

The next line of your program defines a Java class named `Applet1`.

```
public class Applet1 extends java.applet.Applet {
```

A *class* is one of those pieces that goes in a package. Because you're creating an applet, your class needs to *extend* from the `Applet` class in the `java.applet` package. This enables you to reuse many of the different pieces that are already defined for use with applets. If you don't, your program will be much longer. If you're familiar with C++, extending a Java class is the same as inheriting from a base class in C++.

 NOTE *Don't worry if these terms are confusing at the moment—they'll be explained in much greater detail shortly.*

Notice that the package `java.applet` and the class `Applet` are combined to form `java.applet.Applet`. You could have also done the following with the same results:

```
import java.applet.Applet;
public class Applet1 extends Applet {
```

 TIP *If you leave out the* extends *classname from the class definition, Java infers that you're extending from the* `java.lang.Object` *class. Everything eventually extends from the* Object *class.*

The rest of the source tells the program to print the string "Good Morning, JBuilder" on the screen.

```java
public void paint(Graphics g) {
  g.drawString("Good Morning, JBuilder", 40, 50);
  }
}
```

The 40 and 50 represent coordinates on the left side of the baseline of the string. The *baseline* represents an imaginary line to write on. The first coordinate, the *x-position,* is the distance from the left side of the applet's area within the browser. The second coordinate, the *y-position,* is the distance from the top. This is shown in Figure 1-28.

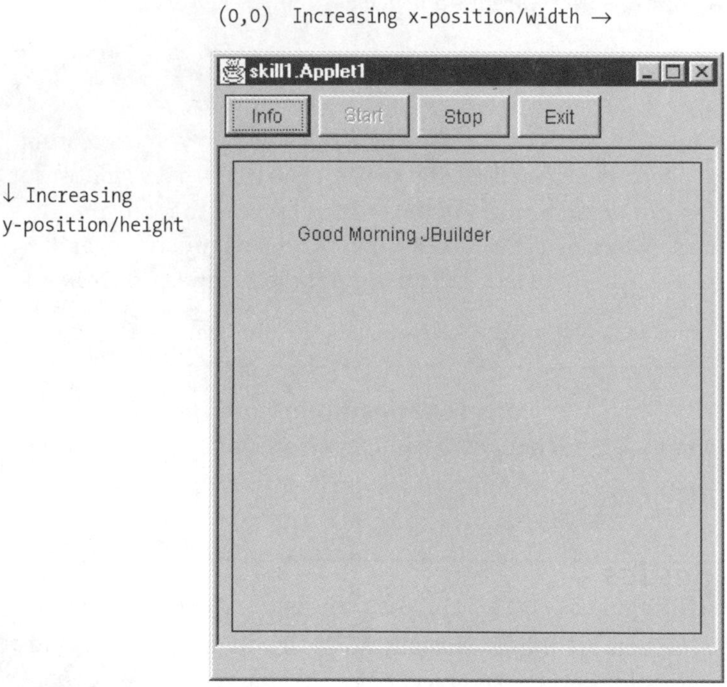

(0,0) Increasing x-position/width →

↓ Increasing
y-position/height

Good Morning JBuilder

Figure 1-28. The Java coordinate system

NOTE *The Java coordinate space is measured in pixels.* Pixels *are display units on a screen. For instance, your desktop's area is probably 800×600, 1024×768, or 1280×1024 pixels. Each little display dot on your screen is a pixel.*

That's really all there is to your applet. The next chapter revisits creating applets and talks more about the Applet Wizard.

> **TIP**   *One of the things you'll notice about JBuilder 6 is that it doesn't support the use of the mouse wheel. This is because Java doesn't provide support of the mouse wheel until Java version 1.4. Because JBuilder 6 runs on top of Java 1.3, the IDE doesn't come with mouse wheel support. However, if you don't mind using some third-party, unsupported software, go to* http://czerwonykapturek.tripod.com/jbWheel/jbwheel.html *to download and install jbWheel. This program will add mouse wheel support under Microsoft Windows. Version 0.90 of the tool is available on the book's companion CD.*

The Basics of Object-Oriented Programming

You've briefly been exposed to a few object-oriented concepts, such as objects and classes. Let's dig into them a little deeper so you can get a better understanding before you move on to bigger things.

> **NOTE**   *This is by no means a complete introduction to object-oriented programming. If you are interested in a more in-depth introduction, consider reading* Beginning Java Objects, *by Jacquie Barker.*

Java Object Basics

In its simplest sense, objects are things—usually nouns if you're strictly looking at parts of speech. At any point in time, an object has a specific state and evokes a specific behavior. An object is a specific instance of a class. A class defines what an object's state and behavior is. A class' variables define its state, while its functions, or methods in object-speak, define its behavior.

To demonstrate, if the class Car exists, it might maintain state for type, color, and amount of fuel in the gas tank. If you were dealing with a specific instance of Car, the type might be a Volkswagen, the color might be purple with pink polka-dots, and the gas tank might be empty. Its behaviors might be start, stop, turn, and reverse.

Methods

Methods define how objects behave. When you declare methods for a class, you create its behavior. If a class doesn't have a particular method, it can't behave in the desired way—you would have to change its behavior by defining another method. In the Car example, there can be methods for start, stop, turn, and reverse. If you want to be able to fill up its gas tank, you can define a method to perform the operation and then have the additional behavior of filling up the tank. If you're familiar with C++, a method is analogous to a member function.

Variables

The state of a class is maintained by its variables. By reserving space in memory, a variable stores the current state of the class.

There are three types of variables: instance, class, and local.

- *Instance variables* maintain the attributes of a specific instance of the class, hence their name. Every object defined for the class will have its own copy of the instance variables. In the previous example, type, color, and gas-tank level are all instance variables. Every car can have a different type, color, and gas-tank level.

- *Class variables* maintain attributes common for all instances of a class. If you ever want to count the number of Car instances created, you can do this with a class variable. In instances of having separate copies of the variable for each class, there is one for all of them.

- *Local variables* are variables declared to be local to some block of code (that is, a method). Outside of the block defined, the local variable doesn't exist.

The actual syntax for creating classes, methods, and variables is described in Skill 3.

Inheritance

Thankfully, programming has advanced to the point where you don't need to create everything from scratch when you need something new. What happens now is you find something that does almost everything you want, and then you customize it for your specific environment. This enables you to take advantage of the vast library of resources already created with minimal effort. When Boeing creates a new airplane, they don't scrap the many years of development effort they already spent and start from scratch. While they may not like Seattle as a base of operations anymore, they still start from some commonality of the last plane they created and build from there.

In object-oriented programming, this customization process is called *inheritance* and involves *subclassing,* or deriving a class. Creating a subclass of an object enables you to build onto another class by altering its behavior or the state it maintains (like your `Applet1` applet). The new class inherits all the behavior from the original and adds functionality onto it. Staying with the `Car` model, if you're working with various electric cars, you can extend `Car` to be `ElectricCar` and add behavior for charging. Then, the electric car can have a type, color, and fuel-level amount (of electricity now instead of gas). `Car` is the *superclass,* or base class, while `ElectricCar` is the *subclass,* or derived class.

Much of the design and development time today is spent creating proper class hierarchies. When you create good, reusable classes that are easily extensible, you enable everyone to work smarter. With the rich core of Java class libraries and several additions that Borland makes available, half of the battle is over for you. You just need to extend these classes for your specific needs. Of course, you have to learn about them first, too.

JavaBeans is another concept worth mentioning here. According to Sun, "JavaBeans components, or Beans, are reusable software components that can be manipulated visually in a builder tool." So, everything that appears on JBuilder's Component palette is a component, and JBuilder is the connect-the-Bean builder tool. You'll work with Beans extensively in Part II of this book.

ARE YOU EXPERIENCED?

Now that you've gotten your feet wet with object-oriented programming terminology, let's wrap up this skill, in which you created a simple program, mostly avoiding the niceties provided with JBuilder. In the next skill, you'll start to take advantage of these JBuilder niceties to automate the more repetitive tasks. Also, you'll learn how to customize your programs at runtime through the use of HTML parameters, command-line parameters, and system properties. All of these things enable you to alter the behavior of Java programs at runtime without having to recode anything.

Now you can

- Use the JBuilder IDE comfortably

- Create a simple applet

- Embed an applet in a Web page

- Understand basic object-oriented programming topics

Employing the JBuilder Applet Wizard

- Using the Project Wizard to create a project

- Working with the Applet Wizard

- Looking at the applet source

- Displaying applet parameters

- Working with the Application Wizard

- Looking at the application source

- Passing application parameters

IN THE LAST SKILL, you toured JBuilder and created your first applet. In this skill, you're going to let JBuilder's wizards do much of the work for you—again, just do not accept all the defaults. Also, you will learn how to provide runtime settings through applet parameters, as well as how to provide command-line options with applications.

> **TIP** *Before you get started, remember to close any open projects by selecting File* ➤ *Close Projects, and then choosing All and the OK button.*

Using the Project Wizard

You'll remember from Skill 1 that when you work with JBuilder, all of your work is contained within a project. If you start one of JBuilder's wizards without an open project, JBuilder reminds you to create one with the Project Wizard before continuing on with the wizard you requested. Selecting File ➤ New Project brings up the first screen of the wizard shown in Figure 2-1.

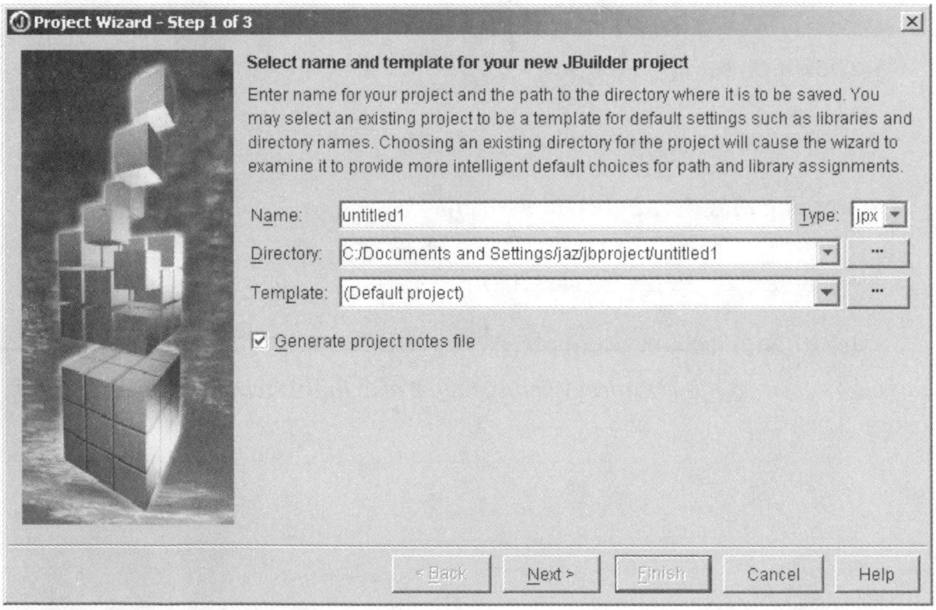

Figure 2-1. The JBuilder Project Wizard, Step 1 of 3. In this window, you configure project basics.

> **TIP**   *You can start the Project Wizard directly from the File menu, or you can select File ➤ New and then click the Project icon.*

As shown in Figure 2-1, the system asks for the project name and where to save the project files. Later screens, shown in Figure 2-2 and Figure 2-3, prompt for project settings as well as author name, company name, and project description.

Figure 2-2. The JBuilder Project Wizard, Step 2 of 3. In this window, you configure project settings.

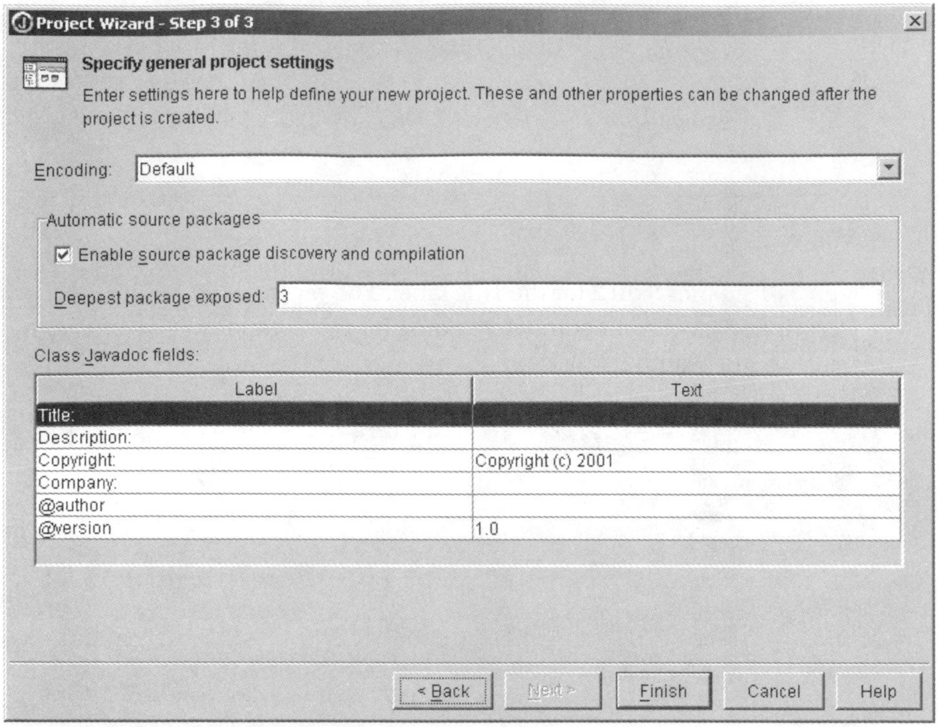

Figure 2-3. The JBuilder Project Wizard, Step 3 of 3. In this window, you provide detail information about the project.

> **NOTE** *In the remaining skills, you are going to save your work under the* C:\skills *directory. If you happen to be using this path for another purpose or are on a UNIX platform, you will need to find another place to save your work (or just accept the default). If you do need to save your work elsewhere, you will have to translate all the skill filenames to the new location. No matter what, don't use a directory with spaces in the name or you will have problems later on.*

Fill in the wizard with the following information. Leave the remaining fields with their defaults by clicking Next between steps.

- Step 1 of 3: Enter **Skill2** into the Name field and **c:\skills\Skill2** into the Directory field.

- Step 2 of 3: Leave all defaults.

- Step 3 of 3: Enter **Skill 2** for the Title label, **The second skill** for the Description label, your company's name for the Company label, and your name for the @author label.

After everything is filled in, click Finish to have JBuilder create the project file. This brings up the AppBrowser window, which has by now become very familiar.

Congratulations! You have now created a project.

NOTE   *The Project Wizard created the file* Skill2.html *to match the project name you specified. The* Skill2.html *file retains a copy of the project information you provided in the Project Wizard.*

Using the Applet Wizard

Now that you have created a project, you can create an applet. The applet will display a message provided as a runtime HTML parameter. Start the Applet Wizard by selecting File ➢ New and double-clicking the Applet icon under the Web tab.

Using the Applet Wizard is a three-part process: you name the applet, you set up runtime parameters, and you decide if an HTML page should be automatically created. The first part (shown in Figure 2-4) prompts you to name the applet's package, class, and superclass, along with some automatic generation options you'll use down the road.

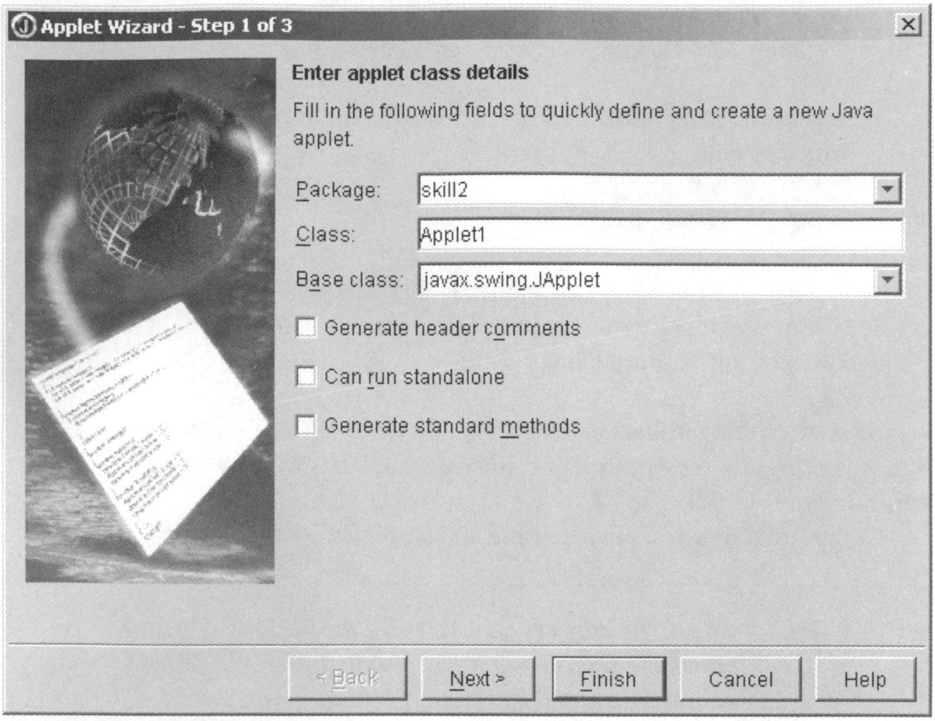

Figure 2-4. The Applet Wizard, Step 1 of 3. In this window, you enter applet class details.

Accept the default package `skill2` and class name `Applet1`, but change the base class to `java.applet.Applet`. Click Next to move to the second part of the process.

The second part (shown in Figure 2-5) asks you to set up any runtime parameters you plan to make available. *Parameters* allow applets to change their behavior without having to recompile the code. Your applet will display a text message provided as an applet parameter, so you need to add one parameter.

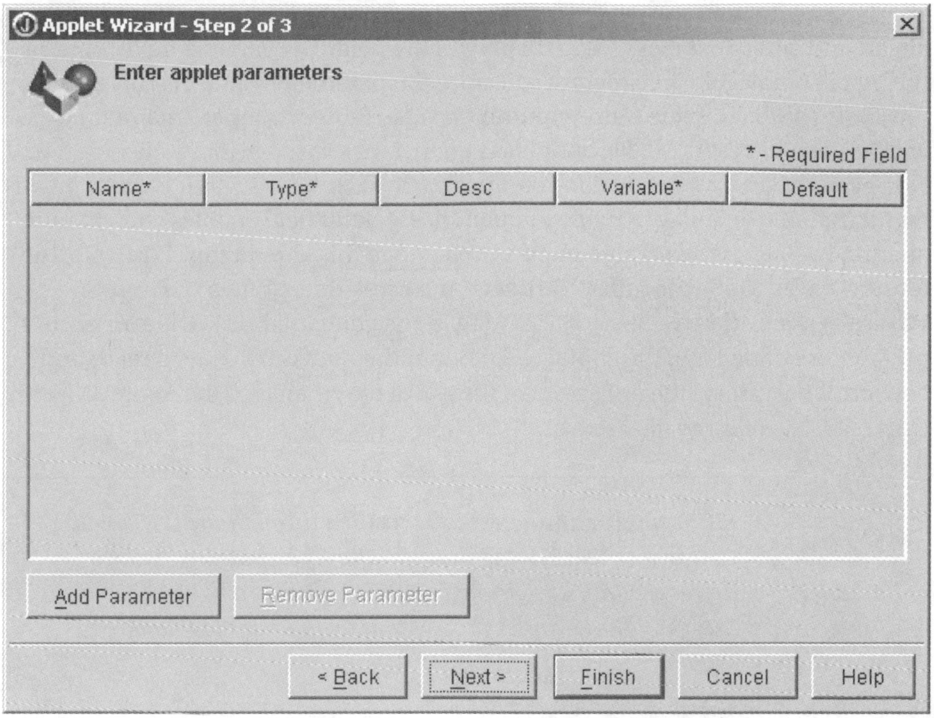

Applet Wizard - Step 2 of 3   ×

Enter applet parameters

* - Required Field

Name*	Type*	Desc	Variable*	Default

Add Parameter   Remove Parameter

< Back   Next >   Finish   Cancel   Help

Figure 2-5. The Applet Wizard, Step 2 of 3. In this window, you enter applet parameters.

To add the parameter, click the Add Parameter button. This adds a row to the table for the parameter. Change the parameter name to **message** to give it more meaning, as param0 doesn't say what the parameter will be used for. Because the message to display is a text message, you can leave the type as a String. When Java gets parameters from HTML files, they are treated as strings. The type selected from the drop-down list determines the data conversion code that the Applet Wizard adds to the applet.

NOTE *In addition to* String *parameters, you can have* boolean, int, hex int, short, long, float, *or* double. *The Applet Wizard automatically generates the code to convert that parameter from a* String *to the appropriate primitive data type.*

Tab over to the Desc field to provide a description of the parameter. Go ahead and enter **Text message to display** in the field. The Variable field contains the instance variable the program will store the parameter value in. This can be the same as what's in the Name column because those names are maintained within the applet's HTML file and this is an instance variable in the class. However, to ensure that you don't confuse the two, enter **msg**, as it is more meaningful than the default var0 name. Finally, the Default field enables you to enter an initial value for the parameter. You can change this later in the HTML file, but for now enter **"Good Morning, JBuilder"** and press Enter. When the Applet Wizard is done, there will be a <PARAM> tag in the generated HTML file for each parameter defined and the applet will contain the necessary code to read (and convert if necessary) the parameter settings. All that thanks to the Applet Wizard. Now click Next for the final screen.

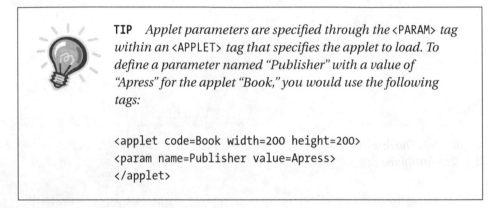

TIP   *Applet parameters are specified through the* <PARAM> *tag within an* <APPLET> *tag that specifies the applet to load. To define a parameter named "Publisher" with a value of "Apress" for the applet "Book," you would use the following tags:*

```
<applet code=Book width=200 height=200>
<param name=Publisher value=Apress>
</applet>
```

The final Applet Wizard screen (shown in Figure 2-6) asks if the Applet Wizard should create the HTML page for you. Instead of having to create an applet loader file yourself, you can have JBuilder do it for you.

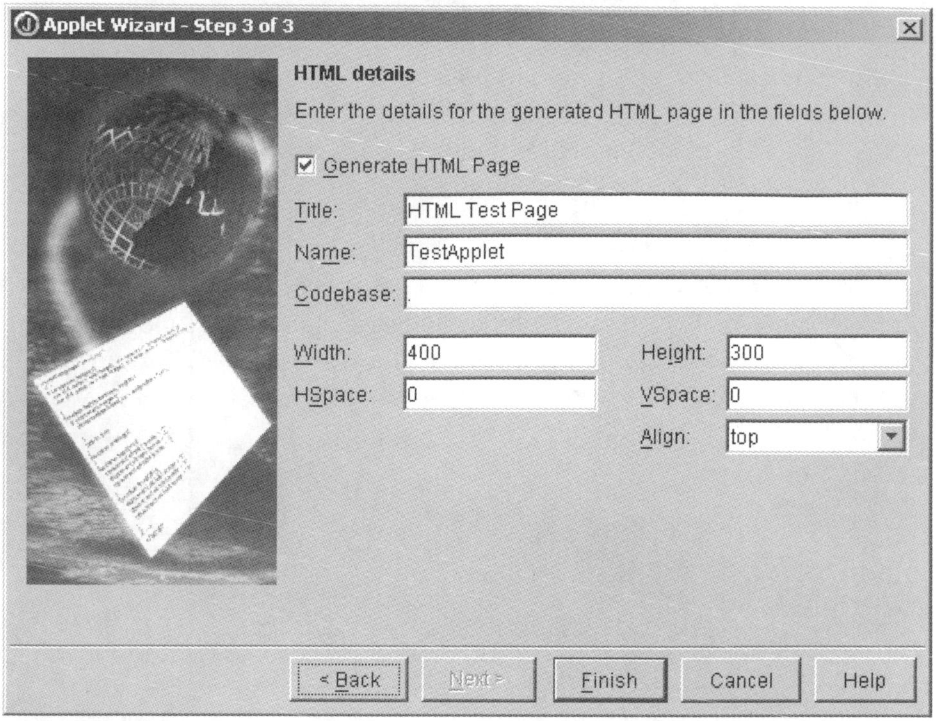

Figure 2-6. The Applet Wizard, Step 3 of 3. In this window, you'll enter information for generating the applet's HTML file.

Leave all the default settings for this form and just click Finish to let the Applet Wizard do its work. Before moving on, though, you should take a quick tour around the options. The Title field contains the HTML page's title, <TITLE>. The remaining fields each map directly to a parameter of the <APPLET>, all of which were explained in Skill 1.

When the Applet Wizard is done, you should see three files in the Navigation pane of the AppBrowser: Applet1.html, Applet1.java, and Skill2.html. To compile the applet, select Project ➢ Make Project "Skill2.jpx." Although the applet doesn't do anything yet, you can run it. Before you run it, you need to remember to save everything by selecting File ➢ Save All. Then select Run ➢ Run Project. This brings up an empty 400×300 screen, as shown in Figure 2-7.

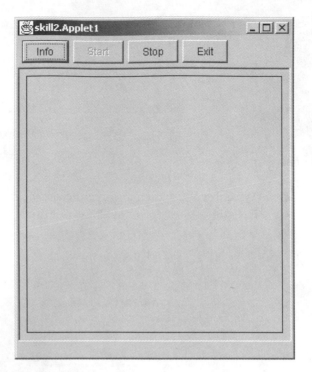

Figure 2-7. Running the initial applet

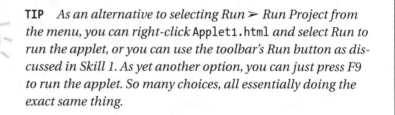

> **TIP** *As an alternative to selecting Run ➢ Run Project from the menu, you can right-click* Applet1.html *and select Run to run the applet, or you can use the toolbar's Run button as discussed in Skill 1. As yet another option, you can just press F9 to run the applet. So many choices, all essentially doing the exact same thing.*

Examining the Applet Source

Before you display the parameter, let's take a look at the code the Applet Wizard generated. All that clicking and typing generated about 50 lines of code in Applet1.java. Let's break it down into code segments and take a look at the parts.

The first line comes from the Package field on the first screen of the Applet Wizard. Although working in separate packages isn't absolutely necessary, it's much simpler when you work on larger projects.

```
package skill2;
```

This next set of statements is included whether you need them yet or not. They include the most frequently used packages of an applet. Remember that you need to explicitly reference classes, such as `java.applet.Applet`, or if you import the necessary package, you can implicitly use the class name by itself— `Applet` in this case.

```
import java.awt.*;
import java.awt.event.*;
import java.applet.*;
```

On the first Applet Wizard screen, you named your class `Applet1` and picked a base class of `Applet`. The other option for a base class is Swing's `JApplet` class.

```
public class Applet1 extends Applet {
```

NOTE *Swing is a set of graphical components introduced with the Java 2 platform, version 1.2. While the components are usable in 1.1-based programs, their usage is not recommended in applets, as you need to provide the Swing classes along with your applet when you execute the applet.*

The `isStandalone` setting refers to the Can run standalone option you didn't select on the first Applet Wizard screen.

```
boolean isStandalone = false;
```

NOTE *If you select the Can run standalone option during the first Applet Wizard step, the Wizard not only sets the flag to true but it also generates code that enables your applet to run as an application as well as an applet.*

On the second screen of the Applet Wizard, the last field in which you entered information was the variable name to use for the parameter passed in from HTML. As demonstrated, the variable name `msg` does not have to match the HTML parameter name `message`. However, you can name the two the same and no conflicts will arise as a result.

```
String msg;
```

Next is a helper routine that the Applet Wizard generates and uses for your applet. You normally don't need to call this version of `getParameter()` yourself because the Applet Wizard automatically generated the parameter-getting code for you. I'll cover what it does internally in just a moment. To use this method, JBuilder automatically generated the call `this.getParameter("message", "Good Morning, JBuilder")` in this example, which asks the method for the parameter setting of key—in this case its `message`. If the parameter isn't specified in the applet loader file, a default value, `def`, is used instead. This is all there is to `getParameter()`. For example, in this case, `key` is `message` and if `message` isn't a parameter in the HTML loader, the returned value is `Good Morning, JBuilder`.

```
//Get a parameter value
public String getParameter(String key, String def) {
  return isStandalone ? System.getProperty(key, def) :
    (getParameter(key) != null ? getParameter(key) : def);
}
```

Next is the constructor for your applet. The constructor is called by the system when it is time to create the applet. Normally, activities in the constructor are reserved for one-time tasks, but with applets, they aren't used for that purpose.

```
//Construct the applet
public Applet1() {
}
```

Instead, with applets, these tasks get done in the init() method:

```
//Initialize the applet
public void init() {
  try {
    msg = this.getParameter("message", "Good Morning, JBuilder");
  }
  catch(Exception e) {
    e.printStackTrace();
  }
  try {
    jbInit();
  }
  catch(Exception e) {
    e.printStackTrace();
  }
}
```

The init() method of an applet is called when the Web page containing the applet is first loaded. Here, the Applet Wizard gets the setting for the msg variable for you. If the data type is something other than String, the Applet Wizard writes the Java code to convert the parameter. If no message parameter is provided in the HTML file, the value you told the Applet Wizard to use as the default is used.

The jbInit() method is called from init() and is used for Java control initialization. Because this applet doesn't have any controls, you can leave the jbInit() method as is. The jbInit() method is not a standard Java method—it is one that JBuilder introduces to make control initialization easier *for JBuilder*. If you weren't using JBuilder, this code would naturally be placed directly in the init() method.

```
//Component initialization
private void jbInit() throws Exception {
}
```

 NOTE   *A* Java control *is a graphic component such as a button or check box. Skill 5 introduces Java controls.*

Finally, you have the getAppletInfo() and getParameterInfo() methods. The getAppletInfo() method shows a short informational string about the applet, usually the author's name and a copyright message. The getParameterInfo() method returns a series of three element arrays, one series entry for each parameter of the applet. The first element of each array is the HTML parameter name. The second is the data type within the Java program. The third and final element is a textual description of the parameter. If you look back to Figure 2-5, you entered these values on the second page of the Applet Wizard. If you were to click the Info button in Figure 2-7, you would see the settings.

```
//Get Applet information
public String getAppletInfo() {
  return "Applet Information";
}
//Get parameter info
public String[][] getParameterInfo() {
  String[][] pinfo =
    {
    {"message", "String", "Text message to display"},
    };
  return pinfo;
}
}
```

Unfortunately, these methods are two of the least frequently used methods around. Hopefully, through automation like the JBuilder wizards, they will be used more because they can be incredibly useful. The reason these methods are provided so infrequently is because neither Netscape Communicator nor Internet Explorer provides the means to automatically call the methods to display the information. For instance, with Netscape Communicator, you would expect to see this information when you select View ➤ Page Info. However, the results of neither appear when you ask about an applet.

Getting Applet Parameters

As long as you use the Applet Wizard, this part is easy—the Applet Wizard does the work for you. You are left with a variable of the proper data type even when a setting of the HTML parameter isn't provided. How easy could life be?

At some point, however, you may want to know how to do this yourself, so let's take a look at some pieces of the generated getParameter() method:

```
public String getParameter(String key, String def) {
  return isStandalone ? System.getProperty(key, def) :
    (getParameter(key) != null ? getParameter(key) : def);
}
```

Let's also examine init():

```
    msg = this.getParameter("message", "Good Morning, JBuilder");
```

Here, the init() method calls the getParameter() helper method. It says, "Get me the value of the message parameter from the HTML loader. If one doesn't exist, return a default setting of 'Good Morning, JBuilder.'" The parameter wouldn't exist if there wasn't a <PARAM name=message value= . . . > tag within the <APPLET> tag that loaded the applet.

In the getParameter() helper routine, the applet's own getParameter() method is called. That version takes a single parameter, String, whose value you are looking for. If the parameter exists in the name field of a <PARAM> tag, within the applet's <APPLET> tag, its value string is returned. If the parameter doesn't exist, getParameter() returns null. Remember, the <PARAM> tag looks like this:

```
<PARAM name=message value="Good Morning, JBuilder">
```

By using the helper routine, JBuilder incorporates the necessary checks to ensure you get a valid setting.

NOTE *Having multiple methods with the same name but different arguments is called* overloading. *The system knows which version to call by matching the number of parameters and their types.*

If the parameter data type is anything other than a String, the Applet Wizard will even add the code to convert the parameter to the proper data type. For example, if you wanted an integer and the <PARAM> tag was

```
<PARAM name=size value=2>
```

the Applet Wizard generates the following to get the integer value of the size setting:

```
try {
   size = Integer.parseInt(this.getParameter("size", "0"));
}
catch(Exception e) {
   e.printStackTrace();
}
```

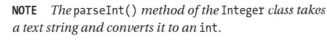

NOTE *The* parseInt() *method of the* Integer *class takes a text string and converts it to an* int.

Now you can update your applet to actually do something with the parameter. Add the following to the Applet1.java source file before the final curly brace (}) of the file:

```
public void paint(Graphics g) {
   g.drawString(msg, 20, 20);
}
```

Once you rebuild and rerun, the result will look like Figure 2-8.

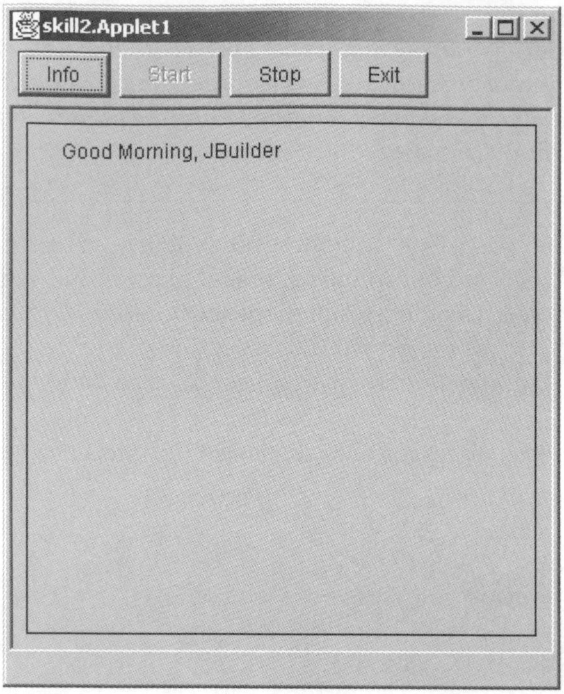

skill2.Applet1

| Info | Start | Stop | Exit |

Good Morning, JBuilder

Figure 2-8. Applet with the message parameter displayed

 NOTE   *At this point, you can also load* Applet1.html *in a Java-enabled Web browser to see the applet working within a browser.*

Using the Application Wizard

Where the Applet Wizard creates programs that run in a browser, such as Internet Explorer, you can create standalone applications with either the Applet Wizard or the Application Wizard.

In the Applet Wizard, you can select the Can run standalone option on the first screen. The Applet Wizard then automatically generates code so your applet will run as a standalone application. While this sounds convincing, using the Applet Wizard to generate purely standalone applications is not the best alternative. Because applets are normally given a display area within a browser, the standalone applet-application works within a similarly constrained area. If you are accustomed to your applications providing a menu or status message area, this is something the applet turned application doesn't have.

A better alternative is to use the Application Wizard. With it, you can automate the creation of a menu bar, toolbar, status message area, or an "about" box. These items make your program look and feel more like a standalone graphical application. Let's walk through the Application Wizard to create a frame that displays a message either from the command line or a system property.

NOTE *A* system property *is an attribute defined automatically for the current Java session. For instance, the location of the Java runtime environment is one of the automatic system properties. In Java, accessing operating system environment variables is illegal. System properties are a standard for providing similar functionality.*

Working from the Skill2 project, select File ➤ New and double-click the Application icon under the New tab. The screen shown in Figure 2-9 appears.

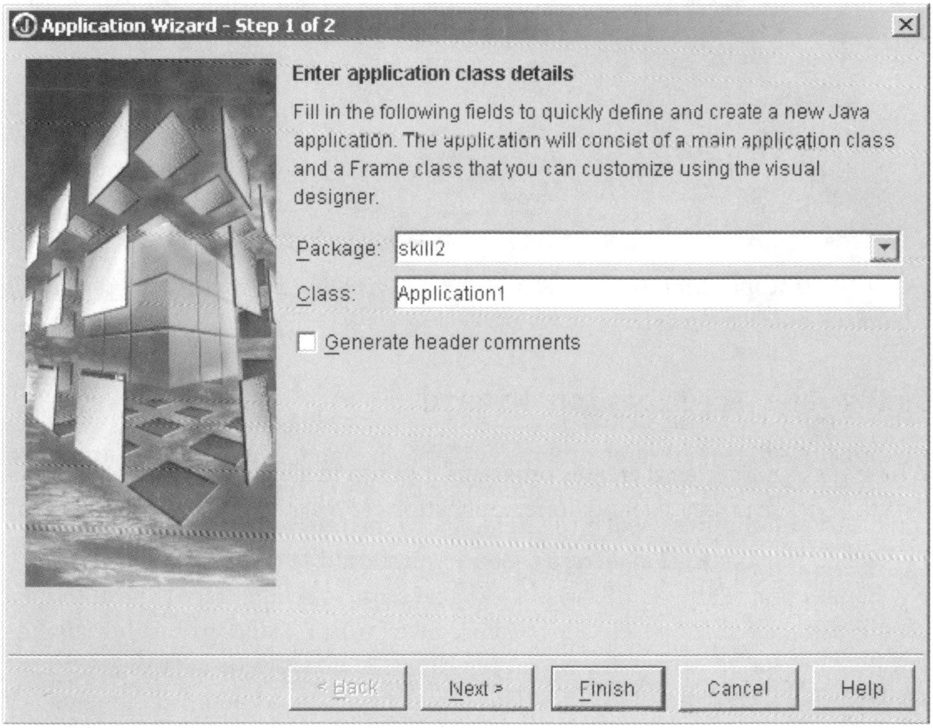

Figure 2-9. *Application Wizard, Step 1 of 2. In this window, you enter basic application information.*

From here, you can change the default package and application class name. However, to keep things simple, accept the defaults and click the Next button to display the screen shown in Figure 2-10. You can automatically generate the basic header comments for an application, which need to be expanded upon manually to describe what the program actually does.

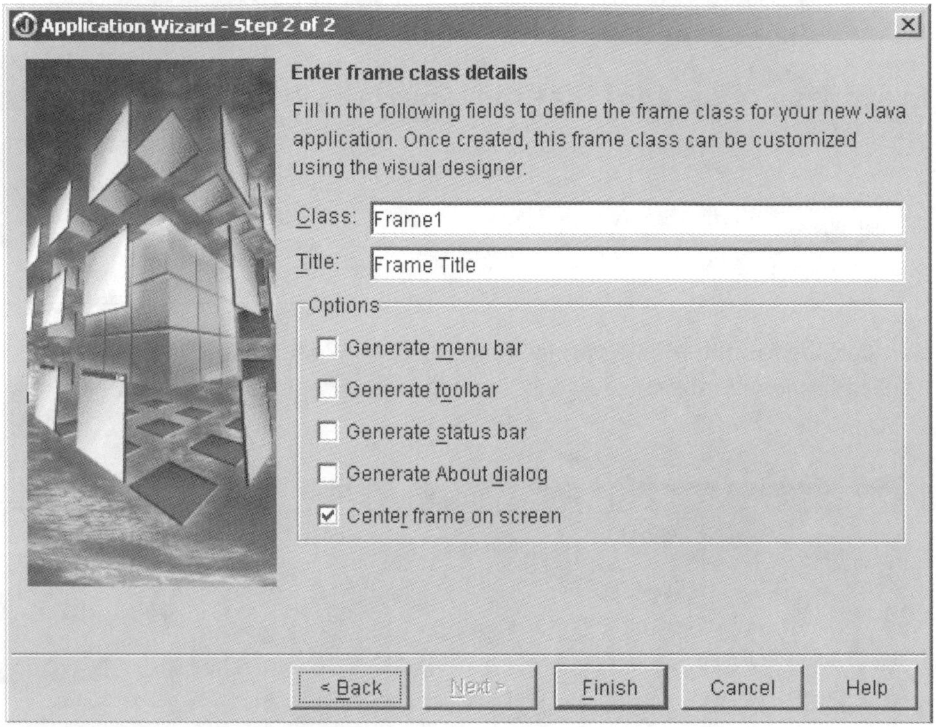

Figure 2-10. Application Wizard, Step 2 of 2. In this window, you enter information about the graphical frame.

For now, accept the defaults again and click Finish. Skill 17 and Skill 18 will demonstrate the other frame options available in Figure 2-10. The defaults create a class named Frame1. Along its window title bar, you'll find the default "Frame Title" text and the frame will be centered when the program runs.

When the Application Wizard is done, you should see two new files in the Navigation pane of the AppBrowser: Application1.java and Frame1.java. To compile the application, select Project ➤ Make Project "Skill2.jpx." Although the application doesn't do much yet, you can run it. To do so, right-click over Application1.java and select Run. This brings up an empty 400×300 screen.

NOTE *While the Applet Wizard prompts you for the screen size, the Application Wizard doesn't. The 400×300 size is automatically placed in the generated source. If you want to change the initial size, you have to edit the generated source code of the* Frame1.java *source file.*

Examining the Application Source

As with the applet, before you display the message, let's take a look at the code generated by the Application Wizard. All that clicking and typing generated about 35 lines of code in Frame1.java. Along with around 40 lines in Application1.java, that's the entire application.

The Application1.java source file shown in Listing 2-1 represents the loader for your application, Frame1. The main() method is what Java runs first for an application. This creates an instance of itself [new Application1()], which in turn creates a Frame1 object, sizes it, centers the window, and places the window on the screen. Its impact is limited to this single function.

Listing 2-1. Application Source Generated by the Application Wizard

```
package skill2;

import javax.swing.UIManager;
import java.awt.*;

public class Application1 {
  boolean packFrame = false;

  //Construct the application
  public Application1() {
    Frame1 frame = new Frame1();
    //Validate frames that have preset sizes
    //Pack frames that have useful preferred size info, e.g. from their layout
    if (packFrame) {
      frame.pack();
    }
    else {
      frame.validate();
    }
```

The jbInit() method sets up the internal panel (content pane), resizes the frame, and sets the title. The setIconImage() method call is commented out, but it allows you to change the image icon shown in the top-left corner of your frame on the title bar.

```
//Component initialization
private void jbInit() throws Exception  {
    //setIconImage(Toolkit.getDefaultToolkit().createImage(
    //  Frame1.class.getResource("[Your Icon]")));
    contentPane = (JPanel) this.getContentPane();
    contentPane.setLayout(borderLayout1);
    this.setSize(new Dimension(400, 300));
    this.setTitle("Frame Title");
}
```

The last method, processWindowEvent(), is used internally to close the application down when you close the frame. By default, the JFrame would be hidden, but the application would continue. This code is executed when you select the Close menu from the system menu, as shown in Figure 2-11 for Microsoft Windows.

```
//Overridden so we can exit when window is closed
protected void processWindowEvent(WindowEvent e) {
    super.processWindowEvent(e);
    if (e.getID() == WindowEvent.WINDOW_CLOSING) {
        System.exit(0);
    }
}
}
```

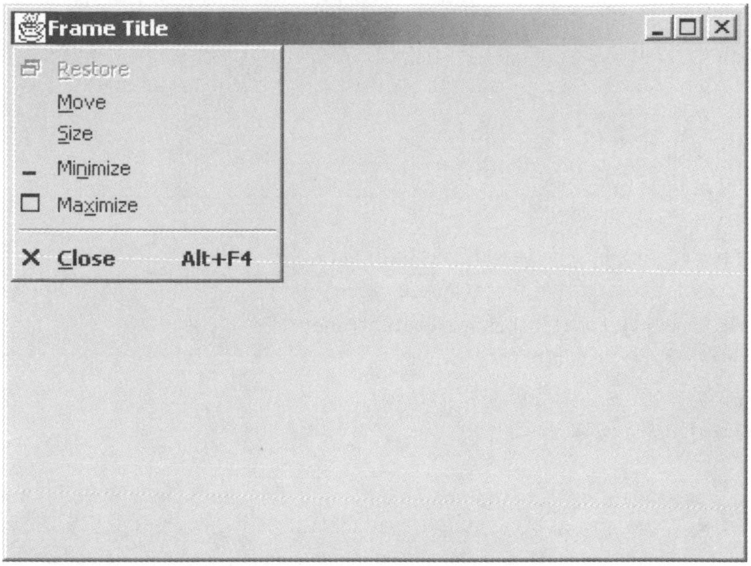

Figure 2-11. Microsoft's Close menu

Setting Application Parameters

There are actually two types of parameters you can use with applications: command-line parameters and system properties. Both are set in the same manner, but you access them inside your application in completely different ways. To set either the command-line parameters or the system properties, you select Project ➤ Project Properties, and then choose the Run tab to display the screen shown in Figure 2-12. You'll see the application's command-line parameters discussed first. The system properties are specified with the Virtual Machine (VM) parameters and are discussed later in this skill.

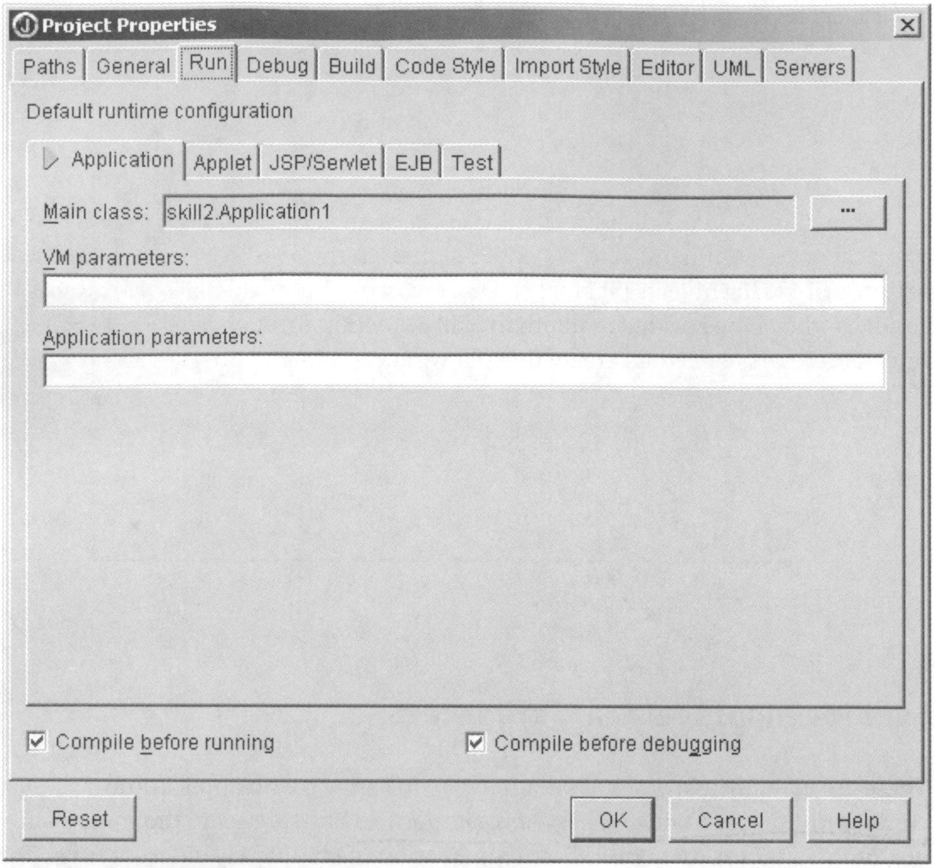

Figure 2-12. Select Project ➤ Project Properties, and then choose the Run tab to configure an application's parameters.

Command-Line Parameters

Command-line parameters get their name from the command-line environment that comes from the Java 2 Software Development Kit. Because you never see a command line with JBuilder, they are shown as "Application parameters" in Figure 2-12.

Java treats the space character as the separator between parameters, so if you enter **one two three**, Java treats that entry as three separate parameters. However, if you quote the string and enter **"one two three,"** Java treats this entry as only one parameter. You'll see shortly how these differ in Table 2-1.

Let's look back at the `main()` method of `Application1`, ignoring the look and feel changing part.

```
//Main method
public static void main(String[] args) {
. . .
  new Application1();
}
```

Because main() is the first thing that Java runs when it starts an application, you access the command-line parameters through the args parameter, which is an array of String objects (String[]). Don't worry about the details of arrays though—they'll be covered in depth in Skill 3. To loop through all the command-line parameters, you could create the following code fragment:

```
for (int count=0; count<args.length; count++) {
    System.out.println(args[count]);
}
```

NOTE *The parameter name* args *has no significance. You can use any parameter name you want. However,* args *is the one generated by the Application Wizard.*

The for statement is one of Java's looping constructs. In this case, the loop enables you to process the command-line arguments individually. The processing in this case is only printing; however, more complex processing could be done if necessary.

The first thing that probably jumps out at you is args.length. Java arrays are objects. Every array knows its size through its length instance variable. You do not have to maintain it separately. Also, Java arrays are *zero-based,* so if you have a ten-element array, you access the entries from 0 through 9.

To demonstrate, look at Table 2-1 to see how unquoted and quoted strings have an effect on the different settings of args. If the arguments are three separate strings, each is spread out among the array elements. However, if it is one quoted string, then that is only one element.

Table 2-1. Command-Line Parameter Demonstration

Arguments	args.length	args[0]	args[1]	args[2]
one two three	3	one	two	three
"one two three"	1	"one two three"	*invalid*	*invalid*

Now, to change your application to display the first command-line argument, you need to make a few changes to the Application1 and Frame1 classes. You need to get the argument from the command line of Application1 over to Frame1. The first thing you need to do is get the parameter from the command line.

```
//Main method
public static void main(String[] args) {
. . .
   String msg;
   if (args.length == 0) {
     msg = "Good Morning, JBuilder";
   } else {
     msg = args[0];
   }
   new Application1(msg);
}
```

The if (args.length == 0) statement checks to see if there are any arguments. You should always check for arguments before you try to access specific elements of the array, because if you try to access an array outside of its boundaries an exception will be thrown. (You'll learn more about exceptions in Skill 3.) After getting a message to display, either a default or the command-line argument, you then pass the message to the Application1 constructor, which needs to notify Frame1.

```
public Application1(String msg) {
   Frame1 frame = new Frame1();
   frame.setMessage(msg);
. . .
```

Here, you changed one line and added another. First, you added the new parameter to the Application1 constructor argument list. This in turn is passed to Frame1 through a new setMessage() method you need to create.

Now you go over to Frame1.java and change a few things. You need a variable to store the current message to display and a setMessage() method to set it.

Finally, you need to draw the string in the frame. You do this by adding a paint() method and having it call the drawString() method of its Graphics argument. Add the following code immediately before the final curly brace (}) character:

```
String message = "Hello";
public void setMessage(String msg) {
  message = msg;
}
public void paint(Graphics g) {
  g.drawString(message, 50, 50);
}
```

If you don't set any command-line parameters and just run Application1 (select Run ➤ Run Project), you'll see the frame in Figure 2-13.

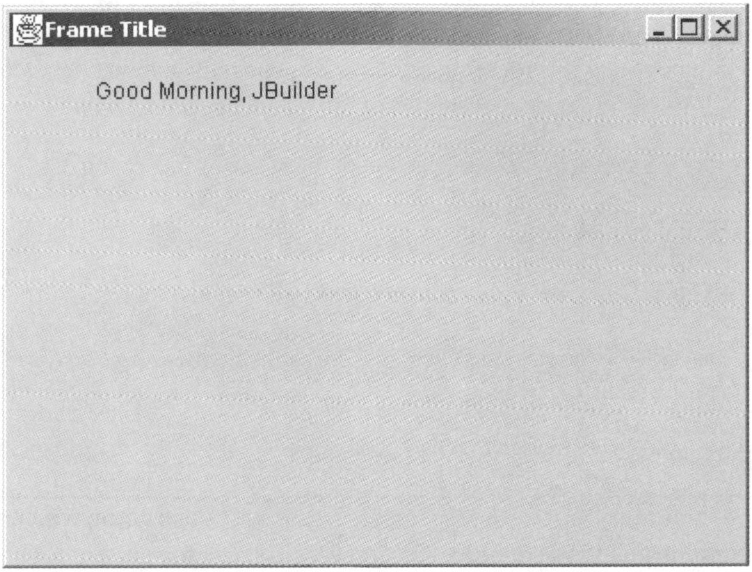

Figure 2-13. The new Application1 program run without parameters

If, instead, you enter something in the Application parameters field in the Project Properties window (see Figure 2-12), you will see the first parameter displayed. For instance, if you enter **"One Two Three"** in the Application parameters field, you see "One Two Three" in the frame instead of "Good Morning, JBuilder."

System Properties

System properties are more similar to HTML parameters than command-line parameters. JBuilder requires that you enter system properties in the VM parameters field of the Project Properties window (see Figure 2-12). Each system property parameter setting begins with –D and is a key-value pair. The following demonstrates one such setting:

```
-Dskill2.message="Welcome to JBuilder"
```

The *D* in –D stands for *define*. The entry before the equal sign is the *key*, while the term after it is called the *value*.

Java VM Parameter Settings

VM parameters get their name because of other available options that can be entered in the VM Parameters field in the Project Properties dialog box. These other options control settings for the Java Virtual Machine (VM). Most likely, you will never need some of these options, but they are available:

- -version shows the current version of the Java runtime being used.

- -help shows a complete list of options available.

- -X shows help for the available nonstandard options.

- -Xms and –Xms enable you to change the available memory size (used for creating really big programs).

You'll see any output in the Message pane.

A key-value pair works in the following way: You ask the system for a particular key, skill2.message in this case, and get its value, Welcome to JBuilder. If it isn't set, null is returned. This works similarly to the getParameter() methods you used with the applet.

```
String s = System.getProperty("skill2.message");
```

You can also provide a default value for when the requested property isn't set:

```
String s = System.getProperty("skill2.message", "Hello");
```

All this works with the help of the `java.util.Properties` class. The system reads in the –D command-line options first and stores them in an internal system property table. From there, the program starts in the `main()` method. If the program ever needs a property, it asks the system for it; otherwise, the properties are ignored.

In addition to enabling developers to set their own properties by defining properties in the VM parameters field, the system comes with a set of 45 properties already set for applications and 19 properties available for applets. For security reasons, there are fewer properties available for applets. For example, while applets do not have access to where Java is installed on the user's machine, they can find out what operating system is being used. Table 2-2 lists the different properties that are available and states whether or not they are available for applets. The set seems to grow with each version of Java.

Table 2-2. Available System Properties

Name	Description	Available from Applet
awt.toolkit	Toolkit class name returned by `Toolkit.getDefaultToolkit()`	No
file.encoding	Mechanism to convert from bytes to characters	No
file.encoding.pkg	Package used for conversion	No
file.separator	Platform-specific file path separator	Yes
java.awt.fonts	Directory to get fonts from	No
java.awt.graphicsenv	Local graphics environment	No
java.awt.printerjob	Name of `java.awt.print.PrinterJob` implementation class	No
java.class.path	Where Java runtime looks for classes	No
java.class.version	Java's class library version	Yes
java.ext.dirs	Where Java runtime looks for extension libraries	No
java.home	Java's installation directory	No
java.io.tmpdir	Directory name for creating temporary files	No
java.library.path	Where Java looks for native libraries	No
java.runtime.name	Name of Java runtime environment	No
java.runtime.version	Version of Java runtime environment	No

(continued)

Table 2-2. Available System Properties (continued)

Name	Description	Available from Applet
java.specification.name	Name of Java specification	Yes
java.specification.vendor	Vendor of Java specification	Yes
java.specification.version	Version of Java specification	Yes
java.vendor	Vendor of Java environment	Yes
java.vendor.url	URL for Java vendor	Yes
java.vendor.url.bug	Where to submit bug reports for Java vendor	No
java.version	Version of Java	Yes
java.vm.info	VM information for Just-in-Time compiler	No
java.vm.name	Name of VM used	Yes
java.vm.specification.name	Specification name for VM	Yes
java.vm.specification.vendor	Specification vendor of VM	Yes
java.vm.specification.version	Specification version of VM	Yes
java.vm.vendor	Vendor of VM	Yes
java.vm.version	Java version of VM	Yes
line.separator	Platform-specific string that separates lines	Yes
os.arch	Machine architecture	Yes
os.name	Operating system name	Yes
os.version	Operating system version	Yes
path.separator	Platform-specific string that separates entries in the paths	Yes
sun.boot.class.path	Where Java runtime looks for system classes	No
sun.boot.library.path	Where Java runtime looks for native system libraries	No
sun.cpu.endian	Internal byte order for numbers	No
sun.cpu.isalist	List of CPU types of user's system	No
sun.io.unicode.encoding	Internal Unicode encoding	No
user.dir	User's working directory	No
user.home	User's home directory	No

(continued)

Table 2-2. Available System Properties (continued)

Name	Description	Available from Applet
user.language	User's language	No
user.name	User's login name	No
user.region	User's geographic region	No
user.timezone	User's time zone	No

To display all current property settings in an application on the Message pane, add the following line to the main() method:

```
System.getProperties().list(System.out);
```

 NOTE *Applets can only fetch single property values with* System.getProperty(name). *They can't ask for all properties with* System.getProperties().

Sample System Property Values

To demonstrate possible values for the different properties, the following entries are displayed on one particular system with the System.getProperties().list(System.out) call just shown.

```
-- listing properties --
awt.toolkit=sun.awt.windows.WToolkit
file.encoding=Cp1252
file.encoding.pkg=sun.io
file.separator=\
java.awt.fonts=
java.awt.graphicsenv=sun.awt.Win32GraphicsEnvironment
java.awt.printerjob=sun.awt.windows.WPrinterJob
java.class.path=C:\skills\Skill2\classes;C:\JB ...
java.class.version=47.0
java.ext.dirs=C:\JBuilder\jdk1.3\jre\lib\ext
java.home=C:\JBuilder\jdk1.3\jre
java.io.tmpdir=C:\WINNT\TEMP\
```

```
java.library.path=C:\JBuilder\jdk1.3\bin;.;C:\WINNT\Syste ...
java.runtime.name=Java(TM) 2 Runtime Environment, Stand ...
java.runtime.version=1.3.0_01
java.specification.name=Java Platform API Specification
java.specification.vendor=Sun Microsystems Inc.
java.specification.version=1.3
java.vendor=Sun Microsystems Inc.
java.vendor.url=http://java.sun.com/
java.vendor.url.bug=http://java.sun.com/cgi-bin/bugreport ...
java.version=1.3.0_01
java.vm.info=mixed mode
java.vm.name=Java HotSpot(TM) Client VM
java.vm.specification.name=Java Virtual Machine Specification
java.vm.specification.vendor=Sun Microsystems Inc.
java.vm.specification.version=1.0
java.vm.vendor=Sun Microsystems Inc.
java.vm.version=1.3.0_01
line.separator=
os.arch=x86
os.name=Windows 2000
os.version=5.0
path.separator=;
sun.boot.class.path=C:\JBuilder\jdk1.3\jre\lib\rt.jar;C:\JB ...
sun.boot.library.path=C:\JBuilder\jdk1.3\jre\bin
sun.cpu.endian=little
sun.cpu.isalist=pentium i486 i386
sun.io.unicode.encoding=UnicodeLittle
user.dir=C:\skills\Skill2
user.home=C:\Documents and Settings\jaz
user.language=en
user.name=jaz
user.region=US
user.timezone=
```

Normally, the output is not sorted—that was done here for readability. Also, some versions of Netscape Communicator and Internet Explorer offer the browser property to applets. This is nonstandard.

Returning to the Application1 example, if you want to display the message in the skill2.message property, you only need to change the main() method to get the same results as the command-line version. To do so, replace the code that looks at the args parameter with code that looks at the system property:

```
  public static void main(String[] args) {
. . .
    String msg;
    msg = System.getProperty("skill2.message", "Good Morning, JBuilder");
    new Application1(msg);
  }
```

ARE YOU EXPERIENCED?

In this skill, you used the Applet Wizard and Application Wizard and concentrated on the basics. While you avoided some of the extra capabilities available from the wizards, you'll learn about them in later skills.

Now you can

- Create a project

- Create an applet using the Applet Wizard

- Access applet parameters

- Use the Application Wizard to create a standalone application

- Access application command-line parameters

- Access system properties

- Provide a list of available system properties

Now that you have a feel for JBuilder, let's take a step back and explore the syntax of the Java language in Skill 3.

Using Java Syntax

- Introducing Java syntax

- Working with data types

- Using flow control

- Declaring classes, methods, and variables

- Understanding access modifiers

- Introducing exception handling

Introducing Java Syntax

The first two skills covered the various capabilities of Java, without much explanation of the syntax of the language. In this skill, you'll look at the language so you'll be able to work through the remaining skills. If you don't grasp something right away, don't worry too much. You'll get more comfortable as you continue to use the various pieces.

The syntax of a language is called its *grammar*. It consists of the *keywords, identifiers*, and *operators* of the language, along with the rules for combining them. First, you'll look at the different parts of the Java programming language, and then you'll see how to put them together.

Comments

First off, let's look at *comments*. You use comments to document your code, so when others read it or you look at it again in a few months, your comments will provide a sense of what you intended the code should do quickly. Java has three styles of comments. Two are from the C++ world, while the third extends a C++ comment style.

- `//` is for single-line comments, where the comment extends to the end of the line.

- `/* comment */` is for multiline comments.

- `/** javadoc comment */` is also for multiline comments; however, these comments are called *documenting comments*. Documenting comments enable you to create documentation directly from the source code. In JBuilder, selecting the Doc tab in the Content pane of the AppBrowser while looking at a class will show you the javadoc-style documentation for that class. Figure 3-1 shows this documentation for the `getParameter()` method of the `Applet` class. This text was placed within javadoc-style comments within the source code for the class. You can do the same thing with your own classes.

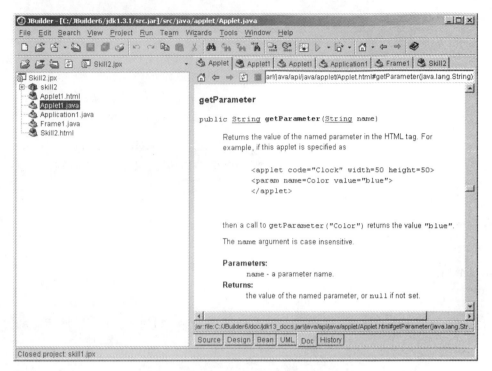

Figure 3-1. The javadoc documentation for the method of a class

To display the javadoc for a class, you can right-click to open the context menu over a class name in your source and select Browse Symbol. This brings up the source code for the class. From there, you can select the Doc tab to see the javadoc documentation (as in Figure 3-1).

NOTE *You can generate the javadoc documentation for your own classes; just follow the instructions on the screen that appears when you click on the Doc tab. For more information on generating javadoc files, visit* `http://java.sun.com/j2se/javadoc/`.

Keywords

Keywords describe the words that a Java compiler will understand. Table 3-1 lists the Java programming language keywords. Out of context, they don't have much meaning, but you'll learn about them as you progress through the book. If you've programmed in another language, many of the keywords in Table 3-1 should look somewhat familiar.

Table 3-1. Java Keywords

abstract	finally	public
boolean	float	return
break	for	short
byte	goto*	static
case	if	strictfp
catch	implements	super
char	import	switch
class	instanceof	synchronized
const*	int	this
continue	interface	throw
default	long	throws
do	native	transient
double	new	try
else	package	void
extends	private	volatile
final	protected	while

* = Reserved as keyword but not used by Java

Identifiers

Identifiers are how Java recognizes classes, variables, and methods. They can start with a letter, an underscore (_), or a dollar sign ($), with remaining positions adding numerals (0-9) to the list of available characters.

Because Java uses the Unicode character set, not just ASCII for U.S. English, the characters used can be outside the typical uppercase and lowercase A-Z range. For instance, façade is a valid variable name. And, you can even use the ideographs in Asian languages in your variable names.

NOTE *If you are not familiar with the Unicode standard, it describes characters for the majority of the international community within a single, 16-bit mapping. With the help of a local font or fonts, appropriate character strings are displayed. Without the fonts, unrecognizable garbage appears. Additional information about Unicode is available from the Unicode Consortium (*http://www.unicode.org/*). For additional information about adding fonts to Java, read the internationalization documentation at* http://java.sun.com /j2se/1.3/docs/guide/intl/index.html.

Operators

Operators are used to transform identifiers and literals (see the upcoming section on literals) within *expressions*. Expressions are statements in which operators function upon variables and return a value. For example, c = a + b; is really two expressions. The first expression takes the value of a and b, performs addition (+ is the addition operator) on them, and returns the sum. The second expression assigns that returned value (the sum of a and b) to the variable c. So, what's a "statement"? Well, a *statement* is a line of Java source code that ends with a semicolon (;). The line may span multiple physical lines within the source code, but it is still considered one statement. For example, the following is one statement:

```
x = 4 * y + 8 / z;
```

This is also a statement:

```
x = 4 *
  y + 8
    / z;
```

The Java programming language consists of operators for math, relational, logical, bit-wise, and assignment operations. In addition to the operators, you can combine operations within parentheses to create larger expressions. Let's take a look at the various operators.

Table 3-2 lists the math operators, which are used for standard math functions.

generates the same result: adding 7 to the original value of y and storing the new value in y. This operator and the other assignment operators are listed in Table 3-5.

Table 3-5. Assignment Operators

Operator	Usage	Normal Operation
=	c = a;	c = a;
+=	c += a;	c = c + a;
-=	c -= a;	c = c - a;
*=	c *= a;	c = c * a;
/=	c /= a;	c = c / a;
%=	c %= a;	c = c % a;
&=	c &= a;	c = c & a;
|=	c |= a;	c = c | a;
^=	c ^= a;	c = c ^ a;
<<=	c <<= a;	c = c << a;
>>=	c >>= a;	c = c >> a;
>>>=	c >>>= a;	c = c >>> a;

Working with Data Types, Literals, and Strings

Now that you know about keywords, identifiers, and operators, let's take a look at how Java manages *data types*, *literals*, and *strings*.

Data Types

A *data type* is the way that Java stores the contents of some value internally. For instance, the letter *c* is a character. Within Java, it would be stored as type char. A Java char is 16-bits/2 bytes because of the Unicode standard for internationalization support. There are actually seven other data types within Java. All the data types are listed in Table 3-6.

Table 3-6. Java Data Types

Data Type	Rule
boolean	true/false
char	16-bit Unicode character
byte	8-bit signed two's complement number
short	16-bit signed two's complement number
int	32-bit signed two's complement number
long	64-bit signed two's complement number
float	32-bit signed floating-point number
double	64-bit signed floating-point number

If you happen to use other programming languages, you may notice a few differences between Java and languages such as C and C++. First and foremost, the size of an int is defined by the language, not by the compiler vendor. You do not have to worry if an int is 16 or 32 bits. In Java, it is always 32 bits. Then there is the boolean data type. Instead of having to worry if 0 is false and non-0 is true or vice versa, Java defines a data type with two distinct values as possible settings. The language designers at Sun did this with you—the programmer—in mind to help reduce programming errors.

The data types listed in Table 3-6 are called primitives. The other data type in Java are *reference types*. Reference types are references to classes, interfaces, and arrays. These will be looked at shortly.

Literals

A literal is taken quite literally by the system, kind of like WYTIWYG (What You Type Is What You Get). Specifically, a literal is a constant. The constant's data type depends on the makeup of the content. Table 3-7 lists available literal data types.

Table 3-7. Literally Speaking

Literal	Possible Values	Value
boolean	true/false	true
byte/short/int	A decimal number	11234
	An octal number (has a leading 0)	0123
	A hexadecimal number (has a leading 0x)	0x8912
long	A decimal number with a trailing l or L	888383L
float	A floating-point number with a trailing f or F	3.14f
double	A floating-point number with an optional trailing d or D	3.141592
char	A single-quoted character	'z'

For characters, in addition to having a single-quoted character to provide a value, there are nine special literals:

- \'   Single quote

- \"   Double quote

- \\   Backslash

- \b   Backspace

- \f   Form feed

- \n   New line

- \r   Carriage return

- \t   Tab

- \xxx   Octal value of character (for example, \101 is the character "A")

Strings

Strings are represented by a series of characters between double quotes ("), instead of the single quotes used for individual characters. A String is actually an object in the system, rather than just a primitive data type. Objects have extra responsibilities that enable developers to perform various operations on the object without the use of operators. These capabilities are available through methods, which I'll discuss shortly. One such method for a `String` class is the `length()` method. The method returns the actual length of the string. For instance, `"Hello, World"` is a string. When asked its length, `"Hello, World".length()` reports 12, because there are 12 characters in the string, including the space.

Declaring Classes, Variables, and Methods

With the help of your friends—identifiers, operators, literals, and the rest—you can now start programming. With some languages, you can create standalone functions and global variables. With Java, that is not the case. Everything you create must be part of a *class*. Classes themselves must exist within a package. If you don't specify a package when you define a class, a default is assigned so that initially you don't need to worry about creating packages much. As you saw in Skill 2, with JBuilder your classes are already placed in packages.

Methods are usually defined next. They enable you to associate behavior with a class—what it does and how it functions. Finally, if the class needs to retain its state, that is done through variables. All methods and variables must be defined within classes.

Classes

I touched on classes briefly in Skill 1. As you may recall, a class defines the state and behavior of an object. In order to define a class in Java, you start a new file with the following line:

```
class SomeName
```

SomeName is the name of the class to create. If you are creating a subclass of something—say, an applet—the line becomes:

```
class SomeName extends java.applet.Applet
```

This line says that the *SomeName* class is a subclass of `Applet`. This is how Java implements the object-oriented concept of inheritance, which was discussed briefly in Skill 1.

After you declare the class, everything else for the class goes between a series of curly braces ({}) that follow.

After you finish defining the class, you save it in a file that matches the class name. If *SomeName* represents class `Bart`, the file to save to is `Bart.java`. If SomeName were actually used, the filename would need to be `SomeName.java`.

Only classes that are public need to be saved in files that match the class name. This enables you to include support classes that nobody knows about within your application definition. Helper classes for the main class of an applet (the class that subclasses `Applet`) or the application (the class that has the `main()` method to start the program) can all reside in the files for applet or application. However, Sun's reference implementation of the Java compiler requires you to put your public classes into separate files, which is a good programming practice and enables you to find things more easily.

 NOTE *For more on what a public class is, see the upcoming "Access Modifiers" section.*

Variables

Variables reserve space for primitive data types and classes. They can also be initialized with literals. The following statement declares the variable x as an `int` with an initial value of 7:

```
int x = 7;
```

To declare a variable, you define a statement that starts with a data type and is followed by an identifier. If you want to initialize it, follow the data type with an equal sign and a literal. For those variables defined outside methods, variables actually get a default initial value. Table 3-8 shows these default values.

Table 3-8. Default Initialization Values

Data Type	Default Initial Value
boolean	false
byte	(byte)0
short	(short)0
int	0
long	0L
float	0.0f
double	0.0d
char	'\u0000'

For variables that are not for the built-in primitive data types but for a reference to a class, the right side of the equal sign can't be a literal. You need to use the new keyword to create a new instance of the class.

```
Bart brat = new Bart();
```

The previous statement declares the variable brat as a Bart and creates a new Bart object. This assumes a class named Bart is defined somewhere.

Arrays

An array is another reference type in Java. They enable you to store multiple values within a single, linear structure. When you create an array, you define its size and data type, and then you fill it to the rim with objects. Let's look at a couple of examples:

```
int x[] = new int[7];
float []y = new float[8];
```

The first thing you may notice is that the square brackets can appear on either side of the variable name. Although Java has this flexibility, you should consistently use the square brackets on whichever side you prefer. Common practice is to place the brackets on the right side of the identifier.

Also, because arrays contain multiple items within a single structure, initialization of arrays is a little more involved than initialization of primitives. Instead of just setting the variable to a literal, you need to do some additional work. You'll also notice the use of the new keyword. Just like when you initialize a variable to a new instance of a class, Java requires you to create new instances of arrays. The new int[7] part of the statement says to create a seven-element array of integers. You can then fill it with lines like the following, which sets the fifth element of the array to 90:

```
x[4] = 90;
```

TIP *All arrays in Java are zero-based, so a seven-element array would be referenced with indices of 0 to 6.*

If you happen to know the values of an array beforehand, you can initialize it at declaration time. In such a case, you don't need to specify the array size, as the number of elements specified is used to determine the size.

```
int z[] = {100, 200, 400, 800};
```

This also allows me to mention an instance variable of arrays. Besides String objects knowing how big they are, arrays in Java know how long they are. The length of an array is found through the length instance variable. For the array z just defined, z.length would be 4.

While, technically speaking, Java doesn't have multidimensional arrays, there is nothing to keep you from creating an array of array objects. This enables you to nest multiple levels of arrays, and each level isn't required to be the same size. For instance, the following demonstrates an array where each subarray is a different size:

```
int w[][] = {{3, 4}, {1, 2, 3, 4, 5, 6, 7, 8, 9, 10}, {11, 12, 13}};
```

Here, w.length is 3, w[0].length is 2, w[1].length is 10, and w[2].length is 3.

Methods

Methods are how you get your programs to work. A method describes the behavior of the class that contains it. You create a method by specifying the return type, method name, and an argument list. If there is no return value, specify void.

```
void setValue(int newValue) {
  . . .
}
```

With this setValue() method, the single parameter is newValue. It represents the local reference for a value passed into the method. Had the method been called with var.setValue(3), newValue would have a setting of 3 within the method. Multiple parameters are specified with a comma-separated list.

If a method has a return value, not only must you specify the type, but you also need to use the return statement to return a value of the appropriate type:

```
int getValue() {
  int value = 1;
  . . .
  return value;
}
```

Interfaces

An interface is a special kind of class. It specifies a template for a set of methods that a class must define. To declare an interface, you use the `interface` keyword.

```
public interface Area {
  public double getArea() {
}
```

When you define an interface, you do not specify the behavior of the method(s). You only specify what the method declaration looks like. Then, when a class chooses to *implement* the interface, it must fill in the details of each method of the interface.

```
public class Rectangle implements Area {
  int height;
  int width;
  . . .
  public double getArea() {
    return (height * width);
  }
  . . .
}
```

The nice thing about an interface is that every class can implement the interface differently, keeping the method declaration fixed.

```
public class Triangle implements Area {
  int height;
  int base;
  . . .
  public double getArea() {
    return (height * base / 2.0);
  }
  . . .
}
```

Then, you use the interface as a parameter to other methods. Because the interface has a known behavior, you can call an interface's methods without knowing the actual class involved.

```
public void printArea(Area a) {
  System.out.println(a.getArea());
}
```

Packages

A *package* is a grouping of related classes. The core Java API provides a set of packages to work with. Each has a focused set of functionality provided by the classes within it. In other language environments, such as C++, this structure may be referred to as *class libraries*. However, other languages, such as Ada, share Java's naming convention and call them "packages."

When you use any class in Java, the runtime environment needs to be able to locate it. At compile time, the compiler needs to be able to find it, too. You can reference each class with its fully qualified name—java.applet.Applet, for instance—every time you need it. Or, you can tell the compiler where things might be—import java.awt.*—and then use just the final piece, the class name (for instance, Graphics), each time. In this case, java.awt is the name of the package within the core Java libraries to reference.

In each of these cases, a package is used. The java.applet package contains classes for applets, while the java.awt package includes classes for interacting with the graphics environment. The Abstract Window Toolkit (AWT) is important for drawing and working with user interface elements.

TIP   *Classes in the* java.lang *package do not need to be imported. The compiler implicitly imports this package because its use is so fundamental. For instance, the* String *class is a commonly used class found in the* java.lang *package.*

You can tell the compiler about an entire package by importing it with an asterisk at the end: import java.applet.*. Or, you can import a specific piece of a package by explicitly specifying the class name: import java.awt.Graphics. The way you import classes tends to be based on personal preference. Neither way has an effect on the runtime performance of the compiled program.

TIP   *Importing is different from the C/C++ #include mechanism. Including header files in C and C++ physically incorporated the header file contents into the program. With Java, on the other hand, importing keeps class files separate. You're just telling the compiler and runtime environment where to look for the current version of the class. This greatly reduces unnecessary recompilations and leaves quite a few checks until runtime.*

To better group classes when you create your own packages, the very first noncomment line of your source code must be this:

```
package packagename;
```

When you use JBuilder wizards, this line is automatically added for you. Then, when you build your program, JBuilder places the `.class` files into the *packagename* directory. For every period in the package name, a subdirectory is created. For example, the `Graphics` class is in the directory `java\awt` (or `java/awt` on Linux). When it's time to install your packages on a Web server, this structure enables you to properly place all the necessary pieces, without clashes with other class names.

> **TIP**   *If you don't like the default package names in the JBuilder Application Wizard or Applet Wizard, you can place your own name in the Package field of the wizard's form. The appropriate package line is then automatically included in your source file.*

Access Modifiers

When classes, variables, and methods are declared, they have a certain visibility in the block they are declared in, as defined by the surrounding set of braces ({}). However, when classes, variables, and methods are defined at the class level, they may be visible beyond the class scope.

In order to control who has access to classes, variables, and methods, you need to specify an access modifier when the class, variable, and method are declared. Java provides three access modifier keywords: `private`, `protected`, and `public`. There is also a fourth behavior when no keyword is specified. Each may be used with a class name, instance variable, or method, with similar results. These access modifiers are described in Table 3-9.

while

In Java, the while statement repeatedly executes a block of code while a certain condition is true. The following example demonstrates the looping construct. Once SomeStuff.x reaches 0, the increase variable will have the necessary count.

```
while (SomeStuff.x != -1) {
  increase++;
  --SomeStuff.x;
}
```

 NOTE *With* while *loops, it is possible to completely pass over the loop without ever executing the internal statements if the initial test condition is false.*

do-while

The do-while loop is for those times when you need to be sure the loop executes at least once. The loop continues until the condition in the while clause is false.

```
do {
  . . .
} while (aCondition);
```

for

A for loop has three separate parts:

```
for (initialization; termination; update) {
  . . .
}
```

The *initialization* part sets things up for the first pass through the loop. Before each run through the loop, the *termination* condition is checked. After each execution of the internal statements, the *update* piece is run. As with a while loop, it is possible that the statements within a for loop are never executed.

Frequently, you'll find a variable defined in the initialization section. This keeps the scope of the variable completely within the for loop. The following example shows this along with a for loop that loops from 0 to 9:

```
for (int i = 0; i < 10; i++) {
  ...
}
```

Trying to access the variable i outside the for loop results in a compilation error.

switch

The switch statement is built for conditional operations with many choices, where the choices are integers or some data type that can be accessed as one. When the system scopes out a switch block for a match, it starts at the top and tries to locate the first matching condition. If it doesn't find one, there is a default entry for nonmatching conditions that can be specified.

Each choice is specified with a case keyword followed by the value and a colon (:). The break statement can also be used to prevent the execution of other test cases. In the event you want to provide behavior for when there is no direct match, you use the default keyword.

```
switch (day) {
  case 0: System.out.println("Sunday"); break;
  case 1: System.out.println("Monday"); break;
  case 2: System.out.println("Tuesday"); break;
  case 3: System.out.println("Wednesday"); break;
  case 4: System.out.println("Thursday"); break;
  case 5: System.out.println("Friday"); break;
  case 6: System.out.println("Saturday"); break;
  default: System.out.println("OOPS!"); break;
}
```

If the break statement is missing, the system continues to execute code until it finds one or until the end of the `switch` block is reached. For example, the following code block will print Thursday, Friday, Saturday, and OOPS if the day passed in was 4:

```
switch (day) {
    case 0: System.out.println("Sunday");
    case 1: System.out.println("Monday");
    case 2: System.out.println("Tuesday");
    case 3: System.out.println("Wednesday");
    case 4: System.out.println("Thursday");
    case 5: System.out.println("Friday");
    case 6: System.out.println("Saturday");
    default: System.out.println("OOPS!");
}
```

NOTE   *The* default *condition does not have to be last. For instance, it could be first. It would still only execute if no other* case *matched. However, conceptually speaking, it makes more sense to put the* default *condition last.*

Using Exception Handling

Prior to C++ and Java, error handling frequently involved functions returning specific values to signify an error and any other value meant success. Alternatively, error handling added an extra parameter to all your functions. Prior to checking the return value of the function call, you needed to check with the extra parameter to see if there were any complications in executing the function. If you forget to check the extra parameter, the value returned could be invalid had there been an error. This led to error-prone code, and numerous tedious and cumbersome extra checks were necessary.

Exception handling is Java's way of handling errors. An *exception* is something that alters the flow of a program. When the exception occurs, code execution is redirected, and you will need to handle the exception or properly pass it along to your caller, who will be expecting it. In order for exception handling to work, you need to tell the caller when to expect an exception. Then you deliver your code to handle the expected exception.

When you are working with a code block that might cause an exception, you place the statement or statements within a try-catch block. The `catch` block part is called the *exception handler.*

```
try {
  // Some statement(s)
} catch (ExceptionType e) {
  // Some error handling code
}
```

If the statements within the block execute successfully, without exceptions, the error-handling code will not be executed. On the other hand, if there is an exception in, for example, the fourth of ten statements, the fifth statement and beyond within the try-catch block will not be executed. This is when the exception handler (catch block) is called. Assuming the exception type that happens does match the exception type listed in the catch block, your program will compile correctly.

There is one more piece to the try-catch block I haven't mentioned yet. It's called the finally clause. If you always want something to happen when code is executed, place the necessary code in the finally block for the try-catch block. This clause is good for ensuring resources are sufficiently released.

```
try {
  // Some statement(s)
} catch (ExceptionType e) {
  // Some error handling code
} finally {
  // Always do it // release resources
}
```

The block makes sure that whether or not there was an error or return statement while executing the code block, the finally block gets executed.

If, on the other hand, you just want to notify your caller that you throw an exception yourself when an error occurs, you don't need a try-catch block—just change the declaration line of the method to show the possible exceptions that it can throw.

This brings the compiler into the picture. By making sure everyone properly calls a method that throws an exception, the compiler ensures they are ready to handle the exception within their own try-catch block.

```
void stuff (int x, int y, int z) throws ExceptionType {
  // Some statement(s)
  throw new ExceptionType("message");
  // Some more statements
}
```

The calling routine then looks something like the following:

```
try {
  stuff (1, 2, 3);
} catch (ExceptionType e) {
  // Handle exception
}
```

There are certain types of problems that aren't serious enough to require try-catch blocks. These are called *runtime exceptions*. They tend to be the result of programmer error. Going beyond the end of an array is an example of a runtime exception. If a runtime exception happens, an exception is thrown and the program stops. You can use try-catch blocks to handle runtime exceptions. If you take care of the non-runtime exceptions, the system can almost take care of itself with the rest.

Looking for More Help

There is much more to the Java language syntax than what is explained here. If you find yourself needing some additional help, consider browsing through the Java Language Specification. To access the document, select Help ➤ Java Reference. From the JBuilder Help window that appears, select Java 2 JDK 1.3 Documentation. You'll need to scroll down to the API & Language Documentation section to find the Java Language Specification link.

ARE YOU EXPERIENCED?

Congratulations! You now know everything you need to know to create anything you want in Java. Of course, putting all these pieces together successfully takes practice.

Now you can

- Comment your code

- Create variables

- Connect variables with operators

- Use Java data types

- Create classes

- Work with Java arrays

- Use packages

- Work with flow control statements

- Handle exceptions

Now that you've learned about the Java programming language syntax, along with the pieces and the rules to connect them, let's move on to Skill 4 and use that knowledge to build an interactive Java form.

Creating a Scrolling Text Applet with Sound

- Working with the Override Method Wizard

- Defining the applet life-cycle methods

- Adding sound to your applet

- Using multithreading

- Working with the Implement Interface Wizard

Getting Started

In Skill 2, you used JBuilder's Applet Wizard to create a welcome applet and JBuilder's Application Wizard to do the same in a standalone application. In this skill, you're going to extend the generated applet to create a scrolling text message across the applet. The moving text gives you the opportunity to learn the basics of multithreading and understand an applet's life-cycle methods.

Instead of editing the applet from the earlier skill, you'll recreate it from scratch to reinforce the skills you learned earlier. After closing any open projects, select File ➤ New and double-click the Applet icon under the Web tab. This brings up the Project Wizard. Fill in the screens as shown in Figure 4-1 and Figure 4-2. On the second Project Wizard screen, just click Next. After you fill in the third screen, click the Finish button to move on to the Applet Wizard screens.

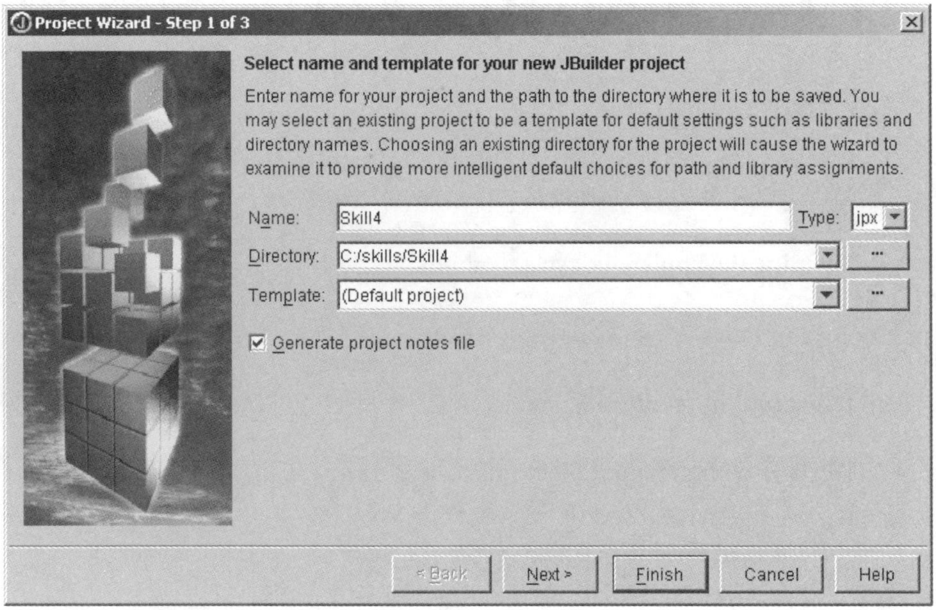

Figure 4-1. The first Project Wizard dialog box is where you enter the project name and path.

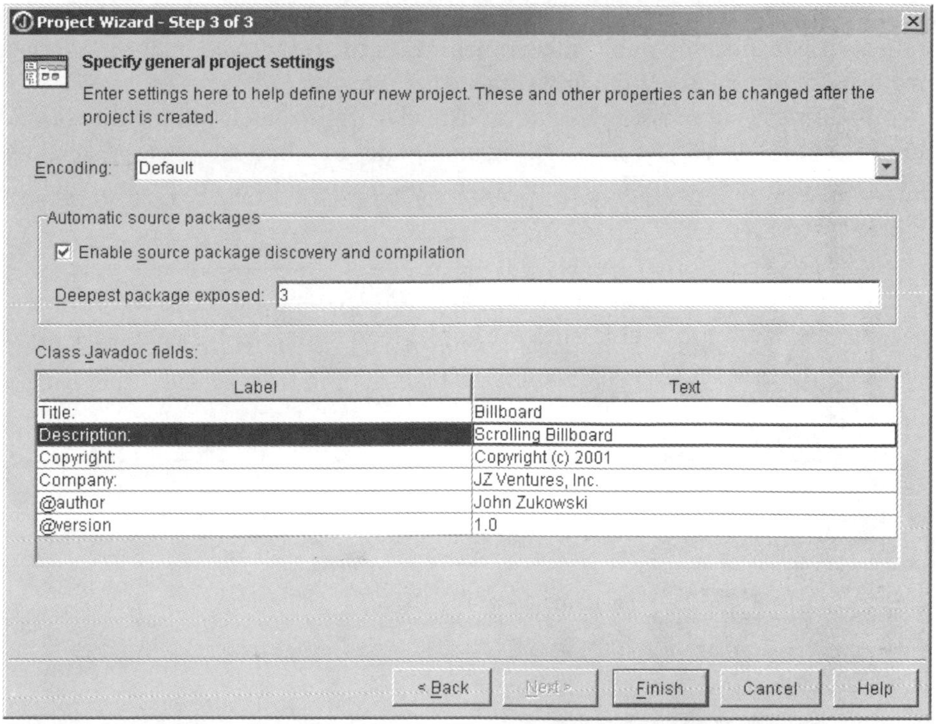

Figure 4-2. In the last Project Wizard dialog box, you enter information for the project notes.

As you remember from Skill 2, there are three dialog boxes to complete for the Applet Wizard. In the first, you change the Class entry to **Billboard**, ensure the Base class is **java.applet.Applet**, check the Generate standard methods option, and then click Next. In the second, you create a parameter named **message** of type **String**. Type in a description—in this case, **Scrolling message**. The parameter should be accessed by the program through the variable **message** with a default setting of **Welcome**. Click Next to move on to the final dialog box. Change the title to **Scrolling Billboard**, its name to **Billboard**, and click the Finish button. Assuming everything went well, you'll notice that you're almost back to where you were in Skill 2 at the end of the "Using the Applet Wizard" section. All that's left to do is add code to display the parameter on the screen.

Using the Override Method Wizard

When you redefine a method in a subclass, you are said to *override* that method. You override methods to provide more specific behavior within subclasses. When you override a method in Java, the name of the method stays the same, as well as the parameter list and return type. In an overridden method, the protection can be made more public (like from private to protected), but it cannot be made more private (like from protected to private).

To display your message this time, instead of immediately editing the source file, select Billboard.java in the Navigation pane, and then select the Wizards ➤ Override Methods menu. This brings up a screen similar to the one shown in Figure 4-3.

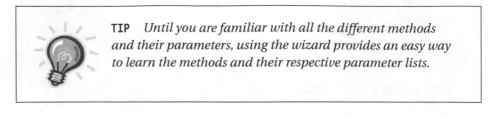

TIP *Until you are familiar with all the different methods and their parameters, using the wizard provides an easy way to learn the methods and their respective parameter lists.*

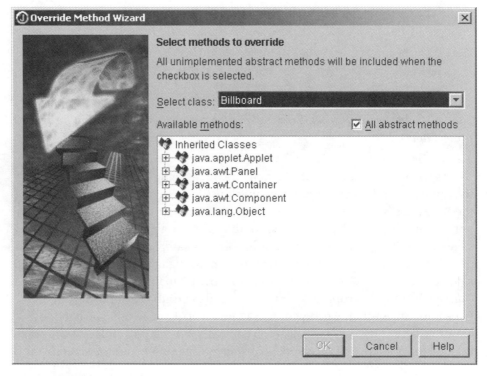

Figure 4-3. Select the method(s) to override from the Override Method Wizard dialog box.

From here, you can select which method you want to override from all of the classes that are in `Billboard`'s class hierarchy tree. Because `Billboard` extends `java.applet.Applet`, that is at the top of the list. The next entry is `java.awt.Panel` because `Applet` is a subclass of `Panel`. Below `Panel` is `java.awt.Container` because `Panel` is its subclass. `Container` is a subclass of `java.awt.Component`, so that is next. At the bottom of all this is `java.lang.Object`. Everything is a subclass of `Object`, eventually. This whole class hierarchy for the Billboard class is shown in Figure 4-4.

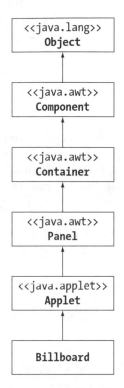

Figure 4-4. The class hierarchy for a user-defined applet

Applet's Object Hierarchy: An Overview

Every program that you want to run within a browser must subclass `java.applet.Applet`. This allows the browser to know what behavior to expect when it sees an `<APPLET>` tag within an `.html` file.

The immediate subclass of `Applet` is `java.awt.Panel`. Because an applet is a subclass of `Panel`, it gets its own drawing area. The superclass of `Panel` is `java.awt.Container`. Because an applet is a subclass of `Container`, it can have other components placed inside of it and it can use a `LayoutManager`. You'll learn about layout management in Skill 6.

Going further up the class hierarchy tree of `Applet`, the `java.awt.Component` class is next. Every graphical control in Java is a subclass of `Component`, and `Applet` is no exception. Because it is a subclass of `Component`, an `Applet` can be grouped together in another `Container` and positioned with a `LayoutManager`. What this means is that an `Applet` can be placed within any `Container`, not just a browser. You'll learn about `Component` in Skill 5.

What does this all mean, then? Well, when you define an applet, there is much behavior already defined and inherited. Frequently, you just need to override an already existing method to offer new behavior. This behavior is what defines an applet and is what the applet's runtime container, the browser, needs. If the behavior isn't there, if you forget to subclass `java.applet.Applet`, the browser cannot run your program.

One final note about applets: If you happen to select `javax.swing.JApplet` as the base class in the Applet Wizard, this doesn't break the rule that all applets must extend from `java.applet.Applet`. `JApplet` happens to be a subclass of `Applet`.

You learned about the `paint()` method of the `java.awt.Component` class in Skill 2 to draw in an applet's drawing area. In this skill, you're going to override the `paint()` method again, but instead of writing all the code yourself, you're going to use the Override Method Wizard. To do this, select the plus sign (+) next to `java.awt.Component` to expand its method list (see Figure 4-5).

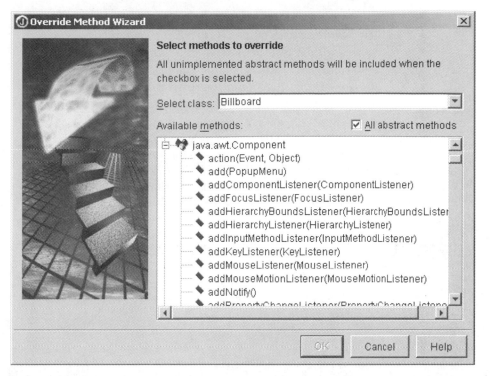

Figure 4-5. In the Available methods list, you select the framework of the method to add.

Scrolling down through the alphabetical listing, around eight screens worth, you'll come upon a paint(Graphics) entry. When you select this entry and click OK, JBuilder inserts the method framework into your source.

> **TIP** *When you use the Override Method Wizard, you can type in the beginning of the method name and the wizard will search for a matching method. This behavior is common across most of the JBuilder IDE, in wizards, dialog boxes, and the Structure pane.*

After you click the OK button, the following appears within your source code:

```
public void paint(Graphics g) {
  /**@todo: Override this java.awt.Component method*/
  super.paint( g);
}
```

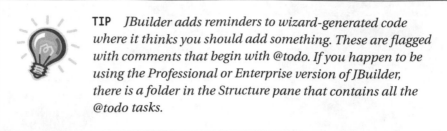

TIP *JBuilder adds reminders to wizard-generated code where it thinks you should add something. These are flagged with comments that begin with @todo. If you happen to be using the Professional or Enterprise version of JBuilder, there is a folder in the Structure pane that contains all the @todo tasks.*

To find where the code was inserted, select the `paint(Graphics g)` entry in the Structure pane in JBuilder, as shown in Figure 4-6. Once the entry is selected, the Content pane jumps to the proper area of the source.

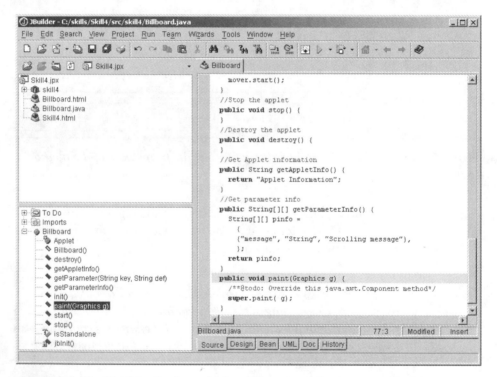

Figure 4-6. The JBuilder Project window. When you select an entry in the Structure pane, you can quickly access that area of the source code in the Content pane.

Admittedly, for this method it may have been easier to just type out the framework. However, if you don't remember the exact parameter list for a method, you can avoid looking it up by using the Override Method Wizard. The Override Method Wizard also maintains the proper access keywords of the method: `public`, `protected`, or `private`. You can change a method to be less protected, but if you try to make a method more protected—for example, if you try to make the paint() method private—the compiler will complain.

Now that you have the framework, let's add the call to drawString() to display the message variable. As mentioned in Skill 2, the second and third parameters are the coordinates of where to display the first. After you add the call, remember to delete the @todo tag that the Wizard added. The paint() method should now look like this:

```
public void paint(Graphics g) {
  super.paint( g);
  g.drawString(message, 20, 20);
}
```

After you save everything (select File ➢ Save All), you can build and run the applet to see how things look so far. Essentially, this will result in an applet that functions identically to the Applet1 applet in Skill 2.

Understanding the Applet Life-Cycle Methods

Before you jump into sound and multithreading to set up your billboard message to scroll, you need to take a look at the life-cycle methods of an applet. The *life-cycle methods* are methods that you do not call directly; instead, the browser calls them for you. There are four methods in the family: init(), start(), stop(), and destroy().

> init(): The init() method of an applet is called once when the applet is first loaded by the browser. For tasks that need to be done once, such as loading support files, this method provides a good place to add such code. Frequently, you will load image and audio files or initialize the screen here.

> start(): The start() method is called every time the page the applet is on is visited by a user. When an applet is first loaded, the browser will call start() after init(). If the user leaves the applet's page to visit another Web site, the start() method will be called again when the user returns. When a program needs additional threads (for example, for animation), the threads are frequently started within the start() method.

TIP *A thread is a section of code that executes independently of other sections. To maintain a high level of interactive performance with the user, lengthy tasks should be executed in separate threads. Imagine trying to drive a car and read a newspaper. Trying to do these tasks at the same time is a risky proposition. However, if there are two people involved, each working in a separate thread, the tasks can easily be done simultaneously.*

stop(): The stop() method of an applet is called whenever a user leaves the Web page that contains the applet. If the user follows a link or exits the browser, the stop() method of the applet will be called. The stop() method is a good place to halt the playing of sound files and the running of any extra threads the program needs. When a user isn't viewing a Web page, the page's applets should not be using resources.

destroy(): The destroy() method is called when the browser removes the applet from its memory. This method could be called before the user exits the browser or when the browser needs to clear out some memory space. It is not a good idea to wait until the browser needs to clear out memory to free up resources. The system needs to use this method for certain tasks. However, you normally should not rely on it being called. When this method is called when the user shuts down the browser, it is possible for the browser to close before the method finishes executing.

Adding Sound

To demonstrate when the different life-cycle methods are called, you're going to have Billboard play a sound whenever one of them is called. The methods for manipulating sound files are part of the java.applet.AudioClip interface.

play(): You call the play() method to play an audio file once.

loop(): You call the loop() method to play an audio file in a continuous loop.

stop(): You call the stop() method when you want to stop the playing of an audio file.

NOTE *The latest version of Java supports playing AIFF, AU, MIDI, RMF, and WAV audio files. Early versions only supported the AU format.*

You get an `AudioClip` to play from the aptly named `getAudioClip()` method of `Applet`. There are two versions of the `getAudioClip()` method:

`getAudioClip(URL url)`: To load a file from an absolute URL, use this version of the method. The URL would need to be of the form `http://www.xxx.yyy/zzz/audiofile.au`.

TIP *An absolute Uniform Resource Locator (URL) is one that contains a fully qualified location of a resource—in this case, an audio file.*

`getAudioClip(URL url, String filename)`: Instead of providing an absolute URL, you can place the sound files in the same directory as the applet and provide the applet's URL as a relative location to work from. Applets actually provide two URLs to work from, depending on your preferences. Using either of these URLs as the first parameter here enables you to specify the sound filenames as the second parameter.

NOTE *To get an* `AudioClip` *to play in an application, you use the* `newAudioClip(URL url)` *method of* `Applet`, *not the* `getAudioClip()` *method.*

Because there are four applet life-cycle methods, you need four different audio files to play a different sound for each of them. If you place the files in the same directory as your `Billboard.html` file, you can use the `getDocumentBase()` method to help load the files and demonstrate when the life-cycle methods are actually called. The `getDocumentBase()` method returns the URL of where the applet was loaded from. For example, if you loaded the applet from `http://www.apress.com/books/jbuilder/applets/billoard.html`, the `getDocumentBase()` method will return `http://www.apress.com/books/jbuilder/applets/`.

For this applet, you'll use some sound files from the samples that come with JBuilder. From the command line, copy the audio files to the appropriate location with the following commands on Windows:

```
copy \jbuilder6\jdk1.3\demo\applets\Animator\audio\1.au
  \skills\Skill4\classes
copy \jbuilder6\jdk1.3\demo\applets\Animator\audio\2.au
  \skills\Skill4\classes
copy \jbuilder6\jdk1.3\demo\applets\Animator\audio\spacemusic.au
  \skills\Skill4\classes
copy \jbuilder6\jdk1.3\demo\applets\Animator\audio\4.au
  \skills\Skill4\classes
```

NOTE *You can acquire many sound files off the Internet. The Sound Ring (`http://www.alexcia.com/`) is a set of Web sites that contain audio files and provide a good starting point for locating them, if you happen to not like the ones suggested here.*

To load the files, make a few changes to your `Billboard`. At the top of your class definition, just under the definition of the message variable, you need to define four variables of type `AudioClip`, one to hold each reference to a sound file:

```
AudioClip one, two, three, four;
```

Because you only want the sound files loaded once, you load the four files in your `init()` method. In addition, you want to play one in `init()`, so you `play()` one there, too. JBuilder provides a basic `init()` method already for its needs, so you can just add the loading and playing to the end of the existing method. Listing 4-1 shows the new `init()` code in the bold font.

Listing 4-1. Updated `init()` Method with Audio File Loading and Playing
```
//Initialize the applet
public void init() {
  try {
    message = this.getParameter("message", "Welcome");
  }
  catch(Exception e) {
    e.printStackTrace();
  }
```

```
try {
  jbInit();
}
catch(Exception e) {
  e.printStackTrace();
}
// Load four audio files
one   = getAudioClip(getDocumentBase(), "1.au");
two   = getAudioClip(getDocumentBase(), "spacemusic.au");
three = getAudioClip(getDocumentBase(), "3.au");
four  = getAudioClip(getDocumentBase(), "4.au");
// Play the first file
if (one != null) {
  one.play();
}
}
```

TIP   *Before calling any* AudioClip *method, it's good practice to check if the* AudioClip *reference is null. The* getAudioClip() *method returns null if it failed to load the audio file.*

For the other three life-cycle methods, you just need to play a file. Because you selected the "Generate standard methods" option in the Applet Wizard, the framework for the start(), stop(), and destroy() methods are generated for you. To be a little different, the sound played in the start() method is looped via the loop() method. Then, the applet's stop() method needs to stop that sound with the stop() method of AudioClip, as well as play its own sound. The destroy() method just needs to play the sound file. The updated methods are provided in Listing 4-2.

CAUTION   *If you don't stop the playing of a looping sound when a user leaves the Web page that started playing the audio file, the sound will continue playing while the user surfs around the Internet. The user must exit the browser to stop the audio file from looping.*

Listing 4-2. Playing Sounds in the Remaining Applet Life-Cycle Methods

```java
//Start the applet
public void start() {
  if (two != null) {
    two.loop();
  }
}
//Stop the applet
public void stop() {
  if (two != null) {
    two.stop();
  }
  if (three != null) {
    three.play();
  }
}
//Destroy the applet
public void destroy() {
  if (four != null) {
    four.play();
  }
}
```

You can now save your work and try things out. As Figure 4-7 shows, the Applet Viewer tool from JBuilder provides Start, Stop, and Exit buttons to help you out. If you listen carefully, you can hear when each sound is played. You will quickly notice that Java doesn't bother waiting for one sound to play completely before starting another.

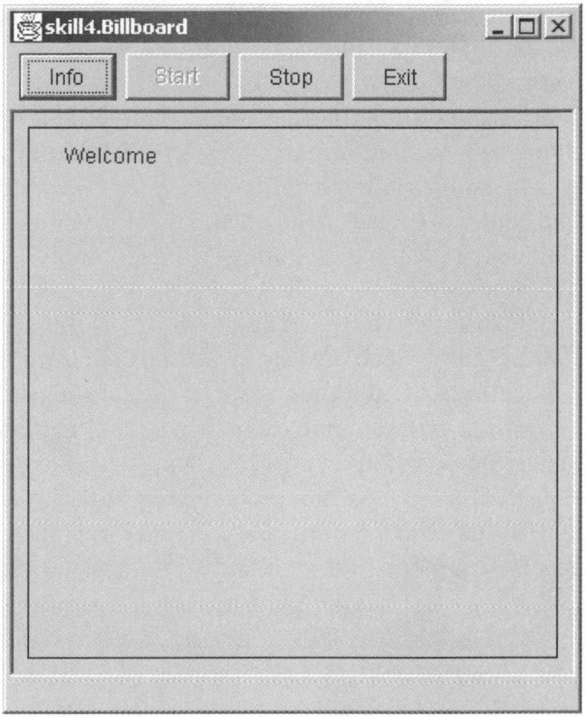

Figure 4-7. In the JBuilder Applet Viewer, you can try out the sounds.

When the applet first starts, you'll hear the init() sound play once and the start() sound playing continuously. Clicking Stop will stop the looping and cause the stop() method's sound to be played. Clicking the Start button then restarts the looping space music. When Exit is called, the looping sound stops and you may or may not hear the stop() and destroy() sounds, as the system is shutting down. Consider loading the Billboard.html file for the applet in a real browser and listen for its behavior there. You'll find the file in the \skills\Skill4\classes directory.

Introducing Multithreading

Now that you know about the different life-cycle methods that Java applets use, you can create programs that use multiple threads to do more than one thing at once. Actually, there are many threads running in your Java program already. Most just happen to be system threads, doing their work behind the scenes, as opposed to the user threads that you control.

When programming in Java, it's necessary to get comfortable with having the system do multiple things at once. This requires special precautions so that your program doesn't step on and corrupt itself. I'll go into more depth on this point in Skill 15 and Skill 21, but for now I'll just cover the basics to get your message scrolling.

Java has a Thread class to support multithreaded programming. You can create lots of threads to go off on their own to do lots of different things. In the movie *Multiplicity*, Michael Keaton's character was too busy to do everything he wanted to do, so he created copies of himself to go off and do other things, while he kept chugging along doing the task at hand. In the end, he gets more work done because the jobs are done simultaneously. And just like the movie, if you're not careful, the copies can interfere with each other.

With Java, it works pretty much the same way: You create and start() an instance of java.lang.Thread, and it goes off on its own to run whatever you tell it to run. You provide what you want it to execute in a run() method, and pass this along to the constructor for Thread.

The Thread constructor has a parameter of type java.lang.Runnable. Runnable is an interface that includes one method called run(). Therefore, your class definition needs to implement the Runnable interface and you need to define a run() method in your class, as in the following example:

```
public class Foo implements Runnable {
  Thread t;
  public void run() { ... }
  ...
  public void someMethod() {
    // Pass in the Runnable to the Thread constructor
    t = new Thread(this);
    // Start thread
    t.start();
    ...
  }
}
```

The call to the start() method of the thread triggers the execution of the run() method of the Runnable passed into the Thread constructor. You don't call the run() method directly, or else it is treated like any other method call and doesn't execute in its own thread.

Defining the Thread Using the Implement Interface Wizard

Because Runnable is an interface, you can use the Implement Interface Wizard in JBuilder to generate the basic code framework. This wizard enables you to pick the interface name from a list and have the wizard add the method framework into your source file to complete. This wizard is really helpful when an interface defines multiple methods—you won't have to type out each by hand. Selecting Wizards ➢ Implement Interface brings up the screen shown in Figure 4-8.

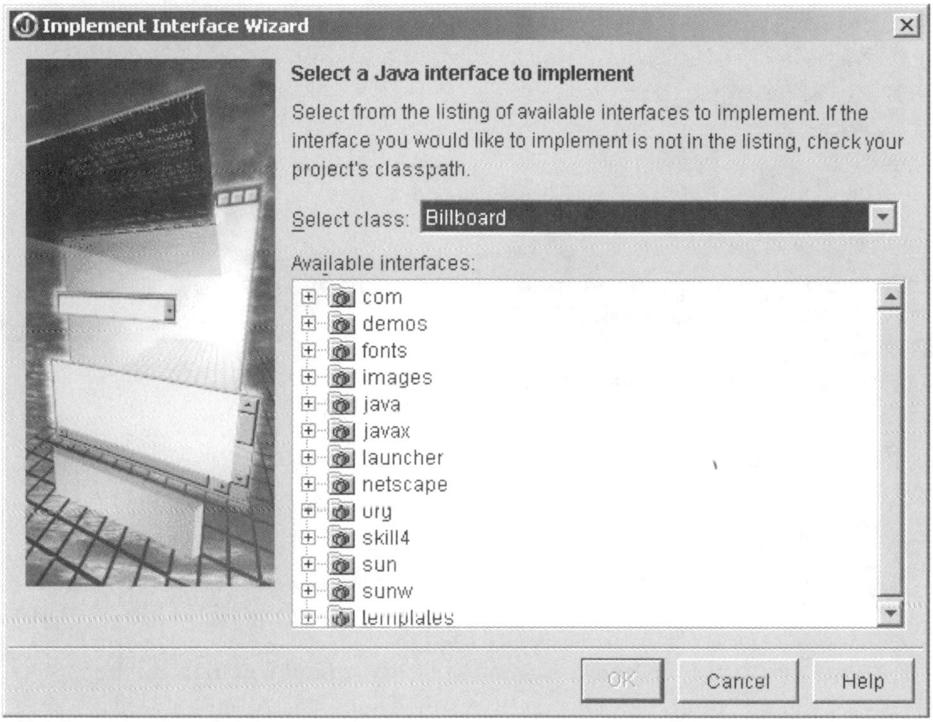

Figure 4-8. The Implement Interface Wizard dialog box

Here, you have to locate the Runnable interface, which happens to be in the java.lang package. Clicking the plus sign (+) next to java and then again next to lang reveals the interface, as shown in Figure 4-9. Select Runnable and then click OK. From there, JBuilder inserts the framework of the run() method into your source and adds implements Runnable to the end of your class declaration. Just providing a run() method within your class definition does not make the class implement the interface. In order to satisfy the compiler that the object passed into the Thread constructor is a Runnable object, the class definition must include implements Runnable.

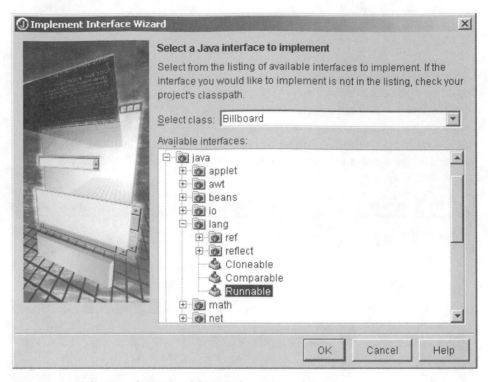

Figure 4-9. Selecting the Runnable interface to implement

```
public void run() {
    /**@todo: Implement this java.lang.Runnable method*/
    throw new java.lang.UnsupportedOperationException(
      "Method run() not yet implemented.");
}
```

In the new run() method you get an @todo to remind you to fix up the method. The exception handling code was mentioned at the end of Skill 3. Essentially, the code says you haven't implemented the method yet so throw the runtime exception named UnsupportedOperationException. Remove all the lines of the method, as you're about to put in the real behavior.

Because you are creating a scrolling billboard, your thread will make the message scroll. Your run() method becomes a continually executing while loop that moves the horizontal drawing position. You do have to include a way to stop the execution, though, so it won't continue to execute when the user leaves the page that loaded the applet. Set the Thread variable to null to signal its time to stop.

First, you'll define an instance variable of type Thread called mover. It will be your worker thread. You can place the definition of the variable underneath your AudioClip variables that you defined earlier.

```
Thread mover;
```

Then, in the run() method, define the task for it to perform. Don't worry about creating the thread just yet. That will be done elsewhere. Replace the default code and todo item that JBuilder placed in the run() method with the following:

```
public void run() {
  while (mover != null) {
    repaint();
    synchronized (this) {
      xpos++;
      if (xpos >= getSize().width) {
        xpos = 0;
      }
    }
    try {
      Thread.sleep(50);
    } catch (InterruptedException ignored) {
    }
  }
}
```

Calling the repaint() method tells the program it's time to update the screen, and the browser eventually places a call to the paint() method. After painting the screen, you need to update the display position for the next time through. Because you are increasing the x position, the message scrolls left to right. You also need to add an instance variable to keep track of the horizontal drawing position. Add this variable underneath the definition of the mover thread.

```
int xpos = 0;
```

You will also notice the new Java construct, the *synchronized block*. For the code encapsulated within the synchronized block, only one thread at a time that checks for the same key (the this variable for this situation) is permitted to execute those statements. Java handles that synchronization for you with the synchronized block.

I should explain the keyword this a little more here: It is a reference to the instance of the object the method belongs to. It is basically a reference to the applet object. By combining `synchronized` and `this`, you're saying to use the applet object as the access lock. The applet then ensures only one thread gets through at a time. Any object can be the lock of a `synchronized` block to serve as the gatekeeper. Also, the same object can guard multiple blocks, possibly ensuring all access is synchronized. However, providing multiple locks means different threads can be executing different `synchronized` blocks, one per lock object.

The `Thread.sleep()` call in `run()` slows down your animation so it moves approximately every 50 milliseconds. The `sleep()` method has the potential to throw an `InterruptedException`, so you need to put the `sleep()` call within a `try-catch` block. Basically, if your sleep is interrupted, you will be notified by an exception. For now, just ignore the exception.

NOTE   *Calling the* `interrupt()` *method of the thread is one way to trigger the sleeping to be interrupted.*

To ensure that the `paint()` method doesn't try to write beyond the end of the screen, you need to control access to the xpos variable. Using the `synchronized(this){ . . . }` block within `run()` and adding a similar fragment to `paint()` ensures that neither accesses the variable at the same time.

```
public void paint(Graphics g) {
   super.paint( g);
   synchronized (this) {
      g.drawString(message, xpos, 20);
   }
}
```

Some Thoughts on Executing Simultaneous Threads

When multiple threads are executing simultaneously, the system could stop one thread at any time and work on another. To ensure the system doesn't leave multistep operations partially complete, you should place `synchronized` blocks around all code that accesses any shared variables of the threads.

To help demonstrate the need for this, imagine two people depositing $200 simultaneously into the same bank account with an initial balance of $500. The end result should be a balance of $900. However, given the following sequence of events, the result could be $700 if balance access isn't controlled properly:

```
5:00 Person A requests balance
5:01 Person B requests balance
5:02 Person B gets balance of $500
5:03 Person A gets balance of $500
5:04 Person A deposits $200
5:05 Person B deposits $200
5:06 Person A computes new balance
5:07 Person B computes new balance
5:08 Person B updates balance to $700
5:09 Person A updates balance to $700
```

Keep in mind that operations happen in milliseconds on a computer system, rather than in seconds or minutes.

Well, you've done the hard part: You've defined the work of the Thread. You haven't created it yet, however. It's time to go back and visit the life-cycle methods.

Creating the Thread

You could create the Thread in the `init()` method and let it go on forever. This isn't ideal, however, because the thread would continue to run when the user is no longer looking at the billboard. (Imagine someone looking at the front of the billboard while you are updating the back. You keep working but nobody sees your results.) Therefore, you should create the thread in the `start()` method and kill it off in the `stop()` method. This way, it will not be running after the user leaves and will be recreated when the user comes back.

You've already defined your Thread variable mover, so now you just have to update `start()` and `stop()`.

```
//Start the applet
public void start() {
  if (two != null) {
    two.loop();
  }
  if (mover == null) {
    mover = new Thread(this);
  }
  mover.start();
}
//Stop the applet
public void stop() {
  if (two != null) {
    two.stop();
  }
  if (three != null) {
    three.play();
  }
  mover = null;
}
```

In start(), you pass into the Thread constructor a class that implements the Runnable interface. It happens to be the Billboard class itself—this—but it could be anything. After the thread is created, the mover.start() statement causes the run() method of the constructor's argument to be called.

In stop(), you added code to set the mover variable to null. This doesn't directly stop the thread. However, it does cause the thread to stop the next time through its loop. You don't want to stop the thread immediately as it could leave the system in an unstable state. Setting the variable to null ensures the thread finishes what it's doing before saying good-bye.

That's really all there is to it. You've created an applet that does all of the following:

- Creates threads

- Plays sounds

- Reads parameters

- Scrolls a text message

If you saved your work and built it, you can see what you've done when you run the program. Just as you did when playing the sound file, you can start and stop your program with the menu choices. Notice that if you restart it, the message continues to scroll from where it left off. Listing 4-3 contains the complete source for the Billboard.java applet.

Listing 4-3. The Billboard.java Scrolling Text Applet

```java
package skill4;

import java.awt.*;
import java.awt.event.*;
import java.applet.*;

public class Billboard extends Applet implements Runnable {
  boolean isStandalone = false;
  String message;
  AudioClip one, two, three, four;
  Thread mover;
  int xpos = 0;

  //Get a parameter value
  public String getParameter(String key, String def) {
    return isStandalone ? System.getProperty(key, def) :
      (getParameter(key) != null ? getParameter(key) : def);
  }

  //Construct the applet
  public Billboard() {
  }
  //Initialize the applet
  public void init() {
    try {
      message = this.getParameter("message", "Welcome");
    }
    catch(Exception e) {
      e.printStackTrace();
    }
    try {
      jbInit();
    }
    catch(Exception e) {
      e.printStackTrace();
    }
```

```java
      // Load four audio files
      one   = getAudioClip(getDocumentBase(), "1.au");
      two   = getAudioClip(getDocumentBase(), "spacemusic.au");
      three = getAudioClip(getDocumentBase(), "3.au");
      four  = getAudioClip(getDocumentBase(), "4.au");
      // Play the first file
      if (one != null) {
        one.play();
      }
    }
    //Component initialization
    private void jbInit() throws Exception {
    }
    //Start the applet
    public void start() {
      if (two != null) {
        two.loop();
      }
      if (mover == null) {
        mover = new Thread(this);
      }
      mover.start();
    }
    //Stop the applet
    public void stop() {
      if (two != null) {
        two.stop();
      }
      if (three != null) {
        three.play();
      }
      mover = null;
    }
    //Destroy the applet
    public void destroy() {
      if (four != null) {
        four.play();
      }
    }
```

```java
//Get Applet information
public String getAppletInfo() {
  return "Applet Information";
}
//Get parameter info
public String[][] getParameterInfo() {
  String[][] pinfo =
    {
    {"message", "String", "Scrolling message"},
    };
  return pinfo;
}
public void paint(Graphics g) {
  super.paint( g);
  synchronized (this) {
    g.drawString(message, xpos, 20);
  }
}
public void run() {
  while (mover != null) {
    repaint();
    synchronized (this) {
      xpos++;
      if (xpos >= getSize().width) {
        xpos = 0;
      }
    }
    try {
      Thread.sleep(50);
    } catch (InterruptedException ignored) {
    }
  }
}
}
```

ARE YOU EXPERIENCED?

Now you can

- Use the Override Method Wizard

- Describe the applet life-cycle methods

- Load audio files

- Play audio files

- Use multithreading within your Java programs

- Define and create threads using the Implement Interface Wizard

In Skill 5, you'll learn how to do even more with Java. You'll start to learn about the various graphical user interface (GUI) controls available through the Abstract Window Toolkit (AWT) and Swing packages, and you'll use them to create interactive programs.

Exploring the Abstract Window Toolkit and Swing

- Learning to use the Abstract Window Toolkit (AWT)

- Learning to use the Project Swing component set

- Adding labels, text fields, and buttons to your program

- Handling actions and keyboard events

- Loading and displaying images

- Creating a Hi-Lo guessing game

Introducing the Abstract Window Toolkit and Swing

One of the Java packages you'll recognize from previous skills is the Abstract Window Toolkit, or AWT for short. AWT provides Java with a simple set of GUI objects to work with. The Java term for each object is "component," because each is a subclass of the Java Component class. However, if you come from another desktop environment, you may call them *controls, widgets,* or *gadgets.*

The primary component set for applets is AWT, as that is what is available in the Java runtime that comes with the browsers. Java's second-generation component set is called Swing. The Swing component set is usable with the Java 1.1 environments, but it is standard with the Java 2 platform. The components that come with Swing provide a richer set of capabilities than the AWT component set. Because of this added richness, Swing is the preferred set of components for Java applications. You tend not to mix visual components from the two sets in the same program.

NOTE *You can use Swing components in applets, but this requires the end user to have something called the Java Plug-in installed. While the Java Plug-in can be downloaded on demand, when users access the applet that needs it, forcing a user to download the Plug-in on a public Internet site is not really a good thing as it is between 5MB and 15MB in size, depending upon the platform and version. You can find details on the Java Plug-in at* http://java.sun.com/products/plugin/. *Another way of delivering Swing-based programs over the Internet is called Java Web Start. You can find details on using Java Web Start in Skill 16.*

Three of the AWT components are Label, TextField, and Button. In this skill, you'll use these components to create a Hi-Lo guessing game. You will learn the skills necessary to create and interact with the components and, finally, you'll be introduced to data conversion, converting string input into numeric values for checking the guesses.

After creating the Hi-Lo game as an applet with AWT, you'll create the same program as an application using the Swing components JLabel, JTextField, and JButton. Most of the basic operations are the same between the two component sets. You'll look at some of the more advanced capabilities of the Swing components, though, to see some of the additional features you can use with them.

The remaining AWT and Swing components behave similarly, so you should be able to extend what you learn in this skill to those components. Many of these components will be covered in later skills, when you use the drag-and-drop GUI builder aspect of JBuilder, which is known as the UI Designer.

NOTE *If you are interested in learning more about the Swing components, consider reading my book,* Definitive Guide to Swing for Java 2, Second Edition *(Apress, 2000).*

Adding Components to Your Program

Java's AWT is a rich set of very simple components. The Swing component set is even richer, and JBuilder provides a still richer component palette with the JavaBeans Component Library (JBCL), which is built on top of Swing. All the components of all three libraries are subclasses of the `java.awt.Component` class. The `Component` class defines the behavior and characteristics of all the other components, across all the component sets. Methods that modify the components' display are shared by all components and appear in Table 5-1. There are actually more than 100 methods of `Component`. Many of the remaining methods will be introduced throughout the other skills. One of the methods, `paint()`, has already been explored.

WARNING *Not to confuse matters, but AWT menu components are the exception to all graphical components being a subclass of* Component. *Although they are graphical components, they do not subclass* Component. *Instead, they subclass* MenuComponent, *which serves as the base of all AWT menu components. To make matters even more confusing, Swing menu components do subclass* Component.

Table 5-1. Common Component Behavior

Methods	Behavior
getBackground()/setBackground()	Fetch/change component background color
getForeground()/setForeground()	Fetch/change component foreground color
getFont()/setFont()	Fetch/change component font
getCursor()/setCursor()	Fetch/change cursor appearing over component
isEnabled()/setEnabled()	Fetch/change component's enabled state

You'll notice that all the methods in Table 5-1 are shown in pairs. This is because they represent JavaBean properties. JavaBeans are discussed in further detail in Part Two of this book.

Now that you know what a component is, you can use some to create the screen for the Hi-Lo game. The Hi-Lo game is a number guessing game. The computer picks a number between 1 and 100, and you have to guess the number with the help of clues provided by the computer. The clues tell you if the number is higher or lower. Figure 5-1 provides a general outline of the layout for the game. If you like the game, as you learn more about Java's graphics features, you can make the screen look much snazzier without affecting the game logic.

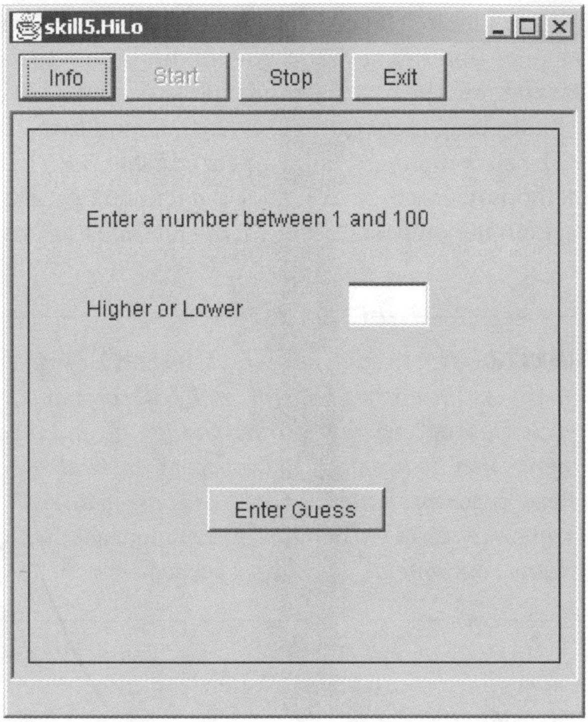

Figure 5-1. The Hi-Lo game screen layout

Using Labels

The first component you'll look at is `java.awt.Label`. The `Label` component provides a component to display a single line of text in a single font. As Figure 5-2 demonstrates, you can change various display characteristics of labels, including alignment.

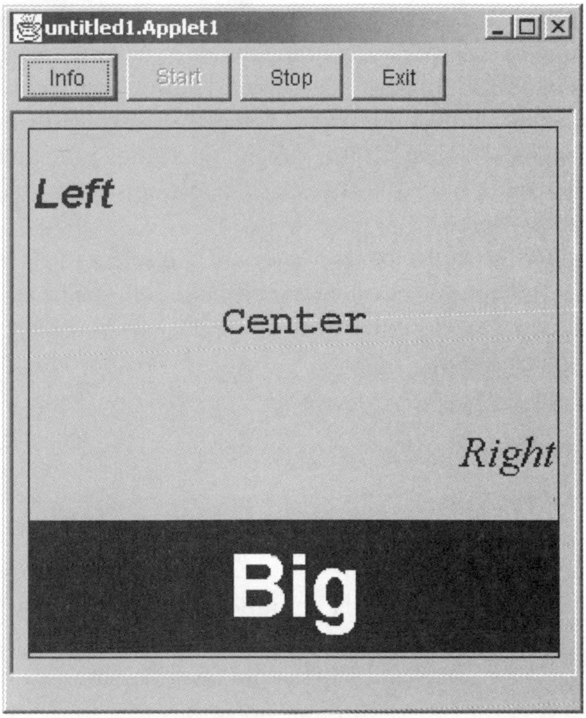

Figure 5-2. Sample labels

Labels are used to display static or fixed text, frequently next to an input field. In your Hi-Lo game, you will need two labels: one for instructions/status and another one next to the input field. When you need to create a new object, you use one of the object's constructors to create it. A *constructor* is a special method of an object that creates an instance of that object. There are three constructors for the Label component.

Unlike a method call, constructors are called through the new keyword. The following list describes the constructors for Label.

```
// To create a Label with no text in it
Label noText = new Label();
// To create a Label with "Message" as its text
Label aMessage = new Label("Message");
// To create the same Label, aligned to the right
// Use Label.LEFT for left aligned, the default setting
// Use Label.CENTER for center alignment
Label alignedMessage = new Label("Message", Label.RIGHT);
```

Before you can create the labels, you need to start up a new project for this skill. Go ahead and save and close anything that is open and create a new project through the Applet Wizard. In the Project Wizard, enter a project name of **Skill5**, a directory of **C:\skills\Skill5**, and then click Finish. The only field that needs to be changed in the Applet Wizard is the class name. Change the default **Applet1** class name to **HiLo**, make sure the Base class is **java.applet.Applet**, and click the Finish button.

Once the Wizard has completed its task, you can select the Content pane and update the source. For starters, declare two variables of type Label. These should be declared at the class level (underneath isStandAlone) because multiple methods will need to access them.

```
Label label1;
Label label2;
```

Now you need to initialize them. If you were not using JBuilder, you would initialize them in the init() method. However, JBuilder keeps component initialization centralized within the jbInit() routine, which is called by the init() method. Within jbInit(), initialize the first variable to be the instruction "Enter a number between 1 and 100" and "Higher or Lower" for the second.

```
label1 = new Label("Enter a number between 1 and 100");
label2 = new Label("Higher or Lower");
```

Instead of specifying the label's text in the constructor, however, you can do the same operation in two steps, as shown here:

```
label1 = new Label();
label1.setText("Enter a number between 1 and 100");
```

This doesn't do anything special that the first way doesn't. However, it does show that you can change the label's text at any time. There is even a getText() method to see what the current label text is, in case you need to check the value.

After you've created the labels, you need to add the objects to the screen so the user can see them. This is done with the help of the add() method. Before I talk about add(), though, I need to briefly discuss positioning and layout managers, a topic that is discussed in greater detail in the next skill.

Components are sized and positioned in Java with the help of layout managers. Layout managers control the display of components on the screen. Because Java programs are meant to work across multiple platforms and are not specific to one platform, you normally do not position objects at specific coordinates. What may look perfectly fine on one platform, in terms of size and placement, could look awful on another. This positioning is the responsibility of the layout manager. Until you learn about layout managers more, you're going to turn them off. This should never be done in a real-world application, but for those beginning to learn Java, disabling the layout managers provides a way to leave that lesson until later. For now, just add the following line to the beginning of your jbInit() method:

```
setLayout(null);
```

Now, it is your responsibility to size and position the components. The setBounds() method of Component is used to control a component's size and position. You can either pass the method the bounding rectangle of where to place the component (as a java.awt.Rectangle) or pass off the x and y coordinates along with the width and height as four separate arguments. For instance, to have the top-left corner of the first label be at (30, 25) with a width of 300 and a height of 50, you would add the following line of code to jbInit():

```
label1.setBounds(30, 25, 300, 50);
```

After positioning the component, the only thing left to do is add the component to the applet. You do this with the add() method, where the single argument is the component to add. A second argument to control positioning is possible, but because you aren't using a layout manager, it would be ignored.

```
add(label1);
```

Similar code is needed to add the label2 component at position (30, 75) with a width of 150 and a height of 50.

```
label2.setBounds(30, 75, 150, 50);
add(label2);
```

NOTE *Unlike the* drawString() *method used in Skill 4, the coordinates specified here are for the top-left corner, not the baseline.*

The complete jbInit() routine follows. At this point, you can save your work and run the applet to see the screen in Figure 5-3.

```
private void jbInit() throws Exception {
  setLayout(null);
  label1 = new Label("Enter a number between 1 and 100");
  label1.setBounds(30, 25, 300, 50);
  add(label1);
  label2 = new Label("Higher or Lower");
  label2.setBounds(30, 75, 150, 50);
  add(label2);
}
```

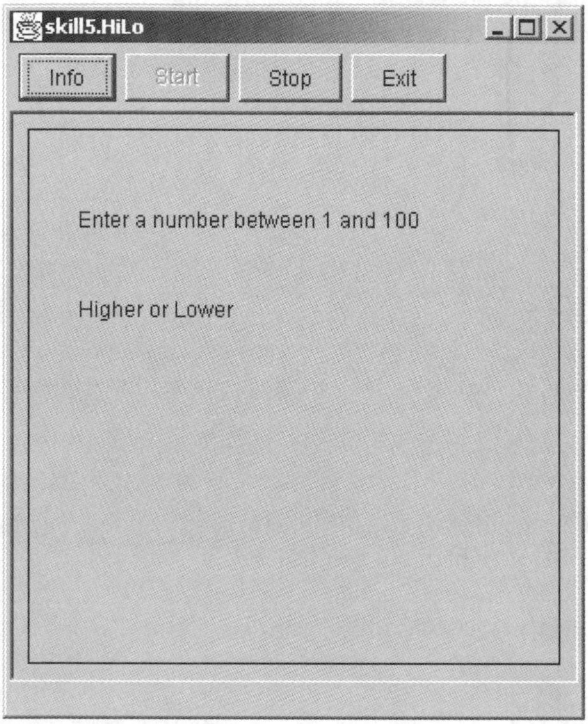

Figure 5-3. Hi-Lo game screen with labels

Using Text Fields

The java.awt.TextField component is similar to the Label component: Both provide for the use of a single line of text. Where the label's text cannot be edited, the text field's primary purpose is for the user to provide its contents.

NOTE *You can make a* TextField *read-only if you need to display a noneditable entry such as a calculated total in what looks like a text field. The method to do this is* setEditable(), *which takes a boolean parameter. If the parameter is false, the* TextField *becomes read-only. To return to the default editable state, use the parameter true.*

The TextField component has four different constructors (shown in the following listing). As with a Label, you can specify the initial text within the object. However, you cannot specify alignment. All text in a TextField is left-justified.

```
// To create a TextField with no text in it
TextFicld noText = new TextField();
// To create a TextField with "Message" as its text
TextField aMessage = new TextField("Message");
// To create the same TextField with a width of 20 average-size characters
TextField aMessage = new TextField("Message", 20);
// To create the same TextField with no text
TextField aMessage = new TextField(20);
```

If you do not specify a width in the constructor but you do specify a message to display, the message may not be fully visible. The system uses an average character width, not the actual message width, to determine how wide to make the text field. It follows then that you should usually specify a width yourself and pad it with a couple of characters to make sure there is enough space for the message. Once you start using a layout manager, though, the specified width can become irrelevant as the layout manager will size the component.

NOTE *The length specified in the* TextField *constructor does not limit the number of characters that a user can input into the field; it is only used to calculate how wide the object is on the screen.*

In addition to the constructors, Table 5-2 lists some other methods of TextField that may prove useful. You will use the getText() routine later in this skill when you need to process the user input.

Table 5-2. Selected TextField Methods

Method	Behavior
setEchoChar(char c)	Change the input mask to c. (This is helpful for password-entry fields.)
setText(String s)	Change the contents to s.
getText()	Get the current contents.
getSelectedText()	Get the currently selected text.

For your Hi-Lo program, you need to create one TextField and place it next to the Higher or Lower label. Like the labels, define an instance variable for the TextField at the top of the class definition:

```
TextField textField1;
```

The next step in the jbInit() method is to create the TextField and add it to the screen. You'll need to size it for about three to four characters and position it next to the appropriate label. Running the applet now will show the text field on the screen, as shown in Figure 5-4.

```
textField1 = new TextField();
textField1.setBounds(175, 85, 50, 25);
add(textField1);
```

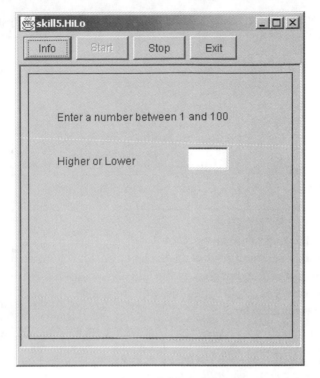

Figure 5-4. Hi-Lo game screen with text field and labels

Using Buttons

The java.awt.Button is the final component to tackle in the Hi-Lo program. In AWT, buttons are used when a user needs to signal the system that he or she is finished with a certain action or needs to submit information. With AWT, buttons are also limited to a single line of text—there are no image buttons. For the button, the single line of text represents the label. Around the button are three-dimensional bevels that make the button appear pressed when clicked with the mouse. This display functionality is automatic, so you don't need to do anything to make a button appear properly to the user.

The Button component has only two constructors: one to create a button without a label and one to create a button with a label. As with the Label or TextField, you can specify the initial value. The only other option is to specify nothing.

```
// To create a Button with no label
Button noText = new Button();
// To create a Button with "Message" as its label
Button aMessage = new Button("Message");
```

Like the other components, `Button` has other routines that may prove helpful. These routines are listed in Table 5-3.

Table 5-3. Selected Button Methods

Method	Behavior
setLabel(String s)	Change the button's label to s.
getLabel()	Get the button's current label.
setActionCommand(String s)	Change the button's command to s.
getActionCommand()	Get the current action command.

The `setActionCommand()` and `getActionCommand()` methods are useful in programs meant to run in multiple languages. They enable you to associate a command with a button but change the label based upon the user's local environment, or locale. Then, you can identify the selected button by looking at the command instead of the label.

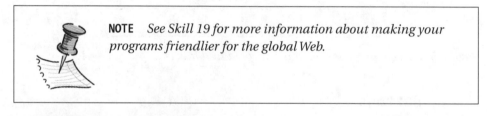

NOTE *See Skill 19 for more information about making your programs friendlier for the global Web.*

In your Hi-Lo program, you'll need to add a button to the screen. User interface guidelines tend to tell you to place action-oriented buttons at the bottom of the screen. Therefore, you need to create a `Button` for the player to signal the entry of a guess, and you need to position it below everything else. As with the other components, you need to define an instance variable for the `Button` at the top of the class.

```
Button button1;
```

Then you add it to the screen using the following code, again in the `jbInit()` method. Now your screen should look complete (see Figure 5-5, which is the same as Figure 5-1).

```
button1 = new Button("Enter Guess");
button1.setBounds(100, 200, 100, 25);
add(button1);
```

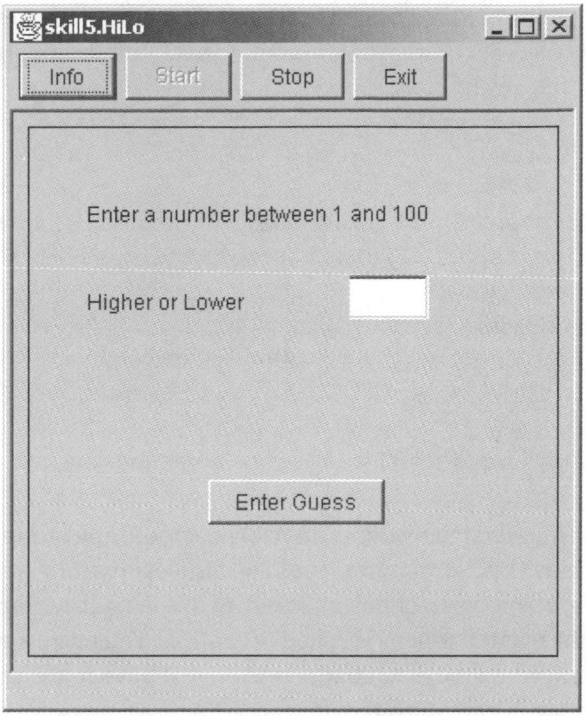

Figure 5-5. Hi-Lo game screen with button, text field, and labels in place

Handling Events

Okay, the screen is done, but you might notice that you have a slight problem on your hands: When you type something into the text field and click the button, nothing happens. To remedy this, you need to add some code that will compare the user's input with the key number when the button is clicked. If the guess is too high, you'll change the label to "Guess Lower." If the guess is too low, you'll change the label to "Guess Higher." If the user guesses the number correctly, you'll have the system beep and pick another number for the next round of guesses.

In addition, you want to make sure the user only enters numerical input into the text field. By doing this, you can be sure that when you convert the text input to a number, there won't be any letters thrown in there.

Before you move on to handling the events, though, you need to initialize the value being guessed. This requires an instance variable, theNum, to retain the number:

```
int theNum;
```

You'll also need a getNextNumber() method to generate the next number to guess and a call to getNextNumber() within the init() method of the applet to generate the first key number:

```
theNum = getNextNumber();
```

Then add the source for the getNextNumber() method as follows:

```
private int getNextNumber() {
  return (int)(Math.random()*100.0) + 1;
}
```

Handling Action Events

Events in Java are generated by the system when something interesting happens with a component. This "something" could be almost anything—the user clicking a button, typing, scrolling, or choosing an entry in a list, for example. The component where the event happens is called the *source.* The event source tells anyone interested when the event happens. You just have to tell the component which operations you are interested in.

When the user clicks the Enter Guess button, you need to perform an operation. In Java, the operation that deals with button clicks is called an *action event,* which is signified by the java.awt.event.ActionEvent class. The system automatically generates an ActionEvent when the user clicks the button. In order to have processing associated with the event, you have to tell the button you are interested in when the event happens. The process of doing this is called *listening,* and you register yourself as a listener of the action event of a Button through its addActionListener() method. Figure 5-6 helps you visualize this interaction.

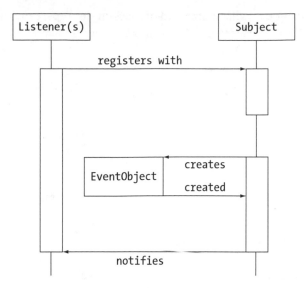

Figure 5-6. Event delegation sequence diagram

The addActionListener() method has one parameter, which is of type
java.awt.event.ActionListener. ActionListener is an interface like the
AudioClip and Runnable interfaces in the last skill. Its single method is
actionPerformed(). So, when the button is selected, it calls the actionPerformed()
method of every registered ActionListener. This leads you to the conclusion that
you must implement the interface and register an ActionListener with the button.

To implement the interface, you'll use the Implement Interface Wizard. The
ActionListener interface is in the java.awt.event package. When you select
the listener and click the OK button, the following code is added to the
HiLo.java program:

```java
public class HiLo extends Applet implements ActionListener {
  . . .
  public void actionPerformed(ActionEvent e) {
    /**@todo: Implement this java.awt.event.ActionListener method*/
    throw new java.lang.UnsupportedOperationException(
      "Method actionPerformed() not yet implemented.");
  }
```

If you create a to-do list composed of five simple steps, providing your implementation of the `actionPerformed()` method becomes easy:

1. Get the text field value.

2. Convert value to `int`.

3. Compare the value entered to the generated value.

4. Change label or beep.

5. Register the listener with the button.

Let's go through the tasks one at a time:

1. You already know how to get the text field value—you use the `getText()` method of `TextField`.

2. Because `getText()` always returns the contents as a string, you need to convert it to a number. The `Integer.parseInt()` method converts strings to integers. If the system determines that the string cannot be converted, a `NumberFormatException` is thrown and the guess is ignored. Don't forget to put in your `try-catch` block around the `parseInt()` method call to deal with the exception.

3. Comparison is easy. Check for equality and if the guess is higher or lower than the number.

4. Once you know the status of the guess, use the `setText()` method of `Label` to notify the user. Or to have the system beep when the guess is correct, use the routine called `beep()` in the `Toolkit` class. To get a `Toolkit` object for use, `Component` has a `getToolkit()` method that `Applet` inherits.

NOTE *The* `Toolkit` *class provides access to information about the user's runtime environment, such as screen size.*

5. With one more addition to the jbInit() method to register the listener, you actually have a working Hi-Lo game.

```
button1.addActionListener(this);
```

Once these steps have been completed, the final actionPerformed() method looks like Listing 5-1.

Listing 5-1. The Complete actionPerformed() Method for the Hi-Lo Game

```
public void actionPerformed(ActionEvent e) {
  String s = textField1.getText();
  int val;
  try {
    val = Integer.parseInt(s);
  } catch (NumberFormatException exp) {
    val = 0;
  }
  if (val == theNum) {
    getToolkit().beep();
    label2.setText("Higher or Lower");
    theNum = getNextNumber();
  } else if (val < theNum) {
    label2.setText("Higher");
  } else {
    label2.setText("Lower");
  }
}
```

> **TIP** *There is no volume control support in Java. You need to adjust the volume from your system-specific volume-control mechanism.*

Handling Keyboard Events

In order to restrict input in the TextField to numerical characters, you need to work with another listener. That listener is called java.awt.event.KeyListener. The KeyListener interface consists of three methods:

- keyPressed(): For any keyboard key that is pressed

- keyReleased(): For any keyboard key that is released

- keyTyped(): For a non-action-oriented key that is pressed and released

NOTE *Action keys are function keys; arrow keys; Ctrl, Shift, and Alt keys; and the like. Nonaction keys are the alphanumeric keys. For instance, to type a capital A, you generate a keypress for Shift and the letter a, a key release for Shift and the letter a, and a keystroke (via* keyTyped()) *for the A.*

The keyTyped() method is the method that enables you to restrict input. However, because you need to implement the KeyListener interface, all three methods need to be created. Using the Implement Interface Wizard simplifies this because you just have to fill in one of the methods—just remember to remove the code to throw an UnsupportedOperationException in the other two. Go ahead and use the Implement Interface Wizard to implement the KeyListener interface now. It, too, is part of the java.awt.event package.

You want to ignore any input that is not numerical. If you check every character as it is typed, you can ignore the ones you don't want. To tell the system to ignore keystrokes, use the consume() method of the KeyEvent argument. If the text field goes through all the listeners and nobody *consumes* the event, the input character is added to the text field.

TIP *Only input events can be consumed with* consume()*. You could not reject the* ActionEvent *for the Enter Guess button.*

```java
public void keyTyped(KeyEvent e) {
  char c = e.getKeyChar();
  if (!Character.isDigit(c)) {
    e.consume();
  }
}
public void keyPressed(KeyEvent e) {
}
public void keyReleased(KeyEvent e) {
}
```

TIP *The* Character *class has over a dozen routines to check for different types of characters: uppercase, lowercase, alphanumeric, and white space, to name a few.*

After you register the KeyListener with the TextField using the addKeyListener() method, you don't have to worry about any more letters in the input field. With one final addition in the jbInit() method, the Hi-Lo game applet is complete. One more thing to mention here is adding the KeyListener doesn't alter the input screen; it is strictly for input validation.

```java
textField1.addKeyListener(this);
```

Listing 5-2 contains the complete code for the Hi-Lo applet.

Listing 5-2. The Complete Hi-Lo Applet Source
```java
package skill5;

import java.awt.*;
import java.awt.event.*;
import java.applet.*;

public class HiLo extends Applet implements ActionListener, KeyListener {
  boolean isStandalone = false;
  Label label1;
  Label label2;
  TextField textField1;
  Button button1;
  int theNum;
```

To convert the program from an AWT applet to a Swing application, you're going to copy everything you added in the applet source to the application. First, you need to copy the instance variables you created. There were five of those. Replace the BorderLayout declaration line (BorderLayout borderLayout1 = new BorderLayout();) with the five lines from the applet. Yes, delete the original line, as you aren't using layout manager until the next skill. Be sure to keep the contentPane variable, as that one will be used in the application.

```
Label label1;
Label label2;
TextField textField1;
Button button1;
int theNum;
```

To have the application use Swing components instead of AWT components, add a **J** before the Label, TextField, and Button declarations—they should be JLabel, JTextField, and JButton.

Next, copy the getNextNum() call from the init() method and place it in the HiLoFrame constructor. Also, copy the getNextNum() method definition.

The next part is a little tricky. Copy the entire contents of the applet's jbInit() method to the end of the jbInit() method of the HiLoFrame. Delete the line that references the previously deleted borderLayout variable. Here's the tricky part: Have the setLayout() and add() methods called off the contentPane variable, as in contentPane.setLayout(...) and contentPane.add(...). Change the creation of the labels, text field, and button to create Swing components instead of AWT components. The resulting jbInit() method is shown in Listing 5-3.

Listing 5-3. The Swing Version of jbInit()

```
private void jbInit() throws Exception  {
//setIconImage(Toolkit.getDefaultToolkit().createImage(
//HiLoFrame.class.getResource("[Your Icon]")));
  contentPane = (JPanel) this.getContentPane();
  this.setSize(new Dimension(400, 300));
  this.setTitle("Hi-Lo Game");
  contentPane.setLayout(null);
  label1 = new JLabel("Enter a number between 1 and 100");
  label1.setBounds(30, 25, 300, 50);
  contentPane.add(label1);
  label2 = new JLabel("Higher or Lower");
  label2.setBounds(30, 75, 150, 50);
  contentPane.add(label2);
  textField1 = new JTextField();
```

```
textField1.setBounds(175, 85, 50, 25);
contentPane.add(textField1);
textField1.addKeyListener(this);
button1 = new JButton("Enter Guess");
button1.setBounds(100, 200, 100, 25);
contentPane.add(button1);
button1.addActionListener(this);
}
```

Next, it's time to copy the event listener implementations. Using the Implement Interface Wizard, have the frame implement the `ActionListener` and `KeyListener` interfaces, and then copy over the interface implementations.

> **TIP** *You can implement both interfaces at once with the wizard by pressing down the Ctrl key when you add the second listener.*

Essentially, you've converted your program from an AWT-based one to a Swing-based one. Not all the AWT components convert to Swing components this easily, but most do. Saving the application and running the program brings up the screen shown in Figure 5-7.

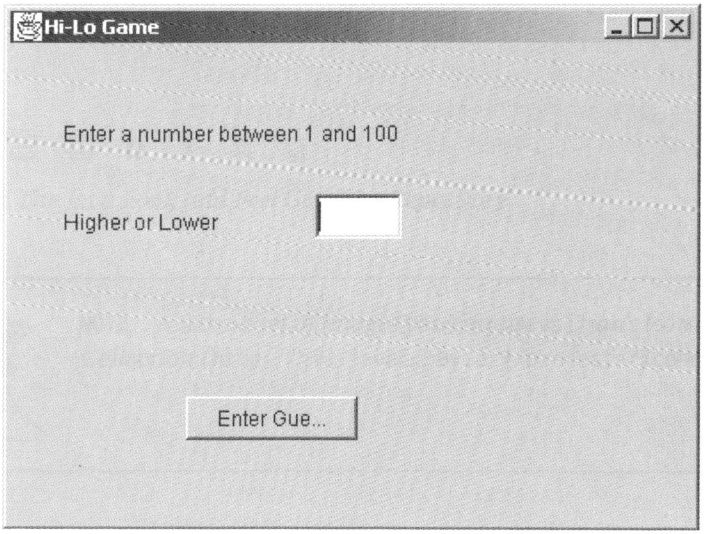

Figure 5-7. Swing-based Hi-Lo game screen

The ImageIcon class relies on the underlying java.awt.Image class to load an image. It just wraps the access to implement the Icon interface so images are easily usable with the Swing components. You can load the image as an Image and pass that to the ImageIcon constructor, or you can pass the URL or filename to the ImageIcon constructor directly.

If you load the Image yourself, there is a getImage() method in the Toolkit class. Just remember to use getToolkit() to get a Toolkit instance. Just pass in a java.net.URL object or the filename as a string. Or, you can pass in the same thing right to the ImageIcon constructor.

If you want to have the Hi-Lo program display up and down images instead of Higher or Lower messages, you can change the program to load a couple of images. First, you need to define two ImageIcon instance variables:

```
ImageIcon up;
ImageIcon down;
```

You then load the images once in the constructor for the class. The images are loaded there because you only need to load them once, not each time you change the message label. You'll also need to import the java.net package for the URL class:

```
import java.net.*;
  . . .
Image image = getToolkit().getImage(
  new URL("http://java.sun.com/jdc/techDocs/hi/repository/" +
    "graphicsRepository/toolbarButtonGraphics/navigation/Up24.gif"));
up = new ImageIcon(image);
down = new ImageIcon(
  new URL("http://java.sun.com/jdc/techDocs/hi/repository/" +
    "graphicsRepository/toolbarButtonGraphics/navigation/Down24.gif"));
```

TIP *In the case of applets,* getImage() *is a method of* Applet. *You would use the two-argument version of* getImage(), *where the first argument is the starting directory to load the image relative to. Use* getCodeBase() *to load the image relative to the applet's* .class *file. Use* getDocumentBase() *to load the image relative to the applet's* .html *loader file. For instance, to load* cup.jpg *from the same directory as* appletloader.html, *use* Image image = getImage(getDocumentBase(), "cup.jpg");.

Displaying Images

Once you have the images loaded, you need to modify the `actionPerformed()`
method so that it displays the appropriate icon at the appropriate time. To display an icon with a `JLabel` (or a `JButton`), just call the `setIcon()` method. Pass in
the icon as an argument. If you need to clear out the icon, pass in a null. As Swing
labels support both images and text, you must clear out the one when setting
the other; otherwise, the wrong text will appear with an image. Here's part of the
updated method:

```
if (val == theNum) {
  getToolkit().beep();
  label2.setText("Higher or Lower");
  label2.setIcon(null);
  theNum = getNextNumber();
} else if (val < theNum) {
  label2.setText(null);
  label2.setIcon(up);
} else {
  label2.setText(null);
  label2.setIcon(down);
}
```

You can now save your updated program and run it. If you then enter a number requiring a higher guess, you'll see something like the screen in Figure 5-9. If
you enter a number that requires a lower guess, you'll see a down arrow instead.

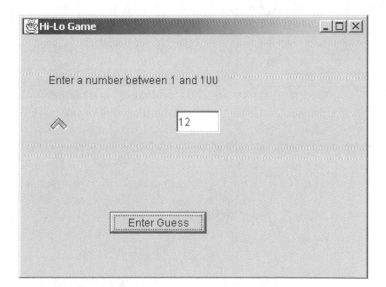

Figure 5-9. The Hi-Lo program needing a higher guess

Listing 5-4 contains the now complete Swing version of the Hi-Lo application.

Listing 5-4. The Complete Hi-Lo Application Source

```java
package skill5;

import java.awt.*;
import java.awt.event.*;
import javax.swing.*;
import java.net.*;

public class HiLoFrame extends JFrame implements ActionListener, KeyListener {
  JPanel contentPane;
  JLabel label1;
  JLabel label2;
  ImageIcon up;
  ImageIcon down;
  JTextField textField1;
  JButton button1;
  int theNum;

  //Construct the frame
  public HiLoFrame() {
    enableEvents(AWTEvent.WINDOW_EVENT_MASK);
    try {
      jbInit();
      theNum = getNextNumber();
      Image image = getToolkit().getImage(
        new URL("http://java.sun.com/jdc/techDocs/hi/repository/" +
          "graphicsRepository/toolbarButtonGraphics/navigation/Up24.gif"));
      up = new ImageIcon(image);
      down = new ImageIcon(
        new URL("http://java.sun.com/jdc/techDocs/hi/repository/" +
          "graphicsRepository/toolbarButtonGraphics/navigation/Down24.gif"));
    }
    catch(Exception e) {
      e.printStackTrace();
    }
  }
```

```java
//Component initialization
private void jbInit() throws Exception  {
  contentPane = (JPanel) this.getContentPane();
  this.setSize(new Dimension(400, 300));
  this.setTitle("Hi-Lo Game");
  contentPane.setLayout(null);
  label1 = new JLabel("Enter a number between 1 and 100");
  label1.setBounds(30, 25, 300, 50);
  contentPane.add(label1);
  label2 = new JLabel("Higher or Lower");
  label2.setBounds(30, 75, 150, 50);
  contentPane.add(label2);
  textField1 = new JTextField();
  textField1.setBounds(175, 85, 50, 25);
  contentPane.add(textField1);
  textField1.addKeyListener(this);
  button1 = new JButton("Enter Guess");
  button1.setBounds(100, 200, 110, 25);
  contentPane.add(button1);
  button1.addActionListener(this);
}
//Overridden so we can exit when window is closed
protected void processWindowEvent(WindowEvent e) {
  super.processWindowEvent(e);
  if (e.getID() == WindowEvent.WINDOW_CLOSING) {
    System.exit(0);
  }
}
private int getNextNumber() {
  return (int)(Math.random()*100.0) + 1;
}
public void actionPerformed(ActionEvent e) {
  String s = textField1.getText();
  int val;
  try {
    val = Integer.parseInt(s);
  } catch (NumberFormatException exp) {
    val = 0;
  }
```

```
        if (val == theNum) {
          getToolkit().beep();
          label2.setText("Higher or Lower");
          label2.setIcon(null);
          theNum = getNextNumber();
        } else if (val < theNum) {
          label2.setText(null);
          label2.setIcon(up);
        } else {
          label2.setText(null);
          label2.setIcon(down);
        }
      }
      public void keyTyped(KeyEvent e) {
        char c = e.getKeyChar();
        if (!Character.isDigit(c)) {
          e.consume();
        }
      }
      public void keyPressed(KeyEvent e) {
      }
      public void keyReleased(KeyEvent e) {
      }
    }
```

ARE YOU EXPERIENCED?

You've now seen how to work with both AWT and Swing components in applets
and applications. You should also understand the basics of event handling. For
most programs, that's really all there is to it: Place some components on the
screen and react to user input. The key is finding the right components and getting your components to look right across all platforms.

Now you can

- Add controls to your program

- Use the Label and JLabel components

- Use the TextField and JTextField components

- Use the `Button` and `JButton` components

- Use the `ImageIcon` to load and display images

- Listen for action events to process requests

- Listen for keyboard events to restrict input

In Skill 6, I'll explain the `LayoutManager` concept and you'll see how Java takes care of platform-independent positioning when you work with the `JTabbedPane`. No more null layout managers.

Understanding Layout Management

- Learning the principles of layout management

- Working with the JTabbedPane control

- Working with FlowLayout

- Setting up a ContainerListener

- Working with GridLayout

- Working with BorderLayout

- Working with BoxLayout, struts, and glue

Introducing Layout Management Principles

Programs created with Java automatically run across multiple platforms. When you compile a Java program, the compiler creates .class files that contain platform-independent byte code. These byte codes are understood by the Java Virtual Machine (JVM) on every platform. This is one of the key benefits of Java: "Write once, run anywhere."

> **NOTE** *The instruction set understood by the JVM is defined by The Java Virtual Machine Specification document (http://java.sun.com/docs/books/vmspec/2nd-edition /html/VMSpecTOC.doc.html). The document is also available under the Help ➢ Java Reference menu that brings up the JBuilder Help window. Just select the Java 2 JDK 1.3 Documentation option.*

For visual programs, you have to do more to make everything look right on every platform. With Java, the size of a component is dependent upon which platform the user is running on. A text field looks different under the different Microsoft Windows flavors (95, 98, Me, NT, 2000), Macintosh, and Motif (UNIX). As a result, your production programs should not use absolute positioning as demonstrated in the previous skill. It works great for testing, so you don't have to worry about platform-specific issues. However, in order to position objects properly across platforms, you need to understand and use Java's layout manager concept.

This skill takes you through the standard layout managers provided with Java and introduces you to Swing's JTabbedPane control, a tabbed pane that enables you to pick from different component sets to display. In addition to introducing the different layout managers, the program you create will resize itself whenever you select a button to better demonstrate the functionality of each layout manager.

Using the JTabbedPane Control

JBuilder contains a JTabbedPane control from the Swing component set for you to fairly easily create screens that look like property sheets. If you've ever changed the Internet Options in Internet Explorer, you've seen the window with the tabbed panels that enable you to alter different groups of settings. Similarly, if you need to display multiple screen types worth of information, JTabbedPane is JBuilder's solution. Figure 6-1, Figure 6-2, and Figure 6-3 show three views of a sample window. When you select one of the tabs at the top—First, Second, or Third—the displayed area below changes to display the components associated with the tab. The Okay and Cancel buttons are not part of the JTabbedPane and are constant throughout.

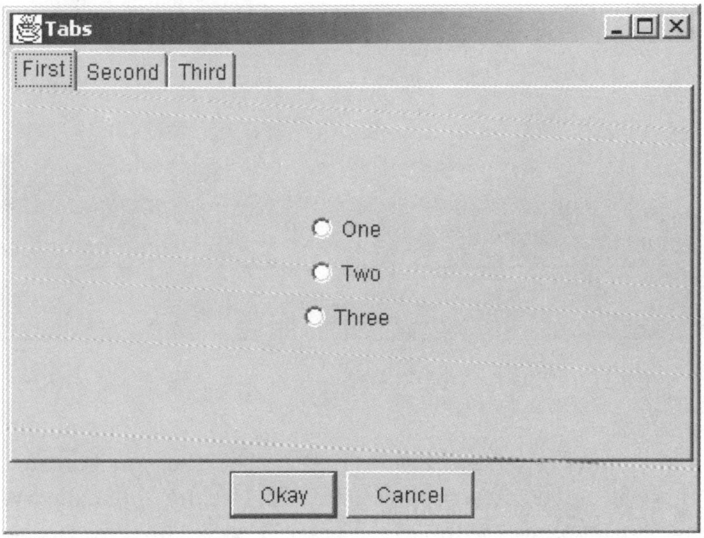

Figure 6-1. The settings on the First tab

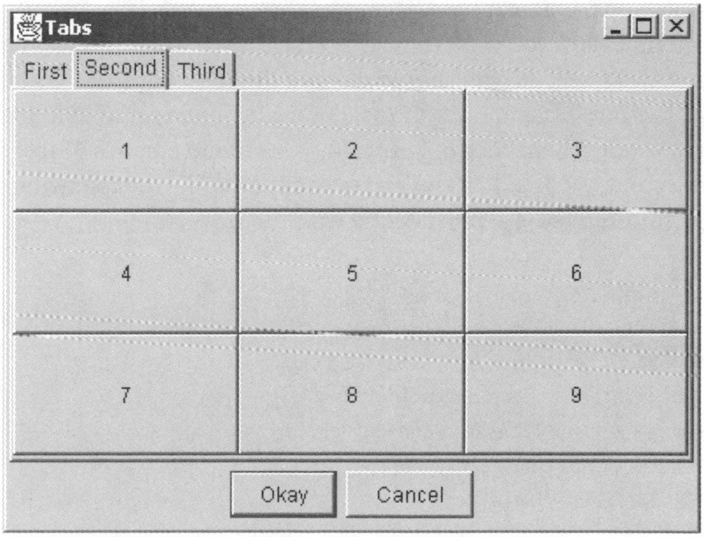

Figure 6-2. The components on the Second tab

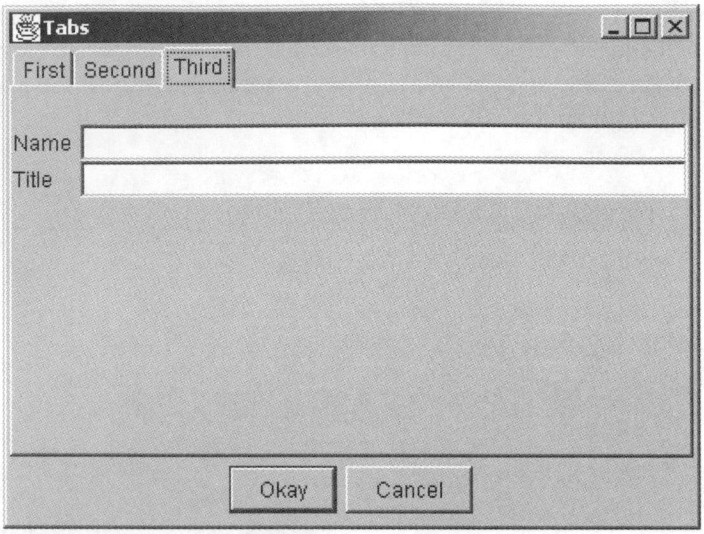

Figure 6-3. The layout of the Third tab

Now that you've been introduced to the JTabbedPane, you'll create one. Close any open projects and create a project for Skill 6. Use the Application Wizard to create a new Project named **Skill6** in the **c:\skills\Skill6** directory then click the Finish button. In the actual Application Wizard dialog boxes, name the frame class **Tabs** on the second screen and click Finish to create the framework to work in. This will create an HTML file named after the project, along with two source files: Tabs.java and Application1.java.

In the source files, you want to work with a JTabbedPane and you want to size the frame yourself. So, you should remove the this.setSize() call in jbInit() of the Tabs class and set the packFrame instance variable to true in the Application1 class. Then, back in jbInit(), you should create a JTabbedPane and add it to the content pane. The method now appears like the following, after you remove the commented-out line dealing with the icon:

```
// In Application1.java
  boolean packFrame = true;
// In Tabs.java
private void jbInit() throws Exception  {
  contentPane = (JPanel) this.getContentPane();
  contentPane.setLayout(borderLayout1);
  this.setTitle("Frame Title");
  JTabbedPane pane = new JTabbedPane();
  contentPane.add(pane, BorderLayout.CENTER);
}
```

The preceding source creates the panel with no tabs. If you build and run the program, it will appear rather small, as shown in Figure 6-4. Because the panel is empty, it takes up no space, so it only leaves the minimal window title line.

Figure 6-4. Packed frame with empty JTabbedPane

 NOTE   *The* JTabbedPane *and all the other Swing classes are located in the* javax.swing *package. This package is automatically imported for the program because the* Tabs *class extends from the Swing* JFrame *class.*

Using FlowLayout

To start exercising the JTabbedPane, you'll add the first component to it. A single component is a JButton or a JLabel. However, you normally see multiple components grouped together. In order for you to be able to group them, you need to use a JPanel. A JPanel is Swing's simplest Java Container that can contain other components. Because a Container is another type of Component, you can embed JPanel components within other JPanel objects.

Every Container within Java has a LayoutManager that controls how components are displayed within the container. For JPanel, the default LayoutManager is called FlowLayout. With FlowLayout, every component within the JPanel will be sized to its preferred size. Every component has a different preferred size, but it tends to be near the minimum space required to display it. For instance, with a JButton, this would essentially be the space for the label with the adornments around it.

 NOTE   *The* Applet *class used in previous skills is a subclass of the AWT* Panel *container. It also has a default layout manager of* FlowLayout.

When multiple components are placed within a JPanel with a FlowLayout manager, they try to appear all on a single row. If there isn't sufficient space, whichever object was the first to not fit completely moves down to the second row and the rest continue on the new line. Add a JPanel with 26 buttons—one button for each letter of the alphabet— to your JTabbedPane to demonstrate. Adding the following to the end of the jbInit() method will do just that:

```
JPanel p = new JPanel();
for (char c = 'a'; c <= 'z'; c++) {
  p.add(new JButton(new Character(c).toString()));
}
pane.add(p, "FlowLayout");
```

The for loop sets the variable c to each letter *a* through *z*. Then, you create a button for each and add it to the panel. Because JButton requires a text label, you have to convert the char to a String. One way to do this is with the help of the Character class, as shown here.

Another way to create appropriately labeled buttons relies on the Java compiler to automatically insert the conversion code for you. If you add a String and a char together, the compiler upgrades the char to a String for you. The button label can also be defined as follows:

```
new JButton ("" + c);
```

Functionally, the new line is identical to the earlier JButton creation code.

If you run the program now, you'll see the image in Figure 6-5, with the only tab, FlowLayout, selected.

Figure 6-5. The initial FlowLayout tab display state

Even though there is only one tab—FlowLayout, in this case—it is visible. If you then resize the window, you'll see in Figure 6-6 how the layout manager wraps the buttons when there isn't sufficient width to display all the buttons on one row.

Figure 6-6. A narrower FlowLayout tab with the buttons wrapped

In addition, if there isn't sufficient space to display everything, you won't be able to see some buttons, as illustrated in Figure 6-7. Resizing the frame to a larger size will return the buttons—so they are not lost forever, just while the screen is too small. Because of the potential danger of losing necessary buttons, FlowLayout containers tend to have very few buttons.

Figure 6-7. A short FlowLayout tab without all the buttons

NOTE *Notice that the* JTabbedPane *sizes itself to the necessary width and height of the components within it. All the areas below the tabs are the same. So, it takes the widest top-level component and the tallest top-level component (within the tabs) and makes that the size of all the top-level components within the tabbed pane.*

Implementing ContainerListener

To have the system (instead of you) change the window size, you can add an ActionListener to every button, similar to what you did in the last skill. If you have this listener call the setSize() method of the frame, it will be resized. You're going to do that but in a slightly roundabout way. Because you're adding your components within a short for loop, the extra work may seem a bit much; however, when you're adding all your components using lots of independent statements, this skill will prove to be very helpful. Also, as you add the other tabs/screens to the JTabbedPane, doing things in this way will require you to do less work with the other tabs.

When you add a component to a container, a ContainerEvent is generated if the Container has a ContainerListener registered. The event tells the listener that a component has been added to the container. What you can do then is listen for components to be added and add the ActionListener (or another listener) if the component happens to be a button. This mechanism works best when the same listener is attached to every component.

In order to do this for the example, you need to attach a ContainerListener to the JPanel p, before any buttons are added to the panel. If the listener had been added after the buttons were added, nothing would have been listening when the buttons were added.

```
JPanel p = new JPanel();
p.addContainerListener(this);
for (char c = 'a'; c <= 'z'; c++) {
```

Then your class needs to implement the ContainerListener interface. If you use the Implement Interface Wizard to add the java.awt.event.ContainerListener interface, the componentAdded() and componentRemoved() methods are added.

When a component is removed from the container (through the remove() method), it isn't necessary to remove the listener, so you should remove the throwing of the UnsupportedOperationException from componentRemoved(). You can leave that method as an empty stub. You just have to fill in the componentAdded() method. The method has one parameter of type ContainerEvent. The event has a property named child that contains the component just added. Using the getChild() method returns this component for you. If the child happens to be a JButton, you can then add the ActionListener to it.

```
public void componentAdded(ContainerEvent e) {
  Component c = e.getChild();
  if (c instanceof JButton) {
    JButton b = (JButton)c;
    b.addActionListener(this);
  }
}
```

TIP *The* (JButton) *part of* JButton b = (JButton)c; *is called* casting. *It changes the way you are referring to an object from one type to another—*Component *to* JButton *in this case. It only works at runtime when the conversion is legal. Because* JButton *is a type of* Component *it will work as long as you know you have a* JButton, *which is what the* instanceof *check is for.*

Now you can implement the ActionListener to resize the window. Using the Implement Interface Wizard again, this time for java.awt.event.ActionListener, you can add an actionPerformed() method to the class. Using Java's random number generator again, you can then resize the window with the setSize() method and validate the screen display.

```
public void actionPerformed(ActionEvent e) {
  int width = (int)(Math.random() * 200 + 150);
  int height = (int)(Math.random() * 200 + 150);
  setSize(width, height);
  validate();
}
```

At this point, you can run your work to see what you've done. Select a few buttons to verify that the screen resizes with every click of a button. Notice that the appearance hasn't changed since Figure 6-5, Figure 6-6, and Figure 6-7.

Using GridLayout

The next tab you will add demonstrates the GridLayout layout manager. As the name implies, GridLayout positions controls within a grid. When you create the layout manager, you specify the grid size. Then, when you add components, the layout manager fills a row at a time, from left to right and top to bottom. One key difference between FlowLayout and GridLayout is that every object within the grid will be sized the same. If there isn't sufficient space to display all the components, they will all be smaller.

WARNING *You cannot specify row-column positions when you add a component with* GridLayout. *You must add components in row order from top-left to bottom-right. If you do not provide enough components to fill the grid (initial row size × initial column size), or if you add too many, the grid will retain the number of rows requested in the* GridLayout *constructor and ignore the columns specified.*

For the example, you'll create the buttons on a telephone keypad, a 4×3 grid. Creating a new JPanel and adding the ContainerListener to the panel allows these buttons to resize the window, too. When you create a JPanel, you can tell it which LayoutManager to use. The statement new GridLayout(4, 3) says to create a layout of 4 rows and 3 columns. Then, when you add the new panel to the JTabbedPane, you will see two tabs, as shown in Figure 6-8. By default, the first tab added is displayed.

```
p = new JPanel(new GridLayout(4, 3));
p.addContainerListener(this);
for (int i = 1; i <= 9; i++) {
  p.add(new JButton("" + i));
}
p.add(new JButton("*"));
p.add(new JButton("0"));
p.add(new JButton("#"));
pane.add(p, "GridLayout");
```

Figure 6-8. Frame with the GridLayout tab added but not displayed

Once you select the GridLayout tab, you'll see the buttons laid out like a telephone keypad (see Figure 6-9). Notice their identical size. If you select a button, the window and buttons will resize, with the buttons maintaining their uniform size. If the window happens to be too narrow for all the tabs of the JTabbedPane, the tabs will appear in separate rows, allowing you to still see them all (see Figure 6-10).

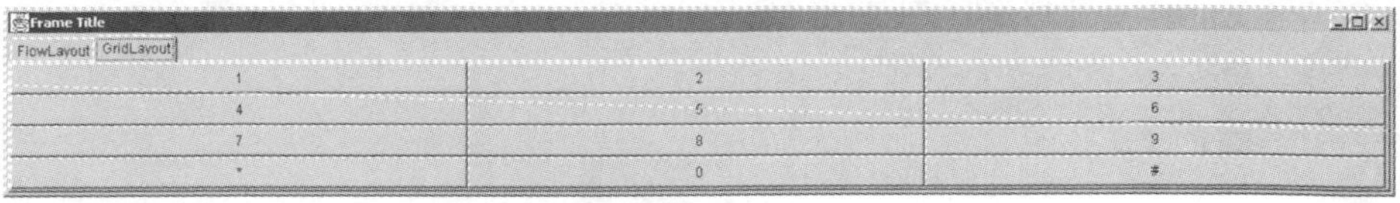

Figure 6-9. The initial GridLayout tab display state

Figure 6-10. A narrow JTabbedPane with the tabs overlapping

Using BorderLayout

For your third tab, you'll demonstrate the BorderLayout layout manager. BorderLayout is the default layout for AWT windows and frames, as well as the content pane of Swing applets, windows, and frames. It works like a quadrant system, with four quadrants around the outside and a fifth in the center occupying any remaining space. If a component is in a quadrant, it uses up the designated space. If there isn't a component in one of the five areas, the occupied areas consume the space. The five areas are called North, South, East, West, and Center.

BorderLayout also has some rather different sizing behaviors. Controls in the North and South quadrants take up the width of the container. Their height is their preferred height, just as with FlowLayout. For controls in the East and West areas, their height is that of the container (less any space taken by North and South, when present). Their width is their preferred width—again, like FlowLayout. The Center area uses up whatever space is left. If there isn't enough space, something won't be shown, though in most cases you don't show something in every area.

Because BorderLayout requires extra quadrant information, you need to use a different version of add( ) to add components to the container. This add( ) method takes two parameters instead of the usual one, where the area to add the component is the second parameter. The BorderLayout class defines five constants, one for each area, to be used as the second parameter: NORTH, SOUTH, EAST, WEST, and CENTER.

```
p = new JPanel(new BorderLayout());
p.addContainerListener(this);
p.add(new JButton("North"), BorderLayout.NORTH);
p.add(new JButton("South"), BorderLayout.SOUTH);
p.add(new JButton("East"), BorderLayout.EAST);
p.add(new JButton("West"), BorderLayout.WEST);
p.add(new JButton("Center"), BorderLayout.CENTER);
pane.add(p, "BorderLayout");
```

The preceding code added buttons with each area name. Again, you create a new JPanel and add the ContainerListener to the panel to allow these buttons to resize the frame, too. Then, when you add the new panel to the JTabbedPane, you will see three tabs, as shown in Figure 6-11. When you select the BorderLayout tab, you'll see the screen shown in Figure 6-12, and if you select a button the window resizes, as shown in Figure 6-13.

Figure 6-11. With the BorderLayout tab added but not displayed

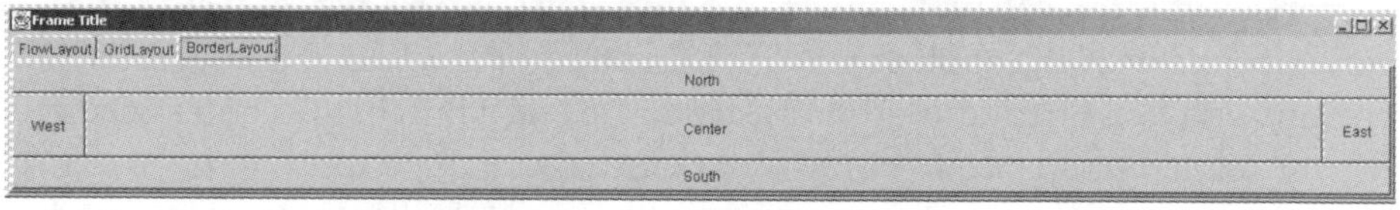

Figure 6-12. The initial BorderLayout tab display state

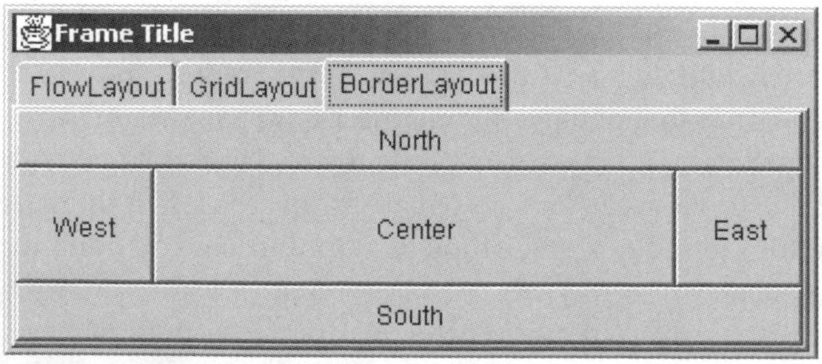

Figure 6-13. A resized BorderLayout tab after selecting a button

Using `BoxLayout`

The `BoxLayout` layout manager was introduced with the Swing component set. It provides for a single row or column of components with two special components, glue and struts, to help with the positioning of the other components. Instead of honoring a component's preferred size, the `BoxLayout` manager works with a component's maximum size. You use the *glue* component to consume extra space to get the other components back to their preferred size. You use the *struts* component to provide fixed size spacers between components.

> **NOTE** *Glue and struts component usage is not limited to `BoxLayout`—you can use them elsewhere. They just don't serve as much use elsewhere.*

In addition to the `BoxLayout` component, there is the `Box` container. `Box` works very much like a `JPanel` with a `BoxLayout` manager, but it is created in one step. You can't just create a `JPanel` with a `BoxLayout` manager in one step, as the constructor for `BoxLayout` requires the panel as an argument:

```
JPanel panel = new JPanel();
BoxLayout layout = new BoxLayout(panel, BoxLayout.X_AXIS);
panel.setLayout(layout);
```

On the other hand, to create the same `Box`, you just need one line of code:

```
Box box = Box.createHorizontalBox();
```

A horizontal `Box` lays out components along the *x* axis like a `FlowLayout`, but with no chance of wrapping components if the window is too narrow.

A vertical `Box` lays out components along the *y* axis like a single-column `GridLayout`, except that each component can be a different size.

Let's add two more panels to the `JTabbedPane`, one with a horizontal layout and one with a vertical layout. In the horizontal box, you'll have three buttons. You'll use glue before and after to make sure the components are centered, but you'll place struts of different sizes between the components so there is a fixed but different distance between them. For the vertical box, you'll have four buttons with glue between each to spread out the components evenly no matter how tall the container.

Creating the glue and struts is a little different than creating most components. To create the glue component, you use the static `createVerticalGlue()` or createHorizontalGlue() method of Box, depending upon the desired direction. If you want to be lazy, you can just createGlue() and it will work in either direction. With struts, the methods are createVerticalStrut(), passing in the height, and createHorizontalStrut(), passing in the width. You can create an invisible component that has a fixed width and height with createRigidArea(), passing in a Dimension to describe the width and height.

Here's the code for the horizontal box shown in Figure 6-14:

```
Box horizontalBox = Box.createHorizontalBox();
horizontalBox.addContainerListener(this);
horizontalBox.add(Box.createHorizontalGlue());
horizontalBox.add(new JButton("One"));
horizontalBox.add(Box.createHorizontalStrut(20));
horizontalBox.add(new JButton("Two"));
horizontalBox.add(Box.createHorizontalStrut(5));
horizontalBox.add(new JButton("Three"));
horizontalBox.add(Box.createHorizontalGlue());
pane.add(horizontalBox, "H Box");
```

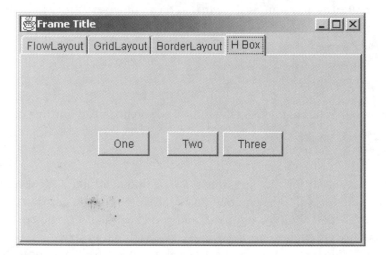

Figure 6-14. The horizontal Box panel

And here's the vertical box source for the screen shown in Figure 6-15:

```
Box verticalBox = Box.createVerticalBox();
verticalBox.addContainerListener(this);
verticalBox.add(new JButton("One"));
verticalBox.add(Box.createVerticalGlue());
```

```
verticalBox.add(new JButton("Two"));
verticalBox.add(Box.createVerticalGlue());
verticalBox.add(new JButton("Three"));
verticalBox.add(Box.createVerticalGlue());
verticalBox.add(new JButton("Four"));
pane.add(verticalBox, "V Box");
```

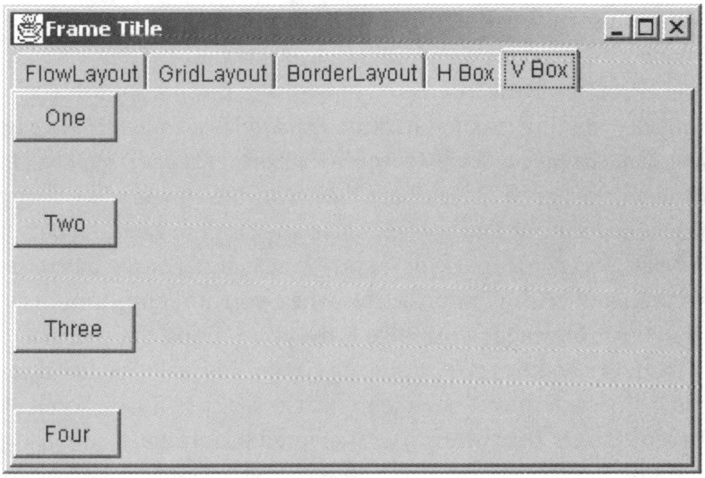

Figure 6-15. The vertical Box panel

> **TIP**   *If you'd like the components in a box to have a different alignment, you can change their x and y alignment with the* setAlignmentX() *and* setAlignmentY() *methods. By default,* JButton *components have an x alignment of 0.0, meaning they're left-justified, and a y alignment of 0.5, meaning they are centered (top to bottom).*

Using Other Layout Managers

There are two other layout managers that come with the standard Java libraries: CardLayout and GridBagLayout. You can find additional layout managers around the Internet. If you're familiar with certain geometry management principles from other languages, someone more than likely has already ported the layout principles to Java as a layout manager.

The CardLayout manager acts like a JTabbedPane without the tabs. If you don't want the tabs, it may be useful. However, you need some way to toggle between the different cards, hence the need for tabs and the JTabbedPane.

The GridBagLayout manager is the most complicated of all the standard layout managers. It relies on a second class, GridBagConstraints, to describe the rules for laying out each component in the container. It provides for the flexibility of having components that span multiple rows and columns as well as which components get extra space when the screen is larger than necessary. Most of the time, you can avoid using GridBagLayout by placing panels inside panels and adjusting the layout manager of each panel. If you are truly interested in learning more about the layout manager consider reading up on it in Sun's *How to Use GridBagLayout* tutorial (http://java.sun.com/docs/books/tutorial/uiswing/layout/gridbag.html).

With JBuilder, you get a handful of other layout managers, too. They are part of the JBuilder Component Library (JBCL). In the com.borland.layout package, you get XYLayout, VerticalFlowLayout, and PaneLayout. The XYLayout manager enables you to specify *x* and *y* coordinates when you add components. The VerticalFlowLayout manager works like FlowLayout along the *y* axis, and the PaneLayout manager enables you to specify constraints relative to other components in the container. Feel free to use these if you'd like. You just need to remember to include them with your delivered programs, as they are nonstandard.

TIP *Once you start using the UI Designer, described in Part Two of the book, you may find yourself creating screens with the* XYLayout *manager then swapping the manager for the* GridBagLayout. *The designer will try to mimic the grid bag constraints as closely as possible for you in the transition.*

Listing 6-1 is the complete source code for creating the JTabbedPane with the different layout managers.

Listing 6-1. The Complete Tabs.java Source
```
package skill6;

import java.awt.*;
import java.awt.event.*;
import javax.swing.*;

public class Tabs extends JFrame implements ContainerListener, ActionListener {
  JPanel contentPane;
  BorderLayout borderLayout1 = new BorderLayout();
```

```
//Construct the frame
public Tabs() {
  enableEvents(AWTEvent.WINDOW_EVENT_MASK);
  try {
    jbInit();
  }
  catch(Exception e) {
    e.printStackTrace();
  }
}
//Component initialization
private void jbInit() throws Exception  {
  contentPane = (JPanel) this.getContentPane();
  contentPane.setLayout(borderLayout1);
  this.setTitle("Frame Title");
  JTabbedPane pane = new JTabbedPane();
  contentPane.add(pane, BorderLayout.CENTER);
  JPanel p = new JPanel();
  p.addContainerListener(this);
  for (char c = 'a'; c <= 'z'; c++) {
    p.add(new JButton(new Character(c).toString()));
  }
  pane.add(p, "FlowLayout");

  p = new JPanel(new GridLayout(4, 3));
  p.addContainerListener(this);
  for (int i = 1; i <= 9; i++) {
    p.add(new JButton("" + i));
  }
  p.add(new JButton("*"));
  p.add(new JButton("0"));
  p.add(new JButton("#"));
  pane.add(p, "GridLayout");

  p = new JPanel(new BorderLayout());
  p.addContainerListener(this);
  p.add(new JButton("North"), BorderLayout.NORTH);
  p.add(new JButton("South"), BorderLayout.SOUTH);
  p.add(new JButton("East"), BorderLayout.EAST);
  p.add(new JButton("West"), BorderLayout.WEST);
  p.add(new JButton("Center"), BorderLayout.CENTER);
  pane.add(p, "BorderLayout");
```

```java
        Box horizontalBox = Box.createHorizontalBox();
        horizontalBox.addContainerListener(this);
        horizontalBox.add(Box.createHorizontalGlue());
        horizontalBox.add(new JButton("One"));
        horizontalBox.add(Box.createHorizontalStrut(20));
        horizontalBox.add(new JButton("Two"));
        horizontalBox.add(Box.createHorizontalStrut(5));
        horizontalBox.add(new JButton("Three"));
        horizontalBox.add(Box.createHorizontalGlue());
        pane.add(horizontalBox, "H Box");

        Box verticalBox = Box.createVerticalBox();
        verticalBox.addContainerListener(this);
        verticalBox.add(new JButton("One"));
        verticalBox.add(Box.createVerticalGlue());
        verticalBox.add(new JButton("Two"));
        verticalBox.add(Box.createVerticalGlue());
        verticalBox.add(new JButton("Three"));
        verticalBox.add(Box.createVerticalGlue());
        verticalBox.add(new JButton("Four"));
        pane.add(verticalBox, "V Box");
    }
    //Overridden so we can exit when window is closed
    protected void processWindowEvent(WindowEvent e) {
        super.processWindowEvent(e);
        if (e.getID() == WindowEvent.WINDOW_CLOSING) {
            System.exit(0);
        }
    }
    public void componentAdded(ContainerEvent e) {
        Component c = e.getChild();
        if (c instanceof JButton) {
            JButton b = (JButton)c;
            b.addActionListener(this);
        }
    }
    public void componentRemoved(ContainerEvent e) {
    }
    public void actionPerformed(ActionEvent e) {
        int width = (int)(Math.random() * 200 + 150);
        int height = (int)(Math.random() * 200 + 150);
        setSize(width, height);
        validate();
    }
}
```

ARE YOU EXPERIENCED?

Congratulations! You can now create programs that will look good across all the different platforms that Java runs on.

Now you can

- Describe layout management

- Position components in a platform-independent manner

- Create tabbed property sheets using the JTabbedPane control

- Use FlowLayout to size components

- Listen for container events

- Use GridLayout to position components

- Work with frames and windows using BorderLayout

- Use glue and struts with Box and BoxLayout

In Skill 7, you'll learn about Java's graphics capabilities and how to create smooth animation sequences.

Drawing with Java

- Drawing to the screen

- Creating event adapters

- Doing double-buffered drawing

- Selecting colors

- Changing line strokes

- Drawing patterns

Drawing Support in Java

In addition to containing the basic GUI components, the java.awt package provides the standard support classes for drawing within the Java libraries. You use the Graphics class for basic drawing operations, telling the system what shapes to draw, where the Color class defines the different shades available for the drawing operation. With Graphics, all drawing operations are for single-pixel-wide lines of a solid color or for a solid fill pattern within the shape. More advanced drawing support is found in the Graphics2D class, with support classes found in the java.awt.geom package. The Graphics2D class is part of the Java 2D capabilities introduced with the Java 2 platform. With the 2D capabilities, you can define a custom line stroke or a fill pattern, so more advanced drawing operations are supported. Unfortunately, you can't use the Java 2D capabilities in an applet without the Java Plug-in, as they aren't available with the standard browser Java runtime. Combining the use of these classes with the Image class demonstrated earlier allows you to create most commonly needed graphical operations.

NOTE *For more information on using the Java Plug-in, see Chapter 16.*

To get started with graphical programming, let's create an applet that draws some basic Java objects. You'll then create an application that uses the Java 2D capabilities, setting up strokes and patterns. As with all skills, close everything first, and create a new skill to work in for Skill 7. Use the Applet Wizard to create the base project and starting applet. In the Project Wizard, enter a project name of **Skill7** and a directory of **C:\skills\Skill7**, and then select Finish. Then, for the Applet Wizard, the only field that needs to be changed is the class name. Change the default **Applet1** name to **Drawing** and select Finish.

So, what will you draw in the applet? Initially, you'll have the program draw filled rectangles in black. Once you have the basic drawing done, you'll add support for stretching the rectangle as it's being drawn. Here's where you'll need to do some extra work in order for the program to look okay. Then you'll randomize the drawing colors. The application will work similarly, but you'll customize the shape outline and fill pattern.

Using the paint() Method to Draw

Once you've gone through the Applet Wizard, it's time to create the program. The first thing to do and understand is drawing. In Skill 5, you worked with Java controls, such as Button and Label. When you needed to use one of those objects, you created it and added it to the screen. Once the control was created, it knew how to display itself.

Drawing on your own is a little different. When Java wants to update the screen, the paint() method is called for the display area to update. In the case of an applet, the applet's paint() method is called. So, because you want to draw something in your applet, you need to add behavior to the paint() method of your applet. First, select Drawing.java in the Navigation pane. Then, using the Override Methods Wizard, you can select the paint(Graphics) method of the java.awt.Container class to have an empty paint method added to our applet. Once you click OK, the following code is added to the applet:

```
public void paint(Graphics g) {
  /**@todo: Override this java.awt.Container method*/
  super.paint( g);
}
```

> **NOTE** *The* paint() *method actually originates with the* Component *class. However, because* Container *overrides the method itself, you're overriding the version that* Container *provides, not* Component.

Once you have the method framework, you can add your own behavior to it. To draw a filled rectangle in Java, use the fillRect() method of Graphics, the parameter to paint(). The method requires a starting point along with a width and height. Almost all drawing operations work in this way. Provide a point in the top-left corner with dimensions, effectively a bounding rectangle, and tell the Graphics object what to do.

Instead of just drawing the rectangle with a fixed location and size, let's create four instance variables representing the two points. This will allow you to more easily support the event handler later to dynamically shape the rectangle. If you add the following line to your code immediately after the class declaration, you'll have your two points to work with, along with initial values:

```
int startX = 0, startY = 0, endX = 100, endY = 100;
```

In addition to creating and initializing the variables, let's add two methods to change them. These will prove beneficial later. Each method will change the location of a point, starting or ending, to the coordinates passed.

```
public void setStartPoint(Point p) {
  startX = p.x;
  startY = p.y;
}

public void setEndPoint(Point p) {
  endX = p.x;
  endY = p.y;
}
```

NOTE *The* Point *class holds the coordinates of a two-dimensional position.*

Then, getting back to the paint() routine, you can determine the top-left corner, width, and height to draw. Because Java's drawing routines want the point to be the top-left corner, you have to determine which position is lowest in both directions. The min() method of the Math class performs this functionality for you. Then, for width and height, the difference between the coordinates needs to be positive. For this, you can use the abs() method (for absolute value) of the Math class. Putting all this together, your paint() method will look like the following listing:

```
public void paint(Graphics g) {
  super.paint(g);
  int x = Math.min(startX, endX);
  int y = Math.min(startY, endY);
  int width  = Math.abs(startX - endX);
  int height = Math.abs(startY - endY);
  g.fillRect(x, y, width, height);
}
```

NOTE *The* Math *class is a collection of common math functions, such as trigonometric functions, a random number generator, and min/max capabilities, among other things.*

When you run this applet, you'll see the screen in Figure 7-1. It's important to point out that paint() isn't called just once. For instance, if the applet's drawing area is invalidated, paint() will be called when the object in front of the applet is removed. In fact, you don't call the method yourself. Instead, the browser calls paint() when necessary to update the display.

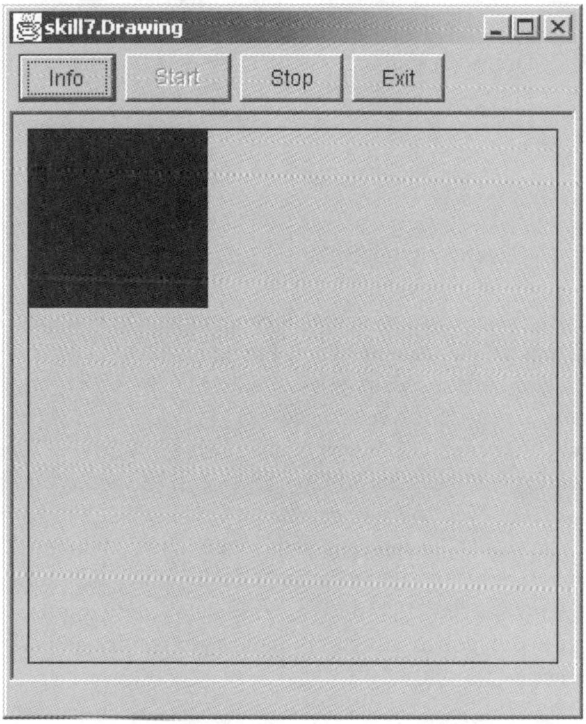

Figure 7-1. The applet drawing a 100×100 rectangle filled in black

TIP *Remember to save your work by selecting File ➢ Save All before you run it.*

Other Drawing Operations

In addition to being able to draw a filled rectangle, you can use the following methods to draw other shapes:

- `drawRect()`: Draws an unfilled rectangle

- `drawRoundRect()`: Draws an unfilled rectangle with rounded corners

- `fillRoundRect()`: Draws a filled rectangle with rounded corners

- `draw3DRect()`: Draws a three-dimensional unfilled rectangle

- `fill3DRect()`: Draws a three-dimensional filled rectangle

- `drawOval()`: Draws an unfilled oval

- `fillOval()`: Draws a filled oval

- `drawArc()`: Draws an arc

- `fillArc()`: Draws an arc filled like a pie chart

You can try to run the program with any of these other shapes, too. Some of these methods require parameters beyond what `fillRect()` or `drawRect()` require. A quick glance at the Help ➤ Java Reference documentation will show the requirements. For instance, `drawRoundRect()` allows you to specify how round you want the corners. Although all methods are a little different, each requires the starting point in the top-left corner and the width and height within which to draw, even to draw an oval.

There are a handful of exceptions to this rule. The text drawing routines, `drawBytes()`, `drawChars()`, and `drawString()`, take a point that serves as the start of the baseline. The line drawing routine, `drawLine()`, only requires two end points. Finally, the polygon `drawPolygon()` and polyline `drawPolyline()` drawing routines take a series of points.

Handling Mouse Events

Because you put all that work into drawing a fixed-sized rectangle, changing its shape to coordinate with different locations is fairly easy. Although it may have seemed like quite a bit of extra work to draw a single rectangle, making your programs more adaptable is good programming practice. It's easier, and cheaper, for the initial designer to add in the capabilities than for someone to come in later to do it. On to the mouse events.

Instead of always drawing the rectangle in one spot, your program should allow the user to specify the coordinates. The most natural way to do this is with the mouse. Pressing the left mouse button signifies the starting point. Then, you drag the mouse to another location and release the button. This new location is the ending point.

The methods that deal with mouse events are part of the MouseListener and MouseMotionListener interfaces. The MouseListener deals with mouse up and down, while the MouseMotionListener deals with movement.

Handling Mouse Events with MouseListener

You'll work with the MouseListener first. Table 7-1 describes the methods that are part of the interface.

Table 7-1. The MouseListener Interface Methods

Methods	Description
mouseClicked()	For when you, the programmer, are interested in when a user presses and releases any mouse button without moving the mouse
mousePressed()	For when a user presses a mouse button
mouseReleased()	For when a user releases a mouse button
mouseEntered()	For when a user moves the mouse into a component's area
mouseExited()	For when a user moves the mouse outside a component's area

So, in order for the applet to get new drawing coordinates for the rectangle, four steps are involved:

1. A MouseListener implementation needs to be created. One way to do this is to have the applet implement the MouseListener interface itself.

2. The MouseListener's mousePressed() method must get the new starting point.

3. The MouseListener's mouseReleased() method must get the ending point and draw the rectangle.

4. The MouseListener must be associated with the applet.

You learned how to implement a listener in Skill 4. Select Wizards ➤ Implement Interface, the name of the interface (java.awt.event.MouseListener in your case), and OK. JBuilder then adds the necessary source code to your program with all the interface methods throwing an UnsupportedOperationException. For the methods you don't define, you'll need to remove the throwing of the exception.

Define the mousePressed() method behavior first. Its signature block looks like the following:

```
public void mousePressed(MouseEvent e)
```

The MouseEvent parameter contains the location of where the event happened. The location is available via the getPoint() method. So, using this point, you can change the starting point with the setStartPoint() method you defined earlier. The mousePressed() method now looks like the following:

```
public void mousePressed(MouseEvent e) {
  setStartPoint(e.getPoint());
}
```

Then, there is the mouseReleased() method. Its signature looks similar:

```
public void mouseReleased(MouseEvent e)
```

Again, you can use the event's coordinates to change the location. This time, you change the ending point using your setEndPoint() method. There's one more thing you have to add, though. In order to update the screen, you need to notify the applet. This is done through a call to the repaint() method, with no parameters. The mouseReleased() method now looks like the following:

```
public void mouseReleased(MouseEvent e) {
  setEndPoint(e.getPoint());
  repaint();
}
```

WARNING   *You cannot call the* paint() *method directly because you don't possess a reference to the required* Graphics *parameter. Using the* repaint() *method ensures that your applet will update the screen with the proper parameter. Otherwise, the screen will only be updated if it becomes invalid—by someone placing another object in front of the screen's area and removing it, or minimizing and reselecting the applet's window.*

With these two methods filled in, remove the comment and throw statement from the remaining three. You now need to associate the listener to the applet so they get called. Similar to associating an ActionListener with a Button, as you did in Skill 5, you can use the addMouseListener() method to associate the applet—the interface implementer—to itself. This can be done in the init() or jbInit() method. Keeping with JBuilder's style of having component initialization in jbInit(), you'll add it there.

```
private void jbInit() throws Exception {
  addMouseListener(this);
}
```

Once this is done, you can run the applet again. If you press and release the mouse at different coordinates, you'll see the program draw various rectangles.

When you run the applet, you'll notice one peculiarity. The rectangle doesn't stretch out as you move the mouse around. You can add this functionality with the help of a MouseMotionListener.

Handling Mouse Events with MouseMotionListener

Table 7-2 lists the methods that are part of the MouseMotionListener interface.

Table 7-2. The MouseMotionListener Interface Methods

Methods	Description
mouseDragged()	For when a user moves the mouse with a button pressed
mouseMoved()	For when a user moves the mouse without a button pressed

Here you only have to perform three steps to deal with the dragging:

1. A MouseMotionListener implementation needs to be created. Like MouseListener, the applet can implement the interface itself.

2. The MouseMotionListener's mouseDragged() method must get the new ending point.

3. The MouseMotionListener must be associated with the applet.

Again, you use the Implement Interface Wizard. This time, you select the java.awt.event.MouseMotionListener and the OK button. Then, you define the mouseDragged() behavior and remove the exception throwing from mouseMoved().

```
public void paint(Graphics g) {
  super.paint(g);
  if (im == null) {
    im = createImage(getSize().width, getSize().height);
    buf = im.getGraphics();
  }
  int x = Math.min(startX, endX);
  int y = Math.min(startY, endY);
  int width  = Math.abs(startX - endX);
  int height = Math.abs(startY - endY);
  if (dragging) {
    g.drawImage(im, 0, 0, this);
    g.fillRect(x, y, width, height);
  } else {
    buf.fillRect(x, y, width, height);
    g.drawImage(im, 0, 0, this);
  }
}
```

NOTE   *The* drawImage() *method takes four parameters. The first is the image to draw. The second is its* x *coordinate, while the third is the* y *coordinate. Both define the top-left corner position. The last parameter is something called an image* observer, *which should be the component on which the image is drawn. As long as your class is a subclass of* Component, *just use the* this *keyword there. The observer is periodically notified as the image is loaded. This is important when loading images over the Internet.*

You set the dragging variable in the MouseListener methods: mousePressed() and mouseReleased(). It isn't necessary to change the value within the mouseDragged() method.

```
public void mousePressed(MouseEvent e) {
  setStartPoint(e.getPoint());
  dragging = true;
}
public void mouseReleased(MouseEvent e) {
  setEndPoint(e.getPoint());
  dragging = false;
  repaint();
}
```

You can run the applet now, but there's one more thing you should add. Because you're forever drawing to the screen, it sure would be nice to eventually clear it. Instead of adding a button or menu to deal with this, let's just have the mouseClick() method (pressing and releasing the mouse button without moving) reset the buffer. Once this is added, your program will appear more like Figure 7-2 after drawing a few rectangles.

```java
public void mouseClicked(MouseEvent e) {
  im = createImage(getSize().width, getSize().height);
  buf = im.getGraphics();
}
```

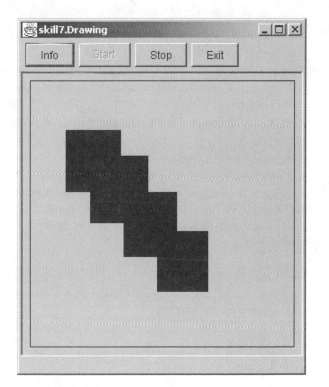

Figure 7-2. The applet after drawing multiple rectangles

Removing the Flash

In order to have the mouse-handling code tell the system to update the display, you called the repaint() method. The repaint() method works by telling the system to call update(), and then the update() method calls paint(), thus updating the display. Herein lies the problem. The update() method clears the screen before the paint() method draws on it. When drawing large objects, this results in a flashing effect because a solid background is shown between screen refreshes. Because you're drawing to a buffer, which happens to be the size of the display, you can stop update() from clearing the screen between buffer drawings. Using the Override Methods Wizard, you can select the update(Graphics) method of java.awt.Component. Changing update() to only notify paint(), without clearing the screen, results in the following source:

```
public void update(Graphics g) {
  paint(g);
}
```

Changing Colors

Working in black and white is fine if you're trying to create screen shots to include in a book. However, you probably would like to see other colors on the screen. Let's have the system change drawing colors whenever the mouse leaves and re-enters the applet's space. This happens to be the mouseEntered() method of the MouseListener interface.

This isn't as easy as it sounds, though. All the earlier drawing operations used the default color, which happened to be black. In order for you to properly change the drawing color, the initial color value must be variable based. Although you could have done it the proper way first, as you did with the drawing points, let's look at all the extra work necessary to go back and fix up everything.

There are four steps involved in this task.

1. Create and initialize a variable to store the current drawing color.

2. Provide a method to change the color.

3. When drawing to either the screen or the buffer, use the current drawing color.

4. Update the mouseEntered() method to use the color changing method.

You've created instance variables for the class a few times already. This one is no different:

```
Color drawingColor = Color.black;
```

You probably noticed Color.black as the initial value and wondered where that came from. The Color class has 13 predefined constants that can be used by name. They're listed in Table 7-3. All other colors must be created manually. You'll see how to create your own shortly.

Table 7-3. The 13 Constants of the java.awt.Color Class

Name						
black	cyan	gray	lightGray	orange	red	yellow
blue	darkGray	green	magenta	pink	white	

The method to change the variable should look somewhat familiar:

```
public void setDrawingColor(Color c) {
  drawingColor = c;
}
```

The reason for these helper methods will become clearer once you learn about JavaBean components in Part Two. Basically, creating them allows a builder tool to use them when it connects various program pieces together.

The third task requires two changes to the paint() method. Because painting is done directly to the screen and the buffer, each must change colors before drawing. Add the following two lines before the if statement, checking on the dragging flag:

```
g.setColor(drawingColor);
buf.setColor(drawingColor);
```

Now, you can actually change the color. If all the previous work was done when the applet was initially created, it wouldn't have to be changed now. Because you're going to change the drawing color when the mouse enters the applet's space, you'll modify the mouseEntered() method of the MouseListener interface. However, your applet already implements the interface, so you only need to add the behavior to the stubbed-out method.

```
public void mouseEntered(MouseEvent e) {
  short r = (short)(Math.random()*256);
  short g = (short)(Math.random()*256);
  short b = (short)(Math.random()*256);
  setDrawingColor(new Color(r, g, b));
}
```

The Color class works similarly to a color computer monitor. There are three color banks—red, green, and blue—that are combined to display a particular color to the user. In Java, each band has 256 possible values, from 0 to 255. The higher the value in each band, the more of that color is shown. For instance, a value of 255 for red, 175 for green, and 175 for blue is the color pink. Unless your video mode supports a color palette of 16.7 million colors (256*256*256), when you ask for a specific color, you may get a slightly different one.

> **WARNING** *Java requires a palette of at least 256 colors. If you like working in 1600×1200 mode but can only display 16 colors with that resolution, you won't be able to run any Java programs. In fact, JBuilder won't even run.*

In case you missed it, you finished your applet. Let's run the program again and see what you got. See Figure 7-3 for a possible screen; yours will more than likely differ. Notice that the initial drawing color isn't black. The very first time the mouse moves into the applet's area, it is reset.

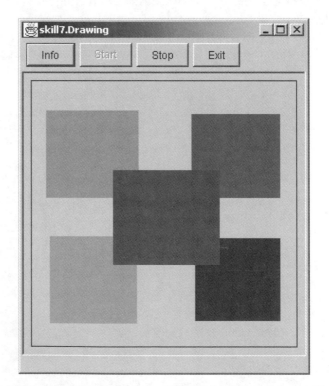

Figure 7-3. A black-and-white example of the multicolor applet you'll see onscreen

Listing 7-1 contains the entire applet source.

Listing 7-1. The Complete Drawing.java Applet Source

```java
package skill7;

import java.awt.*;
import java.awt.event.*;
import java.applet.*;

public class Drawing extends Applet implements MouseListener, MouseMotionListener {

  int startX = 0, startY = 0, endX = 100, endY = 100;
  Image im;
  Graphics buf;
  boolean dragging = false;
  Color drawingColor = Color.black;

  boolean isStandalone = false;
  //Get a parameter value
  public String getParameter(String key, String def) {
    return isStandalone ? System.getProperty(key, def) :
      (getParameter(key) != null ? getParameter(key) : def);
  }

  //Construct the applet
  public Drawing() {
  }
  //Initialize the applet
  public void init() {
    try {
      jbInit();
    }
    catch(Exception e) {
      e.printStackTrace();
    }
  }

  //Component initialization
  private void jbInit() throws Exception {
    addMouseListener(this);
    addMouseMotionListener(this);
  }
```

```java
//Get Applet information
public String getAppletInfo() {
  return "Applet Information";
}
//Get parameter info
public String[][] getParameterInfo() {
  return null;
}
public void paint(Graphics g) {
  super.paint(g);
  if (im == null) {
    im = createImage(getSize().width, getSize().height);
    buf = im.getGraphics();
  }
  int x = Math.min(startX, endX);
  int y = Math.min(startY, endY);
  int width  = Math.abs(startX - endX);
  int height = Math.abs(startY - endY);
  g.setColor(drawingColor);
  buf.setColor(drawingColor);
  if (dragging) {
    g.drawImage(im, 0, 0, this);
    g.fillRect(x, y, width, height);
  } else {
    buf.fillRect(x, y, width, height);
    g.drawImage(im, 0, 0, this);
  }
}

public void setStartPoint(Point p) {
  startX = p.x;
  startY = p.y;
}

public void setEndPoint(Point p) {
  endX = p.x;
  endY = p.y;
}
public void mouseClicked(MouseEvent e) {
  im = createImage(getSize().width, getSize().height);
  buf = im.getGraphics();
}
```

```
  public void mousePressed(MouseEvent e) {
    setStartPoint(e.getPoint());
    dragging = true;
  }
  public void mouseReleased(MouseEvent e) {
    setEndPoint(e.getPoint());
    dragging = false;
    repaint();
  }
  public void mouseEntered(MouseEvent e) {
    short r = (short)(Math.random()*256);
    short g = (short)(Math.random()*256);
    short b = (short)(Math.random()*256);
    setDrawingColor(new Color(r, g, b));
  }
  public void mouseExited(MouseEvent e) {
  }
  public void mouseDragged(MouseEvent e) {
    setEndPoint(e.getPoint());
    repaint();
  }
  public void mouseMoved(MouseEvent e) {
  }
  public void update(Graphics g) {
    paint(g);
  }
  public void setDrawingColor(Color c) {
    drawingColor = c;
  }
}
```

Using the Java 2D API

Okay, your program works fine, but you're stuck working with solid lines and fill patterns. To make your effort more interesting, use the Application Wizard to create a new application. Leave the application class as **Application1** but change the Frame to **FancyDrawing**. Similar to what you did in Skill 5 when you converted an AWT applet to a Swing application, you're going to copy everything you added to the applet to the application.

Starting from the top down, you'll have to copy over the `implements MouseListener, MouseMotionListener` piece:

```
public class FancyDrawing extends JFrame
    implements MouseListener, MouseMotionListener {
```

Next, copy over all the variable declarations:

```
int startX = 0, startY = 0, endX = 100, endY = 100;
Image im;
Graphics buf;
boolean dragging = false;
Color drawingColor = Color.black;
```

Then, copy over the add listener calls in the `jbInit()` method:

```
addMouseListener(this);
addMouseMotionListener(this);
```

Assuming you added all the new code at the bottom of `Drawing`, all the rest of the code should be in the `paint()` method and below. Copy it all and add it to the bottom of `FancyDrawing`.

Because your window is a subclass of `JFrame`, it actually does some double buffering for you, so you can remove some of the added code. In order to reset your program to not flash while dragging, remove the overridden `update()` method and the `super.paint(g)` call, as you no longer want the default behavior of `paint()`.

Saving and running the program at this point essentially returns you to the prior state of the `Drawing` applet.

Using the Graphics2D Object

In order to work with strokes and fill patterns, you have to convert your `paint()` routine to treat the `Graphics` argument as a `Graphics2D` object. This involves a simple casting operation from `Graphics` to `Graphics2D`.

```
Graphics2D g2d = (Graphics2D)g;
```

Because Graphics2D is a subclass of Graphics, you can still call the same fillRect() method. However, to have more fun with the item drawn, you have to create a Shape object. You essentially need to create a Shape from the rectangle coordinates, and then pass that shape into the fill() method of Graphics2D.

```
Shape shape = new Rectangle(x, y, width, height);
g2d.fill(shape);
```

In order for the double buffering to still work, you also have to change the buf variable to a Graphics2D object and cast the return value from getGraphics() on the Image object to a Graphics2D object. Here's the updated paint() and mouseClicked() methods, still keeping the program functionality the same:

```
Graphics2D buf;
  . . .
public void paint(Graphics g) {
  Graphics2D g2d = (Graphics2D)g;
  if (im == null) {
    im = createImage(getSize().width, getSize().height);
    buf = (Graphics2D)im.getGraphics();
  }
  int x = Math.min(startX, endX);
  int y = Math.min(startY, endY);
  int width  = Math.abs(startX - endX);
  int height = Math.abs(startY - endY);
  Shape shape = new Rectangle(x, y, width, height);
  g2d.setColor(drawingColor);
  buf.setColor(drawingColor);
  if (dragging) {
    g2d.drawImage(im, 0, 0, this);
    g2d.fill(shape);
  } else {
    buf.fill(shape);
    g2d.drawImage(im, 0, 0, this);
  }
}
public void mouseClicked(MouseEvent e) {
  im = createImage(getSize().width, getSize().height);
  buf = (Graphics2D)im.getGraphics();
}
```

Other Drawing Shapes

Besides a Rectangle, you can create many other shapes, and you have the ability to define your own paths and combine multiple shapes:

- Arc2D: For arcs

- Area: For combining shapes

- CubicCurve2D: For cubic (Bezier) curve segments

- Ellipse2D: For ellipses

- GeneralPath: For constructing shapes from lines and curves

- Line2D: For drawing lines

- Polygon: For constructing shapes from lines

- QuadCurve2D: For quadratic parametric curve segments

- RoundRectangle2D: For rectangles with rounded corners

See the online documentation under Help ➤ Java Reference for additional information.

Working with Strokes

Now that your program has been converted to draw with the Java 2D API, instead of the basic graphic operations, you can start working with the more interesting Java 2D objects. First, let's add an outline around the rectangle. By default, this will be a single-pixel-wide solid line.

```
buf.setColor(Color.black);
buf.draw(shape);
```

NOTE *Essentially,* draw(aRectangleShape) *would do what the* drawRect() *of* Graphics *does.*

To change the line drawn around the shape to be wider or dashed, you have to define a Stroke object. The Stroke interface is implemented by the BasicStroke class, which offers five constructors that allow you to customize the drawing attributes.

```
// To create a stroke with default attributes
BasicStroke()
// To create a stroke with a different width
BasicStroke(float width)
// To create a stroke with the specified attributes
BasicStroke(float width, int cap, int join)
BasicStroke(float width, int cap, int join, float miterlimit)
BasicStroke(float width, int cap, int join, float miterlimit, float[] dash,
    float dashPhase)
```

The default BasicStroke is like the behavior of drawRect(): a single-pixel-wide solid line. End caps are squared off and path segments can be extended a little so edges meet with neighboring segments. Table 7-4 lists the different constants you can provide for end caps and join settings.

Table 7-4. The Constants for End Cap and Join Settings

Methods	Description
CAP_BUTT	Adds no added decorations
CAP_ROUND	Rounds off ends
CAP_SQUARE	Squares off ends (default)
JOIN_BEVEL	Joins the outer corner of path segments with straight segments
JOIN_MITER	Joins path segments by extending outer edges (default)
JOIN_ROUND	Joins path segments by rounding off the corner

To help you visualize the different styles, see Figure 7-4.

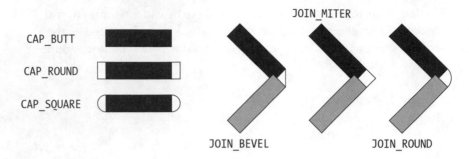

Figure 7-4. Visualizing the stroke end cap and join styles

If you want to have dashed lines, you have to provide an array of dash lengths, including the space between dashes. If all dashes were of equal lengths with the same space between them, you would pass in a one-element array. If they were of different lengths, or you wanted to have a different length between them, you'd create a larger array. The dash phase defines how much of the first dash is ignored.

If you change your program to change the stroke as well as the color when the user enters the program's area, your rectangles can now be framed accordingly. Instead of a random stroke, let's define a set of four to choose from and alternate through them.

```java
Stroke strokes[] = {
// Single pixel
  new BasicStroke(),
// Wider
  new BasicStroke(5),
// Rounded
  new BasicStroke(10, BasicStroke.CAP_ROUND, BasicStroke.JOIN_ROUND),
// Dashed
  new BasicStroke(7, BasicStroke.CAP_SQUARE, BasicStroke.JOIN_BEVEL,
    10, new float[] {20f, 15f}, 0)
};
int strokePos = 0;
Stroke drawingStroke = strokes[strokePos];
```

Then, in the `mouseEntered()` routine, you just have to get the next stroke to use:

```java
public void mouseEntered(MouseEvent e) {
  short r = (short)(Math.random()*256);
  short g = (short)(Math.random()*256);
```

```
  short b = (short)(Math.random()*256);
  setDrawingColor(new Color(r, g, b));
  nextDrawingStroke();
}
public void nextDrawingStroke() {
  strokePos++;
  if (strokePos == strokes.length) {
    strokePos = 0;
  }
  drawingStroke = strokes[strokePos];
}
```

Last, paint() has to be updated to use the stroke:

```
g2d.setStroke(drawingStroke);
buf.setStroke(drawingStroke);
```

When you run the program now, the drawn rectangles get an outline with different stroke patterns, as shown in Figure 7-5.

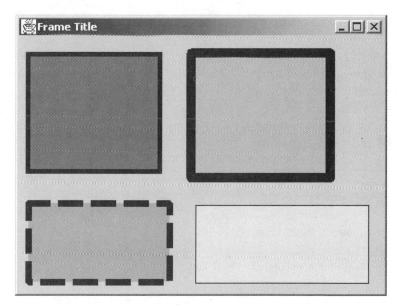

Figure 7-5. Drawn rectangles with different stroke pattern outlines

Working with Arbitrary Fill Patterns

Now that you can change the drawing stroke, let's see how you can change the fill pattern. With the Java 2D API, this fill style is defined by the Paint interface. There are three implementations of the interface: Color, GradientPaint, and TexturePaint. Then, instead of using the setColor() method to change the fill pattern, you use the setPaint() method. So, to change the fill pattern to red, you would use setPaint(Color.red).

 TIP   *For consistency, when you use the* Graphics2D *class, it's best if you consistently change the fill pattern with* setPaint(), *instead of using* setColor() *for solid patterns and* setPaint() *for others.*

A gradient is a gradual change from one color to another. With GradientPaint you get to specify the direction of the change by defining the endpoints of a line, essentially where the colors are solid. So, you can have your shapes filled with a gradient, instead of a solid color.

```
Paint paint = new GradientPaint(point1, color1, point2, color2);
```

With TexturePaint, you define a texture to repeat via a java.awt.image.BufferedImage. This could be an image from disk or the Internet or even a texture you draw yourself. For instance, the following creates a texture from an image on disk, relying on the ImageIcon class shown in Skill 5 to load the image. Just place the image in the project directory, c:\skills\Skill7 here, for it to be loaded properly.

```
ImageIcon icon = new ImageIcon("apresslogo.gif");
Image image = icon.getImage();
int width = image.getWidth(this);
int height = image.getHeight(this);
BufferedImage txtr = new BufferedImage(
  width, height, BufferedImage.TYPE_INT_RGB);
Graphics g = txtr.getGraphics();
g.drawImage(image, 0, 0, this);
Rectangle rect = new Rectangle(0, 0, width, height);
Paint paint = new TexturePaint(txtr, rect);
```

TIP *The* BufferedImage *class works similarly to the* Image *class, as it is a subclass, but it's a bit more flexible when you create images in memory. Of course, here you're just copying an image from disk format to memory format, but you could have drawn on the graphics context, similar to how the double buffer was done.*

Figure 7-6 demonstrates the updated program, now drawing with different fill patterns. The gradient covers almost the entire frame with other rectangles in front of it. Notice that there's a second rectangle with the gradient in the top right. Because the gradient base points remained the same, the fill pattern is essentially identical as the first; so had there been no outline pattern, you would never have been able to tell a second rectangle was drawn over the area.

Figure 7-6. Drawn rectangles with different strokes and fill patterns

Listing 7-2 contains the entire application source.

Listing 7-2. The Complete FancyDrawing.java Application Source

```java
package skill7;

import java.awt.*;
import java.awt.event.*;
import java.awt.image.*;
import javax.swing.*;

public class FancyDrawing extends JFrame
    implements MouseListener, MouseMotionListener {
  JPanel contentPane;
  BorderLayout borderLayout1 = new BorderLayout();

  Stroke strokes[] = {
// Single pixel
    new BasicStroke(),
// Wider
    new BasicStroke(5),
// Rounded
    new BasicStroke(10, BasicStroke.CAP_ROUND, BasicStroke.JOIN_ROUND),
// Dashed
    new BasicStroke(7, BasicStroke.CAP_SQUARE, BasicStroke.JOIN_BEVEL,
      10, new float[] {20, 15}, 0)
  };
  int strokePos = 0;
  Stroke drawingStroke = strokes[strokePos];

  int startX = 0, startY = 0, endX = 100, endY = 100;
  Image im;
  Graphics2D buf;
  boolean dragging = false;

  Paint paints[];
  int paintPos = 0;
  Paint drawingPaint;

  //Construct the frame
  public FancyDrawing() {
    enableEvents(AWTEvent.WINDOW_EVENT_MASK);
    try {
      jbInit();
    }
```

```
      catch(Exception e) {
        e.printStackTrace();
      }
    }
//Component initialization
private void jbInit() throws Exception  {
    contentPane = (JPanel) this.getContentPane();
    contentPane.setLayout(borderLayout1);
    this.setSize(new Dimension(400, 300));
    this.setTitle("Frame Title");
    addMouseListener(this);
    addMouseMotionListener(this);
}
//Overridden so we can exit when window is closed
protected void processWindowEvent(WindowEvent e) {
    super.processWindowEvent(e);
    if (e.getID() == WindowEvent.WINDOW_CLOSING) {
      System.exit(0);
    }
}
public void paint(Graphics g) {
    Graphics2D g2d = (Graphics2D)g;
    if (paints == null) {
      initializePaints();
    }
    if (im == null) {
      im = createImage(getSize().width, getSize().height);
      buf = (Graphics2D)im.getGraphics();
    }
    int x = Math.min(startX, endX);
    int y - Math.min(startY, endY);
    int width  = Math.abs(startX - endX);
    int height = Math.abs(startY - endY);
    Shape shape = new Rectangle(x, y, width, height);
    g2d.setPaint(drawingPaint);
    g2d.setStroke(drawingStroke);
    buf.setPaint(drawingPaint);
    buf.setStroke(drawingStroke);
    if (dragging) {
      g2d.drawImage(im, 0, 0, this);
      g2d.fill(shape);
    } else {
```

```java
      buf.fill(shape);
      buf.setPaint(Color.black);
      buf.draw(shape);
      g2d.drawImage(im, 0, 0, this);
    }
  }

  public void setStartPoint(Point p) {
    startX = p.x;
    startY = p.y;
  }

  public void setEndPoint(Point p) {
    endX = p.x;
    endY = p.y;
  }
  public void mouseClicked(MouseEvent e) {
    im = createImage(getSize().width, getSize().height);
    buf = (Graphics2D)im.getGraphics();
  }
  public void mousePressed(MouseEvent e) {
    setStartPoint(e.getPoint());
    dragging = true;
  }
  public void mouseReleased(MouseEvent e) {
    setEndPoint(e.getPoint());
    dragging = false;
    repaint();
  }
  public void mouseEntered(MouseEvent e) {
    nextDrawingPaint();
    nextDrawingStroke();
  }
  public void nextDrawingStroke() {
    strokePos++;
    if (strokePos == strokes.length) {
      strokePos = 0;
    }
    drawingStroke = strokes[strokePos];
  }
  public void nextDrawingPaint() {
    if (paints == null) {
      initializePaints();
    }
```

```
      paintPos++;
      if (paintPos == paints.length) {
        paintPos = 0;
      }
      drawingPaint = paints[paintPos];
    }
    public void mouseExited(MouseEvent e) {
    }
    public void mouseDragged(MouseEvent e) {
      setEndPoint(e.getPoint());
      repaint();
    }
    public void mouseMoved(MouseEvent e) {
    }
    public Color getRandomColor() {
      short r = (short)(Math.random()*256);
      short g = (short)(Math.random()*256);
      short b = (short)(Math.random()*256);
      return new Color(r, g, b);
    }
    public void initializePaints() {
      paints = new Paint[3];
      paints[0] = getRandomColor();
      paints[1] = new GradientPaint(0, 0, getRandomColor(),
        getSize().width, getSize().height, getRandomColor());
      ImageIcon icon = new ImageIcon("apresslogo.gif");
      Image image = icon.getImage();
      int width = image.getWidth(this);
      int height = image.getHeight(this);
      BufferedImage txtr = new BufferedImage(
        width, height, BufferedImage.TYPE_INT_RGB);
      Graphics g = txtr.getGraphics();
      g.drawImage(image, 0, 0, this);
      Rectangle rect = new Rectangle(0, 0, width, height);
      paints[2] = new TexturePaint(txtr, rect);
      drawingPaint = paints[paintPos];
    }
  }
}
```

ARE YOU EXPERIENCED?

Congratulations! Combining the multithreading you learned in Skill 4 with the drawing and double-buffering capabilities you learned here, you now know the key features of Java needed to do smooth, steady animation.

Now you can

- Draw within Java

- Work with mouse events

- Draw to a buffer

- Display images

- Work with Java colors

- Define line strokes

- Define fill patterns

- Draw with the Java 2D API

You'll revisit multithreading soon to further demonstrate why it's so important to know and appreciate. But next you'll take a look at the Swing JTree component. You'll use it to display the current directory structure graphically and to demonstrate reading from a file.

Accessing Files

- Learning about files

- Creating temporary memory files with `StringWriter`

- Reading a file with `FileReader`

- Listing a directory structure textually

- Displaying disk structure graphically within a `JTree`

Getting File Information

Now that you have a feel for drawing in Java, this skill will teach you how to access the local file system. Java provides access to the file system through classes in the java.io package. The makeup of this package enables you to read and write bytes, characters, and objects and share results with other Java runtime systems without regard for platform-specific data formats. In this skill, you'll sample the pieces of the package to get file information, read files, and display the directory structure—textually and graphically—through JTree.

Access to the local file system in Java is restricted. Standalone Java applications can access it, but untrusted Java applets cannot. Because of this restriction, the program you'll create in this skill is an application.

NOTE *Signing and trusting applets are not covered in this book. Essentially, you digitally sign your applet and distribute the applet with your public encryption key. If the person who receives the applet trusts you, they can register the key and give you extra permissions, such as access to the local file system. For additional information about signing applets and the Java 2 platform's security architecture, you can read* Code Signing for Java Applets *(*http://www.javacommerce.com/tutorial/signing/*),* Securing Java—Beyond the Sandbox: Signed Code in JDK 1.2 *(*http://www.securingjava.com/chapter-three/*),* and *Sun's* Java Tutorial—Trail: Security in Java 2 SDK 1.2 *(*http://java.sun.com/docs/books/tutorial/security1.2/*). However, you should know that signing and trusting applets are different for Internet Explorer, Netscape browsers, and the Java 2 Plug-in.*

As always, to get started, close any open projects and create a project for Skill 8. Use the Application Wizard to create a new project named **Skill8** in the **C:\skills\Skill8** directory. Once you're in the actual Application Wizard dialog boxes, click Next and name the frame class **DirReader**, and then click Finish to create the framework to work in. This will create an HTML file named after the project, Skill8.html, along with two source files, DirReader.java and Application1.java.

The first class you need to know about when accessing the file system is the aptly named File class. File enables you to find out information about the specific file-system resource—answers to questions such as "Does it exist?", "Is it a directory?", and "What size is it?" Table 8-1 lists the information querying methods of File. There are other File methods not listed in Table 8-1 that are more action-oriented.

Table 8-1. Information Methods of File

Methods	Description
canRead()	Is the file readable?
canWrite()	Is the file writable?
exists()	Does the file exist?
getAbsoluteFile()	What is the absolute path to the file (as a File)?
getAbsolutePath()	What is the absolute path to the file (as a String)?
getCanonicalFile()	What is the absolute path to the file, without any relative pieces in the name (as a File)?
getCanonicalPath()	What is the absolute path to the file, without any relative pieces in the name (as a String)?
getName()	What is the filename?
getParent()	What is the parent directory (as a String)?
getParentFile()	What is the parent directory (as a File)?
getPath()	What is the directory path to the file?
isAbsolute()	Is the name absolute?
isDirectory()	Is the file a directory?
isFile()	Is the file normal?
isHidden()	Is the file hidden?
lastModified()	When was the file last changed?
length()	How big is the file?

NOTE   *One thing you may notice about all these methods is that none of them look at the contents of the file. This means that the File class does not open the file—it only looks at the directory information. Also, starting with version 1.2, methods were added to the File class to return File objects instead of String objects. This made things easier as you frequently just created File objects from the String returned.*

Next, you'll create a program that displays all the information for any filename entered. You'll use the methods that return strings instead of `File` objects, as you are only displaying the information for now, not traversing the directory tree.

Using a StringWriter

To demonstrate the different methods of `File`, you're going to create a program that gets a filename from a `JTextField` and calls all the appropriate `File` methods to learn about the specific file. The information will be displayed in a `JTextArea`.

 NOTE *A* `JTextArea` *is similar to a* `JTextField` *except that a* `JTextArea` *provides multiple lines for display, whereas a* `JTextField` *only offers one.*

As you'll find with most interactive programs, the first thing you want to do is create the user interface. Here, you need a `JTextField` and `JTextArea`, so create them where the Application Wizard created the other instance variables of the `DirReader` program. To name them after their purpose, you'll call the `JTextField` "input," and you'll call the `JTextArea` "output." The variable section of the program now looks like the following:

```
JPanel contentPane;
BorderLayout borderLayout1 = new BorderLayout();
JTextField input = new JTextField();
JTextArea output = new JTextArea();
```

In order to complete the interface, you need to modify the `jbInit()` method. Select the `jbInit()` method in the Structure pane to move the cursor in the Content pane to the appropriate location. Here, you need to add `input` and `output` to the screen.

To add the components, call the `add()` method for the content pane. The `JTextField` `input` looks best in the north area of the `BorderLayout`, while the `JTextArea` `output` looks best in the center. You want the `JTextField` to be only as tall as necessary and as wide as possible. This is what the north area of the `BorderLayout` pane does. On the other hand, you want the `JTextArea` for results output to be as big as possible. That is exactly what the center area does.

For Swing components that require scrolling when their contents get too large—`JTextArea`, for example—you need to place them in a `JScrollPane`.

If you don't, they won't get a scrollbar, and they will always be positioned at the top of their contents. Making the JTextArea scrollable is as simple as passing the component to scroll to the JScrollPane constructor [JScrollPane pane = new JScrollPane(output)] and then adding the JScrollPane to the screen instead of the component. Also, because the JTextArea is strictly for output, you should make it read-only by calling setEditable(false).

After deleting the commented-out line, the jbInit() method now looks like the following:

```
private void jbInit() throws Exception  {
  contentPane = (JPanel) this.getContentPane();
  contentPane.setLayout(borderLayout1);
  this.setSize(new Dimension(400, 300));
  this.setTitle("Frame Title");
  output.setEditable(false);
  JScrollPane pane = new JScrollPane(output);
  contentPane.add(input, BorderLayout.NORTH);
  contentPane.add(pane, BorderLayout.CENTER);
}
```

That's it for the interface for now. It isn't too snazzy, but it serves its purpose. When you get to the "Reading Files" section, you'll add some buttons along the bottom of the screen to differentiate the functionality. For now, there is only one thing to do: Get the file information.

Getting the File Information

As you'll remember from the Hi-Lo game in Skill 5, in order to get action events from the JTextField, you need to listen for an ActionEvent. In order to listen, you need something to implement the ActionListener interface. So, you'll have the DirReader class implement ActionListener and associate it with the text field. With the help of the Implement Interface Wizard, select java.awt.event.ActionListener and then click OK to add an actionPerformed() method to the source, along with an implements ActionListener clause to the class.

Now you need to call all the informational File methods for the filename entered. By itself, this is easy, but what's the best way to get the results and display them to the JTextArea? Java provides what can be thought of as an in-memory, temporary file class called StringWriter. The class enables you to store any information in memory until you need it. When you need it, you ask for the contents back through the toString() method.

TIP *If you truly want to save the information in a temporary disk file, you can ask for an unused name with the* createTempFile() *method of* File. *This will return a filename for the platform-specific temporary file directory. You then call the* deleteOnExit() *method of the returned object to have the file deleted on program termination [*File file = File.createTempFile("prefix", "suffix"); file.deleteOnExit();*]. In Windows, the file would be created in something like* C:\Windows\temp *or* C:\WinNT\temp, *whereas UNIX would most likely save it to* /tmp. *With the Macintosh platform, you'll probably find the files created in the* Temporary Items *folder.*

That sounds great, but how do you write to the StringWriter? Well, I'm actually going to sidestep that question and show you an easier way. Instead of writing to StringWriter directly, you're going to wrap around it a PrintWriter object:

```
StringWriter sw = new StringWriter();
PrintWriter pw = new PrintWriter(sw);
```

You can use the methods of PrintWriter and what you write to the PrintWriter pw will be saved in the StringWriter sw, because that's what was passed into the PrintWriter constructor. I'll say that again: When you write to the PrintWriter, it's written to the StringWriter. PrintWriter has two methods of interest: print() and println(). These methods print any single argument and send it to the PrintWriter's destination—in this case, the StringWriter. The println() version of the method adds a platform-specific line termination, some combination of carriage return and new line, though you don't need to know the details of which.

```
pw.println("something of interest");
```

Once you are done sending the output through the PrintWriter, you ask the StringWriter for its contents [sw.toString()] and display the results in the JTextArea with its setText() method.

```
output.setText(sw.toString());
```

The code in Listing 8-1 does what I just described, getting the file information for the filename entered in the text field. The code for outputting the file information is in a helper method called infoFile(). Also, be sure to add the import statement of the java.io package to the top of the source with the other import statements.

Listing 8-1. The Initial actionPerformed() Method for DirReader

```java
import java.io.*;
 . . .
public void actionPerformed(ActionEvent e) {
  StringWriter sw = new StringWriter();
  PrintWriter pw = new PrintWriter(sw);
  File f = new File(input.getText());
  infoFile(pw, f);
  output.setText(sw.toString());
}
private void infoFile(PrintWriter out, File f) {
  out.println("canRead() " + f.canRead());
  out.println("canWrite() " + f.canWrite());
  out.println("exists() " + f.exists());
  out.println("getAbsolutePath() " + f.getAbsolutePath());
  try {
    out.println("getCanonicalPath() " + f.getCanonicalPath());
  } catch (IOException ex) {
    out.println("getCanonicalPath() unknown");
  }
  out.println("getName() " + f.getName());
  out.println("getParent() " + f.getParent());
  out.println("getPath() " + f.getPath());
  out.println("isAbsolute() " + f.isAbsolute());
  out.println("isDirectory() " + f.isDirectory());
  out.println("isFile() " + f.isFile());
  out.println("isHidden() " + f.isHidden()),
  out.println("lastModified() " + new java.util.Date(f.lastModified()));
  out.println("length() " + f.length());
}
```

NOTE *There is one point worth mentioning: The* File.lastModified() *method returns the modification date as a* long, *which is twice as big as an* int. *To display the modification date in some meaningful manner, you need to convert it to a* Date *object:* new java.util.Date(f.lastModified()).

Now that you've programmed the functionality, you need to listen for the user pressing the Enter key in the `JTextField`. To do this, you need to associate the `ActionListener` with `input` in the `jbInit()` method—anywhere will do, but try putting the statement last: `input.addActionListener(this);`. You can now save everything and run the program. Figure 8.1 shows you a sample of the output for the skill's project file.

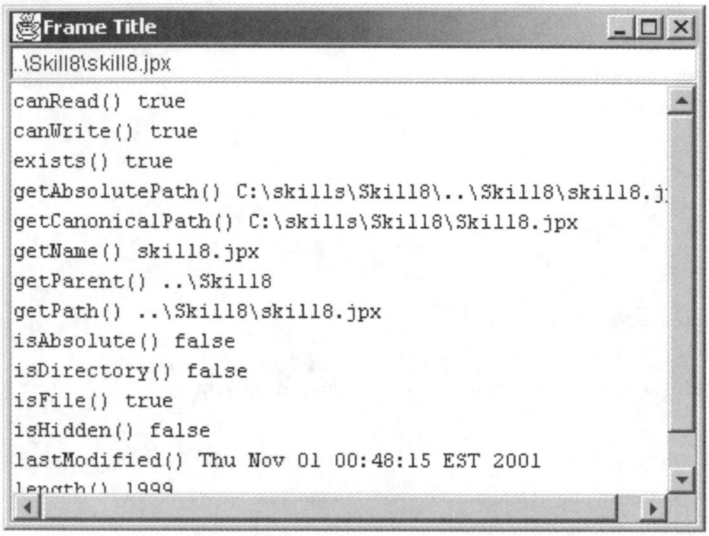

```
Frame Title                                    _ □ ×
..\Skill8\skill8.jpx
canRead() true
canWrite() true
exists() true
getAbsolutePath() C:\skills\Skill8\..\Skill8\skill8.j
getCanonicalPath() C:\skills\Skill8\Skill8.jpx
getName() skill8.jpx
getParent() ..\Skill8
getPath() ..\Skill8\skill8.jpx
isAbsolute() false
isDirectory() false
isFile() true
isHidden() false
lastModified() Thu Nov 01 00:48:15 EST 2001
length() 1999
```

Figure 8-1. Enter different names in the JTextField to see different results. This screen shows the results for ..\Skill8\skill8.jpx.

Reading Files

Once you are able to access the file information, you can find out if the file is worth reading. The class responsible for reading files is `FileReader`. Given a `File` or a filename (a `String`), you can read the file one character at a time until you get to the end. However, just as with `StringWriter`, there is an easier way. If you want to read a line at a time, you need the help of a `BufferedReader`. Given a source (the `FileReader` in this case), you can use a `BufferedReader` to read in the contents and display them in the `JTextArea`.

NOTE *This concept of building on an I/O class with some-thing that offers more capabilities is called* daisy chaining. *It is very common in the Java libraries. The basic input and output classes are very simple. If you do not need extra capa-bilities, there is no overhead involved; if you need the extra capabilities, you chain the basic class within a richer one to get more functionality. This chaining is not limited to just two classes: You can keep chaining more and more capabili-ties on top of one another. If you are into design patterns, this kind of daisy chaining is called the* Decorator *pattern.*

There are a few changes you need to make to your existing program now.

1. You need to add two buttons to the screen: Info and Read. These buttons enable the user to select what functionality he or she wants to perform.

2. You need to associate the listener with each button and remove the cur-rent listener from the JTextField, because you don't know which action should be done anymore.

3. Because there is one listener for two buttons, you need to check which button is selected in the action handler. If the Info button is selected, you keep the current capabilities.

4. If the user selects the Read option, you need to add in the necessary code to read in the file if it is a regular file.

First, perform step 1 and step 2. You'll add the buttons to the south area of the frame's content pane. In order to add multiple components into one area, you need to group them together. The JPanel class provides the most common way to do this. Basically, create a JPanel, create each button, stuff each button into the panel, and add the panel to the frame. Be sure to associate an ActionListener with each button along the way. Listing 8-2 contains the updated jbInit() method.

Listing 8-2. The Updated jbInit() Method for DirReader

```
private void jbInit() throws Exception  {
  contentPane = (JPanel) this.getContentPane();
  contentPane.setLayout(borderLayout1);
  this.setSize(new Dimension(400, 300));
  this.setTitle("Frame Title");
  output.setEditable(false);
  JScrollPane pane = new JScrollPane(output);
  contentPane.add(input, BorderLayout.NORTH);
  contentPane.add(pane, BorderLayout.CENTER);
  JPanel panel = new JPanel();
  JButton info = new JButton("Info");
  info.addActionListener(this);
  panel.add(info);
  JButton read = new JButton("Read");
  read.addActionListener(this);
  panel.add(read);
  contentPane.add(panel, BorderLayout.SOUTH);
}
```

For step 3 and step 4, you need to update your existing actionPerformed()
method. To determine which button was selected, the ActionEvent parameter
has a getActionCommand() method. When the event source is a button, the action
command tells you the label of the button selected. For the Info button, you need
to check if the action command is the "Info" string. If it is, you just do what you
did before—call infoFile().

For the Read button behavior, You'll write the code to read the contents of
the file first in a helper method called readFile(). In the method, you check if the
filename provided is a normal file and, if it is, you read its contents. The isFile()
method of File reports on the file status. When the file status is normal, you pass
in the File object to the FileReader and then the FileReader into the
BufferedReader, daisy chaining the three objects together. Now, when you read
with the BufferedReader's readLine() method, you are getting your contents from
the File. When the BufferedReader gets to the end of the file, readLine() returns
null. This signifies there is nothing left to read. The file-reading code follows in
Listing 8-3.

Listing 8-3. The New readFile() Method for DirReader

```
private void readFile(PrintWriter out, File f) {
  if (f.isFile()) {
    try {
      FileReader fr = new FileReader(f);
      BufferedReader br = new BufferedReader(fr);
      String line;
      while ((line = br.readLine()) != null) {
        out.println(line);
      }
    } catch (IOException e) {
      out.println("Problem reading file");
    }
  } else {
    out.println("not a normal file");
  }
}
```

Now you have the readFile() method defined. Listing 8-4 contains the updated actionPerformed() method.

Listing 8-4. The Updated actionPerformed() Method for DirReader

```
public void actionPerformed(ActionEvent e) {
  StringWriter sw = new StringWriter();
  PrintWriter pw = new PrintWriter(sw);
  if (e.getSource() instanceof JButton) {
    File f = new File(input.getText());
    String command = e.getActionCommand();
    if (command.equals("Info")) {
      infoFile(pw, f);
    } else {
      readFile(pw, f);
    }
  }
  output.setText(sw.toString());
}
```

The second phase of your program is done. It can now read the file information and read files. If you save everything and run the program, you'll see the results shown in Figure 8-2 if you read the program's source.

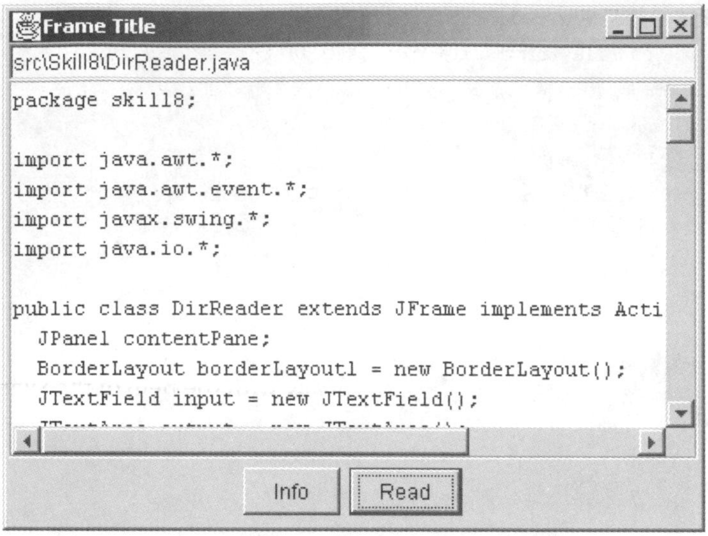

Figure 8-2. This screen shows the results of reading the program's source.

Listing a Directory

The third button you'll add to the program will enable you to get a directory listing. The File class has a list() method. This returns an array of strings with one entry for each file in the current File, if it is a directory. Adding this button to the screen in jbInit():

```
JButton dir = new JButton("Dir");
dir.addActionListener(this);
panel.add(dir);
```

and adding code to the actionPerformed() method enables you to display the directory. Add the following code immediately after the call to infoFile(), before the else and call to readFile():

```
} else if (command.equals("Dir")) {
  pw.println(f.getAbsolutePath());
  if (f.isDirectory()) {
    String files[] = f.list();
    for (int i=0, n=files.length; i < n; i++) {
      pw.println(i + ": " + files[i]);
    }
  }
```

> **NOTE** *Of course, you could break out the directory listing code into its own method. That's shown in the final code listing (Listing 8-7) in this chapter.*

Showing a Directory Graphically

For this skill's final task, you're going to combine everything you've learned so far and display the directory structure graphically with the help of the Swing JTree component, as shown in Figure 8-3. In the graphical representation, if the user selects an entry, the file information, contents, or directory will be displayed in the JTextArea based upon the entry type selected.

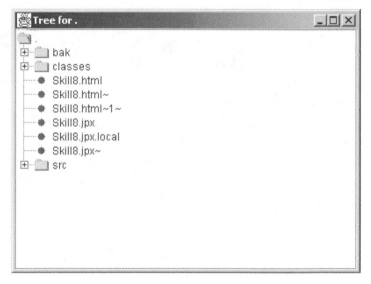

Figure 8-3. The initial Tree screen for the current directory

Defining the Tree Node

The key to using the JTree component is to know all the pieces. The first thing you need is something to place in the tree. You do this with a class that implements the TreeNode interface. Instead of implementing the interface completely by yourself, though, Swing provides a default implementation that is nearly sufficient for your needs: the DefaultMutableTreeNode. The class enables you to store any object within it, a File object in this case, but it relies on the object's toString() implementation as the text to show within the tree representing the node. In the case of the File object, toString() will display the full path of the object. Normally, in a tree you only want to display the name, not the full path, so you need to subclass DefaultMutableTreeNode and override its toString().

To define a new class, select File ➤ New Class. You'll leave your new class in the skill8 package, but change the class name to **FileTreeNode** and have it extend from **DefaultMutableTreeNode** (found in the javax.swing.tree package—either select the package by clicking the . . . button or type the package name with the class name). Also, the only options you need checked are Public and Generate Default Constructor, so uncheck the others. This leaves you with the screen shown in Figure 8-4. Click the OK button to move on.

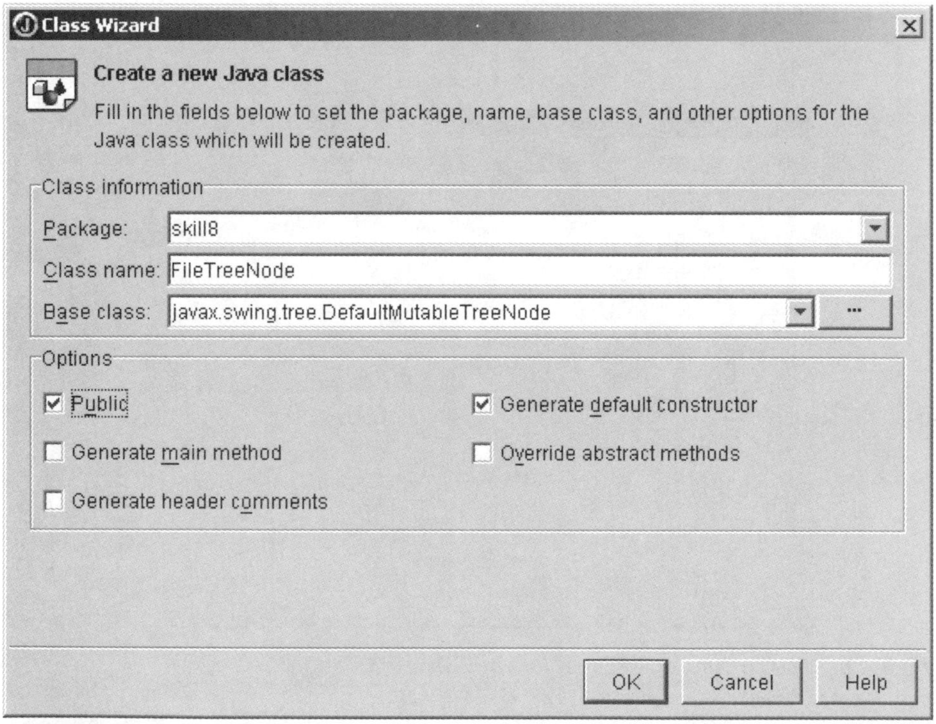

Figure 8-4. The new Class Wizard screen

Now, in your class definition, you need to change the default constructor generated to accept a File object and pass that file object into the DefaultMutableTreeNode constructor. Passing an object to your superclass' constructor is done with a call to the super() method, as in super(object).

You also have to override the toString() method to return that object's name. You don't have to keep a reference to the object passed into the constructor because the DefaultMutableTreeNode also does, in a protected variable named userObject. So, all you have to do is cast the object to a File and call getName() in the toString() method.

With those two tasks done, you have your completed FileTreeNode class definition, as shown in Listing 8-5.

Listing 8-5. The FileTreeNode Class Definition

```
package skill8;

import javax.swing.tree.DefaultMutableTreeNode;
import java.io.File;

public class FileTreeNode extends DefaultMutableTreeNode {

  public FileTreeNode(File file) {
    super(file);
  }
  public String toString() {
    return ((File)userObject).getName();
  }
}
```

Building the Tree

Once you have the node defined, you can build the tree. Using a simple recursive algorithm, you create a node for the File passed in, and then if the file is a directory, you create a child node for each of its entries. This repeats forever until there are no more directories. The only thing that should appear new to you in the following code is the add() method FileTreeNode inherited from DefaultMutableTreeNode. This is how you associate a child to a node in a tree. Just add the following method to the DirReader class:

```
private FileTreeNode buildTree(File file) {
  FileTreeNode root = new FileTrecNode(file);
  if (file.isDirectory()) {
    File files[] = file.listFiles();
    for (int i=0, n=files.length; i < n; i++) {
      FileTreeNode child = buildTree(files[i]);
      root.add(child);
    }
  }
  return root;
}
```

NOTE Recursion *is the process of breaking down complex tasks down into simpler ones through a common algorithm. For instance, 6! (six factorial) is 1*2*3*4*5*6. You can program this in one of two ways. In the first way, you loop from 1 to 6 and multiply the numbers together. This is the nonrecursive, or* iterative, *way. In the second way, you use recursion. 6! is 6*5!, but what is 5!? 5! is 5*4!. And 4! is 4*3!. Next, 3! is 3*2!. Then, 2! is 2*1!. Finally, 1! is 1. This then backtracks to give you 6! is 720. Some algorithms are easy to implement recursively, while others may be* representable *recursively but are best left to the nonrecursive realm.*

Displaying the Tree

Now that you can build the tree, or at least the root node for the tree, you need to add another button to your screen. This one you'll naturally call "Tree." When the user selects it, it will create and display the tree. In jbInit() you add three lines that should be somewhat familiar to you by now:

```
JButton tree = new JButton("Tree");
tree.addActionListener(this);
panel.add(tree);
```

You'll put the tree showing code in a new method showTree(). Creating the tree is then a simple call of passing the root node to the JTree constructor:

```
private void showTree(File f) {
  FileTreeNode root = buildTree(f);
  JTree tree = new JTree(root);
```

As with the JTextArea component, you need to place the JTree component in a JScrollPane to support scrolling. Then, you can place the tree in its own window to display the tree. As with the DirReader, you'll use a JFrame for this, adding the JScrollPane to the center of its content pane. You then tell the frame to close when the user goes to close the window. By default, the frame would be just hidden, not disposed of, leaving resources used but unavailable. Finally, you size the window and show it.

```
JScrollPane pane = new JScrollPane(tree);
JFrame frame = new JFrame("Tree for " + f.getName());
Container contentPane = frame.getContentPane();
contentPane.add(pane, BorderLayout.CENTER);
frame.setDefaultCloseOperation(JFrame.DISPOSE_ON_CLOSE);
frame.setSize(400, 300);
frame.show();
}
```

Finally, you have to put the code in `actionPerformed()` to deal with the new Tree button. Add the following code immediately after the code previously added to handle the Dir button, right before the `else` and call to `readFile()`:

```
} else if (command.equals("Tree")) {
  showTree(f);
```

Putting all these pieces together, you can then run the program and enter a directory, such as "." to signify the current directory, in the text field and select Tree. This will bring up a screen like the one shown in Figure 8-3. After selecting several of the plus signs (+) to open up the subdirectories, you'll see the screen shown in Figure 8-5. You did not need to add any code to handle the opening and closing operations with the plus sign (+) or minus sign (-) graphics.

WARNING *While the program will work fine if you enter a directory such as* C:\, *consider using a smaller directory instead. If you enter a directory such as* C:\, *the recursive algorithm will have to create a tree for everything on your hard drive. It will just take some time to read through all the directories on some of the larger hard drives out there.*

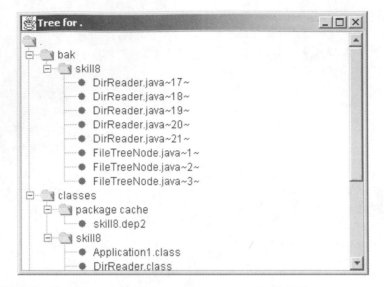

Figure 8-5. The directory tree after opening up several subfolders

MVC: Model-View-Controller

This is your first introduction to MVC, the Model-View-Controller architecture, which is used often within the Swing component set. The MVC design originated with Smalltalk to help create more reusable interfaces. It is composed of three pieces.

- The *Model* defines the state of the system. In the case of the example, the model is the root tree node, which consists of a collection of nodes with children. At a particular instance of time, there is only one model for the system.

- The *View* is how the user sees the model. In the example program, it is in the JTree. However, if you want to display the model differently, the model does not change, only your view of it does. Imagine a flattened-out version of the tree nodes within a scrollable list or some other component.

- The *Controller* is how the user interacts with the model. With Swing components, the controller and view are combined into a something called a *delegate*. For the example tree, that delegate is the JTree. Because of the close ties between the display and interaction with that display, the two pieces are combined.

In order to use the Swing components in an optimized fashion, it is best to get a good grasp of their MVC design and architecture. For additional information about this architecture, see my book, *Definitive Guide to Swing for Java 2, Second Edition* (Apress, 2000).

Handling Selection in the Tree

Returning to the tasks described at the beginning of the chapter, this leaves you with the final task of handling selection of an entry in the JTree to show the contents of the selected node. In order to handle selection of a node in the tree, you need to attach a TreeSelectionListener to the tree. It isn't necessary to attach the same listener to each node in the tree. Using the Implement Interface Wizard, you can have the DirReader class implement the listener, which you can find in the javax.swing.event package. This will add a dummy valueChanged() method.

To find out the node that was selected, you need to ask the tree what the last selected component was. You do this with the getLastSelectedPathComponent() method of JTree. However, you don't yet have a reference to your tree in valueChanged(). Thankfully, to find the tree, you can just ask for the source of the event passed into the method with getSource(). Every event has a source, and in the case of a TreeSelectionEvent, that source is the JTree.

Once you have the node from the tree, you can ask that node for the File object associated with it. This is retrieved from the getUserObject() method that FileTreeNode inherited from DefaultMutableTreeNode. Using that file, you can then read it, list it, or get its information based upon its type. This leaves you with Listing 8-6 for the implementation of valueChanged().

Listing 8-6. The valueChanged() Method Implementation for TreeSelectionListener

```java
public void valueChanged(TreeSelectionEvent e) {
  StringWriter sw = new StringWriter();
  PrintWriter pw = new PrintWriter(sw);
  JTree tree = (JTree)e.getSource();
  FileTreeNode node = (FileTreeNode)tree.getLastSelectedPathComponent();
  if (node != null) {
    File file = (File)node.getUserObject();
    if (file.isFile()) {
      readFile(pw, file);
    } else if (file.isDirectory()) {
      listDir(pw, file);
    } else {
      infoFile(pw, file);
    }
    output.setText(sw.toString());
  }
}
```

You need to attach the listener to the tree and do one other thing. By default, trees can have multiple nodes selected. You want to only support single selection, so you have to change the tree selection model in jbInit(). The three available models are CONTIGUOUS_TREE_SELECTION, DISCONTIGUOUS_TREE_SELECTION, and SINGLE_TREE_SELECTION. You want the last.

```java
import javax.swing.tree.*;
 . . .
tree.getSelectionModel().setSelectionMode
  (TreeSelectionModel.SINGLE_TREE_SELECTION);
tree.addTreeSelectionListener(this);
```

Now, save and run the program. After you display a directory tree, select a node and you'll notice that the appropriate file data appears in the JTextArea. Listing 8-7 contains the entire listing of the application you created in this skill.

Listing 8-7. The Complete DirReader.java Application Source

```java
package skill8;

import java.awt.*;
import java.awt.event.*;
import javax.swing.*;
import java.io.*;
import javax.swing.tree.*;
import javax.swing.event.TreeSelectionEvent;
import javax.swing.event.TreeSelectionListener;

public class DirReader extends JFrame implements ActionListener,
    TreeSelectionListener {
  JPanel contentPane;
  BorderLayout borderLayout1 = new BorderLayout();
  JTextField input = new JTextField();
  JTextArea output = new JTextArea();

  //Construct the frame
  public DirReader() {
    enableEvents(AWTEvent.WINDOW_EVENT_MASK);
    try {
      jbInit();
    }
    catch(Exception e) {
      e.printStackTrace();
    }
  }
```

```
//Component initialization
private void jbInit() throws Exception  {
  contentPane = (JPanel) this.getContentPane();
  contentPane.setLayout(borderLayout1);
  this.setSize(new Dimension(400, 300));
  this.setTitle("Frame Title");
  output.setEditable(false);
  JScrollPane pane = new JScrollPane(output);
  contentPane.add(input, BorderLayout.NORTH);
  contentPane.add(pane, BorderLayout.CENTER);
  JPanel panel = new JPanel();
  JButton info = new JButton("Info");
  info.addActionListener(this);
  panel.add(info);
  JButton read = new JButton("Read");
  read.addActionListener(this);
  panel.add(read);
  JButton dir = new JButton("Dir");
  dir.addActionListener(this);
  panel.add(dir);
  JButton tree = new JButton("Tree");
  tree.addActionListener(this);
  panel.add(tree);
  contentPane.add(panel, BorderLayout.SOUTH);
}
//Overridden so we can exit when window is closed
protected void processWindowEvent(WindowEvent e) {
  super.processWindowEvent(e);
  if (e.getID() == WindowEvent.WINDOW_CLOSING) {
    System.exit(0);
  }
}
public void actionPerformed(ActionEvent e) {
  StringWriter sw = new StringWriter();
  PrintWriter pw = new PrintWriter(sw);
  if (e.getSource() instanceof JButton) {
    File f = new File(input.getText());
    String command = e.getActionCommand();
    if (command.equals("Info")) {
      infoFile(pw, f);
    } else if (command.equals("Dir")) {
      listDir(pw, f);
```

```
          } else if (command.equals("Tree")) {
            showTree(f);
          } else {
            readFile(pw, f);
          }
        }
        output.setText(sw.toString());
      }
      private void listDir(PrintWriter out, File f) {
        out.println(f.getAbsolutePath());
        if (f.isDirectory()) {
          String files[] = f.list();
          for (int i=0, n=files.length; i < n; i++) {
            out.println(i + ": " + files[i]);
          }
        }
      }
      private void infoFile(PrintWriter out, File f) {
        out.println("canRead() " + f.canRead());
        out.println("canWrite() " + f.canWrite());
        out.println("exists() " + f.exists());
        out.println("getAbsolutePath() " + f.getAbsolutePath());
        try {
          out.println("getCanonicalPath() " + f.getCanonicalPath());
        } catch (IOException ex) {
          out.println("getCanonicalPath() unknown");
        }
        out.println("getName() " + f.getName());
        out.println("getParent() " + f.getParent());
        out.println("getPath() " + f.getPath());
        out.println("isAbsolute() " + f.isAbsolute());
        out.println("isDirectory() " + f.isDirectory());
        out.println("isFile() " + f.isFile());
        out.println("isHidden() " + f.isHidden());
        out.println("lastModified() " + new java.util.Date(f.lastModified()));
        out.println("length() " + f.length());
      }
      public void readFile(PrintWriter out, File f) {
        if (f.isFile()) {
          try {
            FileReader fr = new FileReader(f);
            BufferedReader br = new BufferedReader(fr);
            String line;
```

```
          while ((line = br.readLine()) != null) {
            out.println(line);
          }
        } catch (IOException e) {
          out.println("Problem reading file");
        }
      } else {
        out.println("not a normal file");
      }
    }
    private FileTreeNode buildTree(File file) {
      FileTreeNode root = new FileTreeNode(file);
      if (file.isDirectory()) {
        File files[] = file.listFiles();
        for (int i=0, n=files.length; i < n; i++) {
          FileTreeNode child = buildTree(files[i]);
          root.add(child);
        }
      }
      return root;
    }
    private void showTree(File f) {
      FileTreeNode root = buildTree(f);
      JTree tree = new JTree(root);
      tree.getSelectionModel().setSelectionMode
        (TreeSelectionModel.SINGLE_TREE_SELECTION);
      tree.addTreeSelectionListener(this);
      JScrollPane pane = new JScrollPane(tree);
      JFrame frame = new JFrame("Tree for " + f.getName());
      Container contentPane = frame.getContentPane();
      contentPane.add(pane, BorderLayout.CENTER);
      frame.setDefaultCloseOperation(JFrame.DISPOSE_ON_CLOSE);
      frame.setSize(400, 300);
      frame.show();
    }
    public void valueChanged(TreeSelectionEvent e) {
      StringWriter sw = new StringWriter();
      PrintWriter pw = new PrintWriter(sw);
      JTree tree = (JTree)e.getSource();
      FileTreeNode node = (FileTreeNode)tree.getLastSelectedPathComponent();
      if (node != null) {
        File file = (File)node.getUserObject();
        if (file.isFile()) {
```

```
        readFile(pw, file);
      } else if (file.isDirectory()) {
        listDir(pw, file);
      } else {
        infoFile(pw, file);
      }
      output.setText(sw.toString());
    }
  }
}
```

ARE YOU EXPERIENCED?

Wow—you made it! You've now been introduced to the daisy chaining parts of the java.io package to exchange data within your Java program. You also looked at MVC and Swing's JTree component.

Now you can

- Display file information

- Use StringWriter for temporary storage

- Use PrintWriter for easy writing of any data

- Use FileReader to read a file

- Use BufferedReader to buffer file accesses

- Use JTree to display a graphical hierarchy

- Use JScrollPane to deal with scrollable components

- Describe the MVC architecture

- Respond to selection events within the JTree

In Skill 9, you'll move into the JavaBeans pieces of JBuilder and you'll start to see how JBuilder isn't just an IDE—it's a true RAD tool.

Part Two

Digging into JavaBeans

Understanding JavaBeans

- Explaining bean basics

- Exploring the IDE's role

- Using drag and drop to build screens

- Changing bean properties with the Inspector

- Adding event listeners through the Inspector

What's a Bean?

According to Sun's JavaBeans FAQ (Frequently Asked Questions), "*JavaBeans components, or Beans, are reusable software components that can be manipulated visually in a builder tool.*" A formal definition is all well and good, but what does it mean and what good are beans? Well, the use of reusable components means that the software industry is finally maturing. In fields such as electrical engineering and manufacturing, products are built from various components. For instance, if you want to build a computer, you don't go off and design a disk controller, graphics controller, and keyboard. Instead, you buy the pieces from the component makers and put them together. Now, in software development, you can do the same thing with JavaBean components.

Instead of creating monolithic applications that take 2 years to develop and are out-of-date before they're even deployed, you can play connect-the-beans to create programs from component parts, the beans. With the Internet life cycle running in dog years, you no longer have the luxury of taking your sweet time to deliver a solution to customers. They want it yesterday, and they want it fully tested, or they'll go elsewhere. With JavaBean components, that reality is closer.

What's Inside a Bean?

So, what defines a bean, and what makes it work so well with other beans? A bean is defined by its structure. By following a certain set of design rules, a builder tool like JBuilder can discover all it needs to know about a bean for you to visually program it.

Beans need to know how to handle events. When something happens, the bean must be able to react as well as cause events to happen. A bean must be visually configurable, without which a builder tool wouldn't function very well. Beans must also be able to save and restore their state. This allows each to continue functioning over time, after restarting from a stopped application.

Properties, Methods, and Events

Inside a bean, the first thing to look at is its *properties*. Each property is a named attribute of a bean. A pair of specially named methods reads or sets a property's value. When using a builder tool, a property editor enables the application developer to modify the properties.

Next are *methods*. Methods are just what their name implies—they provide the means to manipulate a bean and access properties. A builder tool will have access to all the public methods of a bean or to a subset if you choose to restrict its access.

Finally, there are *events*. Events serve as the notification mechanism between beans. If a bean wants to know when an event happens, it registers itself with the source of the event. Then, when the event happens, the source notifies everyone registered as a listener.

Skill 11 discusses the specifics of working with beans and events, and Skill 12 discusses beans and properties.

Customization and Introspection

When a bean is created, you publish its capabilities. This exposes the names of all the supported properties and events. The publishing process is called *customization*. When a bean is reused within a builder tool, the tool needs to discover what has been published. This discovery process is called *introspection*.

Skill 13 and Skill 14 explain the introspection and customization processes, respectively.

Persistence

For beans to be useful, they need a way to store their state. If the same bean is reused in 20,000 applications without *persistence,* the bean will look the same in all 20,000 applications. However, with persistence, you can customize each bean to be different for each of the applications. Then, after the bean has been configured (outside the application), it can be saved separately and reused for each application instance.

Skill 15 discusses the details of persistence.

What Does JBuilder Have to Do with All This?

As stated earlier, "JavaBeans components are reusable software components that can be manipulated visually in a builder tool." As its name implies, JBuilder is such a builder tool. It helps you both create beans and manipulate them visually. Let's look at the part of JBuilder that we've avoided so far, the UI (User Interface) Designer (sometimes known as the Visual Designer). You will see that the UI Designer can automate the generation of a lot of the code that you have been writing in previous skills. Why didn't you just use this tool earlier, then? Well, with many code-generation tools, to fully appreciate what the tool is doing, you must have an understanding of what the tool is trying to achieve.

Using the UI Designer

At this point, close all your open projects and create a new application with the New Application Wizard. Create a project called **Skill9** in the directory **C:\skills\Skill9** and click Finish. Then, within the actual Application Wizard, click Next, rename the class from Frame1 to **ListBuilder**, and click Finish. Now, if you select the ListBuilder.java file in the Navigation pane and the Design tab at the bottom of the Content pane, the UI Designer will appear, as shown in Figure 9-1. To the right of the UI Designer is the Inspector, which I'll explain shortly. Using the UI Designer, you can drag any component from the palette and drop it into your system.

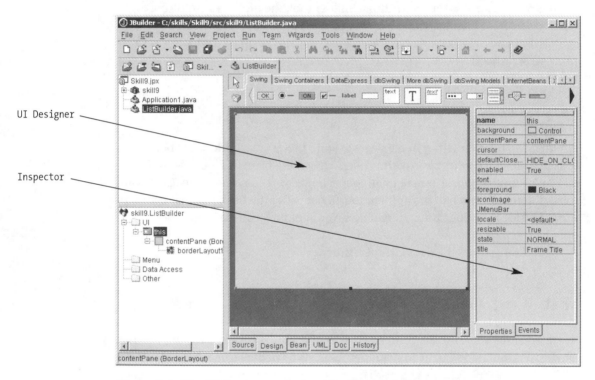

Figure 9-1. The UI Designer window for drag-and-drop screen creation

To the right of the UI Designer window is the Inspector. The Inspector displays the property and event settings of the currently selected bean. To toggle between the two, select the appropriate tab at the bottom of the Inspector screen, as shown in Figure 9-2. Essentially, these are all the methods from event listeners that the currently selected component can respond to. For instance, if you double-click the componentMoved line, you can add code that will be called when the user moves the frame.

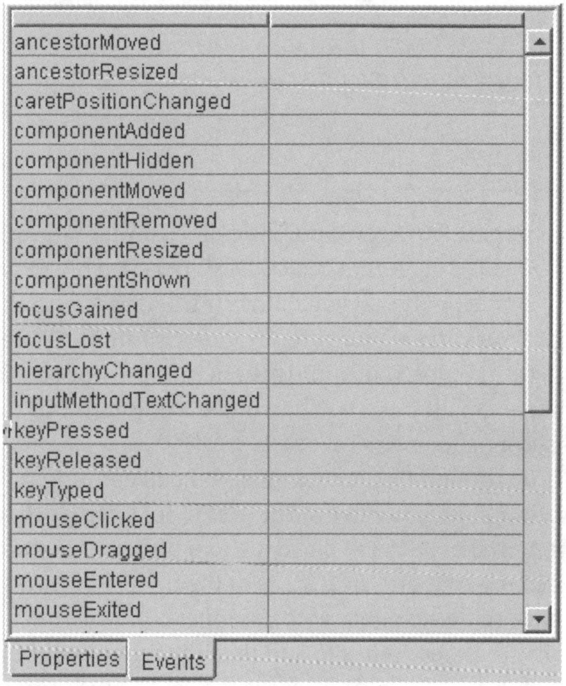

ancestorMoved
ancestorResized
caretPositionChanged
componentAdded
componentHidden
componentMoved
componentRemoved
componentResized
componentShown
focusGained
focusLost
hierarchyChanged
inputMethodTextChanged
keyPressed
keyReleased
keyTyped
mouseClicked
mouseDragged
mouseEntered
mouseExited
Properties
Events

Figure 9-2. The Events tab of the Inspector for a component

Dragging Components and Dropping Them into Your System

To get a feel for the UI Designer, let's create a program with a `JTextField` for input, two `JButton` components that say what to do with the input (add or remove), and a `JList` for maintaining an input history list. First, you'll create the screen. Then, you'll add the code to do the work. Figure 9-3 shows the Swing Component palette you'll be using.

JButton
JToggleButton
JLabel
JTextArea
JEditorPane
JComboBox
JSlider
JScrollBar
JTable
Glue
V-Strut
JRadioButton
JCheckBox
JTextField
JTextPane
JPasswordField
JList
JProgressBar
JTree
ButtonGroup
H-Strut

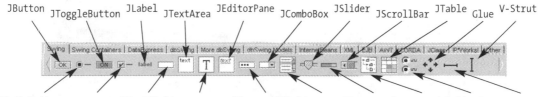

Figure 9-3. The Swing Component palette

NOTE *By selecting another tab in the Component palette, components from other libraries become available.*

To create the program's screen, you basically just pick something from the Component palette and drag it into the UI Designer. The big gray area represents the frame's inner content pane, so you'll drop it there. Because the content pane uses BorderLayout, you can lay out the components into the different areas of the layout manager by strategically dropping them into the appropriate area of the screen. Of course, if you miss, you can move things around to get them into the right position.

If you put a little thought into the layout, you can get it right with the initial component drop. It makes sense to put the JTextField across the top, as you want to limit its height. It makes sense to place the two buttons either in a shared panel on the bottom or in the east and west areas of the pane. For now you'll do the latter so you don't have to figure out how to combine components into their own area. Then, it makes the most sense to add the JList to the middle of the screen, consuming the remaining space. This leaves the south area empty. After dragging the components to the window, your screen should look something like the one in Figure 9-4. If you missed positioning a component properly, just literally drag it to the proper area of the screen. (Select the component with your mouse and move the component while keeping the left mouse button depressed.)

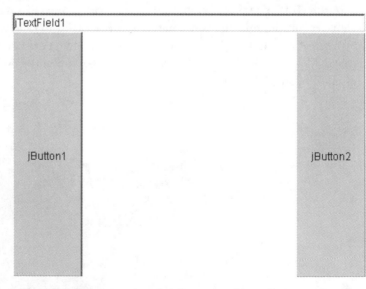

Figure 9-4. The initial input screen for the example program

TIP   *If you aren't sure of the components in the palette yet, you can rest your mouse over the component and its name will appear in a tool tip.*

With the initial layout complete, you can continue with the screen setup. By default, JBuilder relies on a counter to name each component added to the screen. For buttons, then, that name is used as the label. For text fields, that name is the initial content. You need to change the button labels and clear out the text field content. To change a button's label, select the component, find the text attribute of the Properties tab in the Inspector, and type in a new label. After you press Enter, the new label is shown in the UI Designer. In the screen, for the left button, change the label to **Add**, and for the right button, change the label to **Remove**. For the JTextField, select the text property again but delete the current contents. After making these changes, the screen setup is now complete and will look like the screen in Figure 9-5.

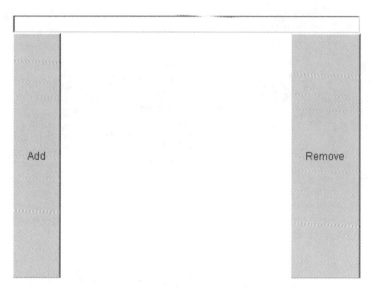

Figure 9-5. The final input screen for the example program

Bringing the Screen to Life

Now that the screen is in place, you need to make it work. If the Add button is selected, you want to get the text field content and add it to the JList. When Remove is selected, you get the content and try to remove it. In either case, if nothing is in the text field, nothing is done.

To define the Add button's action, first select Add in the UI Designers and then select the Events tab in the Inspector. Selecting this tab shows all possible events that could happen to a button, as shown in Figure 9-6. Each entry is for a specific method call. When the event happens, the event's source notifies anyone interested, calling the method listed in the second column.

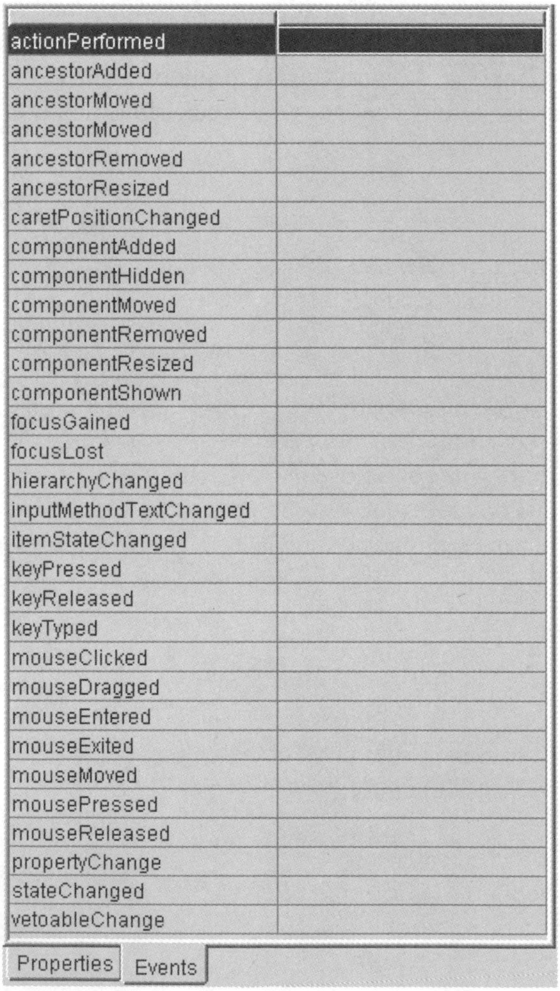

actionPerformed	
ancestorAdded	
ancestorMoved	
ancestorMoved	
ancestorRemoved	
ancestorResized	
caretPositionChanged	
componentAdded	
componentHidden	
componentMoved	
componentRemoved	
componentResized	
componentShown	
focusGained	
focusLost	
hierarchyChanged	
inputMethodTextChanged	
itemStateChanged	
keyPressed	
keyReleased	
keyTyped	
mouseClicked	
mouseDragged	
mouseEntered	
mouseExited	
mouseMoved	
mousePressed	
mouseReleased	
propertyChange	
stateChanged	
vetoableChange	

Properties | Events

Figure 9-6. The JButton event list

If you double-click in the right column of one of these events, JBuilder will associate an appropriate listener to the component. It is then your responsibility to fill in what happens when the event occurs. In the case of the button, the method that reacts to button selection is `actionPerformed()`, the first entry. After you double-click in the field next to `actionPerformed()`, you will be placed in the source code for the `ListBuilder` class. Then, you can fill in the appropriate source code. By default, the code added is just the framework of the method.

```
void jButton1_actionPerformed(ActionEvent e) {

}
```

Notice that this isn't the specific method of the event listener, `ActionListener`. Instead, the listener implementation calls this method. The code to map the calls was automatically generated by JBuilder and added to your class.

```
jButton1.addActionListener(new java.awt.event.ActionListener() {
  public void actionPerformed(ActionEvent e) {
    jButton1_actionPerformed(e);
  }
});
```

NOTE *The* `ActionListener` *implementation here is what is called an* anonymous *class. It has no name. You could have done something similar in earlier chapters, but instead I chose to implement the interface at the class level. Creating listeners in this manner enables you to not have to check which action triggered the listener calling (as you did in Skill 8) and have a separate listener for each button/component.*

You need to add code to the `jButton1_actionPerformed()` method to perform its Add action. So, you have to get the `JTextField` contents and display it in the `JList` if the text field isn't empty. You've already seen the `getText()` method of `JTextField`. Just check the `length()` of the string returned to see if it is empty. To add an element to the list, you have to look at the component's MVC architecture. The model for the `JList` is a `ListModel`, which is retrievable from `getModel()`. Assuming your actual model is a `DefaultListModel` (the only concrete implementation of the `ListModel` interface in the Swing classes), you can add your element with the `addElement()` method.

```
void jButton1_actionPerformed(ActionEvent e) {
  String s = jTextField1.getText();
  if (s.length() > 0) {
    DefaultListModel model = (DefaultListModel)jList1.getModel();
    model.addElement(s);
  }
}
```

There's one additional change you have to make to the code. In order for a JList to support dynamic changes to its content, you have to initialize its data model. By default, the data model is empty and immutable (not changeable), so you have to create your own model that *can* be changed. Somewhere in the jbInit() method you have to create a data model for the component and associate the model to the JList.

```
private void jbInit() throws Exception  {
  . . .
  ListModel model = new DefaultListModel();
  jList1.setModel(model);
  . . .
}
```

Going back to the UI Designer, you can do practically the same thing for the Remove button. Select the button and double-click the actionPerformed() entry again. Here the code is similar, but you use the removeElement() method of DefaultListModel to remove the element.

```
void jButton2_actionPerformed(ActionEvent e) {
  String s = jTextField1.getText();
  if (s.length() > 0) {
    DefaultListModel model = (DefaultListModel)jList1.getModel();
    model.removeElement(s);
  }
}
```

That's all there is to it. You can now save and compile the program to see how it works. Figure 9-7 shows how the program looks when it's running. Listing 9-1 provides the ListBuilder.java source.

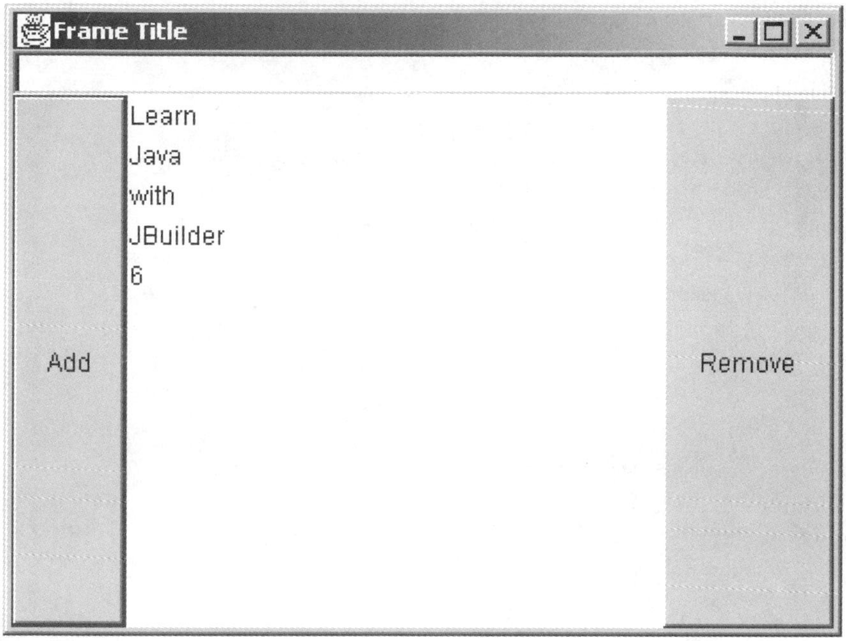

Figure 9-7. Executing the program after entering and removing a few entries

Listing 9-1. The Complete ListBuilder.java Source

```java
package skill9;

import java.awt.*;
import java.awt.event.*;
import javax.swing.*;

public class ListBuilder extends JFrame {
  JPanel contentPane;
  BorderLayout borderLayout1 = new BorderLayout();
  JButton jButton1 = new JButton();
  JButton jButton2 = new JButton();
  JTextField jTextField1 = new JTextField();
  JList jList1 = new JList();

  //Construct the frame
  public ListBuilder() {
    enableEvents(AWTEvent.WINDOW_EVENT_MASK);
    try {
      jbInit();
    }
```

```
      catch(Exception e) {
        e.printStackTrace();
      }
    }
    //Component initialization
    private void jbInit() throws Exception  {
      contentPane = (JPanel) this.getContentPane();
      jButton1.setText("Add");
      jButton1.addActionListener(new java.awt.event.ActionListener() {
        public void actionPerformed(ActionEvent e) {
          jButton1_actionPerformed(e);
        }
      });
      contentPane.setLayout(borderLayout1);
      this.setSize(new Dimension(400, 300));
      this.setTitle("Frame Title");
      jButton2.setText("Remove");
      jButton2.addActionListener(new java.awt.event.ActionListener() {
        public void actionPerformed(ActionEvent e) {
          jButton2_actionPerformed(e);
        }
      });
      ListModel model = new DefaultListModel();
      jList1.setModel(model);
      contentPane.add(jButton1, BorderLayout.WEST);
      contentPane.add(jTextField1, BorderLayout.NORTH);
      contentPane.add(jList1, BorderLayout.CENTER);
      contentPane.add(jButton2, BorderLayout.EAST);
    }
    //Overridden so we can exit when window is closed
    protected void processWindowEvent(WindowEvent e) {
      super.processWindowEvent(e);
      if (e.getID() == WindowEvent.WINDOW_CLOSING) {
        System.exit(0);
      }
    }

    void jButton1_actionPerformed(ActionEvent e) {
      String s = jTextField1.getText();
      if (s.length() > 0) {
        DefaultListModel model = (DefaultListModel)jList1.getModel();
        model.addElement(s);
      }
    }
```

```
void jButton2_actionPerformed(ActionEvent e) {
  String s = jTextField1.getText();
  if (s.length() > 0) {
    DefaultListModel model = (DefaultListModel)jList1.getModel();
    model.removeElement(s);
  }
}

}
```

NOTE *Like the* JTree *in Skill 8, the* JList *should be placed in a* JScrollPane *if you want scrollbars added when the component contents exceed available space. In this example, if you add more elements to the list than space permits, a scrollbar will not be added. Feel free to experiment with the UI Designer to get the proper behavior with a* JScrollPane. *Adding a component into a* JScrollPane *is demonstrated in Skill 13.*

ARE YOU EXPERIENCED?

Congratulations! You should now have a feel for using drag and drop to create your screens.

Now you can

- Describe a JavaBean component

- Describe what's inside a bean

- Use the UI Designer

- Change properties with the Inspector

- Add event listeners through the Inspector

- Add and remove elements from the JList component

Skill 10 will show you how to find and add more beans to the Component palette, so you can drag and drop your way into the future.

Configuring the Palette

- Working with beans not on the palette

- Adding beans to the palette

- Customizing palette entries

- Deleting beans from the palette

- Finding beans

Setting Up the Component Palette

After playing connect-the-beans in the last skill and showing off some of the various standard components on the Component palette, this skill will show you how to extend the palette so that even more beans are available. You need to extend the palette because you've either licensed some beans (purchased or open source) or created your own and want to reuse them more easily. If you're experimenting with various beans from the Web and you need to get rid of them, I'll also discuss the extra steps necessary to completely remove them. Finally, I'll wrap up the skill by showing you where to look for more beans.

Working with Beans Not on the Palette

Before you jump into working with the Component palette, you'll need to close up the last skill's project and create a new one. Using the Application Wizard, call the new project **Skill10** with a directory of **C:\skills\Skill10**, and call the frame class **PaletteTester**. At this point, select the Design tab for PaletteTester to see the UI Designer and the Component palette.

While the Component palette for JBuilder comes with quite a few components already installed, it doesn't include everything. If you want to work with something not on the palette, you have to either manually add in the necessary code or select the class with the Bean Chooser button, as shown in Figure 10-1.

Figure 10-1. The JBuilder Bean Chooser button

When you click the Bean Chooser button, a menu appears. After you choose the Select option, the Bean Chooser pop-up window appears (see Figure 10-2), and you can select a component to add to your program. (All classes can be treated as components. It's just a matter of how easy it is to work with them through the Inspector versus manually coding component behavior.) For instance, I talked about the Swing components working in the MVC world. However, only the "View" components are on the palette. If you didn't want to manually add the line creating the DefaultListModel in Skill 9, you could have selected the class with the help of the Bean Chooser. Once you select a component from the pop-up window, you drop the component into the UI Designer area, just like if you had selected the component from the Component palette.

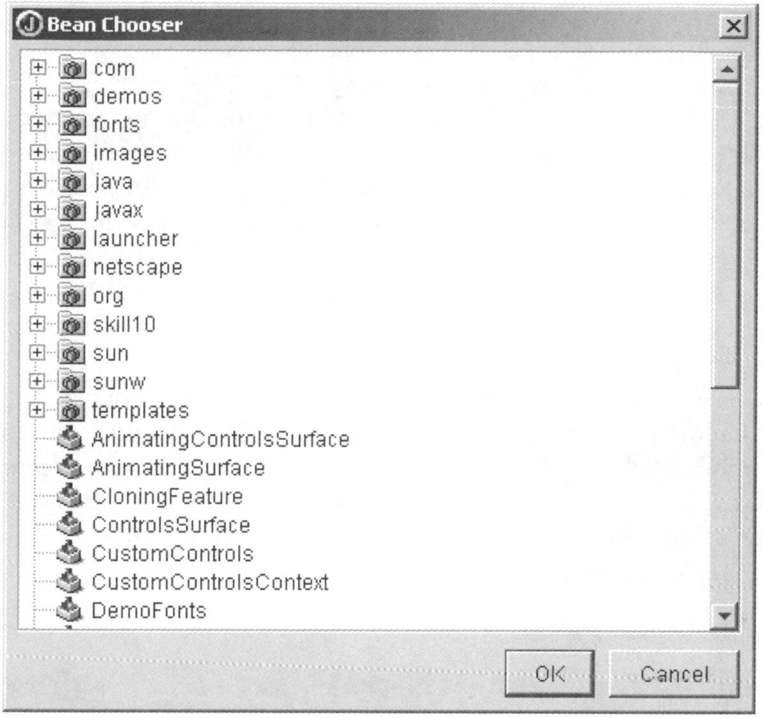

Bean Chooser ☒

- ⊞ 📷 com
- ⊞ 📷 demos
- ⊞ 📷 fonts
- ⊞ 📷 images
- ⊞ 📷 java
- ⊞ 📷 javax
- ⊞ 📷 launcher
- ⊞ 📷 netscape
- ⊞ 📷 org
- ⊞ 📷 skill10
- ⊞ 📷 sun
- ⊞ 📷 sunw
- ⊞ 📷 templates
  - 🝆 AnimatingControlsSurface
  - 🝆 AnimatingSurface
  - 🝆 CloningFeature
  - 🝆 ControlsSurface
  - 🝆 CustomControls
  - 🝆 CustomControlsContext
  - 🝆 DemoFonts

[OK] [Cancel]

Figure 10-2. The JBuilder Bean Chooser pop-up window

Initially, only the Select option is available from the Bean Chooser menu, but as you manually select more components, each gets added to the menu for the specific project.

 TIP *If you ever want to remove items from the menu, when JBuilder is closed, edit the project's* `.jpx` *file and remove the line with the* `palette.bean.chooser.beans` *settings.*

To demonstrate, drop a `JSplitPane` from the Swing Containers tab into the `PaletteTester` frame. The `JSplitPane` is a panel that provides a user-movable divider between two components. You add two components, one to each side, and then allow the user (or the programmer) to move the divider.

Before adding the components, you'll make a slight modification to the split pane behavior. The change you'll make is to the `continuousLayout` property. By default, this setting is False, meaning that as the user drags the divider, the components are not redrawn until the divider is dropped. As long as the components aren't too complex to redraw, it's more interesting to have this property be True. Also, be sure the split pane is in the center of the Content pane.

You can now add the components. You'll use some of the demo components to drop into the split pane. For the first component, you'll take the Tree component, which you can find in the demos.Fonts package. This component displays the letters "AB" in an interesting, tree-like structure, rotating and resizing the letters for different branches. To add the component, select the Bean Chooser button, and then choose the Select option to bring up the Bean Chooser screen. From there, open up the appropriate package and double-click the Tree item. You'll need to drop the component into the JSplitPane for it to be added into your program. Do the same thing with the BezierAnim demo, which you can find in the demos.Arcs_Curves package. This demo draws a different Bezier curve with each resizing of the component.

With everything added, the only thing left to do is run the program. Figure 10-3 shows what the screen might look like after moving the divider. The right side of the screen will likely be different for you. Notice how the components redraw themselves as you move the divider. This is because the continuousLayout property is true. Change the setting to false if you'd like to see the default behavior. You'll find the source for the program in Listing 10-1.

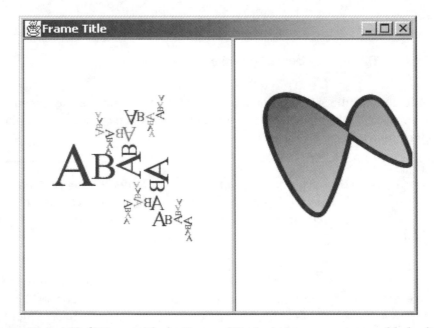

Figure 10-3. A JSplitPane with the Tree and BezierAnim components added, after moving the divider

> **NOTE** *You can find the source for the demo components in the* jre/demo/jfc *directory, under the JBuilder installation directory. If you aren't familiar with Bezier curves, you can draw them with the help of the* CubicCurve2D *class. You specify two end points and two control points, where the line between the end points is pulled toward the control points.*

Listing 10-1. The Complete PaletteTester.java Source

```java
package skill10;

import java.awt.*;
import java.awt.event.*;
import javax.swing.*;
import demos.Fonts.*;
import demos.Arcs_Curves.*;

public class PaletteTester extends JFrame {
  JPanel contentPane;
  BorderLayout borderLayout1 = new BorderLayout();
  JSplitPane jSplitPane1 = new JSplitPane();
  Tree tree1 = new Tree();
  BezierAnim bezierAnim1 = new BezierAnim();

  //Construct the frame
  public PaletteTester() {
    enableEvents(AWTEvent.WINDOW_EVENT_MASK);
    try {
      jbInit();
    }
    catch(Exception e) {
      e.printStackTrace();
    }
  }
  //Component initialization
  private void jbInit() throws Exception  {
    contentPane = (JPanel) this.getContentPane();
    contentPane.setLayout(borderLayout1);
    this.setSize(new Dimension(400, 300));
    this.setTitle("Frame Title");
    jSplitPane1.setContinuousLayout(true);
    contentPane.add(jSplitPane1, BorderLayout.CENTER);
```

```
    jSplitPane1.add(tree1, JSplitPane.LEFT);
    jSplitPane1.add(bezierAnim1, JSplitPane.RIGHT);
  }
  //Overridden so we can exit when window is closed
  protected void processWindowEvent(WindowEvent e) {
    super.processWindowEvent(e);
    if (e.getID() == WindowEvent.WINDOW_CLOSING) {
      System.exit(0);
    }
  }
}
```

Adding Beans to the Palette

Moving beyond the preinstalled components and manual selection, let's say you're Wile E. Coyote and you've just purchased the Acme Bean Collection. You want to add the beans to JBuilder so you can hunt down your nemesis, the Road Runner. Adding a new bean—or an entire set of beans—to JBuilder is as easy as following Wile E.'s blueprints for a Road Runner trap. Thankfully, with JBuilder the process always works as expected in the end.

To add beans to JBuilder, the first step is to get the collection, which may involve downloading files from the Web or placing a CD into your CD-ROM drive. Once you've installed the product, you'll end up with the beans in either a ZIP file or a JAR file.

 NOTE   *JAR files are* Java Archives. *They are similar to ZIP files, but they contain something called a* manifest *that describes the contents of the files. You'll learn more about these files in Skill 16.*

Adding from an Archive

For this skill, you'll actually use a collection that comes with JBuilder, so you don't have to bother with downloading something off the Internet. The demos from Sun that you just used are in the `SwingSet2.jar` file in `/jdk1.3/demo/jfc/SwingSet2`, under the JBuilder installation directory. You'll add one of the components you just used to the Other tab, so next time that component can be more easily used.

Once you have the collection available, select Tools ➤ Configure Palette (or right-click over the palette and select Properties) to bring up the dialog box shown in Figure 10-4. The first tab you see is the Pages tab, which shows a list of each tab, or page, on the Component palette.

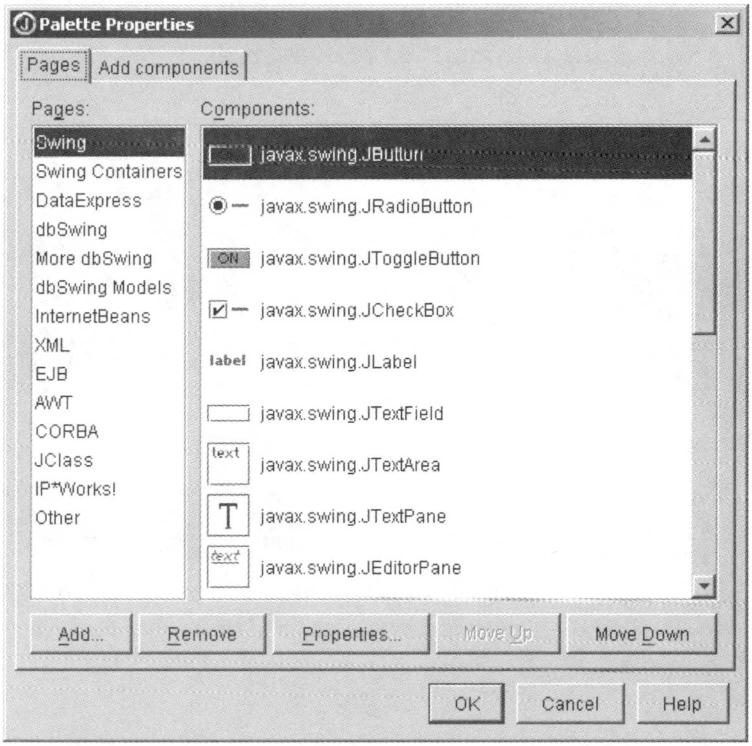

Figure 10-4. From the Palette Properties dialog box, you can add, remove, or reorder components on the Component palette.

To add a bean from either a .jar file or a straight .class file, select the Add components tab. You'll then see the dialog box shown in Figure 10-5.

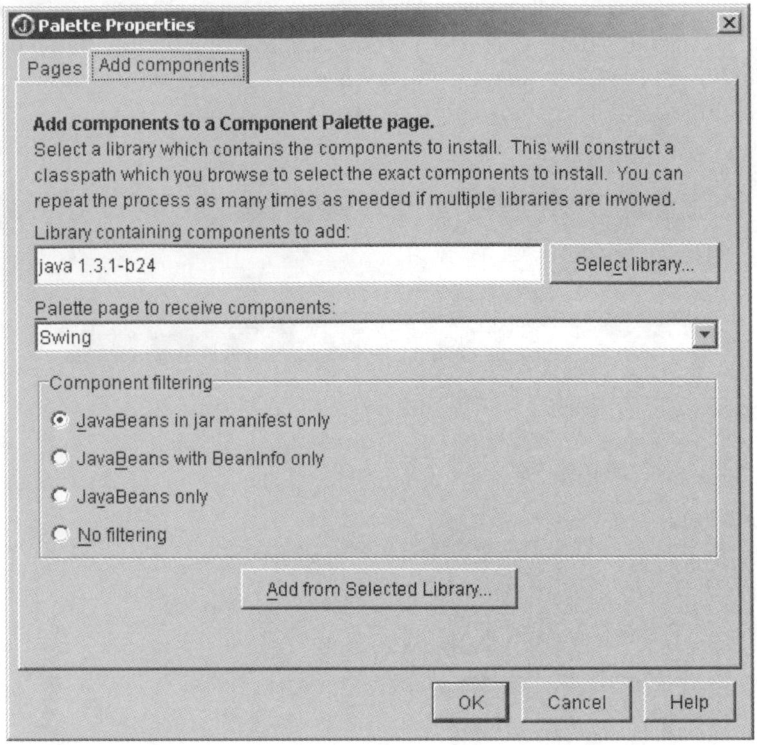

Figure 10-5. From the Add components tab of the Palette Properties dialog box, you choose an archive or directory, select a page, and then select the beans to install.

To find the JAR file from which to select the beans, click the Select library button to bring up the Select a different library window shown in Figure 10-6.

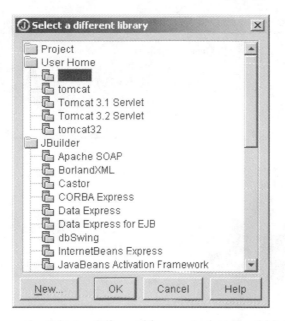

Figure 10-6. You use the Select a different library window to add help components to the JBuilder Component palette.

From here, you can select one of the libraries that comes with JBuilder or add a new library. If you choose to add a new library, where that library is available depends on which folder is selected when you click the New button. If the Project folder is selected, the library will be available only to the current project. If the User Home folder is selected, the library is available whenever you're logged in and using JBuilder from this machine. For the JBuilder folder, it's whenever anyone is logged in and using JBuilder from this machine.

The demo programs you added aren't in one of the existing libraries, so you need to add them yourself. You'll add them at the User Home level, but you don't have to select the User Home folder here. Just click New to bring up the New Library Wizard dialog box, as shown in Figure 10-7.

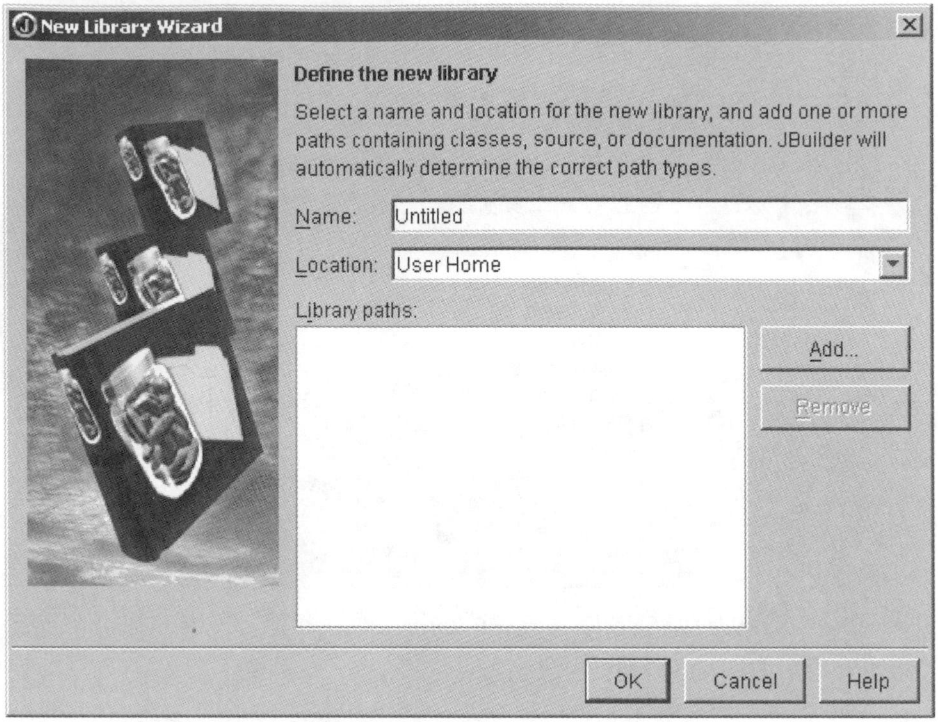

Figure 10-7. You use the New Library Wizard dialog box to make new libraries available when you add components to the palette.

In this dialog box, enter **SwingSet** in the Name field and select **User Home** in the Location field. You'll then need to click the Add button to find the SwingSet2.jar file that you just saw in the /jdk1.3/demo/jfc/SwingSet2 directory. After selecting the .jar file, click the OK button. Because you're adding components right from a .jar file and not from a .class file, the system reports that it can't detect source, documentation, and class paths (see Figure 10-8), so you just want to click the Add as Class Path button and then click OK.

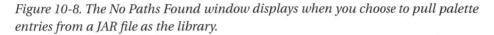

Figure 10-8. *The No Paths Found window displays when you choose to pull palette entries from a JAR file as the library.*

You're now back at the Select a different library window, where you need to click OK one more time to get back to the Palette Properties dialog box.

Now that you've selected the library from which to get the bean, you need to select the Palette tab to receive the component—**Other**, in your case—and then you can finally add the bean from the selected library. Before you click the Add from Selected Library button, though, one more thing requires explanation. There are four methods of Component filtering displayed right above that button. One method automatically adds all the beans in the JAR file, while the other three let you filter the contents to various degrees. For now, just select No filtering, as manifests and BeanInfo haven't been covered sufficiently for you to try to use those, and the JavaBeans only option doesn't buy you much with this JAR file.

NOTE *I'll address* BeanInfo *in Skill 13. Basically, it's an optional support class provided to help builder tools work with beans in a more effective manner.*

After you click the Add from Selected Library button, the Browse for Class window appears, as shown in Figure 10-9. From here you can select the BezierAnimationPanel class, which is what you used earlier. Select the class name and click OK. Assuming everything went okay, the confirmation window shown in Figure 10-10 appears and your component is almost available on the palette.

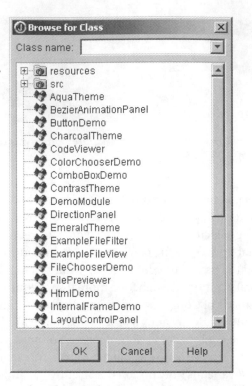

Figure 10-9. The Browse for Class dialog box enables you to pick the bean to add to the Component palette.

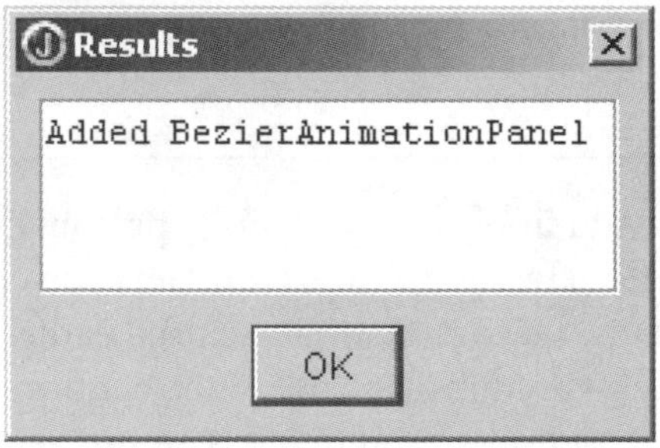

Figure 10-10. A confirmation window appears after you successfully add a component to the palette.

If the Other tab on the Component palette is visible in the background, you'll notice the new component isn't there yet. Until you actually click the OK button from the Palette Properties dialog box, no change is made. Once you click OK again, you'll find the new bean added to the palette. Having added the component to the Other tab, that tab now looks like Figure 10-11.

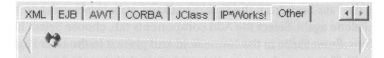

Figure 10-11. The Other tab on the Component palette with the new BezierAnimationPanel bean

Adding from a Package

Adding a bean from a package isn't much different than adding one from a JAR file. To demonstrate, you'll add to the Other tab the Tabs frame you created in Skill 6. As a refresher, Figure 10-12 shows you what the Tabs frame looks like.

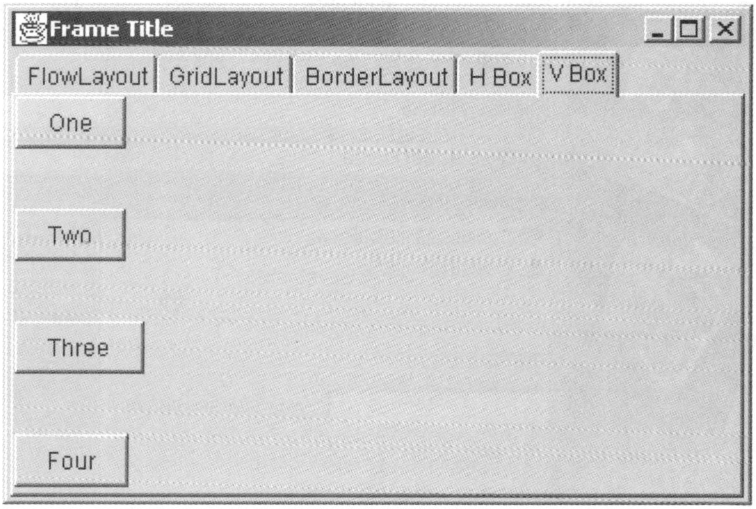

Figure 10-12. The Tabs frame created in Skill 6

>  **TIP** *One thing to remember: Although you're working with visual beans, not all beans have to be visual. You can create beans that have no visual representation. When you drop these beans into JBuilder, they'll just appear in the Component tree (located in the same area of the screen as the Structure pane, but when the UI Designer is shown).*

icon to the left of the Select Image toggle (see Figure 10-15). Click OK to return to the Palette Properties dialog box and click OK one more time to return to the tool. The Component palette now shows the new icon for the Tabs component (see Figure 10-16).

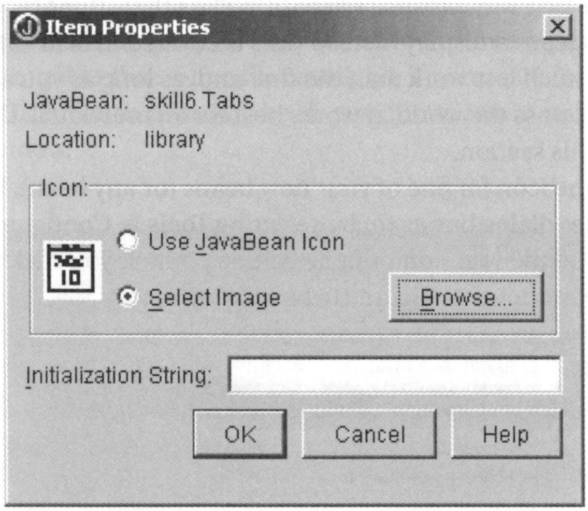

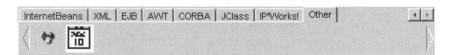

Figure 10-15. *The Item Properties dialog box with the new Tabs icon*

InternetBeans | XML | EJB | AWT | CORBA | JClass | IP*Works! | Other |

Figure 10-16. *The Component palette with the new Tabs icon*

TIP *If you want to create your own icon images, you need to use a program other than JBuilder to create them. Paint Shop Pro (http://www.visitorinfo.com/software/paint.htm) is a good shareware program that supports creating GIF-formatted images.*

Deleting Beans from the Palette

Removing a bean from the Component palette is straightforward. Just select Tools ➤ Configure Palette, find the bean, and select Remove. There is one catch, though: Make sure you have the bean selected in the right column, not the page in the left column. If you just select Remove, the page is removed but not the selected component. You'll notice a light yellow box around the selected object once you select the component.

TIP *If you accidentally select Remove on a page that you'd like to keep around, just select Cancel. The page isn't really removed until you click OK.*

Finding Beans

Now that you know how to integrate new beans into JBuilder, where can you find them? Well, there are several different places to look, and each has its own benefits. Instead of listing specific vendors, I'll point out some of the component warehouses.

Sitraka Software

To get your first set of beans you don't even have to go anywhere. The JClass family of components from Sitraka Software (formerly KL Group) comes with JBuilder. It consists of several Swing-like components and a charting component. While most of the components have similar controls within the Swing component set, you may find some of them useful. Figure 10-17 lists the components available under the JClass tab of the Components palette.

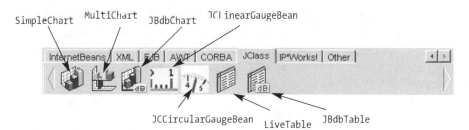

Figure 10-17. The JClass palette of components

You can find the JClass Web site at
`http://parker.sitraka.com/software/jclass/`, and additional support is also
available from the Sitraka JClass Documentation under JBuilder's Help ➤ Help
Topics menu.

> **TIP** *While the Sitraka JClass Chart library is available with
> JBuilder, it isn't necessarily the best charting package out
> there.* JavaPro *selected Visual Mining's NetCharts as the "Best
> Pure Java Packaged Client Application" in 2001. For more
> information on Visual Mining's charting product, visit*
> `http://www.visualmining.com/.`

JavaBeans Home

The official home page for JavaBeans technology is `http://java.sun.com/beans`.
From there, you can find documentation on the technology and Sun's Solutions
Marketplace (`http://industry.java.sun.com/solutions/beans/`), which is
a directory of JavaBean components. In addition, in Sun's Marketing Your Beans
resource, Sun lists three places that allow you to sell your beans and hence find
beans for sale.

- Component Planet (`http://www.componentplanet.com/`)

- ComponentSource (`http://www.componentsource.com/java`)

- Flashline.com (`http://www.flashline.com/components/javabeans.jsp`)

Java Review Service (JARS)

What started out as the "Java Applet Rating Service," JARS
(`http://www.jars.com/`) is a catalog of user-submitted resources for peer review.
Among the many things rated are JavaBean components. If you click the JARS
Top 1% link from the home page, you'll find what JARS' reviewers think are the
best beans in the business. You may get lucky and find some that even include
source code.

alphaBeans

IBM provides a virtual treasure trove of components at their alphaWorks Web site (http://alphaworks.ibm.com/alphaBeans). Serving as a virtual testing ground for many new and interesting components, you'll find several components that rated in the JARS Top 1% list. Some of alphaWorks' more popular components are the Calendar Bean Suite, XML Bean Suite, and Spinner control. Some have graduated into commercial products that you can buy at Flashline.com or ComponentSource.

Borland

JBuilder's maker maintains a list of JavaBean components at http://www.borland.com/jbuilder/resources/jbtools.html#jbcompon. You'll also find several other tools that integrate into the JBuilder development environment listed on the page.

ARE YOU EXPERIENCED?

Now you can

- Use the Configure Palette tool

- Add beans to the Component palette

- Remove beans from the Component palette

- Customize beans on the Component palette

- Fill your hard drive with more beans

Now that you know how to add already existing beans to JBuilder, you'll start creating your own. Skill 11 begins the process by exploring the events aspect of bean creation.

Creating Beans: Events

- Creating your first bean

- Explaining Java's delegation-based event model

- Working with nonrectangular beans

- Generating event-handling code with BeansExpress

SO FAR, YOU'VE GOTTEN A FEEL for using some of the existing beans. Starting in this skill, and continuing in the next four skills, I'll explain the different pieces necessary to create your own beans. You don't need to read all the skills to create simple beans. However, as the complexity of a bean increases, you may want to provide more pieces so the developer using the bean has an easier time. In each skill, after you look at how to manually create each of the different pieces, you'll see how JBuilder's BeansExpress helps automate many of the tasks.

To demonstrate, let's start by creating a simple bean. This bean will be a basic blue box. Wherever you place the bean, you'll see a blue box on the screen. First, close any open projects. Then, create a new project named **Skill11** in **C:\skills\Skill11** with the Project Wizard.

After you create the new project, create a new class with the Class Wizard by selecting File ➤ New and then double-clicking the Class icon on the New tab, as shown in Figure 11-1. Alternatively, you can just select File ➤ New Class.

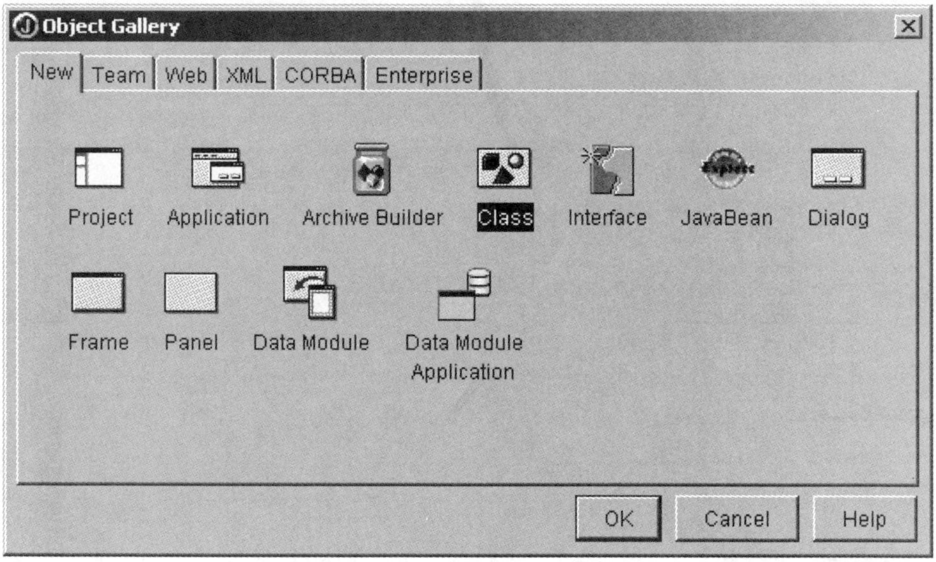

Figure 11-1. Creating a new class with the Class Wizard

The Class Wizard dialog box appears, as shown in Figure 11-2. There are no specific naming requirements for beans, so you'll enter a class name of **BlueBox**. Because you're creating a visual bean, in the Base class chooser you need to enter or select **javax.swing.JPanel** to extend it. With Swing components, JPanel is the natural one to extend, whereas with AWT components, you usually extend Canvas. If you click the " . . . " button, you can manually locate the class to extend. Once you've extended from the class, it will be added to the list of choices shown when you click the down arrow at the right-hand side of the text box. The

Public check box is already selected, as is the Generate default constructor, so just click the OK button to generate the class. You should also be sure to check the Generate header comments check box, and if there have been any abstract methods, you should check the Override abstract methods box, too.

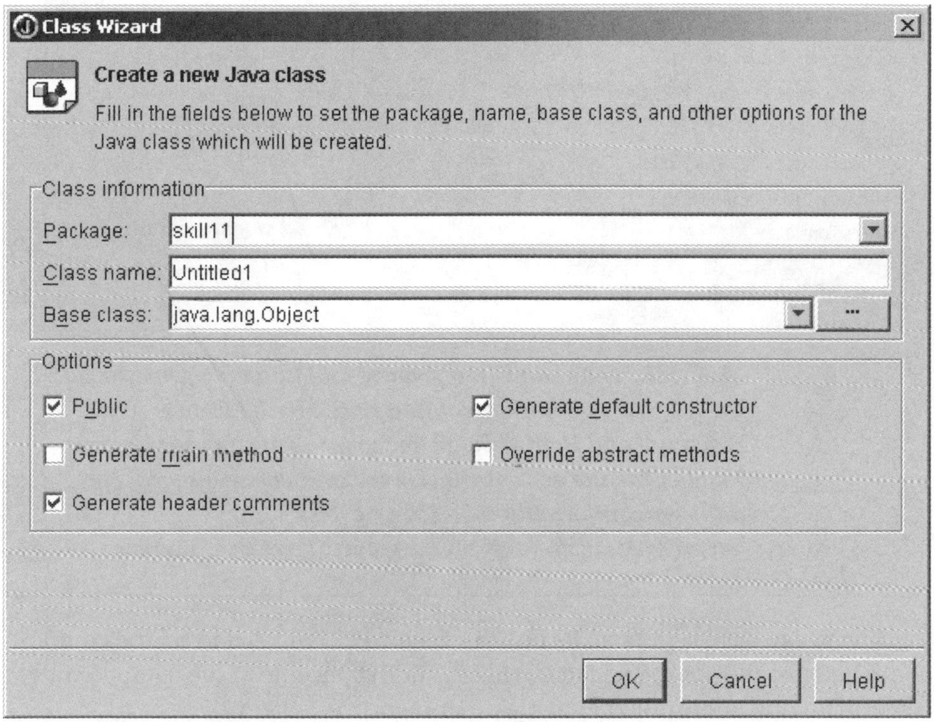

Class Wizard ⊗

Create a new Java class

Fill in the fields below to set the package, name, base class, and other options for the Java class which will be created.

Class information

Package: skill11

Class name: Untitled1

Base class: java.lang.Object

Options

☑ Public   ☑ Generate default constructor

☐ Generate main method   ☐ Override abstract methods

☑ Generate header comments

OK   Cancel   Help

Figure 11-2. The Class Wizard dialog box for creating new classes

TIP   *All beans must be public classes. It's easiest to work with them if they have no argument constructors, though that is not an absolute requirement according to the JavaBeans Specification (*http://java.sun.com/products/javabeans /docs/spec.html*). The no-argument constructor is considered the default constructor.*

The first thing you'll notice in the generated source is the javadoc framework for the class. These lines should be filled so that others will understand your class after you've moved on to bigger and better things. The lines with an @ symbol before a word are special and can be placed in the generated API documentation for the class.

```
/**
 * <p>Title: BlueBox</p>
 * <p>Description: A rectangular JavaBean component that is blue.</p>
 * <p>Copyright:   Copyright (c) 2001</p>
 * <p>Company: JZ Ventures, Inc.</p>
 * @author John Zukowski
 * @version 1.0
 */
```

> **NOTE** *The command-line* javadoc *tool is used to generate all the API documentation. You can find it under Help ➤ Java Reference and Help ➤ Swing Reference. You can use the same tool to generate documentation for your classes as well. For additional information on* javadoc, *visit* http://java.sun.com/j2se/1.3/docs/tooldocs/javadoc/.

In order to have your bean be one big, blue area, you need to set the component's background color. You can do this by adding one line to the component's constructor and importing the java.awt package.

```
import java.awt.*;
 . . .
  public BlueBox() {
    setBackground(Color.blue);
  }
```

At this point, your bean is essentially done. Save and compile it to make sure everything is okay. You can't run the program yet because the bean hasn't been used. In order to make it useable by another program, it's best to just drop it into the Component palette.

> **NOTE** *To compile a single class, right-click over the filename in the Navigation pane and select Make. Alternatively, you can press Ctrl-Shift-F9.*

From Bean to Program

Going from bean to program involves two steps. First you must add the bean to the Component palette, and then you create a test program.

Adding Your First Bean to the Palette

As you learned in the last skill, select Tools ➤ Configure Palette to bring up the Palette Properties dialog box. From there, add the BlueBox to the palette just like the component from Skill 6. First select the Add components tab, and then click the Select library button. You'll need to create a new library by clicking the New button and add the **C:\skills\Skill11** directory to the library path, as shown in Figure 11-3.

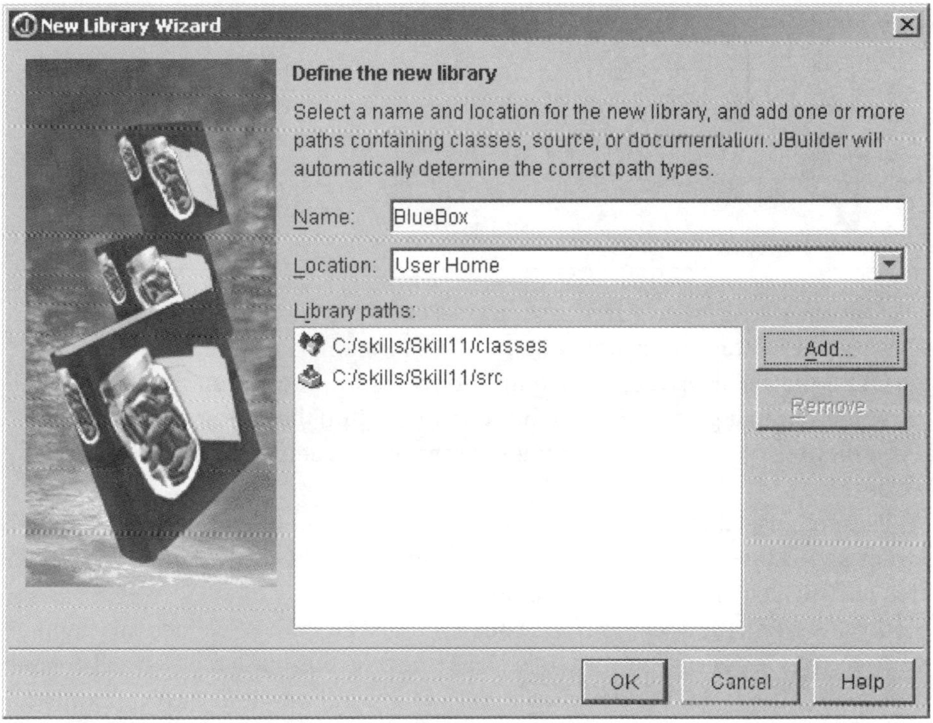

Figure 11-3. The New Library Wizard with the appropriate directory added for the BlueBox bean

From here, click OK once to create the library. Then click the OK button a second time to select the library. After you select the Other palette to add the bean to, you can select either the JavaBeans only or No filtering option to choose how to filter the selected CLASSPATH. Next, click the Add from Selected Library button to bring up the list of classes found, find the BlueBox bean in the skill11 package, click the OK button on the Browse for Class window, click the OK button on the Results window, and then click the OK button on the Palette Properties window. Okay? Yes, that's five different OK buttons there.

Using the BlueBox Bean

Now it's time to show off your new bean. You'll need to create a new project to do the testing. Close the Skill11 project and start up the Application Wizard. In the Project Wizard, you'll name this one **Skill11b** and place it in the **C:\skills\Skill11b** directory as usual. In the Application Wizard, name the frame class **BlueBoxTester** and click Finish.

TIP *When testing out your beans, it's best to test them from a different project. This provides a more realistic testing environment and verifies that proper access keywords, such as* private, protected, *and* public, *were used.*

Once you select the Design tab for BlueBoxTester and the Other tab on the Component palette, you can try out the BlueBox bean. Select the bean from the Other tab and drop it into the frame. At this point, your frame's screen should turn blue, assuming you dropped the component into the center of the frame. If you didn't, make sure the component's constraints setting in the Inspector is Center.

Now change the layout manager of the frame's Content pane from BorderLayout to FlowLayout. Select the contentPane in the Component tree screen area and then change its layout property to FlowLayout.

At this point, the screen reverts back to almost all gray. Why does this happen when the blue box is in the container? Well, the blue box has a really small default size. If you'd like to see your box again, select the component in the Component tree and change the component's preferredSize property. The property is a comma-separated list of width and height. So, if you make the size something like **25, 50**, you will see the box back on the screen.

TIP *If you find a component doesn't immediately reflect your property changes, double-click the component in the Component tree area.*

To make the screen a little more interesting, drop a few more blue boxes onto the screen and resize each to a new setting. After saving and running the program, you may end up with a screen similar to the one shown in Figure 11-4.

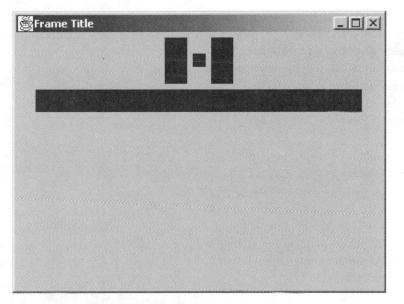

Figure 11-4. Run BlueBoxTester after you drop in a few beans. Your screen will more than likely differ from the one in this figure, depending upon the size and number of the BlueBox beans you place.

NOTE *If you have more than one bean on the Other tab without an associated image icon, and you aren't sure which one is the BlueBox, briefly rest your mouse over each bean to see the class name displayed. For this example,* skill11.BlueBox *is the right one.*

The source for the BlueBoxTester follows in Listing 11-1. Yours will more than likely differ, unless you selected the exact same number of beans and size.

Listing 11-1. The Complete BlueBoxTester.java Source

```java
package skill11b;

import java.awt.*;
import java.awt.event.*;
import javax.swing.*;
import skill11.*;

public class BlueBoxTester extends JFrame {
  JPanel contentPane;
  BlueBox blueBox1 = new BlueBox();
  FlowLayout flowLayout1 = new FlowLayout();
  BlueBox blueBox2 = new BlueBox();
  BlueBox blueBox3 = new BlueBox();
  BlueBox blueBox4 = new BlueBox();

  //Construct the frame
  public BlueBoxTester() {
    enableEvents(AWTEvent.WINDOW_EVENT_MASK);
    try {
      jbInit();
    }
    catch(Exception e) {
      e.printStackTrace();
    }
  }
  //Component initialization
  private void jbInit() throws Exception  {
    contentPane = (JPanel) this.getContentPane();
    contentPane.setLayout(flowLayout1);
    this.setSize(new Dimension(400, 300));
    this.setTitle("Frame Title");
    blueBox1.setPreferredSize(new Dimension(25, 50));
    blueBox2.setPreferredSize(new Dimension(15, 15));
    blueBox3.setPreferredSize(new Dimension(25, 50));
    blueBox4.setPreferredSize(new Dimension(350, 25));
    contentPane.add(blueBox1, null);
    contentPane.add(blueBox2, null);
    contentPane.add(blueBox3, null);
    contentPane.add(blueBox4, null);
  }
```

```
//Overridden so we can exit when window is closed
protected void processWindowEvent(WindowEvent e) {
  super.processWindowEvent(e);
  if (e.getID() == WindowEvent.WINDOW_CLOSING) {
    System.exit(0);
  }
 }
}
```

Java's Delegation-Based Event Model

Okay, now that you have a bean to play with, I can move on to explain Java's event model. As you learned in Skill 9, events serve as the notification mechanism between beans. If a bean wants to know when an event happens, it registers itself with the source of the event as an observer. Then, when the event happens, the source notifies anyone registered, or listening. The event itself must be a subclass of java.util.EventObject, while the listener implements the java.util.EventListener interface. All of the AWT and Swing events work this way, so implicitly all AWT and Swing components are beans. The whole scenario looks something like Figure 11-5.

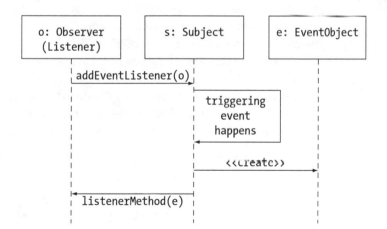

Figure 11-5. Message diagram of the Event source, listener, and object cycle

Maintaining Listener Lists

If you want to add some event handling to the BlueBox, you need to pick an event for it to generate, maintain the listener list, and notify those listeners when the event is triggered. You can create your own event type—however, with all the work the Java team put into creating the AWT/Swing event structure, it's much easier to just reuse what they created. For general events, this is sufficient. You'll also give creating custom events a go later in this skill.

Once you reopen the Skill11 project, you can add some event handling to the BlueBox. The most common event handler to add is for the ActionEvent class. The ActionEvent serves as a general-purpose event type that reports when some action happens. You saw it used with a JButton when it was selected, and it can be used with a JTextField when the user presses Enter after entering some text.

There are many different ways to manage a list of listeners. It seems that with each release of Java, a new way is added. You'll use the latest mechanism, which works with any event listener type. It is based off the EventListenerList class, which is part of Swing.

TIP *If you are curious about other ways to manage listener lists, and if you want to do all the work yourself, including dealing with multithreading, you can manage the list in a data structure such as a* Vector/ArrayList. *This method works, but it is the most error-prone. Another mechanism is to manage the listener lists with the help of the* AWTEventMulticaster. *This is the simplest method, but it only works for predefined AWT-related events. The latter is described in my Swing book,* Definitive Guide to Swing for Java 2, *while the former is what JBuilder generates and is described more fully in my* Java Collections Framework *book.*

In order to process an event within a class, you need to maintain a list of listeners. No matter what the event type, you need to create an instance variable of type EventListenerList and create an empty instance of the class to start.

```
private EventListenerList actionListenerList = new EventListenerList();
```

The EventListenerList class happens to be in the javax.swing.event package, so you should import that package. Right after the other import lines, add the following line:

```
import javax.swing.event.*;
```

So someone can listen for when an event happens, the event source—BlueBox—has to add and remove listeners from the EventListenerList. The add and remove methods need to be named a certain way to follow the JavaBeans Specification and for JBuilder, or any bean-connection tool, to find them and recognize their purpose. The method names always follow the same naming pattern, where you only fill in the specific listener type. The method name patterns, or signatures, are as follows:

```
public void addListenerType(ListenerType l)
public void removeListenerType(ListenerType l)
```

In the case of the BlueBox, because you'll be managing a list of ActionListener objects, the methods need to be named addActionListener() and removeActionListener(). Naming the methods is the easy part, but now you need to maintain the lists. Thankfully, EventListenerList does all the hard stuff internally, and you just have to call the add() and remove() methods, respectively.

```
public void addActionListener(ActionListener actionListener) {
  actionListenerList.add(ActionListener.class, actionListener);
}
public void removeActionListener(ActionListener actionListener) {
  actionListenerList.remove(ActionListener.class, actionListener);
}
```

This time be sure to import the java.awt.event package for the ActionListener class.

```
import java.awt.event.*;
```

Both the add() and remove() methods take two parameters: the listener type and the listener to add or remove. An EventListenerList *can* be used to maintain multiple listener type lists in one list object, so you need to pass in what type you want each listener to be used as.

Notifying Listeners

At this point, your BlueBox bean maintains the listener lists fine, but that is only half the story. It doesn't notify the listeners. To complete the process, the bean needs to notify them. Before I describe what activates the notification, you'll create a method to notify the listeners. With the help of the `EventListenerList` support class, the method is rather simple. There is no formal naming standard for the notification method, but it tends to be fire*ListenerMethodName*(*ListenerEvent*), where *ListenerMethodName* is the name of the listener method and *ListenerEvent* is the event type.

For your `ActionListener`, then, the method is named `fireActionPerformed()` and it accepts an `ActionEvent` argument.

The basic method structure is nearly identical for all event listener types: Get the list of listeners for the specific type and notify each of them. The only part that's tricky is that the array of listeners returned from the getter method (`getListeners()`) has two items per entry, so your `for` loop has to jump by two each time. Here's what the method looks like, with an added import line for `EventListener`:

```
import java.util.*;
  . . .
protected void fireActionPerformed(ActionEvent actionEvent) {
  EventListener list[] =
    actionListenerList.getListeners(ActionListener.class);
  for (int i=0, n=list.length; i < n; i++) {
    ((ActionListener)list[i]).actionPerformed(actionEvent);
  }
}
```

> **TIP** *Make sure the event notification method isn't public, as you do not want just anyone calling this method. The JavaBeans event-handling requirements state that the list of listeners cannot change while listeners are being notified. Because you copy the list out of the listener list, if the original listener list changes, your list doesn't because you've copied them out of the original.*

No matter what event you're handling, the majority of the code is identical. The only thing that really changes is which listener to get with `getListeners()` and which interface method to call.

You still need to add the code to trigger the calling of the listeners. For the blue box component, you'll have it notify listeners when the user double-clicks the mouse over it.

TIP *Keep in mind that a click is when the mouse doesn't move between press and release.*

In order for the blue box to respond to mouse clicks, it needs to register a `MouseListener` with itself that calls `fireActionPerformed()`. Instead of using the Implement Interface Wizard, though, you're going to use JBuilder templates. Position the mouse in the `BlueBox` constructor, on a new line after `setBackground(Color.blue);`, and press Ctrl-J to bring up the template list shown in Figure 11-6. Because you want to add a `MouseListener`, you'll need to scroll down until you find `addmouse`, with its description `add MouseListener`. When you find it, press Enter.

addaction	add ActionListener
addadjust	add AdjustmentListener
addanc	add AncestorListener
addawt	add AWTEventListener
addbeanm	add BeanContextMembershipListene
addbeans	add BeanContextServicesListener
addcaret	add CaretListener
addcell	add CellEditorListener

Figure 11-6. JBuilder's template selection window

NOTE *For a complete list of available templates to add your own, or to see exactly what code a template adds, select the Template tab on the Editor Options dialog box (Tools ➤ Editor Options). Adding your own template is demonstrated in Skill 20.*

The template code for the mouse listener follows in Listing 11-2. This is what is called an *anonymous listener* because the class created has no name. It's defined right in the `addMouseListener()` call. Essentially, this is one long line of code, as the close parenthesis and the semicolon to end the `addMouseListener()` line are at the very end.

Listing 11-2. The Code Added by the addmouse Template

```
addMouseListener(new MouseAdapter() {
  public void mouseClicked(MouseEvent e) {
  }

  public void mousePressed(MouseEvent e) {
  }

  public void mouseReleased(MouseEvent e) {
  }

  public void mouseEntered(MouseEvent e) {
  }

  public void mouseExited(MouseEvent e) {
  }
});
```

Now, once you find the mouseClicked() method, you can add in a call to fireActionPerformed(). Because fireActionPerformed() requires an ActionEvent argument, you need to create one. But you have to make sure it's a double-click event, which is available from the MouseEvent. Just ask with getClickCount(). Here's what the final version looks like:

```
public void mouseClicked(MouseEvent e) {
  if (e.getClickCount() == 2) {
    ActionEvent action = new ActionEvent(
      e.getSource(), ActionEvent.ACTION_PERFORMED, "");
    fireActionPerformed(action);
  }
}
```

Because mouseClicked() is the only MouseListener method you are interested in, you can actually delete the other four empty stubs. This is possible because the addActionListener() line created a MouseAdapter (addMouseListener(new MouseAdapter() . . .), which provides empty stubs for all the listener methods.

Now you can save and recompile BlueBox. It isn't necessary to add the component again to the palette, as it is already there.

The complete source for BlueBox appears in Listing 11-3.

Listing 11-3. The Complete BlueBox.java Source

```java
package skill11;

import javax.swing.*;
import java.awt.*;
import javax.swing.event.*;
import java.awt.event.*;
import java.util.*;

/**
 * <p>Title: BlueBox</p>
 * <p>Description: A rectangular JavaBean component that is blue.</p>
 * <p>Copyright:   Copyright (c) 2001</p>
 * <p>Company: JZ Ventures, Inc.</p>
 * @author John Zukowski
 * @version 1.1
 */

public class BlueBox extends JPanel {

  private EventListenerList actionListenerList = new EventListenerList();

  public BlueBox() {
    setBackground(Color.blue);
    addMouseListener(new MouseAdapter() {
      public void mouseClicked(MouseEvent e) {
        if (e.getClickCount() == 2) {
          ActionEvent action = new ActionEvent(
            e.getSource(), ActionEvent.ACTION_PERFORMED, "");
          fireActionPerformed(action);
        }
      }
    });
  }
  public void addActionListener(ActionListener actionListener) {
    actionListenerList.add(ActionListener.class, actionListener);
  }
  public void removeActionListener(ActionListener actionListener) {
    actionListenerList.remove(ActionListener.class, actionListener);
  }
```

```
    protected void fireActionPerformed(ActionEvent actionEvent) {
      EventListener list[] =
        actionListenerList.getListeners(ActionListener.class);
      for (int i=0, n=list.length; i < n; i++) {
        ((ActionListener)list[i]).actionPerformed(actionEvent);
      }
    }
  }
}
```

Creating a New Tester

You can now create a new test program to try out the new and improved BlueBox. Instead of adding to the tester in Skill11b, close any open projects and run the Application Wizard again. Create a project called **Skill11c** in **C:\skills\Skill11c** and name the main frame class **BlueBoxActionTester**.

You'll need a blue box and a text field on your screen. When the user double-clicks the blue box, the text field will display "I've been hit" with a counter. Select BlueBoxActionTester.java in the Navigation pane, and then select the Design tab in the Content pane to set up the screen.

First, drop a JTextField into the North area of the screen. On the Swing tab, select the JTextField. This should be the sixth icon from the left. Just drop this one onto the top of the screen.

To place the blue box on the screen, select the Other tab of the Component palette. Then, select the blue box and drop it into the middle of the frame. Notice that the rest of the frame turns blue.

To register an ActionListener with the BlueBox, double-click the BlueBox in the UI Designer. This is the same as selecting the Events tab on the Inspector and double-clicking in the actionPerformed() method as you've done in the past. Double-clicking BlueBox adds the component's *default* event. A bean's default event can be customized in the BeanInfo for that class, but it defaults to the first event. When the action event happens, just call the setText() method for the text field to display the "I've been hit" message. You'll need to add in a variable to count the hits.

```
int counter;
void blueBox1_actionPerformed(ActionEvent e) {
  jTextField1.setText("I've been hit: " + ++counter);
}
```

NOTE *The ++ is an autoincrement operator. It will increment the value of the variable by one before it is used. Because* int *variables are automatically initialized to 0, the first* setText() *call will display the value 1.*

You should also change the initialization of the JTextField component from "jTextField1" to nothing, as it doesn't need to have an initial value set.

Saving and running the program demonstrates the updated BlueBox bean and its notification of the action listener. Listing 11-4 provides the new testing program source, and Figure 11-7 shows the program in action.

Listing 11-4. The Initial BlueBoxActionTester.java Source

```java
package skill11c;

import java.awt.*;
import java.awt.event.*;
import javax.swing.*;
import skill11.*;

public class BlueBoxActionTester extends JFrame {
  JPanel contentPane;
  BorderLayout borderLayout1 = new BorderLayout();
  JTextField jTextField1 = new JTextField();
  BlueBox blueBox1 = new BlueBox();

  //Construct the frame
  public BlueBoxActionTester() {
    enableEvents(AWTEvent.WINDOW_EVENT_MASK);
    try {
      jbInit();
    }
    catch(Exception e) {
      e.printStackTrace();
    }
  }
  //Component initialization
  private void jbInit() throws Exception  {
    contentPane = (JPanel) this.getContentPane();
    contentPane.setLayout(borderLayout1);
    this.setSize(new Dimension(400, 300));
```

```
      this.setTitle("Frame Title");
      blueBox1.addActionListener(new java.awt.event.ActionListener() {
        public void actionPerformed(ActionEvent e) {
          blueBox1_actionPerformed(e);
        }
      });
      contentPane.add(jTextField1, BorderLayout.NORTH);
      contentPane.add(blueBox1, BorderLayout.CENTER);
    }
    //Overridden so we can exit when window is closed
    protected void processWindowEvent(WindowEvent e) {
      super.processWindowEvent(e);
      if (e.getID() == WindowEvent.WINDOW_CLOSING) {
        System.exit(0);
      }
    }
    int counter;
    void blueBox1_actionPerformed(ActionEvent e) {
      jTextField1.setText("I've been hit: " + ++counter);
    }
}
```

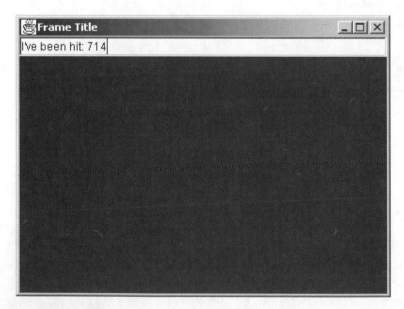

Figure 11-7. The BlueBoxActionTester in action after selecting the BlueBox a few times

WARNING *In this project, you repeatedly hop between differ-ent projects, changing classes in package X that are being used in package Y. If you find that the Design tool is con-fused, meaning it doesn't seem to be picking up changes in a class version from the other package, save everything and restart the tool. This will ensure that the latest class versions are used.*

Making a Red Triangle

Creating a new bean that is rectangular doesn't involve much work: You just define how to draw it, maintain your event list, and determine when to generate the events. Then, whenever the event happens, you notify the event listener lists. If the event has to do with mouse clicks, the click can happen anywhere within the bean. If you want to restrict where the click triggers the event, you have to do a little extra work. In this section, you'll convert the blue box to a red triangle so you can see what I mean.

You'll create the new class in Skill11, so reopen the project. You can use File ➢ Reopen to easily find the project. Create a new class with the Class Wizard and call it **RedTriangle**. Have it extend from **skill11.BlueBox** so you only have to add the customized behavior. Instead of duplicating all the functionality of BlueBox in RedTriangle, you're going to inherit it and just change the undesirable behavior. Click OK after you make the name changes.

First, fill in the javadoc comments for the new class. Use your name and company.

```
/**
 * <p>Title: RedTriangle </p>
 * <p>Description: A red triangular component (with blue background). </p>
 * <p>Copyright:   Copyright (c) 2001 </p>
 * <p>Company: JZ Ventures, Inc. </p>
 * @author John Zukowski
 * @version 1.0
 */
```

As far as the class definition goes, the essential difference between BlueBox and RedTriangle is the painting. For the triangle, you need to define a Polygon that contains the different points of the triangle. Then, you can rely on the fillPolygon() method of Graphics to draw the triangle filled.

A Polygon is another class of AWT. You use it to describe closed figures through a series of points. Your polygon will have three points for the triangle. They can be anywhere within the bean, but you'll use the top-left, bottom-left, and bottom-right corners.

Override the paintComponent() method. While AWT components and applets have you override paint(), with Swing components you override paintComponent(). Swing components can have borders and can contain other components, so you have to make sure paint() still calls paintBorder() and paintChildren(). This is easily accomplished by just overriding the paintComponent() method.

Using the Override Methods Wizard, select the paintComponent(Graphics) method under the javax.swing.JComponent list and click OK. You want to call the superclass' (BlueBox's) paintComponent() method to ensure the background color is drawn, so leave the super.paintComponent() call. Then declare a polygon and place three points in it with addPoint(). Finally, draw it filled with fillPolygon().

```
protected void paintComponent(Graphics g) {
  super.paintComponent(g);
  Dimension d = getSize();
  Polygon p = new Polygon();
  p.addPoint(0, 0);
  p.addPoint(0, d.height);
  p.addPoint(d.width, d.height);
  g.fillPolygon(p);
}
```

NOTE *The reason you have to size the polygon each time is that the screen, and hence the component, may have been resized.*

For the drawing color, set the foreground color in the constructor.

```
public RedTriangle() {
  setForeground(Color.red);
}
```

Working with Nonrectangular Beans

At this point, the RedTriangle works exactly like the BlueBox, but as you would expect, it looks a little different. For the functionality to be distinct—so only double-clicking within the actual triangle triggers the action event—you need to override the contains() method of Component. By default, contains() always returns true, meaning the event happened within the rectangular coordinate space of the component. If you change contains() to only return true while double-clicking within the triangle, you've accomplished your mission. Thankfully, Polygon has a contains() method too. Because it reports if a point is within the polygon, you only need to return what it returns.

Using the Override Methods Wizard, select Component's contain(int, int) method and click OK. Moving the polygon creation code out of paintComponent() and into a shared helper routine, getTriangle(), results in the completed source in Listing 11-5.

Listing 11-5. The Complete RedTriangle.java Source

```java
package skill11;

import javax.swing.*;
import java.awt.*;

/**
 * <p>Title: RedTriangle</p>
 * <p>Description: A red triangular component (with blue background).</p>
 * <p>Copyright:    Copyright (c) 2001</p>
 * <p>Company: JZ Ventures, Inc.</p>
 * @author John Zukowski
 * @version 1.0
 */

public class RedTriangle extends BlueBox {

  public RedTriangle() {
    setForeground(Color.red);
  }
  private Polygon getTriangle() {
    Dimension d = getSize();
    Polygon p = new Polygon();
    p.addPoint(0, 0);
    p.addPoint(0, d.height);
    p.addPoint(d.width, d.height);
    return p;
  }
```

```
protected void paintComponent(Graphics g) {
  super.paintComponent(g);
  Polygon p = getTriangle();
  g.fillPolygon(p);
}
public boolean contains(int x, int y) {
  Polygon p = getTriangle();
  return p.contains(x, y);
}
}
```

At this point, save and compile RedTriangle. Once it's error-free, add it to the Component palette next to the BlueBox by following these steps:

1. Select Tools ➤ Configure Palette.

2. Select the Add components tab.

3. Click the Select library button.

4. Select the BlueBox library.

5. Click the OK button.

6. Enter **Other** in the Palette page.

7. Select the JavaBeans only component filtering option.

8. Click the Add from Selected Library button.

9. Open the skill11 folder and select RedTriangle.

10. Click the OK button.

11. Click the OK button.

12. Click the OK button.

The RedTriangle is now on the Component palette.

Updating the New Tester

If you return to Skill11c, you can add a `RedTriangle` to the test program. Select the `BlueBoxActionTester` in the Navigation pane. Then select the Design tab in the Content pane and choose the Other tab on the Component palette. Next, pick the `RedTriangle` from the Component palette and drop it on the `contentPane` in the Component tree (lower left). If you drop the red triangle into the UI Designer, you may end up dropping the component into the blue box, which you don't want. (You'll correct this behavior when you learn about `BeanInfo` in Skill 13.) Because `BlueBox` and `RedTriangle` are of the subclass `JPanel`, they are considered containers, so other components can be added into them.

After you dropped the `RedTriangle` into the Component tree, the UI Designer probably placed the triangle in the north area and moved the text field to the south. Put the `JTextField` back in the **North** area and move the `RedTriangle` in the **East** area through the Inspector.

The initial size of the red triangle is 10×10. In order for the screen to be a little more interesting, make the preferred size of the triangle 200×1 by entering **200, 1** in the `preferredSize` property of the Inspector. This will effectively give the triangle half the initial screen size (400, 300). Even though you set the height to 1, the component in the east area of a `BorderLayout` container will be as high as the component space allows. Your screen should now look like the one in Figure 11-8.

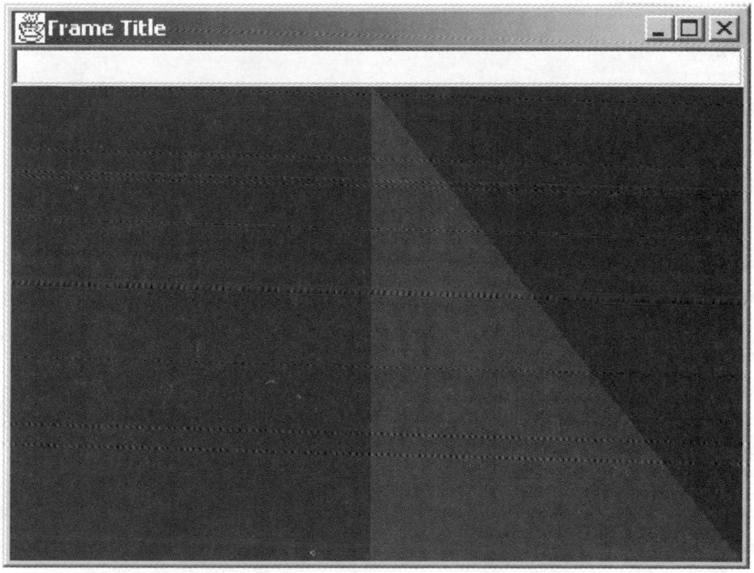

Figure 11-8. The updated BlueBoxActionTester with a BlueBox and a RedTriangle

The last thing to do to wrap up this version of the testing program is to add an action listener to the component. Before double-clicking the component, you're going to change the way JBuilder adds in event handlers. By default, JBuilder will create an anonymous listener for the event handler. If instead you prefer JBuilder to generate standard adapters, full-blown classes, there is a switch within JBuilder you can turn on. If you open up the Project Properties dialog box by selecting Project ➤ Project Properties, you'll see the window in Figure 11-9.

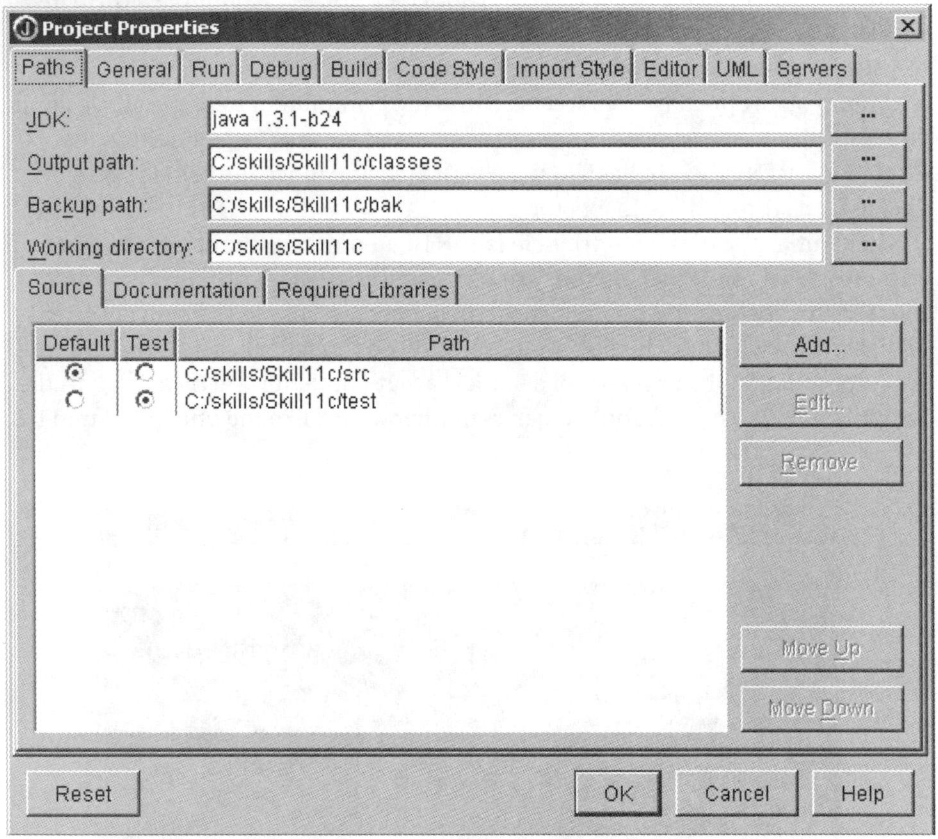

Figure 11-9. The Project Properties dialog box

Select the Code Style tab (see Figure 11-10). From here, if you select Standard adapter, each time you attach a new listener type to the component, a newly named class will be generated and added. Listeners already added aren't changed. The separate adapter classes enable you to more cleanly separate the adapters from the main class, as the definition isn't buried inside another. In the end, the overall number of .class files is not reduced, though, so it tends to be a personal preference thing. After you select Standard adapter, click the OK button and you'll generate the next adapter with the new format.

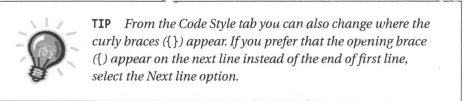

Figure 11-10. The Code Style tab of the Project Properties dialog box

> **TIP** *From the Code Style tab you can also change where the curly braces ({}) appear. If you prefer that the opening brace ({) appear on the next line instead of the end of first line, select the Next line option.*

If you double-click the triangle, you'll make the frame listen for action events within the RedTriangle. Like the BlueBox, you'll change the text in the text field and count the number of hits. The actual action-handling code is minimal.

```
int triCounter;
void redTriangle1_actionPerformed(ActionEvent e) {
  jTextField1.setText("I'm not square: " + ++triCounter);
}
```

The major difference is in the listener attachment. With the default Anonymous adapter behavior, the blue box listener was attached with the following:

```
blueBox1.addActionListener(new java.awt.event.ActionListener() {
  public void actionPerformed(ActionEvent e) {
    blueBox1_actionPerformed(e);
  }
});
```

However, with the new Standard adapter behavior, the red triangle listener was attached with two slightly larger blocks:

```
redTriangle1.addActionListener(
    new BlueBoxActionTester_redTriangle1_actionAdapter(this));
```

and

```
class BlueBoxActionTester_redTriangle1_actionAdapter
    implements java.awt.event.ActionListener {
  BlueBoxActionTester adaptee;

  BlueBoxActionTester_redTriangle1_actionAdapter(BlueBoxActionTester adaptee) {
    this.adaptee = adaptee;
  }
  public void actionPerformed(ActionEvent e) {
    adaptee.redTriangle1_actionPerformed(e);
  }
}
```

While the class name is a little long, it's automatically generated (and used) so you don't have to know it. However, if you look closely, you'll notice an obvious mapping from program, component, and listener to method name.

If you save everything and run the program again, you'll notice that when you double-click the mouse over the red triangle, the text changes in the text field. However, when you double-click in the blue area—still within the triangle's bounding box—the text does not change. Be sure to resize the frame to demonstrate that the size change is tracked properly.

Generating Event-Handling Code with BeansExpress

Now that you've seen how to manually deal with an event set for a component by managing a list of listeners and notifying those listeners when the event happens, let's look into how JBuilder supports automating the process. To demonstrate, you'll build up your box of Lucky Charms and create a green oval. For each click in the oval, an ActionEvent will be generated. For each double-click in the oval, a DoubleActionEvent will be generated. To support the DoubleActionEvent, you'll need to define a DoubleActionListener, too.

For starters, return to the Skill11 project and start the Class Wizard. Call the class **GreenOval** and have it extend from JPanel, like BlueBox. In the constructor, set the background to blue and the foreground to green. In the paintComponent() method, draw a filled oval the size of the component. Add the component to the Other tab of the Component palette. You now have your basic component.

```java
package skill11;

import java.awt.*;
import javax.swing.JPanel;

/**
 * <p>Title: GreenOval</p>
 * <p>Description: A green oval component (with blue background).</p>
 * <p>Copyright: Copyright (c) 2001</p>
 * <p>Company: JZ Ventures, Inc.</p>
 * @author John Zukowski
 * @version 1.0
 */

public class GreenOval extends JPanel {

  public GreenOval() {
    setBackground(Color.blue);
    setForeground(Color.green);
  }
  protected void paintComponent(Graphics g) {
    super.paintComponent(g);
    Dimension d = getSize();
    g.fillOval(0, 0, d.width, d.height);
  }
}
```

For simplicity's sake, you're not going to override `contains()`, so the entire bounding rectangle of the oval is "selectable" once you attach listeners.

Adding Existing Event Sets

In addition to the Source and Design tabs within JBuilder, there is a Bean tab. Selecting the Bean tab brings up the BeansExpress train. The Events tab of BeansExpress is where you find the event-handling support for your bean components. From here, beans can easily be made to listen for events and fire them off when they happen. The only code you have to add is the calling of the firing method. BeansExpress generates the rest for you. Figure 11-11 displays the Events tab of BeansExpress.

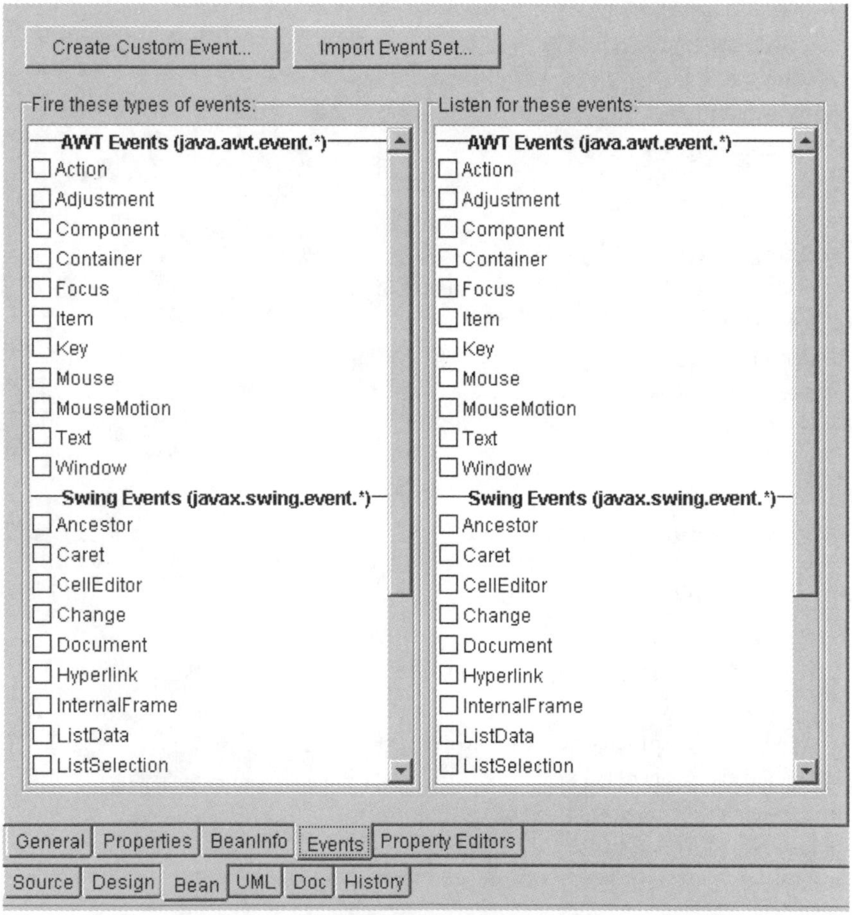

Figure 11-11. The Events tab of BeansExpress generates code so your beans can easily generate and listen for events.

The display is broken up into two areas. The left half of the screen enables you to easily generate events. This is what you did in the earlier "Maintaining Listener Lists" and "Notifying Listeners" sections. The right half of the screen is for listening for events happening in other beans. Essentially, this would be the source you added in the tester program. In both halves, the list of events shown consists of all those in the AWT and Swing event packages: `java.awt.event` and `javax.swing.event`, respectively.

If you select one of the events in the left column, your bean will have add/remove listener methods for that event and a fire method for each of the methods in the listener interface. Because you want your bean to generate ActionEvent objects, select Action in the left column. The generated source that was added to the GreenOval class appears in Listing 11-6.

Listing 11-6. The BeansExpress Generated Source for AWT's ActionEvent

```java
public synchronized void removeActionListener(ActionListener l) {
  if (actionListeners != null && actionListeners.contains(l)) {
    Vector v = (Vector) actionListeners.clone();
    v.removeElement(l);
    actionListeners = v;
  }
}
public synchronized void addActionListener(ActionListener l) {
  Vector v = actionListeners == null ?
    new Vector(2) : (Vector) actionListeners.clone();
  if (!v.contains(l)) {
    v.addElement(l);
    actionListeners = v;
  }
}
private transient Vector actionListeners;
protected void fireActionPerformed(ActionEvent e) {
  if (actionListeners != null) {
    Vector listeners = actionListeners;
    int count = listeners.size();
    for (int i = 0; i < count; i++) {
      ((ActionListener) listeners.elementAt(i)).actionPerformed(e);
    }
  }
}
```

> **NOTE** *Notice that the JBuilder generated code relies on a* Vector *for managing the listener list. There is nothing wrong with that, but the code has some synchronized blocks that weren't necessary when you used* EventListenerList.

Just selecting that one box on the screen is all that is necessary for a bean to generate an event. Because you need to listen for mouse clicks, you can also select Mouse on the right side. The oval will now be a listener for mouse clicks. You still have to add yourself as the listener (addMouseListener(this); in the constructor) and fill in mouseClicked(), but selecting Mouse is the same as picking the event listener interface with the Implement Interface Wizard.

```
public void mouseClicked(MouseEvent e) {
  ActionEvent action = new ActionEvent(
    e.getSource(), ActionEvent.ACTION_PERFORMED, "");
  fireActionPerformed(action);
}
```

You've now essentially duplicated all the non-drawing-related code you manually wrote for the entire BlueBox with two mouse clicks.

Creating Custom Event Sets

One of the buttons on the Events tab I haven't explained yet is labeled "Create Custom Event." When clicked, this button brings up the dialog box in Figure 11-12, which enables you to automate the generation of a new event listener and its related event object. If you find the existing AWT/Swing events aren't sufficient or don't seem appropriate, you can define your own.

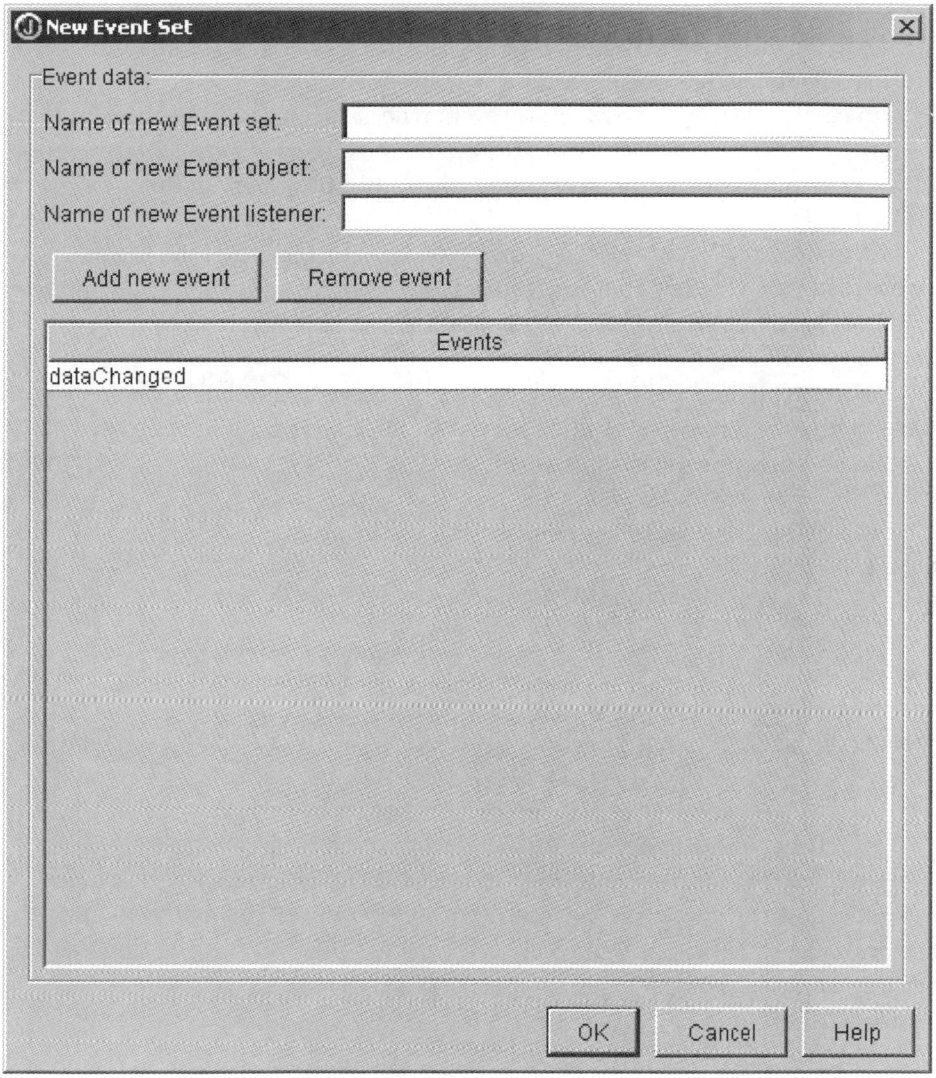

Figure 11-12. You can create custom event sets in the New Event Set dialog box.

Because your green oval needs to generate a DoubleActionEvent and support maintaining a DoubleActionListener list, the event set to generate is DoubleAction. Enter **DoubleAction** in the Name of new Event set field. Notice the other two (read-only) text fields become DoubleActionEvent and DoubleActionListener for you.

The bottom half of the New Event Set dialog box is the type(s) of event in the set. For instance, with the MouseEvent/MouseListener pair, the event types were mouseClicked(), mousePressed(), mouseReleased(), mouseEntered(), and mouseExited(). You just need one event, and you'll call it doubleActionHappened for lack of a better name. Usually, the event types are named with the event set name first followed by some verb (in the past tense). This is not a requirement—it's just something that makes working with events easier.

To create a doubleActionHappened event type, select dataChanged and type over the name. You can also remove the event and add a new one. Once you click OK, you'll notice two additions to your project and a new entry in the BeansExpress screen.

To fire the new event set, select the new DoubleAction under the Custom Events setting on the left and revisit source mode. There will now be add/remove methods for the DoubleActionListener and a fireDoubleActionHappened() method for the single event set.

To finish off the GreenOval, add to its mouseClicked() method a call to fireDoubleActionHappened() when the mouse clicking is a double-click event. Listing 11-7 presents the complete source.

Listing 11-7. The Complete GreenOval.java Source

```java
package skill11;

import javax.swing.JPanel;
import java.awt.*;
import java.awt.event.*;
import java.util.*;

/**
 * <p>Title: GreenOval</p>
 * <p>Description: A green oval component (with blue background).</p>
 * <p>Copyright:   Copyright (c) 2001</p>
 * <p>Company: JZ Ventures, Inc.</p>
 * @author John Zukowski
 * @version 1.0
 */

public class GreenOval extends JPanel implements MouseListener {

  public GreenOval() {
    setBackground(Color.blue);
    setForeground(Color.green);
    addMouseListener(this);
  }
  protected void paintComponent(Graphics g) {
    super.paintComponent(g);
    Dimension d = getSize();
    g.fillOval(0, 0, d.width, d.height);
  }
```

```
public synchronized void removeActionListener(ActionListener l) {
  if (actionListeners != null && actionListeners.contains(l)) {
    Vector v = (Vector) actionListeners.clone();
    v.removeElement(l);
    actionListeners = v;
  }
}
public synchronized void addActionListener(ActionListener l) {
  Vector v = actionListeners == null ?
    new Vector(2) : (Vector) actionListeners.clone();
  if (!v.contains(l)) {
    v.addElement(l);
    actionListeners = v;
  }
}
private transient Vector actionListeners;
private transient Vector doubleActionListeners;
protected void fireActionPerformed(ActionEvent e) {
  if (actionListeners != null) {
    Vector listeners = actionListeners;
    int count = listeners.size();
    for (int i = 0; i < count; i++) {
      ((ActionListener) listeners.elementAt(i)).actionPerformed(e);
    }
  }
}
public void mouseClicked(MouseEvent e) {
  ActionEvent action = new ActionEvent(
    e.getSource(), ActionEvent.ACTION_PERFORMED, "");
  fireActionPerformed(action);
  if (e.getClickCount() == 2) {
    DoubleActionEvent doubleAction = new DoubleActionEvent(e.getSource());
    fireDoubleActionHappened(doubleAction);
  }
}
public void mousePressed(MouseEvent e) {
}
public void mouseReleased(MouseEvent e) {
}
public void mouseEntered(MouseEvent e) {
}
public void mouseExited(MouseEvent e) {
}
```

```java
public synchronized void removeDoubleActionListener(DoubleActionListener l) {
  if (doubleActionListeners != null && doubleActionListeners.contains(l)) {
    Vector v = (Vector) doubleActionListeners.clone();
    v.removeElement(l);
    doubleActionListeners = v;
  }
}
public synchronized void addDoubleActionListener(DoubleActionListener l) {
  Vector v = doubleActionListeners == null ?
    new Vector(2) : (Vector) doubleActionListeners.clone();
  if (!v.contains(l)) {
    v.addElement(l);
    doubleActionListeners = v;
  }
}
protected void fireDoubleActionHappened(DoubleActionEvent e) {
  if (doubleActionListeners != null) {
    Vector listeners = doubleActionListeners;
    int count = listeners.size();
    for (int i = 0; i < count; i++) {
      ((DoubleActionListener) listeners.elementAt(i)).doubleActionHappened(e);
    }
  }
}
}
```

You should now save your project and compile everything to make sure it compiles correctly. Pressing Ctrl-Shift-A for Save All and Ctrl-F9 for Make Project will do this for you.

For completeness, the automatically generated DoubleActionEvent and DoubleActionListener class definitions follow, without header comments.

```java
package skill11;

import java.util.*;

public class DoubleActionEvent extends EventObject {

  public DoubleActionEvent(Object source) {
    super(source);
  }
}
```

and

```
package skill11;

import java.util.*;

public interface DoubleActionListener extends EventListener {
  public void doubleActionHappened(DoubleActionEvent e);
}
```

Updating the New Tester Again

You can now update your test program in Skill11c. Returning to the Skill11c project, add a GreenOval into the south area of the screen and give it a preferred size of **1,100**. This will give you the screen shown in Figure 11-13.

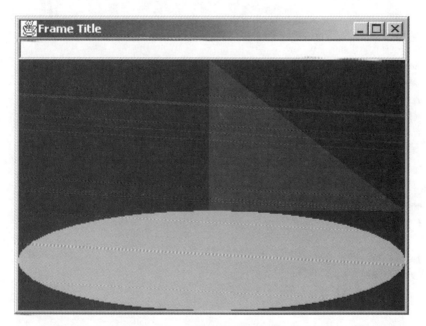

Figure 11-13. The third generation of BlueBoxActionTester, with a BlueBox, RedTriangle, and GreenOval

NOTE *Before you add new listeners, you may want to reset the Code Style tab in the Project Properties dialog box to be of the Anonymous adapter type.*

Double-click the green oval to add an `ActionListener`. As with the other action listeners, set the text field's value and include another counter.

To attach a `DoubleActionListener`, first select the `GreenOval` in the UI Designer. Then select the Events tab in the Inspector. Double-clicking in the doubleActionHappened line will attach a `DoubleActionListener` for you. Just fill in this listener method by setting the text field and maintaining another counter.

You can now save everything and run the program. Clicking in each of the components generates a specific message.

Listing 11-8 presents the final source for the program.

Listing 11-8. The Final `BlueBoxActionTester.java` Source

```
package skill11c;

import java.awt.*;
import java.awt.event.*;
import javax.swing.*;
import skill11.*;

public class BlueBoxActionTester extends JFrame {
  JPanel contentPane;
  BorderLayout borderLayout1 = new BorderLayout();
  JTextField jTextField1 = new JTextField();
  BlueBox blueBox1 = new BlueBox();
  GreenOval greenOval1 = new GreenOval();
  RedTriangle redTriangle1 = new RedTriangle();

  //Construct the frame
  public BlueBoxActionTester() {
    enableEvents(AWTEvent.WINDOW_EVENT_MASK);
    try {
      jbInit();
    }
    catch(Exception e) {
      e.printStackTrace();
    }
  }
  //Component initialization
  private void jbInit() throws Exception  {
    contentPane = (JPanel) this.getContentPane();
    contentPane.setLayout(borderLayout1);
    this.setForeground(Color.red);
    this.setSize(new Dimension(400, 300));
    this.setTitle("Frame Title");
    blueBox1.addActionListener(new java.awt.event.ActionListener() {
```

```java
      public void actionPerformed(ActionEvent e) {
        blueBox1_actionPerformed(e);
      }
    });
    redTriangle1.setPreferredSize(new Dimension(200, 1));
    redTriangle1.addActionListener(
      new BlueBoxActionTester_redTriangle1_actionAdapter(this));
    greenOval1.setPreferredSize(new Dimension(1, 100));
    greenOval1.addDoubleActionListener(new skill11.DoubleActionListener() {
      public void doubleActionHappened(DoubleActionEvent e) {
        greenOval1_doubleActionHappened(e);
      }
    });
    greenOval1.addActionListener(new java.awt.event.ActionListener() {
      public void actionPerformed(ActionEvent e) {
        greenOval1_actionPerformed(e);
      }
    });
    contentPane.add(jTextField1,  BorderLayout.NORTH);
    contentPane.add(blueBox1, BorderLayout.CENTER);
    contentPane.add(redTriangle1,  BorderLayout.EAST);
    contentPane.add(greenOval1,  BorderLayout.SOUTH);
  }
  //Overridden so we can exit when window is closed
  protected void processWindowEvent(WindowEvent e) {
    super.processWindowEvent(e);
    if (e.getID() == WindowEvent.WINDOW_CLOSING) {
      System.exit(0);
    }
  }
  int counter;
  void blueBox1_actionPerformed(ActionEvent e) {
    jTextField1.setText("I've been hit: " + ++counter);
  }

  int triCounter;
  void redTriangle1_actionPerformed(ActionEvent e) {
    jTextField1.setText("I'm not square: " + ++triCounter);
  }

  int ovalCounter;
  void greenOval1_actionPerformed(ActionEvent e) {
    jTextField1.setText("I'm feeling green: " + ++ovalCounter);
  }
```

```
    int doubleCounter;
    void greenOval1_doubleActionHappened(DoubleActionEvent e) {
      jTextField1.setText("I'm feeling doubly green: " + ++doubleCounter);
    }
  }


class BlueBoxActionTester_redTriangle1_actionAdapter
    implements java.awt.event.ActionListener {
  BlueBoxActionTester adaptee;

  BlueBoxActionTester_redTriangle1_actionAdapter(BlueBoxActionTester adaptee) {
    this.adaptee = adaptee;
  }
  public void actionPerformed(ActionEvent e) {
    adaptee.redTriangle1_actionPerformed(e);
  }
}
```

ARE YOU EXPERIENCED?

Congratulations on completing Skill 11! You've made your way through the first of five important skills for creating beans.

Now you can

- Create beans

- Add events to beans manually

- Make visual beans nonrectangular

- Add events to beans with BeansExpress

- Create custom event sets

- Generate anonymous event adapters

- Generate standard event adapters

Now that you're able to add events to your beans, manually or with BeansExpress, it's time to move on to Skill 12, where you'll learn about bean properties. Properties are named attributes of beans. You've actually already used them for the system components.

Creating Beans: Properties

- Creating simple properties

- Creating indexed properties

- Creating bound properties

- Creating constrained properties

- Generating properties with BeansExpress

Introducing Properties

As you learned back in Skill 9, a *property* is a named attribute of a bean. A pair of specially named methods read or set a property's value. While an application developer is within a builder tool, a property editor enables that developer to modify the properties. In JBuilder, this property editor is called the Inspector.

There are different types of properties:

- Simple

- Indexed

- Bound

- Constrained

In this skill, you'll learn about the four different types of bean properties. You'll learn how to create them by hand and how to have JBuilder create them for you with BeansExpress. To demonstrate, you'll start with a simple CyanBox component, which is essentially the initial version of the BlueBox component from the last skill without all the event-handling code and with a different background color.

To create the CyanBox component, first close any open projects. Then start the Project Wizard, not the Application Wizard. Call the project **Skill12** and save it to **C:\skills\Skill12**. Next, start the Class Wizard. Name the class **CyanBox** and have it subclass **javax.swing.JPanel**, just like BlueBox. Leave the four options other then "Generate main method" selected and click OK. After filling in the header comments and adding the line to set the background to cyan, you'll have the beginning of your CyanBox component shown in Listing 12-1.

Listing 12-1. The Initial CyanBox.java Source

```
package skill12;

import javax.swing.JPanel;
import java.awt.*;

/**
 * <p>Title: CyanBox</p>
 * <p>Description: A rectangular JavaBean component that is cyan.</p>
 * <p>Copyright: Copyright (c) 2001</p>
 * <p>Company: JZ Ventures, Inc.</p>
 * @author John Zukowski
```

```
 * @version 1.0
 */


public class CyanBox extends JPanel {

  public CyanBox() {
    setBackground(Color.cyan);
  }
}
```

Working with Simple Properties

As their name implies, *simple properties* are the simplest to work with. A simple property is defined by a set of routines: one called set and one called get. The rest of the method signature defines the property name and data type. The set routine enables you to change the property value, while the get routine enables you to retrieve the value.

```
public DataType getPropertyName()
public void setPropertyName(DataType value)
```

There are many different properties you can add to the CyanBox to make the component more interesting. One such property you can add to the CyanBox is a text label. Instead of just being a solid color, your box can have a text label in the middle of the component. Then, when someone uses the component, that person can define what he or she wants the box label to be.

To add a text label property to the component, you need to create an instance variable to save the property value, define the set and get methods for the property, and draw the property setting, as follows:

1. Add an instance variable to save the value of the text label. As a general rule of thumb, all instance variables for properties should be private.

    ```
    private String textLabel;
    ```

2. Add a setText() method.

    ```
    public void setText(String value) {
      textLabel = value;
      repaint();
    }
    ```

TIP *Whenever you change a visible aspect of a component, don't forget to tell the component to* repaint() *the display.*

3.   Add a getText() method.

```
public String getText() {
   return textLabel;
}
```

NOTE *If the data type of the property is* boolean, *the name of the* get *routine can have the prefix of* is *instead of* get. *For instance, for a property named* active *of type* boolean, *the set method would be* setActive() *and the get routine would be* isActive().

4.   Override paintComponent() to draw the text label. To find out the size of the label, you need to convert the method's Graphics argument to a Graphics2D, ask for the font, and then ask the font for the bounds of the label and the metrics of the label. Based on those bounds and the line metrics, you can center the label horizontally. Drawing a string requires the baseline for the string, not the middle of the string, so there are a few extra calculations necessary.

```
import java.awt.font.*;
import java.awt.geom.*;
  . . .
public void paintComponent(Graphics g) {
   super.paintComponent(g);
   Graphics2D g2d = (Graphics2D)g;
   if (textLabel != null) {
      FontRenderContext fontRenderContext = g2d.getFontRenderContext();
      Font font = g.getFont();
      Rectangle2D bounds = font.getStringBounds(textLabel,
      fontRenderContext);
      double stringWidth = bounds.getWidth();
      double stringHeight = bounds.getHeight();
      LineMetrics lineMetrics =
```

```
    font.getLineMetrics(textLabel, fontRenderContext);
  float x = (float)((getWidth() - stringWidth)/2.0);
  float y = (float)((getHeight() + stringHeight)/2.0) -
    lineMetrics.getDescent() - lineMetrics.getLeading();
  g2d.drawString(textLabel, x, y);
 }
}
```

NOTE *The name of the property added is* text. *Its name arrives from the* set/get *method names, not from the instance variable (*textLabel, *in this case).*

Now, save and compile the bean, and then add it to the Component palette. Select Tools ➤ Configure Palette. Select Other in the Pages column in the Palette Properties window, and then select the Add components tab. Click the Select library button, and then click New. Name the library **Skill12** and add the base directory for the skill, **C:\skills\Skill12**. Click OK until you are back at the Palette Properties window, select the JavaBeans only Component filtering option, and then click Add from Selected Library. Find and select the CyanBox component, and then click OK three more times. Your button is now on the palette.

Because CyanBox is a bean component and not an application, you'll need to create a program to run it. Instead of creating a new project to test the bean, just run the Application Wizard here. Name the frame class **CyanTester** on the second screen and click Finish to create the testing framework. With CyanTester, select the Design tab and drop a CyanBox into the center of the frame.

First, if you look in the Inspector, you'll see that there is a text property for the CyanBox (see Figure 12-1). This is the one you just created. Second, JBuilder actually initialized the property for you to the name of the component. This is a "feature" of JBuilder limited to properties named text. Had the property had another name it would not have been initialized. If you run the program now, you'll see that the label is indeed centered (see Figure 12-2). Feel free to change the label before running the program or change the frame size once the frame is displayed and the text label will remain centered.

name	cyanBox1
constraints	Center
actionMap	
alignmentX	0.5
alignmentY	0.5
background	☐ Cyan
border	
debugGraphicsOptio...	<default>
doubleBuffered	True
enabled	True
font	"Dialog", 0, 12
foreground	■ Black
inputVerifier	
layout	<default layout>
maximumSize	32767, 32767
minimumSize	10, 10
nextFocusableComp...	
opaque	True
preferredSize	10, 10
requestFocusEnabled	True
text	cyanBox1
toolTipText	
verifyInputWhenFocu...	True

Properties | Events

Figure 12-1. The Inspector for the CyanBox with the text property available

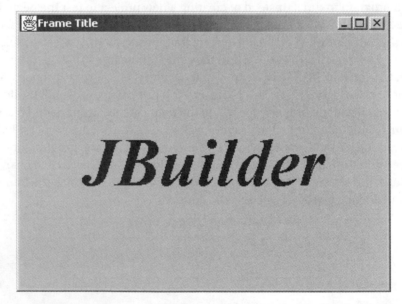

Figure 12-2. The CyanTester program with a CyanBox in the middle and a text label of JBuilder in a 72-point, bold, italic, Serif font

Working with Indexed Properties

An *indexed property* is a property that can hold an array of values within a single property. When creating your own properties to be indexed, there are four methods you need to define:

```
public DataType[ ] getPropertyName()
public DataType getPropertyName(int position)
public void setPropertyName(DataType value[ ])
public void setPropertyName(DataType value, int position)
```

An example of an indexed property is the items property of the com.borland.dbswing.JdbList component (the tenth component on the dbSwing tab of the Component palette). When setting an indexed property, JBuilder can provide a different interface (shown in Figure 12-3) to support entering multiple items—String objects in the case of the items property here.

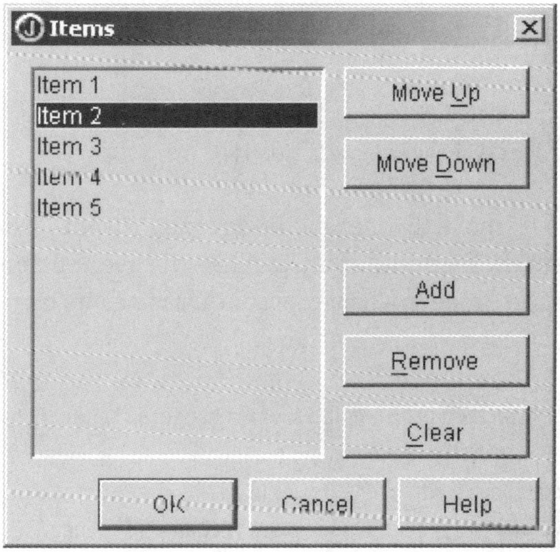

Figure 12-3. The property editor for an indexed property in JBuilder

There aren't any obvious indexed properties for the CyanBox, so move on to the next type of property, bound, instead of trying to force the issue.

Working with Bound Properties

A *bound property* is for when you want property changes to propagate from bean to bean to bean. For instance, if there are ten cyan boxes on a screen, and they all should have the same label, you can make the text property a bound property and register each box as interested when the property changes. Then, only one text label change is necessary and that one change will propagate out to the other beans, keeping the label consistent across all the components. However, there has to be a way to change the property at runtime for this to really be useful. Imagine changing color schemes in a program as a useful application of this.

In order to demonstrate, let's change the text property of CyanBox to be bound. For every class with a bound property, the same code needs to be added. Later in the chapter you'll learn how to make JBuilder do this for you.

1. Create a property-change listener list to manage the list of listeners. The java.beans package has a support class for this called PropertyChangeSupport. The variable name can be anything.

   ```
   import java.beans.*;
     . . .
      private transient PropertyChangeSupport propertyChangeListeners =
         new PropertyChangeSupport(this);
   ```

2. Create add/remove listener methods for a PropertyChangeListener. Fortunately, these methods are just like the event listener add/remove methods. The PropertyChangeSupport class has its own pair of add/remove listener methods to call.

   ```
   public synchronized void addPropertyChangeListener(PropertyChangeListener
   l) {
      super.addPropertyChangeListener(l);
      propertyChangeListeners.addPropertyChangeListener(l);
   }
   public synchronized void
   removePropertyChangeListener(PropertyChangeListener l) {
      super.removePropertyChangeListener(l);
      propertyChangeListeners.removePropertyChangeListener(l);
   }
   ```

NOTE *It is necessary to call the superclass' add/remove listener methods in case the parent class manages its own list of listeners. In the case of any* `java.awt.Component` *subclass, these methods are actually public and you don't have to provide your own methods or listener list. However, here you're learning how to manage the listener lists yourself, for when you're not using a* `Component` *subclass.*

3. Modify the set*Property*() method to notify the listeners. Notification is done through the `firePropertyChange()` method of `PropertyChangeSupport`.

```java
public void setText(String value) {
    String  oldText = textLabel;
    textLabel = value;
    propertyChangeListeners.firePropertyChange("text", oldText, textLabel);
    repaint();
}
```

NOTE *It isn't necessary to check if the property value actually changed. The* `firePropertyChange()` *method does this internally for you.*

There are two things to point out here in the property setter method. First, the `firePropertyChange()` method passes along the name of the property that changed. This means that any listener needs to check the name before it can react to the event. Otherwise, it might be responding to a bound property change of the wrong property. Second, it passes both the old and new value. This means that you have to save the old value before you change it. The notification happens after the property value has changed. If you need notification prior to the change happening, see the next section, "Working with Constrained Properties."

At this point, save and compile the CyanBox so you can test it.

Returning to the test program, CyanTester, place two additional cyan box components on the screen (add one with a North constraint and another with a South constraint). The way the program will work is when the text property of the first box changes, the change propagates to the other two boxes. If the text property of either of the other two boxes changes, this change doesn't propagate, meaning each can change its property without the change propagating.

Each component *should* register its own `PropertyChangeListener` with the interested party so that it can handle the change accordingly:

```
import java.beans.*;
. . .
cyanBox1.addPropertyChangeListener(new java.beans.PropertyChangeListener() {
  public void propertyChange(PropertyChangeEvent e) {
    if (e.getPropertyName().equals("text")) {
      String newValue = (String)e.getNewValue();
      cyanBox2.setText(newValue);
    }
  }
});
cyanBox1.addPropertyChangeListener(new java.beans.PropertyChangeListener() {
  public void propertyChange(PropertyChangeEvent e) {
    if (e.getPropertyName().equals("text")) {
      String newValue = (String)e.getNewValue();
      cyanBox3.setText(newValue);
    }
  }
});
```

However, the JBuilder interface doesn't support having multiple listeners like this, so you'll need to merge the two together. If you double-click in the propertyChange entry on the Events tab for the first cyan box, you can add the following code:

```
if (e.getPropertyName().equals("text")) {
  String newValue = (String)e.getNewValue();
  cyanBox2.setText(newValue);
  cyanBox3.setText(newValue);
}
```

Now any change to the text property of cyanBox1 will propagate to cyanBox2 and cyanBox3. In order to demonstrate something, it's necessary to add code to change the label. If you double-click in mousePressed for each box, you can add the appropriate source. In the case of the "trigger" box, it's necessary to alternate the label change or else once the label changes once, future calls to setText() won't propagate because the property won't be changing.

```
void cyanBox3_mousePressed(MouseEvent e) {
  cyanBox3.setText("Third");
}
```

```
void cyanBox2_mousePressed(MouseEvent e) {
  cyanBox2.setText("Second");
}

void cyanBox1_mousePressed(MouseEvent e) {
  int rand = (int)(Math.random()*10);
  cyanBox1.setText("First"+rand);
}
```

Listing 12-2 shows the current version of the source for the testing program. Figure 12-4 shows the test program in action.

Listing 12-2. The Current CyanTester.java Source

```
package skill12;

import java.awt.*;
import java.awt.event.*;
import javax.swing.*;
import java.beans.*;

public class CyanTester extends JFrame {
  JPanel contentPane;
  BorderLayout borderLayout1 = new BorderLayout();
  CyanBox cyanBox1 = new CyanBox();
  CyanBox cyanBox2 = new CyanBox();
  CyanBox cyanBox3 = new CyanBox();

  //Construct the frame
  public CyanTester() {
    enableEvents(AWTEvent.WINDOW_EVENT_MASK);
    try {
      jbInit();
    }
    catch(Exception e) {
      e.printStackTrace();
    }
  }
  //Component initialization
  private void jbInit() throws Exception  {
    contentPane = (JPanel) this.getContentPane();
    contentPane.setLayout(borderLayout1);
    this.setSize(new Dimension(400, 300));
    this.setTitle("Frame Title");
```

```java
      cyanBox1.setFont(new java.awt.Font("Serif", 3, 72));
      cyanBox1.setText("JBuilder");
      cyanBox1.addMouseListener(new java.awt.event.MouseAdapter() {
        public void mousePressed(MouseEvent e) {
          cyanBox1_mousePressed(e);
        }
      });
      cyanBox1.addPropertyChangeListener(new java.beans.PropertyChangeListener() {
        public void propertyChange(PropertyChangeEvent e) {
          cyanBox1_propertyChange(e);
        }
      });
      cyanBox2.setText("cyanBox2");
      cyanBox2.addMouseListener(new java.awt.event.MouseAdapter() {
        public void mousePressed(MouseEvent e) {
          cyanBox2_mousePressed(e);
        }
      });
      cyanBox3.setText("cyanBox3");
      cyanBox3.addMouseListener(new java.awt.event.MouseAdapter() {
        public void mousePressed(MouseEvent e) {
          cyanBox3_mousePressed(e);
        }
      });
      contentPane.add(cyanBox1,  BorderLayout.CENTER);
      contentPane.add(cyanBox2,  BorderLayout.NORTH);
      contentPane.add(cyanBox3, BorderLayout.SOUTH);
    }
    //Overridden so we can exit when window is closed
    protected void processWindowEvent(WindowEvent e) {
      super.processWindowEvent(e);
      if (e.getID() == WindowEvent.WINDOW_CLOSING) {
        System.exit(0);
      }
    }
    void cyanBox1_propertyChange(PropertyChangeEvent e) {
      if (e.getPropertyName().equals("text")) {
        String newValue = (String)e.getNewValue();
        cyanBox2.setText(newValue);
        cyanBox3.setText(newValue);
      }
    }
```

```
void cyanBox3_mousePressed(MouseEvent e) {
  cyanBox3.setText("Third");
}

void cyanBox2_mousePressed(MouseEvent e) {
  cyanBox2.setText("Second");
}

void cyanBox1_mousePressed(MouseEvent e) {
  int rand = (int)(Math.random()*10);
  cyanBox1.setText("First"+rand);
}
}
```

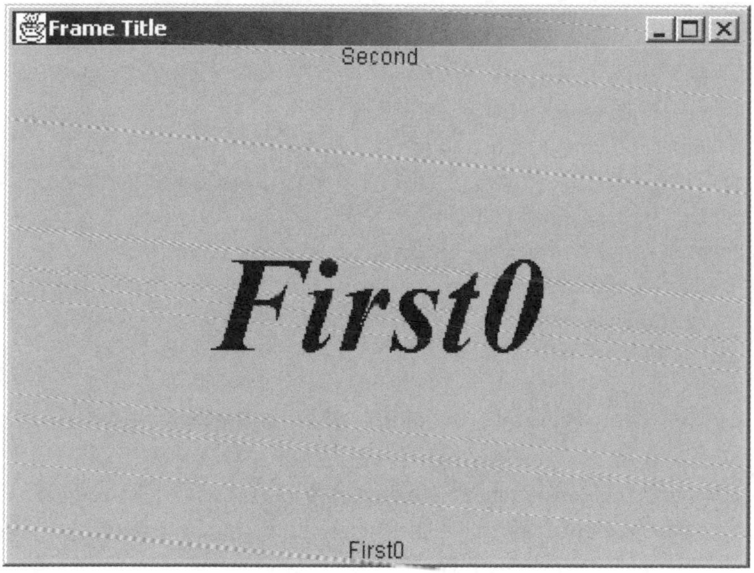

Figure 12-4. The CyanTester text program with the text property bound between boxes

Working with Constrained Properties

The fourth type of property is *constrained.* Constrained properties take bound properties one level further. When the set method of a bound property is called, the bean asks anyone interested if the new value is okay before it changes the actual value. If the new value isn't appropriate for some reason, the listener can reject the change, and the original change request will be aborted. What frequently happens next is the constrained property is also bound, so anyone interested in successful property changes will be notified.

Similar to bound properties, for every constrained property, the same code needs to be added. Perform the following steps to make the text property of CyanBox constrained as well as bound:

1. Create a vetoable-change listener list to manage the list of listeners. The java.beans package has a support class for this called VetoableChangeSupport. The variable name can be anything.

```
private transient VetoableChangeSupport vetoableChangeListeners =
    new VetoableChangeSupport(this);
```

2. Create add/remove listener methods for a VetoableChangeListener. Like PropertyChangeSupport, VetoableChangeSupport has the appropriate add and remove listener methods to call.

```
public synchronized void addVetoableChangeListener(VetoableChangeListener
l) {
    super.addVetoableChangeListener(l);
    vetoableChangeListeners.addVetoableChangeListener(l);
}
public synchronized void
removeVetoableChangeListener(VetoableChangeListener l) {
    super.removeVetoableChangeListener(l);
    vetoableChangeListeners.removeVetoableChangeListener(l);
}
```

3. Modify the set*Property*() method to notify the listeners. Notification is done through the fireVetoableChange() method of VetoableChangeSupport. The fireVetoableChange() method can throw a PropertyVetoException. This means all callers of the method must do so within a try-catch block.

```
public void setText(String text) throws PropertyVetoException {
    String  oldText = textLabel;
    vetoableChangeListeners.fireVetoableChange("text", oldText, text);
    textLabel = text;
    propertyChangeListeners.firePropertyChange("text", oldText, text);
    repaint();
}
```

If a VetoableChangeListener rejects the change, a PropertyVetoException is thrown and the line textLabel = text; is never reached. Save and compile the CyanBox class. The source for the class follows in Listing 12-3.

Listing 12-3. The Final Hand-Created CyanBox.java Source

```java
package skill12;

import javax.swing.JPanel;
import java.awt.*;
import java.awt.font.*;
import java.awt.geom.*;
import java.beans.*;

/**
 * <p>Title: CyanBox</p>
 * <p>Description: A rectangular JavaBean component that is cyan.</p>
 * <p>Copyright: Copyright (c) 2001</p>
 * <p>Company: JZ Ventures, Inc.</p>
 * @author John Zukowski
 * @version 3.0
 */  [Easier to cut and paste . . . no code changes, just comments.]
public class CyanBox extends JPanel {

  private String textLabel;
  private transient PropertyChangeSupport propertyChangeListeners =
    new PropertyChangeSupport(this);
  private transient VetoableChangeSupport vetoableChangeListeners =
    new VetoableChangeSupport(this);

  public CyanBox() {
    setBackground(Color.cyan);
  }

  public void setText(String text) throws PropertyVetoException {
    String  oldText = textLabel;
    vetoableChangeListeners.fireVetoableChange("text", oldText, text);
    textLabel = text;
    propertyChangeListeners.firePropertyChange("text", oldText, text);
    repaint();
  }

  public String getText() {
    return textLabel;
  }
```

```java
public synchronized void addPropertyChangeListener(PropertyChangeListener l) {
  super.addPropertyChangeListener(l);
  propertyChangeListeners.addPropertyChangeListener(l);
}

public synchronized void removePropertyChangeListener(PropertyChangeListener l) {
  super.removePropertyChangeListener(l);
  propertyChangeListeners.removePropertyChangeListener(l);
}

public synchronized void addVetoableChangeListener(VetoableChangeListener l) {
  super.addVetoableChangeListener(l);
  vetoableChangeListeners.addVetoableChangeListener(l);
}

public synchronized void removeVetoableChangeListener(VetoableChangeListener l) {
  super.removeVetoableChangeListener(l);
  vetoableChangeListeners.removeVetoableChangeListener(l);
}

public void paintComponent(Graphics g) {
  super.paintComponent(g);
  Graphics2D g2d = (Graphics2D)g;
  if (textLabel != null) {
    FontRenderContext fontRenderContext = g2d.getFontRenderContext();
    Font font = g.getFont();
    Rectangle2D bounds = font.getStringBounds(textLabel, fontRenderContext);
    double stringWidth = bounds.getWidth();
    double stringHeight = bounds.getHeight();
    LineMetrics lineMetrics =
      font.getLineMetrics(textLabel, fontRenderContext);
    float x = (float)((getWidth() - stringWidth)/2.0);
    float y = (float)((getHeight() + stringHeight)/2.0) -
      lineMetrics.getDescent()-lineMetrics.getLeading();
    g2d.drawString(textLabel, x, y);
  }
}
}
```

Now that there is something to veto, you can veto any specific changes to the text label you don't like. For instance, if you don't like the number 7 as part of the text label, veto the change. Select the vetoableChange entry in the Event tab of the Inspector for the first box and enter in the following source:

```
if (e.getPropertyName().equals("text")) {
  String newText = (String)e.getNewValue();
  if (newText.endsWith("7")) {
    throw new PropertyVetoException("7 is an unlucky number", e);
  }
}
```

This essentially says if the property to change is the "text" property and the last character of the next text label is "7", then reject the change.

Another change you'll need to make is to add try-catch blocks around all calls to setText(). This is a necessary evil when using constrained properties. Listing 12-4 lists the final version of the testing program.

Listing 12-4. The Final CyanTester.java Source

```
package skill12;

import java.awt.*;
import java.awt.event.*;
import javax.swing.*;
import java.beans.*;

public class CyanTester extends JFrame {
  JPanel contentPane;
  BorderLayout borderLayout1 = new BorderLayout();
  CyanBox cyanBox1 = new CyanBox();
  CyanBox cyanBox2 = new CyanBox();
  CyanBox cyanBox3 = new CyanBox();

  //Construct the frame
  public CyanTester() {
    enableEvents(AWTEvent.WINDOW_EVENT_MASK);
    try {
      jbInit();
    }
    catch(Exception e) {
      e.printStackTrace();
    }
  }
```

```
//Component initialization
private void jbInit() throws Exception  {
  contentPane = (JPanel) this.getContentPane();
  contentPane.setLayout(borderLayout1);
  this.setSize(new Dimension(400, 300));
  this.setTitle("Frame Title");
  cyanBox1.setFont(new java.awt.Font("Serif", 3, 72));
  cyanBox1.setText("JBuilder");
  cyanBox1.addVetoableChangeListener(new java.beans.VetoableChangeListener() {
    public void vetoableChange(PropertyChangeEvent e)
        throws PropertyVetoException {
      cyanBox1_vetoableChange(e);
    }
  });
  cyanBox1.addMouseListener(new java.awt.event.MouseAdapter() {
    public void mousePressed(MouseEvent e) {
      cyanBox1_mousePressed(e);
    }
  });
  cyanBox1.addPropertyChangeListener(new java.beans.PropertyChangeListener() {
    public void propertyChange(PropertyChangeEvent e) {
      cyanBox1_propertyChange(e);
    }
  });
  cyanBox2.setText("cyanBox2");
  cyanBox2.addMouseListener(new java.awt.event.MouseAdapter() {
    public void mousePressed(MouseEvent e) {
      cyanBox2_mousePressed(e);
    }
  });
  cyanBox3.setText("cyanBox3");
  cyanBox3.addMouseListener(new java.awt.event.MouseAdapter() {
    public void mousePressed(MouseEvent e) {
      cyanBox3_mousePressed(e);
    }
  });
  contentPane.add(cyanBox1,  BorderLayout.CENTER);
  contentPane.add(cyanBox2,  BorderLayout.NORTH);
  contentPane.add(cyanBox3, BorderLayout.SOUTH);
}
```

```
//Overridden so we can exit when window is closed
protected void processWindowEvent(WindowEvent e) {
  super.processWindowEvent(e);
  if (e.getID() == WindowEvent.WINDOW_CLOSING) {
    System.exit(0);
  }
}
void cyanBox1_propertyChange(PropertyChangeEvent e) {
  if (e.getPropertyName().equals("text")) {
    String newValue = (String)e.getNewValue();
    try {
      cyanBox2.setText(newValue);
      cyanBox3.setText(newValue);
    } catch (PropertyVetoException propertyVetoException) {
      System.err.println("Unable to change button 2&3");
    }
  }
}


void cyanBox3_mousePressed(MouseEvent e) {
  try {
    cyanBox3.setText("Third");
  } catch (PropertyVetoException propertyVetoException) {
    System.err.println("Unable to change button 3");
  }
}


void cyanBox2_mousePressed(MouseEvent e) {
  try {
    cyanBox2.setText("Second");
  } catch (PropertyVetoException propertyVetoException) {
    System.err.println("Unable to change button 2");
  }
}


void cyanBox1_mousePressed(MouseEvent e) {
  try {
    int rand = (int)(Math.random()*10);
    cyanBox1.setText("First"+rand);
  } catch (PropertyVetoException propertyVetoException) {
    System.err.println("Unable to change button 1");
  }
}
```

```
      void cyanBox1_vetoableChange(PropertyChangeEvent e)
         throws PropertyVetoException {
      if (e.getPropertyName().equals("text")) {
        String newText = (String)e.getNewValue();
        if (newText.endsWith("7")) {
          throw new PropertyVetoException("7 is an unlucky number", e);
        }
      }
    }
  }
}
```

Generating Properties with BeansExpress

Now that you've seen how to manually create properties for beans, let's look into how JBuilder can automate this for you. To demonstrate, you'll recreate the CyanBox component and run the CyanTester program against that component instead.

Run the Class Wizard to create a component called **CyanBox2**. Have its base class be javax.swing.JPanel, just like the original CyanBox. Once the class is generated, click the Bean tab at the bottom for CyanBox2, and then select the Properties subtab. This will bring you to the screen shown in Figure 12-5.

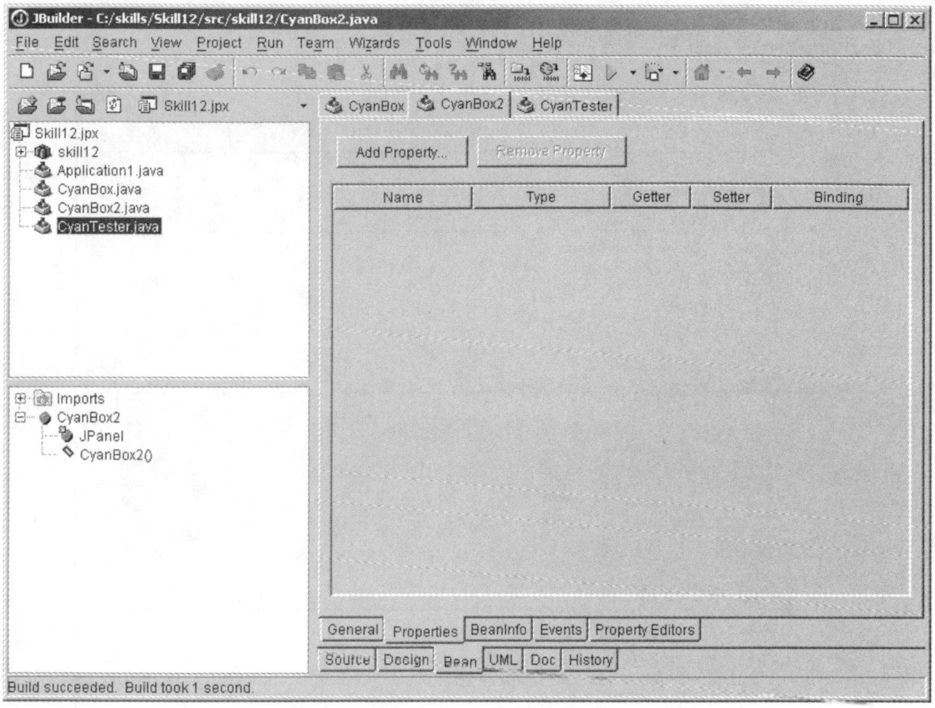

Figure 12-5. JBuilder's property editor from BeansExpress

The original CyanBox had a text property of type String, so you'll need to add the same property here. Clicking the Add Property button brings up the New Property window (see Figure 12-6).

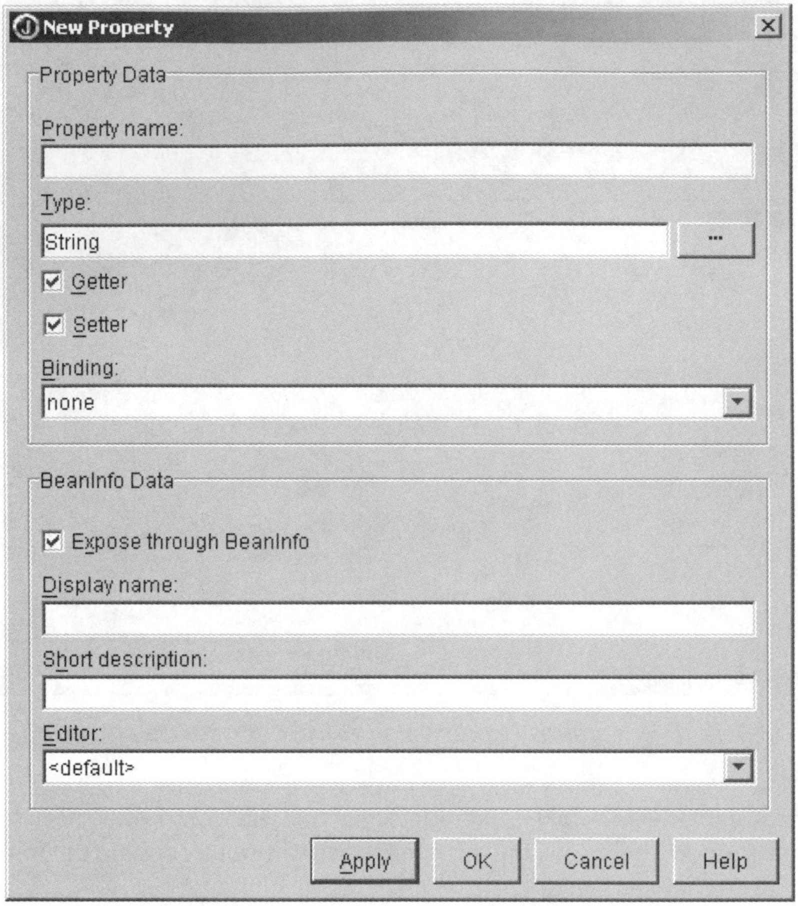

New Property ×

Property Data

Property name:

Type:

String ...

☑ Getter

☑ Setter

Binding:

none ▼

BeanInfo Data

☑ Expose through BeanInfo

Display name:

Short description:

Editor:

<default> ▼

Apply OK Cancel Help

Figure 12-6. The New Property dialog box for creating new properties

NOTE *BeansExpress doesn't support creating indexed proper-ties—it only supports simple, bound, and constrained.*

Enter a Property name of **text**, leave the default Type of String, and select a binding of **constrained** from the binding options. When you click OK all the source code you previously created by hand to make a bound/constrained property for the component is automatically generated. You're left with four things you'll have to manually add to the source. In the constructor, add the call to setBackground(Color.cyan). Next, you'll need to add in the repaint() call to the end of the setText() method. Also, you'll have to copy the paintComponent()

method to draw the text. In `paintComponent()`, you'll need to change the reference to the `textLabel` variable to `text`. JBuilder automatically uses the property name as the variable name. Finally, don't forget to pull over the import lines for the `java.awt`, `java.awt.font`, and `java.awt.geom` packages.

At this point, you can return to the `CyanTester` program and change the three lines at the top to create `CyanBox2` objects instead of `CyanBox` objects, as follows:

```
CyanBox2 cyanBox1 = new CyanBox2();
CyanBox2 cyanBox2 = new CyanBox2();
CyanBox2 cyanBox3 = new CyanBox2();
```

If you run the program again, everything will work fine. And, you hardly had to write any code. The complete version of the `CyanBox2` source follows in Listing 12-5.

Listing 12-5. The Complete System-Generated CyanBox2.java Source

```java
package skill12;

import javax.swing.JPanel;
import java.beans.*;
import java.awt.*;
import java.awt.font.*;
import java.awt.geom.*;

/**
 * <p>Title: CyanBox2</p>
 * <p>Description:  A rectangular JavaBean component that is cyan.
 *                  Includes bound/constrained text property. </p>
 * <p>Copyright: Copyright (c) 2001 </p>
 * <p>Company: JZ Ventures, Inc. </p>
 * @author John Zukowski
 * @version 4.0
 */

public class CyanBox2 extends JPanel {

  public CyanBox2() {
    setBackground(Color.cyan);
  }
  private String text;
  private transient PropertyChangeSupport propertyChangeListeners =
    new PropertyChangeSupport(this);
```

```
        private transient VetoableChangeSupport vetoableChangeListeners =
          new VetoableChangeSupport(this);
        public String getText() {
          return text;
        }
        public void setText(String text) throws java.beans.PropertyVetoException {
          String  oldText = this.text;
          vetoableChangeListeners.fireVetoableChange("text", oldText, text);
          this.text = text;
          propertyChangeListeners.firePropertyChange("text", oldText, text);
          repaint();
        }
        public synchronized void removePropertyChangeListener(PropertyChangeListener l) {
          super.removePropertyChangeListener(l);
          propertyChangeListeners.removePropertyChangeListener(l);
        }
        public synchronized void addPropertyChangeListener(PropertyChangeListener l) {
          super.addPropertyChangeListener(l);
          propertyChangeListeners.addPropertyChangeListener(l);
        }
        public synchronized void removeVetoableChangeListener(VetoableChangeListener l) {
          super.removeVetoableChangeListener(l);
          vetoableChangeListeners.removeVetoableChangeListener(l);
        }
        public synchronized void addVetoableChangeListener(VetoableChangeListener l) {
          super.addVetoableChangeListener(l);
          vetoableChangeListeners.addVetoableChangeListener(l);
        }
        public void paintComponent(Graphics g) {
          super.paintComponent(g);
          Graphics2D g2d = (Graphics2D)g;
          if (text != null) {
            FontRenderContext fontRenderContext = g2d.getFontRenderContext();
            Font font = g.getFont();
            Rectangle2D bounds = font.getStringBounds(text, fontRenderContext);
            double stringWidth = bounds.getWidth();
            double stringHeight = bounds.getHeight();
            LineMetrics lineMetrics =
              font.getLineMetrics(text, fontRenderContext);
```

```
      float x = (float)((getWidth() - stringWidth)/2.0);
      float y = (float)((getHeight() + stringHeight)/2.0) -
        lineMetrics.getDescent()-lineMetrics.getLeading();
      g2d.drawString(text, x, y);
    }
  }
}
```

ARE YOU EXPERIENCED?

Congratulations! Your beans are getting better. Now they can have events and properties. After working your way through manually creating simple, indexed, bound, and constrained properties, you worked your way up to creating properties automatically through BeansExpress.

Now you can

- Add simple, index, bound, and constrained properties to beans

- Calculate text size through the FontRenderContext and LineMetrics

- Handle bound and constrained properties

- Use BeansExpress to create properties

Now it's time to move on to Skill 13, where you'll learn about introspecting classes and using BeanInfo to have your beans present themselves in a friendlier manner.

Creating Beans: Introspection

- Understanding introspection

- Looking into reflection

- Examining the BeanInfo interface

- Turning off container status

- Working with property and event set descriptors

Introducing Introspection

Skill 9 described introspection as the process of discovering information about a bean. The bean-connection tool, JBuilder, does this to decide what to show in the Inspector window when a developer is using the UI Designer. By default, JBuilder lists a property for each set of set*PropertyName*() and get*PropertyName*() methods. Under the Inspector's Event tab, JBuilder lists the methods for each event listener defined by a pair of add*EventTypeListener*() and remove*EventTypeListener*() methods. JBuilder examines the bean class file for all the different methods. For each pair that follows the appropriate naming pattern, a property or event is defined. This inspection process is called *introspection.*

In this skill, you'll see how introspection works and look into the BeanInfo interface to restrict what is sent back during introspection. Unless you override the default behavior, BeanInfo relies on reflection to inspect a class.

Introducing Reflection

By default, bean inspection uses the java.lang.reflect package to discover and use bean information. To demonstrate how reflection works, you'll create a program that displays a JFrame instance and prompts for a command in a text field. Three actions will be supported:

- bigger: To make the frame 10 percent larger

- smaller: To make the frame 5 percent smaller

- *Anything else:* The program checks to see if the command is a predefined Color. If so, it changes the frame background to that color; otherwise, nothing is done.

This program sounds rather simple and could be done completely without reflection. However, the way you're going to create the program will demonstrate the magic that JBuilder performs to work with classes it never knew about when Borland created it.

Let's start by creating the basics of the program, and then I'll talk about reflection and add in all the magic. Close any open projects in JBuilder and run the Application Wizard. Name the project **Skill13** and place it in **C:\skills\Skill13**. On the second page of the Application Wizard, name the class **Lookup**. Next, go into the UI Designer for Lookup.java and drop a JTextField from the Swing tab into the top of the screen. Make sure it ends up with a constraints property setting of North, and clear out the initial text setting.

Now, if you create `bigger()` and `smaller()` methods, you can use reflection to execute the methods without directly calling them.

```
public void bigger() {
  Dimension dim = getSize();
  int width = (int)(dim.width * 1.1);
  int height = (int)(dim.height * 1.1);
  setSize(width, height);
  validate();
}
public void smaller() {
  Dimension dim = getSize();
  int width = (int)(dim.width * 0.95);
  int height = (int)(dim.height * 0.95);
  setSize(width, height);
  validate();
}
```

At this point, you could add an action listener to the text field: If the input is **bigger**, call the `bigger()` method, and if it's **smaller**, call the `smaller()` method. Instead, you're going to use reflection to locate a method with the name entered and call it indirectly.

When you work with reflection, the first class you need to know about is the `java.lang.Class` class. Every instance of a class has a `Class` associated with it. The `Class` class holds the keys for unlocking access to the properties and methods of a class instance. There are two ways to get the `Class` instance associated with a specific class:

- `getClass()`: This method is part of the `java.lang.Object` class, so everyone inherits it from there.

- *ClassName*`.class`: When you specify the `.class` filename associated with a class, you gain access to the `Class` associated with the class—in this case, `ClassName`.

Once you have a `Class`, you can discover its fields and methods, among many other pieces of information. Table 13-1 describes some of this information.

Table 13-1. Some of the Useful Methods of Class

Method	Description
getDeclaredFields()	Gets array of variables declared within class
getDeclaredField()	Gets specific variable if declared in class
getFields()	Gets array of declared and inherited fields
getField()	Gets specific field, if declared locally or inherited
getConstructor()	Gets constructor with specific argument list, if declared in class
getConstructors()	Gets array of constructors declared in class
getDeclaredMethods()	Gets array of methods declared within class
getDeclaredMethod()	Gets specific method, with specific argument list, if declared in class
getMethods()	Gets array of declared and inherited methods
getMethod()	Gets specific method, with specific argument list, if declared locally or inherited
getName()	Gets fully qualified name of class

Notice that there is no mention of properties or events here, only of methods and fields. In the Lookup program, you'll need to find the method bigger() or smaller(), so you should ask getDeclaredMethod(String name, Class parameterTypes[ ]) to see if the method exists for the user's input. Because both bigger() and smaller() do not require arguments, the second parameter to getDeclaredMethod(String name, Class parameterTypes[ ]) can be null. Otherwise, you would need to create an array of the different argument class types and pass that along as the second argument.

NOTE   *To create an array of class types, just add* .class *to each argument type and make an array. For instance, if your method accepted arguments of type* int, String, *and* float[], *the array declaration would look like this:* Class args[] = {int.class, String.class, and float[].class};. *Yes, some of those look a little weird, but that's how you do it.*

Once you have a specific `Method`, you can use the methods of the `java.lang.Method` class to find out about that method. To do the equivalent of a method call, the method of the `Method` class to call is `invoke()`. You need to pass in to the `invoke()` method the specific instance of the class to execute the method against and the actual argument list, this time as an `Object` array or null if there are none. Putting this all together, you can now add an action listener to the text field. If you double-click the text field, JBuilder will make the connection. Then, you need to add the appropriate action, as shown in Listing 13-1.

Listing 13-1. The `ActionListener` for the `TextField` to Invoke the Method for the `String` Entered

```java
import java.lang.reflect.*;
 . . .
  void jTextField1_actionPerformed(ActionEvent e) {
    String command = e.getActionCommand();
    System.out.println("Command: " + command);
    Class c = getClass();
    try {
      Method method = c.getDeclaredMethod(command, null);
      method.invoke(this, null);
    } catch (NoSuchMethodException exception) {
      System.err.println("Invalid input");
    } catch (Exception exception) {
      System.err.println("Invocation error");
    }
  }
```

Because of the "anything else" case mentioned earlier in the chapter, you're interested in when the `NoSuchMethodException` gets thrown by `getDeclaredMethod()`. You'll have to add something to find the color later. However, you don't need to differentiate between the other exceptions that `invoke()` throws, hence the second catch block is generic.

At this point, if you save and run `Looker` you can enter **bigger** or **smaller** into the text field. When you press Enter the screen will resize. Figure 13-1 shows one possible screen. If you look in the Message window after entering an invalid name, you'll see `Invalid input`.

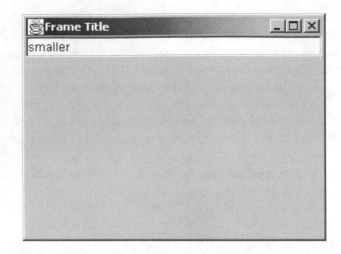

*Figure 13-1. The Looker class screen after inputting **smaller** and **bigger** a few times*

Adding the Color-Handling Code

The final piece you need to add to the program is the ability to enter a string, such as **red**, into the input field, and check to see if the string is a valid color. Because the Color class has 13 predefined color constants, you can check the string against the constants. If the user enters one that exists, you want to change the frame background to the color. Within the jTextField1_actionPerformed() method just created, in the catch (NoSuchMethodException exception) block, remove the print statement and follow these steps:

1. Get an instance of the Color class.

   ```
   Class colorClass = Color.class;
   ```

2. Check to see if it has a field of the input string.

   ```
   Field field = colorClass.getDeclaredField(command);
   ```

3. Get the value. Although you are getting a static variable of Color, the get() method of Field requires an instance of the class. Also, it's necessary to cast the return value of get() to the appropriate class.

   ```
   Color color = (Color)field.get(Color.white);
   ```

4. Use the color to change the background.

```
contentPane.setBackground(color);
```

5. Add a try-catch block around the whole block of code.

```
try {
   . . .
} catch (NoSuchFieldException exception2) {
   System.out.println("Invalid input");
} catch (IllegalAccessException exception2) {
   System.err.println("Access violation");
}
```

Now you can save and run the program, which Listing 13-2 provides in its entirety. In addition to entering **bigger** or **smaller** to resize the window, you can enter any of the colors in Table 13-2 to change the background of the frame's Content pane.

Table 13-2. Constants of the Color Class

Constant	
black	magenta
blue	orange
cyan	pink
darkGray	red
gray	white
green	yellow
lightGray	

Listing 13-2. The Complete Looks.java Application Source

```java
package skill13;

import java.awt.*;
import java.awt.event.*;
import javax.swing.*;
import java.lang.reflect.*;

public class Lookup extends JFrame {
  JPanel contentPane;
  BorderLayout borderLayout1 = new BorderLayout();
  JTextField jTextField1 = new JTextField();

  //Construct the frame
  public Lookup() {
    enableEvents(AWTEvent.WINDOW_EVENT_MASK);
    try {
      jbInit();
    }
    catch(Exception e) {
      e.printStackTrace();
    }
  }
  //Component initialization
  private void jbInit() throws Exception  {
    contentPane = (JPanel) this.getContentPane();
    contentPane.setLayout(borderLayout1);
    this.setSize(new Dimension(400, 300));
    this.setTitle("Frame Title");
    jTextField1.addActionListener(new java.awt.event.ActionListener() {
      public void actionPerformed(ActionEvent e) {
        jTextField1_actionPerformed(e);
      }
    });
    contentPane.add(jTextField1, BorderLayout.NORTH);
  }
  //Overridden so we can exit when window is closed
  protected void processWindowEvent(WindowEvent e) {
    super.processWindowEvent(e);
    if (e.getID() == WindowEvent.WINDOW_CLOSING) {
      System.exit(0);
    }
  }
}
```

```
public void bigger() {
  Dimension dim = getSize();
  int width = (int)(dim.width * 1.1);
  int height = (int)(dim.height * 1.1);
  setSize(width, height);
  validate();
}
public void smaller() {
  Dimension dim = getSize();
  int width = (int)(dim.width * 0.95);
  int height = (int)(dim.height * 0.95);
  setSize(width, height);
  validate();
}

void jTextField1_actionPerformed(ActionEvent e) {
  String command = e.getActionCommand();
  System.out.println("Command: " + command);
  Class c = getClass();
  try {
    Method method = c.getDeclaredMethod(command, null);
    method.invoke(this, null);
  } catch (NoSuchMethodException exception) {
    try {
      Class colorClass = Color.class;
      Field field = colorClass.getDeclaredField(command);
      Color color = (Color)field.get(Color.white);
      contentPane.setBackground(color);
    } catch (NoSuchFieldException exception2) {
      System.out.println("Invalid input");
    } catch (IllegalAccessException exception2) {
      System.err.println("Access violation");
    }
  } catch (Exception exception) {
    System.err.println("Invocation error");
  }
}
}
```

Although this program doesn't demonstrate all the capabilities of reflection, it does show the essentials of what JBuilder does to support the Inspector window.

Using the BeanInfo Introspector

With JavaBean components, a support class does all the reflection lookups. Instead of using the low-level methods in java.lang.reflect, JBuilder asks a class called the Introspector for the information associated with a bean. Then, by working through an interface named BeanInfo, JBuilder can find out about the properties and events of a bean. By providing one level of indirection for the inspection, you, the bean creator, can restrict what the bean builder tool, JBuilder, sees. Table 13-3 shows what is available through the BeanInfo interface.

Table 13-3. The BeanInfo Interface

Method	Description
getAdditionalBeanInfo()	Allows a bean to have multiple BeanInfo objects
getBeanDescriptor()	Gets a bean's BeanDescriptor
getDefaultEventIndex()	Gets index of default event
getDefaultPropertyIndex()	Gets index of default property
getEventSetDescriptors()	Gets array of EventSetDescriptor objects
getIcon()	Gets a bean's icon
getMethodDescriptors()	Gets array of MethodDescriptor objects
getPropertyDescriptors()	Gets array of PropertyDescriptor objects

To demonstrate how the Introspector works for JBuilder, let's create a new program that has a button and text area. When the button is selected, all of the method names for the button are listed in the text area. Close any open projects and run the Application Wizard again. Name the project **Skill13b** and save it in **C:\skills\Skill13b**. Name the frame class **Inspect**.

To set up the screen, go into the UI Designer for Inspect.java. Here you want to add a JTextArea in the Center and a JButton in the South. However, if you remember from Skill 8, in order for the JTextArea to support scrolling, you actually have to place the component in a JScrollPane. So, add the JScrollPane to the Center and drop the JTextArea into the JScrollPane.

TIP *None of the Swing components directly supports scrolling. If you need them to be scrollable, you add them to the* JScrollPane. *This is necessary for the* JList, JTree, JTextArea, JTextPane, *and* JEditorPane, *among other components.*

If you double-click the button, you can then add an action event handler. In Skill 8, you learned how to use a `StringWriter` to buffer input into a `JTextArea`. You'll do the same thing here by following these steps:

1. Import the `java.io` and `java.beans` packages.

    ```
    import java.io.*;
    import java.beans.*;
    ```

2. Create a `StringWriter` and chain it to a `PrintWriter`.

    ```
    StringWriter sw = new StringWriter();
    PrintWriter pw = new PrintWriter(sw);
    ```

3. Get the `BeanInfo` for the `JButton`.

    ```
    BeanInfo beanInfo = Introspector.getBeanInfo(jButton1.getClass());
    ```

4. Get the `MethodDescriptor` array for the button.

    ```
    MethodDescriptor methodDescriptor[] = beanInfo.getMethodDescriptors();
    ```

5. Loop through each, printing out the method name. Instead of printing, you could get the specific `Method` with `getMethod()` and `invoke()` it. Then, you're executing methods without having to know method names at all.

    ```
    for (int i=0, n=methodDescriptor.length; i<n; i++) {
      pw.println(methodDescriptor[i].getName());
    }
    ```

6. Display the results in the `JTextArea`.

    ```
    String methodList = sw.toString();
    jTextArea1.setText(methodList);
    ```

7. Because the `Introspector` can throw an `IntrospectionException` when getting the bean information, you'll need to place the source from steps 3 through 5 within a try-catch block. Step 5 doesn't need to be in the try-catch block, but the variable used there does.

    ```
    try {
      . . .
    } catch (IntrospectionException exception) {
      pw.println("Error inspecting");
    }
    ```

TIP *To indent a block of code more, highlight the code block and press the Tab key. This will move the code block in two spaces. To move the code out two spaces, press Shift-Tab.*

If you save the program, run it, and press the button, you'll see the method list for the button shown in Figure 13-2.

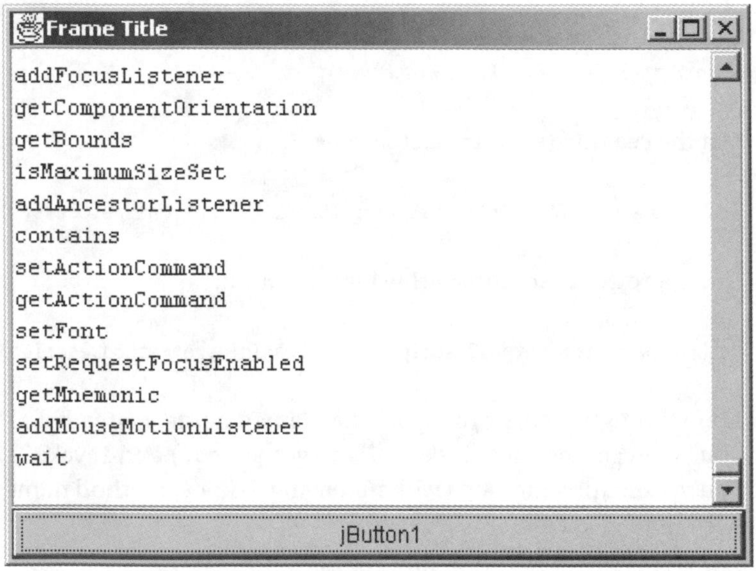

```
Frame Title                                          _ □ ×
addFocusListener                                          ▲
getComponentOrientation
getBounds
isMaximumSizeSet
addAncestorListener
contains
setActionCommand
getActionCommand
setFont
setRequestFocusEnabled
getMnemonic
addMouseMotionListener
wait                                                      ▼
                         jButton1
```

Figure 13-2. The Inspect program with the method list unsorted

To make the method list a little more useful, you should list the methods in sorted order. While the `Introspector` doesn't provide the methods to you in an ordered list, you can sort the array of `MethodDescriptor` objects. The `java.util.Arrays` class provides a `sort()` method to order the element sort arrays.

If the elements of the array you want to sort implement the Comparable interface, you can just pass them to sort() and they'll be sorted in their natural order. If, however, the elements don't implement the Comparable interface, you must provide the sort() method with an implementation of the Comparator interface. When you implement Comparator, you need to define a public int compare(Object, Object) method, specifying how you want the elements of your class ordered. The method will return a negative number if the first object comes before the second, a zero if they are equal, and a positive number if the second object comes first.

In your Comparator implementation, you're going to order the elements by method name: getName(). Because the name is a String object, and String implements Comparable, all you need to do is pass back the return value of calling compareTo() for the two strings. The compareTo() method is the method from the Comparable interface.

Thus, immediately before the for loop to print the array, order the elements as follows:

```
Comparator comparator = new Comparator() {
  public int compare(Object first, Object second) {
    MethodDescriptor one = (MethodDescriptor)first;
    MethodDescriptor two = (MethodDescriptor)second;
    return (one.getName().compareTo(two.getName()));
  }
};
Arrays.sort(methodDescriptor, comparator);
```

Because the Arrays and Comparator classes are defined in the java.util package, you'll need to import the package.

```
import java.util.*;
```

Now if you run the program and press the button, you'll see the methods listed in alphabetical order, as shown in Figure 13-3. If you notice the same name multiple times, it means the method exists in the class multiple times, just with different argument lists.

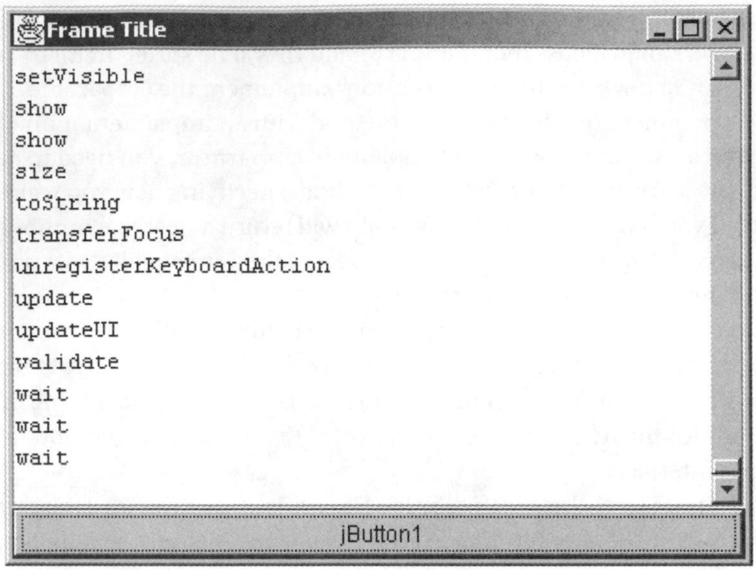

Figure 13-3. The Inspect program with the method list sorted

Listing 13-3 contains the complete source for Inspect.java.

Listing 13-3. The Complete Inspect.java Application Source

```java
package skill13b;

import java.awt.*;
import java.awt.event.*;
import javax.swing.*;
import java.io.*;
import java.beans.*;
import java.util.*;

public class Inspect extends JFrame {
  JPanel contentPane;
  BorderLayout borderLayout1 = new BorderLayout();
  JButton jButton1 = new JButton();
  JScrollPane jScrollPane1 = new JScrollPane();
  JTextArea jTextArea1 = new JTextArea();

  //Construct the frame
  public Inspect() {
    enableEvents(AWTEvent.WINDOW_EVENT_MASK);
    try {
      jbInit();
    }
```

```
    catch(Exception e) {
      e.printStackTrace();
    }
  }
//Component initialization
private void jbInit() throws Exception  {
  contentPane = (JPanel) this.getContentPane();
  jButton1.setText("jButton1");
  jButton1.addActionListener(new java.awt.event.ActionListener() {
    public void actionPerformed(ActionEvent e) {
      jButton1_actionPerformed(e);
    }
  });
  contentPane.setLayout(borderLayout1);
  this.setSize(new Dimension(400, 300));
  this.setTitle("Frame Title");
  jTextArea1.setText("jTextArea1");
  contentPane.add(jButton1, BorderLayout.SOUTH);
  contentPane.add(jScrollPane1, BorderLayout.CENTER);
  jScrollPane1.getViewport().add(jTextArea1, null);
}
//Overridden so we can exit when window is closed
protected void processWindowEvent(WindowEvent e) {
  super.processWindowEvent(e);
  if (e.getID() == WindowEvent.WINDOW_CLOSING) {
    System.exit(0);
  }
}


void jButton1_actionPerformed(ActionEvent e) {
  StringWriter sw = new StringWriter();
  PrintWriter pw = new PrintWriter(sw);
  try {
    BeanInfo beanInfo = Introspector.getBeanInfo(jButton1.getClass());
    MethodDescriptor methodDescriptor[] = beanInfo.getMethodDescriptors();
    Comparator comparator = new Comparator() {
      public int compare(Object first, Object second) {
        MethodDescriptor one = (MethodDescriptor)first;
        MethodDescriptor two = (MethodDescriptor)second;
        return (one.getName().compareTo(two.getName()));
      }
    };
```

```
      Arrays.sort(methodDescriptor, comparator);
      for (int i=0, n=methodDescriptor.length; i<n; i++) {
        pw.println(methodDescriptor[i].getName());
      }
    } catch (IntrospectionException exception) {
      pw.println("Error inspecting");
    }
    String methodList = sw.toString();
    jTextArea1.setText(methodList);
  }
}
```

> **NOTE** *You can easily change this program to look at the* PropertyDescriptor *list for the button or the* EventSetDescriptor *list. The methods to get the appropriate lists are* getPropertyDescriptors() *and* getEventSetDescriptors(), *respectively.*

Overriding BeanInfo

Now that you've seen how to use reflection and how reflection is used, it's time to override the default behavior. When you ask the Introspector for the BeanInfo for a class, it first looks for a specific supporting class. The supporting class is the name of the bean followed by BeanInfo. Therefore, if you had a bean called MyButton, the BeanInfo for it would be in MyButtonBeanInfo. Then, if MyButtonBeanInfo isn't found, the Introspector goes off and uses the default behavior: reflection.

To demonstrate this, let's create a subclass of JButton. You only want it to have one property—the text—and one event set—action. Close any open projects and create a new one by running the Project Wizard (not the Application Wizard). Name this project **Skill13c** and save it in **C:\skills\Skill13c**. Next, run the Class Wizard to create the **MyButton** class, and have it extend from **javax.swing.JButton**. Uncheck all the options but the Public option and click Finish. You now have your complete MyButton class, which you're going to create a BeanInfo object for.

```
package skill13c;

import javax.swing.JButton;

public class MyButton extends JButton {
}
```

To generate the `BeanInfo` interface, you could subclass `java.lang.Object` and define each method of the interface yourself (see Table 13-3). However, this requires lots of unnecessary work; you only want to customize some behavior, in this case the property and event set descriptors. The `java.beans` package provides a support class called `SimpleBeanInfo`. If you subclass this, you only have to override the pieces to provide your custom behavior.

Instead of running the Class Wizard to create the `BeanInfo` for `MyButton`, select the Bean tab on the bottom of the Source pane. Then, click the BeanInfo subtab. If you click the Generate BeanInfo button you'll get the framework for extending `SimpleBeanInfo` to do whatever you want. There are some helper methods defined—for example, for loading icons to display images on the Component palette—but essentially you're free to add whatever you need to the class to customize the Introspector behavior for the `MyButton` component. Listing 13-4 presents the initial autogenerated `MyButtonBeanInfo.java` source.

Listing 13-4. The Initial Autogenerated MyButtonBeanInfo.java Source

```
package skill13c;

import java.beans.*;

/**
 * <p>Title: </p>
 * <p>Description: </p>
 * <p>Copyright:    Copyright (c) 2001</p>
 * <p>Company: </p>
 * @author unascribed
 * @version 1.0
 */

public class MyButtonBeanInfo extends SimpleBeanInfo {
  Class beanClass = MyButton.class;
  String iconColor16x16Filename;
  String iconColor32x32Filename;
  String iconMono16x16Filename;
  String iconMono32x32Filename;
```

```
public MyButtonBeanInfo() {
}
public PropertyDescriptor[] getPropertyDescriptors() {
  PropertyDescriptor[] pds = new PropertyDescriptor[] { };
  return pds;
}
public java.awt.Image getIcon(int iconKind) {
  switch (iconKind) {
  case BeanInfo.ICON_COLOR_16x16:
      return iconColor16x16Filename != null ?
        loadImage(iconColor16x16Filename) : null;
  case BeanInfo.ICON_COLOR_32x32:
      return iconColor32x32Filename != null ?
        loadImage(iconColor32x32Filename) : null;
  case BeanInfo.ICON_MONO_16x16:
      return iconMono16x16Filename != null ?
        loadImage(iconMono16x16Filename) : null;
  case BeanInfo.ICON_MONO_32x32:
      return iconMono32x32Filename != null ?
        loadImage(iconMono32x32Filename) : null;
      }
  return null;
  }
}
```

Limiting Properties

To limit the available properties of a bean, it's necessary to override the
getPropertyDescriptors() method. Notice that an overridden version is already
provided for you—it just returns no properties for the component, limiting component properties considerably to start. You'll need to add one entry for each
property you want available.

 To create a single PropertyDescriptor, the constructor requires the property
name and the bean's Class object. Once you have a single PropertyDescriptor,
you need to place it in an array and return that array. Because the
PropertyDescriptor could throw an IntrospectionException (for when
the property isn't available/valid), the entire source code needs to be in
a try-catch block, returning null on error.

```
public PropertyDescriptor[] getPropertyDescriptors() {
  try {
    PropertyDescriptor textDescriptor =
      new PropertyDescriptor("text", MyButton.class);
    PropertyDescriptor pds[] = {textDescriptor};
    return pds;
  } catch (IntrospectionException exception) {
    return null;
  }
}
```

Limiting Events

Limiting the available event set of a bean is similar to limiting properties.
You start by overriding the getEventSetDescriptors() method. This method
returns an EventSetDescriptor array, with one entry for each available event
listener method.

To create a single EventSetDescriptor, the constructor requires the bean
Class object, the event set name, the listener type Class, and the listener method
name. Again, once you have the descriptor, you need to place it in an array and
return the array. Because the constructor can throw an IntrospectionException
(when the event set isn't really available), the source needs to be in a try-catch
block, returning null on error.

```
public EventSetDescriptor[] getEventSetDescriptors() {
  try {
    EventSetDescriptor actionDescriptor = new EventSetDescriptor(
      MyButton.class, "action", ActionListener.class, "actionPerformed");
    EventSetDescriptor eds[] = {actionDescriptor};
    return eds;
  } catch (IntrospectionException exception) {
    return null;
  }
}
```

Because the ActionListener class is in the java.awt.event package, you also
need to import the java.awt.event package.

```
import java.awt.event.*;
```

Limiting Containment

There's one other thing that you will do with the BeanInfo for the MyButton component, though it isn't necessary for this specific component. Because JComponent is a subclass of Container, any subclass of JComponent you create is also considered a container. This is true even if you subclass JButton, which you wouldn't think of as a container.

In the system-provided BeanInfo for JButton and other Swing components that aren't really containers, there is a magical method called isContainer(). You can consider it a magical method because it isn't part of the BeanInfo interface. It's just there. In the system-provided BeanInfo for Swing components, isContainer() returns false, meaning JButton isn't really a container, even though it's still a subclass of Container. This holds true for all concrete Swing components. But, if you subclass JComponent (or JPanel) directly, and you don't want your component to be considered a container, the BeanInfo for your class must provide the method and return false. When isContainer() is used in this manner, you won't be able to accidentally drop components into something that you shouldn't, as you learned in Skill 11 in the BlueBox and RedTriangle exercise.

So, add the following to your MyButtonBeanInfo:

```
public boolean isContainer() {
  return false;
}
```

> **NOTE** *Using* isContainer() *in this manner doesn't stop you from programmatically adding components to the container. It only prevents you from using the designer to add components.*

Setting Icons

One thing you won't do but easily can is configure the bean's palette icon. If you are interested in having your bean appear in the Component palette with a predefined icon other than the default, you can set one of the four filename variables in the generated SimpleBeanInfo subclass to the appropriate icon file. The filenames describe the size (in pixels) for the icon and whether or not it should be color or black and white. These files are usually GIFs, but any Java-supported image format will work.

```
String iconColor16x16Filename;
String iconColor32x32Filename;
String iconMono16x16Filename;
String iconMono32x32Filename;
```

You're now done creating the BeanInfo. Take a look at the complete source in Listing 13-5 before you go on to use it.

Listing 13-5. The Final MyButtonBeanInfo.java Source

```
package skill13c;

import java.beans.*;
import java.awt.event.*;

/**
 * <p>Title: The MyButtonBeanInfo</p>
 * <p>Description: Single event/property demonstration</p>
 * <p>Copyright:    Copyright (c) 2001</p>
 * <p>Company: JZ Ventures, Inc. </p>
 * @author John Zukowski
 * @version 1.0
 */

public class MyButtonBeanInfo extends SimpleBeanInfo {
  Class beanClass = MyButton.class;
  String iconColor16x16Filename;
  String iconColor32x32Filename;
  String iconMono16x16Filename;
  String iconMono32x32Filename;

  public MyButtonBeanInfo() {
  }
  public PropertyDescriptor[] getPropertyDescriptors() {
    try {
      PropertyDescriptor textDescriptor =
        new PropertyDescriptor("text", MyButton.class);
      PropertyDescriptor pds[] = {textDescriptor};
      return pds;
    } catch (IntrospectionException exception) {
      return null;
    }
  }
}
```

process becomes much easier as unnecessary pieces are hidden away. And, when the user is done connecting the beans, it becomes unnecessary to deliver the BeanInfo class with the final deliverable to run the program. It is only necessary at design time.

ARE YOU EXPERIENCED?

Now you can

- Use reflection to discover class information

- Invoke methods indirectly through reflection

- Sort arrays

- Use the Introspector

- Examine a bean's BeanInfo

- Customize a bean's properties and event sets

You've now seen how JBuilder uses reflection and the Introspector to dig inside the beans and how you can restrict that through BeanInfo. In Skill 14, you'll move on to customizing how properties will be shown to the bean developer.

SKILL 14

Creating Beans:
Customization

- Using property editors with beans

- Implementing selection property editors

- Implementing custom property editors

Getting Started

In this skill you're going to create a bean that draws one of four shapes within its available area: an oval, a circle, a rectangle, or a square. By itself, that doesn't sound too complicated. The class has two properties (the shape and a filled versus unfilled setting), four constants for the different shapes, and a paintComponent() routine.

A problem arises, though, when the bean users want to change the shape property. How do they change it? If the property was saved internally as an integer, users might have to type **0** for an oval, **1** for a circle, **2** for a rectangle, or **3** for a square. But how do they know what value is for what shape? Instead, it would be better if they could just pick from a drop-down list in which the choices were the available shapes. Or, even better, you could show the shapes graphically, and let users see the shape they're picking. All these options—integer input, drop-down list, and graphical selection—are handled by offering a *property editor* to the builder tool. This skill shows you how to create each of these options.

Creating the ShapeBox

At this point, start up JBuilder, close any open projects, and run the Project Wizard, not the Application Wizard. Name the project **Skill14**, set the directory to **C:\skills\Skill14** and click Finish. Next, use the New Class Wizard to create the **ShapeBox**, and have the class subclass **javax.swing.JPanel**. Leave just the Public and Generate default constructor options checked and click OK to create the beginning of your new bean.

```
package skill14;

import javax.swing.JPanel;

public class ShapeBox extends JPanel {

  public ShapeBox() {
  }
}
```

Now you have three steps to perform: Add the constants for the different shapes you support, add the properties for the current shape and fill status, and draw the component. Next, you'll look at what's involved in each step.

1. Define the constants:

    ```
    public static final int OVAL = 0;
    public static final int CIRCLE = 1;
    public static final int RECTANGLE = 2;
    public static final int SQUARE = 3;
    ```

2. Add the properties. Click the Bean tab and then the Properties tab. Add one property named **shape** of type **int** and one named **filled** of type **boolean**. Because each of the properties will affect what is drawn, add a call to repaint() at the end of each generated setter method. This will ensure the display is updated. The generated code with the updated methods is shown in Listing 14-1.

Listing 14-1. The Code Generated for the shape and filled Properties of ShapeBox, with the Added repaint() Calls

```
private int shape;
private boolean filled;
  . . .
public void setShape(int shape) {
  this.shape = shape;
  repaint();
}
public int getShape() {
  return shape;
}
public void setFilled(boolean filled) {
  this.filled = filled;
  repaint();
}
public boolean isFilled() {
  return filled;
}
```

3. Draw the shape. Here's where you determine which shape the user wants to draw, and then draw it empty or filled. For the circle or square, you need to make sure the height and width are the same. For all of them, you'll leave a little room around the edges. Remember, with Swing components, you override paintComponent() to draw within the component, not paint(). The full method is shown in Listing 14-2, with the necessary import statements.

Listing 14-2. The paintComponent() Method to Draw the Appropriate ShapeBox

```
import java.awt. *;
import java.awt.geom.*;
  . . .
public void paintComponent(Graphics g) {
  super.paintComponent(g);
  Graphics2D g2d = (Graphics2D)g;
  Dimension dim = getSize();
  int min = Math.min(dim.width, dim.height);
  Shape s;
  switch (shape) {
    case CIRCLE:
      s = new Arc2D.Float(2, 2, min-4, min-4, 0, 360, Arc2D.OPEN);
      break;
    case RECTANGLE:
      s = new Rectangle(2, 2, dim.width-4, dim.height-4);
      break;
    case SQUARE:
      s = new Rectangle(2, 2, min-4, min-4);
      break;
    case OVAL:
    default:
      s = new Arc2D.Float(2, 2, dim.width-4, dim.height-4, 0, 360, Arc2D.OPEN);
      break;
  }
  if (filled) {
    g2d.fill(s);
  } else {
    g2d.draw(s);
  }
}
```

NOTE *For a refresher on drawing, revisit Skill 7. The only thing really new here is the arc. When you create an* Arc2D *to draw, there are seven arguments. The first of four is the familiar bounding rectangle for the drawing. Yes, even when drawing arcs you work with a bounding rectangle and not a center point. The next two parameters are the starting and ending angle. Zero degrees is at 3 o'clock, directly to the right, and the angles increase counterclockwise, where 12 o'clock would be 90 degrees, 9 o'clock would be 180 degrees, and 6 o'clock would be 270 degrees, returning back to 3 o'clock for 360 or a complete oval. The last argument is one of three values,* Arc2D.OPEN, Arc2D.CHORD, *or* Arc2D.PIE, *and represents how to connect the end points.* OPEN *means don't connect,* CHORD *means connect with a line, and* PIE *means connect like a pie chart, with two lines, each from an end point to the center. The last argument only has meaning when the arc is not a complete oval.*

That's the whole bean. At this point, save your class, compile the bean, and add it to the Other tab of the Component palette.

1. Select Tools ➤ Configure Palette.

2. Select the Other option from the Pages list.

3. Select the Add components tab.

4. Click the Select libraries button.

5. Click the New button.

6. Name the library **Skill14**.

7. Click the Add button.

8. Double-click the C:\skills folder.

9. Single-click the Skill14 folder.

10. Click the OK button. This will add C:/skills/Skill14/classes and C:/skills/Skill14/src to the Library paths.

TIP   *If you don't get the* C:/skills/Skill14/classes *direc-tory added, that means you didn't compile the bean first. Compile the bean, and then return to Step 1 to add the bean to the palette.*

11. Click the OK button again.

12. Click the OK button a third time.

13. Select the JavaBeans only option under Component filtering.

14. Click the Add from Selected Library button.

15. Open the skill14 folder.

16. Double-click the ShapeBox bean.

17. Select OK on the Results window that says Added skill14.ShapeBox.

18. Select OK on the Palette Properties window.

The ShapeBox is now on the Component palette. The entire source for the component appears in Listing 14-3. For the rest of this skill, the component will not change one bit. All the changes will be done by manipulating the BeanInfo for the component.

Listing 14-3. The Final ShapeBox Component Source

```
package skill14;

import javax.swing.JPanel;
import java.awt.*;
import java.awt.geom.*;

public class ShapeBox extends JPanel {

  public static final int OVAL = 0;
  public static final int CIRCLE = 1;
  public static final int RECTANGLE = 2;
  public static final int SQUARE = 3;
  private int shape;
  private boolean filled;
```

```
public ShapeBox() {
}
public void paintComponent(Graphics g) {
  super.paintComponent(g);
  Graphics2D g2d = (Graphics2D)g;
  Dimension dim = getSize();
  int min = Math.min(dim.width, dim.height);
  Shape s;
  switch (shape) {
    case CIRCLE:
      s = new Arc2D.Float(2, 2, min-4, min-4, 0, 360, Arc2D.OPEN);
      break;
    case RECTANGLE:
      s = new Rectangle(2, 2, dim.width-4, dim.height-4);
      break;
    case SQUARE:
      s = new Rectangle(2, 2, min-4, min-4);
      break;
    case OVAL:
    default:
      s = new Arc2D.Float(2, 2, dim.width-4, dim.heighl-4, 0, 360,
        Arc2D.OPEN);
      break;
  }
  if (filled) {
    g2d.fill(s);
  } else {
    g2d.draw(s);
  }
}
public void setShape(int shape) {
  this.shape = shape;
  repaint();
}
public int getShape() {
  return shape;
}
public void setFilled(boolean filled) {
  this.filled = filled;
  repaint();
}
```

```
    public boolean isFilled() {
      return filled;
    }
  }
}
```

Using the Default Property Editor

Now that you have your bean with the two properties of type int and boolean, you can test the bean to see how JBuilder presents the properties to the developer or bean user. Close the Skill14 project and run the Application Wizard. Create the new project in **C:\skills\Skill14b**, this time naming it **Skill14b**. On the second page of the Application Wizard, name the frame class **ShapeFrame**.

Once the Application Wizard does its magic, you can add a ShapeBox to the ShapeFrame. Select the Design tab in the UI Designer and drop the ShapeBox into the center of the frame. At this point, your AppBrowser window will look like the screen shown in Figure 14-1. Because ShapeBox.OVAL is equivalent to 0, that is the default shape.

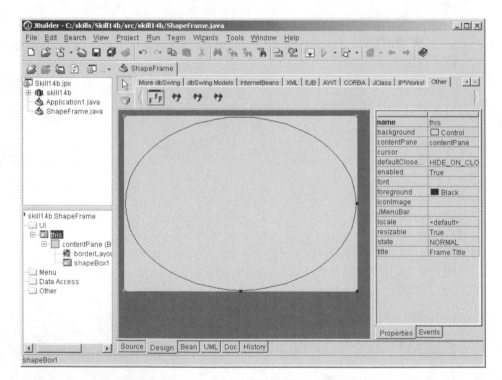

Figure 14-1. The AppBrowser window with the ShapeBox drawn in the frame

If you select shapeBox1 in the Structure pane and look in the Inspector window, you'll notice the shape property is set to 0 and the filled property is False. Figure 14-2 shows the Inspector window.

name	shapeBox1
constraints	Center
filled	False
shape	0

Properties | Events

Figure 14-2. The Inspector window for a ShapeBox

To see what 0 means, you have to go back to the ShapeBox.java source and see that 0 is an oval, 1 is a circle, 2 is a rectangle, and 3 is a square. If you change the shape property to 1, 2, or 3, you'll notice that the box changes to the appropriate shape. Saving and running the application draws the appropriate shape and filled status within the ShapeFrame, as shown in Figure 14-3.

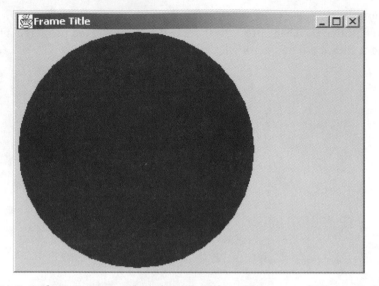

Figure 14-3. A ShapeFrame with a ShapeBox shape property of 1 for a circle and a filled property of True

Listing 14-4 has the automatically generated JBuilder source code of ShapeFrame.java. Essentially, this will stay the same throughout the rest of this skill. What will change is how you change the shape property setting in the Inspector.

Listing 14-4. The Final ShapeFrame Source

```
package skill14b;

import java.awt.*;
import java.awt.event.*;
import javax.swing.*;
import skill14.*;

public class ShapeFrame extends JFrame {
  JPanel contentPane;
  BorderLayout borderLayout1 = new BorderLayout();
  ShapeBox shapeBox1 = new ShapeBox();

  //Construct the frame
  public ShapeFrame() {
    enableEvents(AWTEvent.WINDOW_EVENT_MASK);
    try {
      jbInit();
    }
```

```
    catch(Exception e) {
      e.printStackTrace();
    }
  }
  //Component initialization
  private void jbInit() throws Exception  {
    contentPane = (JPanel) this.getContentPane();
    contentPane.setLayout(borderLayout1);
    this.setSize(new Dimension(400, 300));
    this.setTitle("Frame Title");
    shapeBox1.setFilled(true);
    shapeBox1.setShape(1);
    contentPane.add(shapeBox1, BorderLayout.CENTER);
  }
  //Overridden so we can exit when window is closed
  protected void processWindowEvent(WindowEvent e) {
    super.processWindowEvent(e);
    if (e.getID() == WindowEvent.WINDOW_CLOSING) {
      System.exit(0);
    }
  }
}
```

Getting Shape Names As Input

One problem with the previous example arises if you don't know what value is
used for which shape. In this simple example, you can easily try out the different
numbers to get the different values. What would happen, though, if the developer
used numbers such as 83214243, 187, 381028934, and 1348774 for the different
shapes? Unless these values were well documented somewhere, before you were
able to guess 187 to get the first shape, you would probably have given up.

There is one alternative. If you provide your bean without the source code to
a developer, JBuilder can examine the class file to get a best guess of its contents.
The process of examining the compiled class file to regenerate the source is
called *decompiling,* though all JBuilder does is list the methods and variables, not
the decompiled source. Listing 14-5 shows what JBuilder would generate if the
ShapeBox.java source file was not available.

Listing 14-5. The JBuilder-Generated Stub Source for the ShapeBox Class

```
// JBuilder API Decompiler stub source generated from class file
// Dec 25, 2001
// -- implementation of methods is not available

package skill14;

// Imports
import javax.swing.JPanel;
import java.awt.Graphics;

public class ShapeBox extends JPanel {

  // Fields
  public static final int OVAL = 0;
  public static final int CIRCLE = 1;
  public static final int RECTANGLE = 2;
  public static final int SQUARE = 3;
  private int shape;
  private boolean filled;

  // Constructors
  public ShapeBox() { }

  // Methods
  public int getShape() { }
  public void setShape(int p0) { }
  public void setFilled(boolean p0) { }
  public boolean isFilled() { }
  public void paint(Graphics p0) { }
  static  { }

  // Inner classes
}
```

TIP *If you right-click over a variable and select Browse Symbol, JBuilder will load the source code for the respective class. If the source file can't be found, JBuilder will decompile the class' definition file (.class file).*

The nice thing about the decompiled source is that it lists the mappings between constants and shapes. So, had you used 83214243, 187, 381028934, and 1348774 instead of 0, 1, 2, and 3, you would at least know what to enter. This still isn't the best option, though.

Returning to Skill14, you can make some changes so this would be easier. What you need to do is add a property editor to the ShapeBox. The nice thing about property editors, or any other BeanInfo-related support classes, is you never need to change the original bean. The support classes are only necessary when designing screens, so when the developers who are connecting the beans are done, they don't need to deliver the support classes to their users. This keeps deliverable size to a minimum. The next sections will show how to implement and use a property editor to prompt the developer for the shape, versus the shape value, from a pick list.

Creating the Property Editor

As with adding events and properties to beans, JBuilder has built-in support for generating most of the necessary code for building a property editor. Actually, after you enter a name and choose a type from a pick list, it will generate everything.

To bring up the Property Editor generator for the ShapeBox component, select the Bean tab at the bottom of the AppBrowser. Then select the Property Editors subtab. This brings up the screen shown in Figure 14-4.

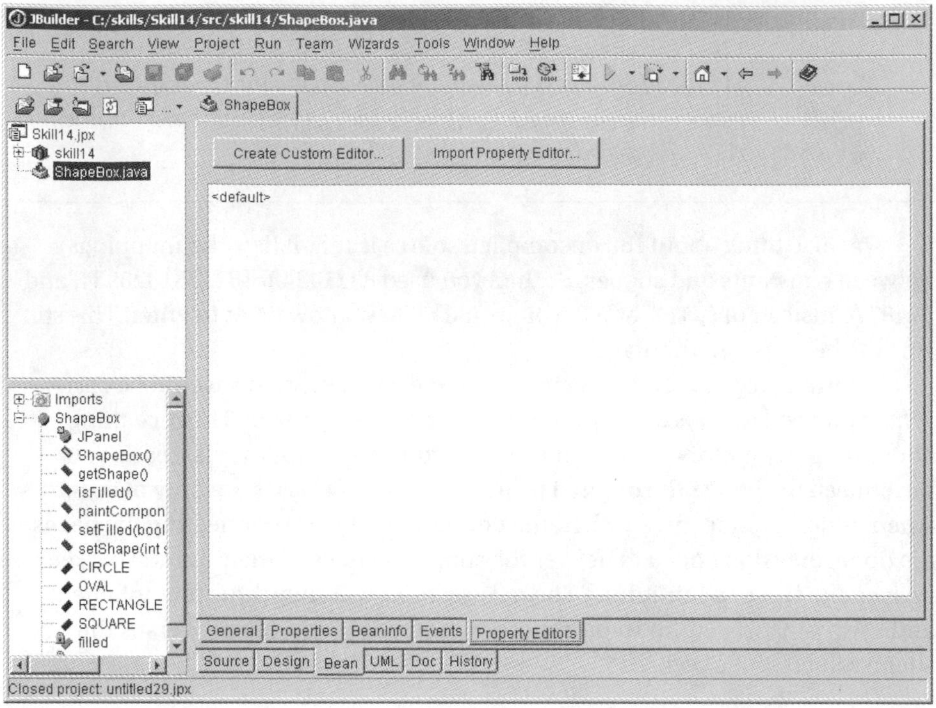

Figure 14-4. The JBuilder Beans Express Property Editors management screen

Because you want to create a property editor, the obvious thing to do is click the Create Custom Editor button, which opens the New Property Editor dialog box shown in Figure 14-5.

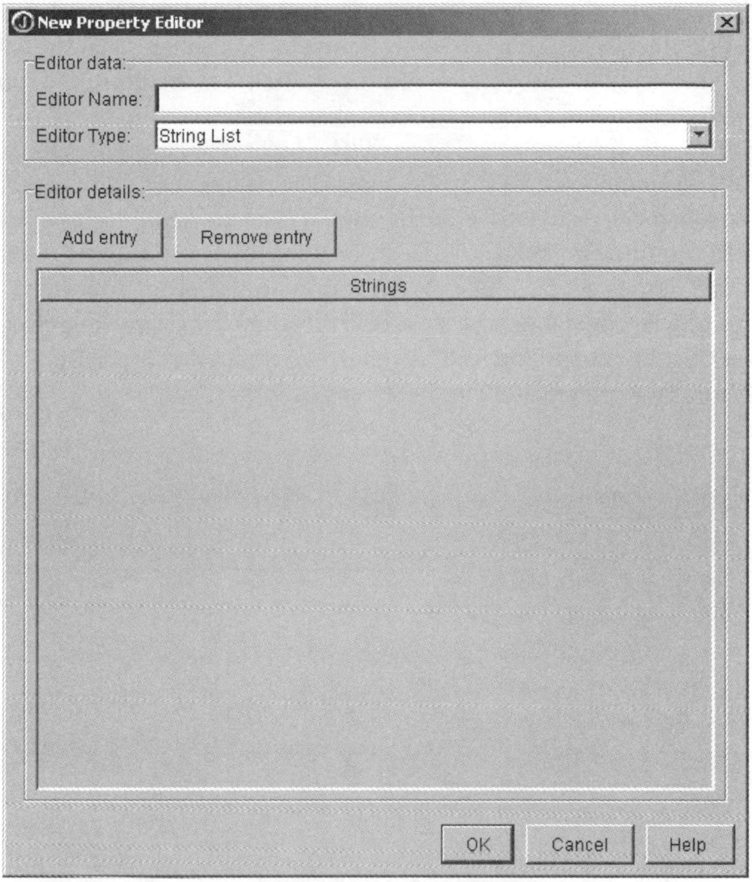

Figure 14-5. JBuilder's New Property Editor dialog box

Under Editor Type are four different types of property editors that JBuilder can generate for you. In this skill, you'll demonstrate the most complex, the last two.

- *String List:* For when you want the user to select from a list of strings and the selected value is the string you want your program to use

- *String Tag List:* For when you want the user to select from a list of strings and the selected value is not the string you want your program to use

- *Integer Tag List:* For when you want the user to select from a list of strings and the selected value maps to an integer value and integer string expression

- *Custom Editor Component:* For when you want the editor to appear in a pop-up window

For the first property editor, name the editor **ShapeEditor** and select Integer Tag List. You'll need to enter in four entries, one for each shape that the ShapeBox can draw. Click the Add entry button four times. In the first column, Resource string, you'll need to enter the name of the shapes you want the user to pick from: **Oval**, **Circle**, **Rectangle**, and **Square**. The second column is for the integer values for the constants in the ShapeBox class. The values of 0, 1, 2, and 3 are entered automatically and happen to be correct. The final column, Java initialization string, is the string representing an int that you want JBuilder to place in the source code to set the property. For your four properties you want JBuilder to use the constants in ShapeBox; so the four strings are **ShapeBox.OVAL**, **ShapeBox.CIRCLE**, **ShapeBox.RECTANGLE**, and **ShapeBox.SQUARE**. The completed properties for the editor are shown in Figure 14-6.

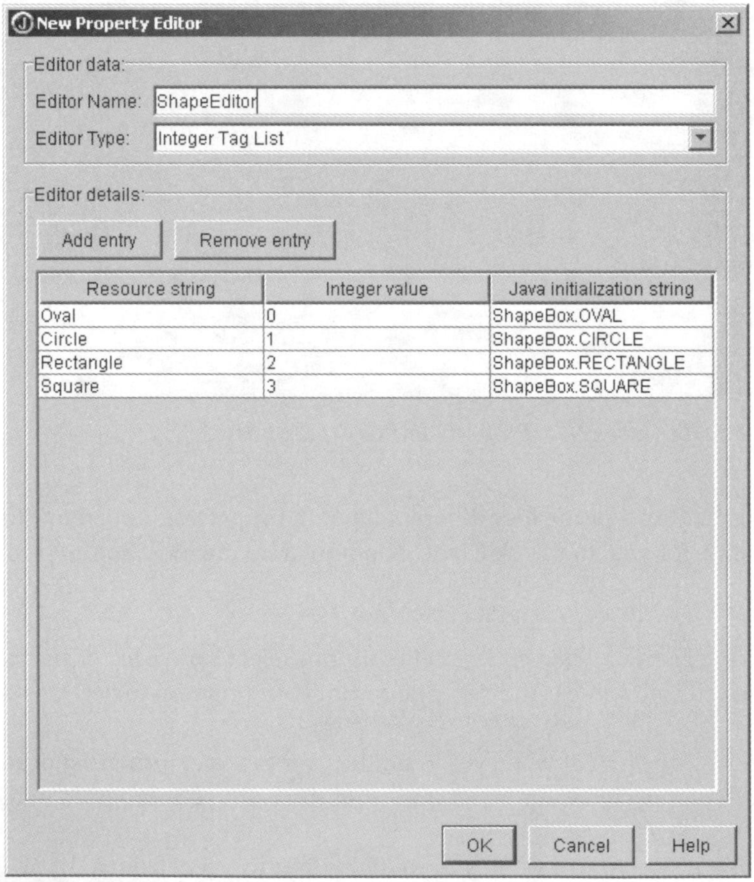

Figure 14-6. The ShapeEditor dialog box with all the necessary options entered. Just click the OK button to create the property editor.

Once you click OK, the editor is created. After you fill in the header comments, you'll get the source shown in Listing 14-6.

Listing 14-6. The Initial ShapeEditor.java Property Editor Source

```java
package skill14;

import java.beans.*;

/**
 * <p>Title: Editor for shape property of ShapeBox</p>
 * <p>Description: Permit user to pick shape from string vs. int</p>
 * <p>Copyright: Copyright (c) 2001</p>
 * <p>Company: JZ Ventures, Inc.</p>
 * @author John Zukowski
 * @version 1.0
 */

public class ShapeEditor extends PropertyEditorSupport {
  private static String[] resourceStrings =
     { "Oval", "Circle", "Rectangle", "Square", };
  private static int[] intValues =
     { 0, 1, 2, 3, };
  private static String[] sourceCodeStrings =
     { "ShapeBox.OVAL", "ShapeBox.CIRCLE", "ShapeBox.RECTANGLE",
       "ShapeBox.SQUARE", };

  public ShapeEditor() {
  }
  public String[] getTags() {
    return resourceStrings;
  }
  public String getJavaInitializationString() {
    Object value = getValue();
    for (int i = 0; i < intValues.length; i++) {
      if (value.equals(new Integer(intValues[i]))) {
        return sourceCodeStrings[i];
      }
    }
    return null;
  }
```

```java
public String getAsText() {
  Object value = getValue();
  for (int i = 0; i < intValues.length; i++) {
    if (value.equals(new Integer(intValues[i]))) {
      return resourceStrings[i];
    }
  }
  return null;
}
public void setAsText(String text) throws IllegalArgumentException {
  for (int i = 0; i < resourceStrings.length; i++) {
    if (text.equals(resourceStrings[i])) {
      setValue(new Integer(intValues[i]));
      return;
    }
  }
  throw new IllegalArgumentException();
}
}
```

Creating the BeanInfo Class

Now that the editor is created, it's time to connect the editor to the property. First select the ShapeBox.java file. Then, if you click the Bean tab and then the BeanInfo tab, you can enter **ShapeEditor** in the last column for the shape property, as shown in Figure 14-7.

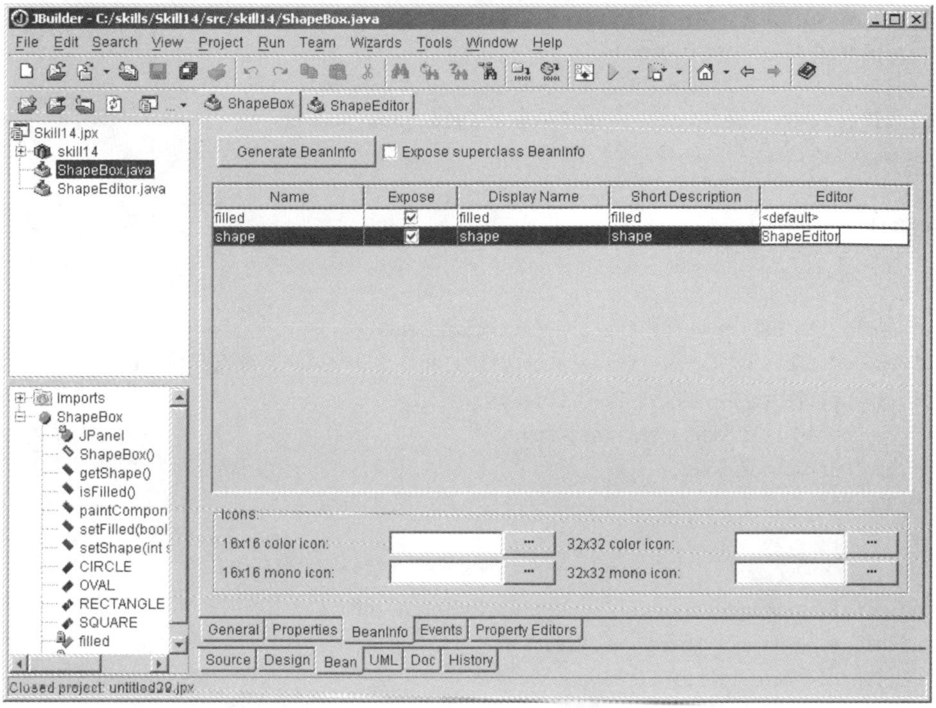

Figure 14-7. Associate the ShapeEditor with the shape property in the ShapeBox. Then click Generate BeanInfo.

If you click the Generate BeanInfo button, you'll have a `BeanInfo` class for the ShapeBox. The one line of source that makes the association between property and editor is shown here, where `_shape` is the `PropertyDescriptor` for the shape property:

```
_shape.setPropertyEditorClass(ShapeEditor.class);
```

You'll add one thing, though. The filling of the shape is done with the foreground color for the component. You want to make this property visible to the designer. For this, you need to create another `PropertyDescriptor` in `ShapeBoxBeanInfo.java` and add it to the `pds` array:

```
PropertyDescriptor _foreground = new PropertyDescriptor("foreground", beanClass);
_foreground.setDisplayName("foreground");
_foreground.setShortDescription("foreground");
PropertyDescriptor[] pds = new PropertyDescriptor[] {
  _filled, _foreground, _shape};
```

The complete source for the BeanInfo class appears in Listing 14-7, with the completed header comments.

Listing 14-7. The Final ShapeBoxBeanInfo.java Source

```java
package skill14;

import java.beans.*;

/**
 * <p>Title: BeanInfo for the ShapeBox component</p>
 * <p>Description: Expose three properties and connect one to custom editor</p>
 * <p>Copyright: Copyright (c) 2001</p>
 * <p>Company: JZ Ventures, Inc.</p>
 * @author John Zukowski
 * @version 1.0
 */

public class ShapeBoxBeanInfo extends SimpleBeanInfo {
  Class beanClass = ShapeBox.class;
  String iconColor16x16Filename;
  String iconColor32x32Filename;
  String iconMono16x16Filename;
  String iconMono32x32Filename;

  public ShapeBoxBeanInfo() {
  }
  public PropertyDescriptor[] getPropertyDescriptors() {
    try {
      PropertyDescriptor _filled =
        new PropertyDescriptor("filled", beanClass, "isFilled", "setFilled");
      _filled.setDisplayName("filled");
      _filled.setShortDescription("filled");
      PropertyDescriptor _shape =
        new PropertyDescriptor("shape", beanClass, "getShape", "setShape");
      _shape.setDisplayName("shape");
      _shape.setShortDescription("shape");
      _shape.setPropertyEditorClass(ShapeEditor.class);
      PropertyDescriptor _foreground =
        new PropertyDescriptor("foreground", beanClass);
      _foreground.setDisplayName("foreground");
      _foreground.setShortDescription("foreground");
```

```
        PropertyDescriptor[] pds = new PropertyDescriptor[] {
            _filled,
            _foreground,
            _shape};
        return pds;
    }
    catch(IntrospectionException ex) {
      ex.printStackTrace();
      return null;
    }
  }
  public java.awt.Image getIcon(int iconKind) {
    switch (iconKind) {
    case BeanInfo.ICON_COLOR_16x16:
        return iconColor16x16Filename != null ?
          loadImage(iconColor16x16Filename) : null;
    case BeanInfo.ICON_COLOR_32x32:
        return iconColor32x32Filename != null ?
          loadImage(iconColor32x32Filename) : null;
    case BeanInfo.ICON_MONO_16x16:
        return iconMono16x16Filename != null ?
          loadImage(iconMono16x16Filename) : null;
    case BeanInfo.ICON_MONO_32x32:
        return iconMono32x32Filename != null ?
          loadImage(iconMono32x32Filename) : null;
        }
    return null;
  }
}
```

At this point, select Project ➤ Make Project "Skill14.jpx" and the three classes, ShapeBox, ShapeEditor, and ShapeBoxBeanInfo, will be compiled.

Using the Property Editor

Now that you have a property editor, you can reopen the Skill14b project and use it. Return to the UI Designer for ShapeFrame and select shapeBox1. You'll get an updated Inspector window with the newly exposed foreground property available, as shown in Figure 14-8. Without any code changes, the shape property is now Circle instead of 1.

name	shapeBox1
constraints	Center
filled	True
foreground	■ Black
shape	Circle

Properties Events

Figure 14-8. The updated Inspector window for the ShapeBox component

If you click the shape property setting (Circle), you'll notice that a drop-down list of choices is now available, as displayed in Figure 14-9. If you change the setting, the shape drawn in the ShapeBox will change, too.

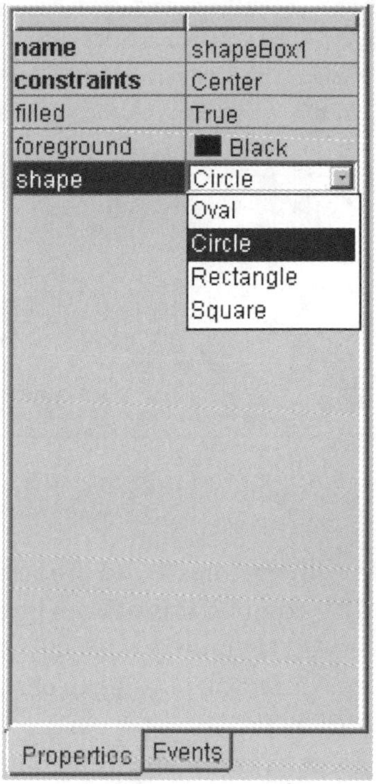

Figure 14-9. Picking from the list of shape choices made available through the property editor

Creating a Custom Property Editor

In most cases, textual input or a drop-down list of choices is sufficient for a developer to pick a property. However, what do you do when you need something more complicated? For instance, if you click the " . . . " next to the foreground property, a window pops up where you can select the different attributes of a single property and even get a preview panel for the color, as shown in Figure 14-10.

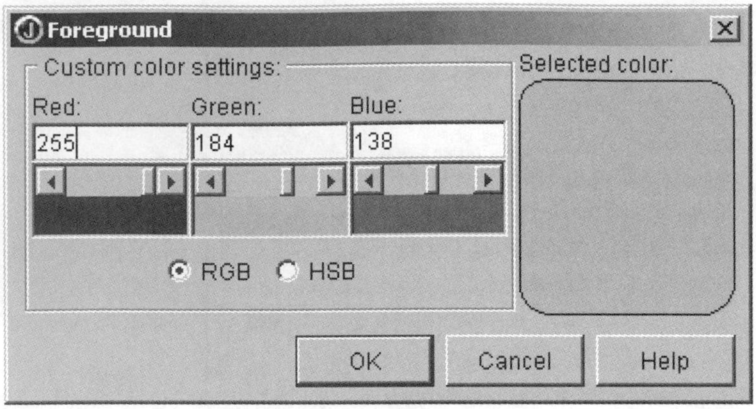

Figure 14-10. The custom editor for any Color property

This is a *custom editor*. With the foreground property, there's also a drop-down list to choose from. This combination of both is what you'll do for the shape property. Return now to the Skill14 project.

In creating your custom editor, you're going to cheat a little. You want to create a custom editor, but you already have a property editor. So, you'll have JBuilder create a dummy property editor and a custom editor. From the dummy property editor, you'll copy over the necessary code and place it in your ShapeEditor. You'll then finish up the custom editor and the two will be linked, leaving you to delete the dummy editor.

Return now to the Property Editors tab for the ShapeBox component. Click the Create Custom Editor button and select the Custom Editor Component option under Editor Type. You'll now see the screen shown in Figure 14-11.

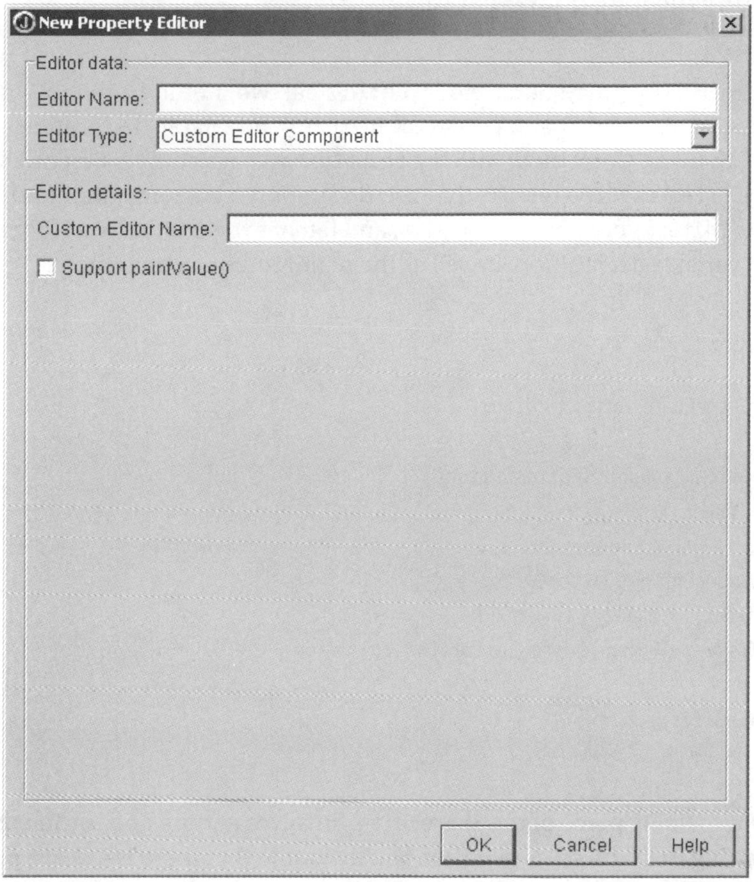

Figure 14-11. JBuilder's New Property Editor dialog box for a custom editor component

The Editor Name here is the dummy editor you're going to create, so enter **DummyEditor**. The Custom Editor Name is the custom editor class you're going to actually use—name that **ShapeCustomEditor**. You're not going to use the final option, Support paintValue(), so leave it unchecked. If you support paintValue(), that means you have to add code to paint the current setting of the property in the little area of the Inspector. The area is a little tight to try to draw an oval, circle, rectangle, or square and be able to tell them apart. After you click OK, the DummyEditor and ShapeCustomEditor classes are generated.

Updating the Property Editor

In the DummyEditor.java source, you want to steal two methods
(supportsCustomEditor() and getCustomEditor()), a variable declaration, and an
import statement. Copy them into the ShapeEditor.java source. Essentially,
supportsCustomEditor() reports that you do support a custom editor and
getCustomEditor() creates, if necessary, and fetches the editor. Don't forget to
copy the variable declaration as well as the required import statement.

```java
import java.awt.*;
 . . .
private ShapeCustomEditor editor;
 . . .
public boolean supportsCustomEditor() {
  return true;
}
public Component getCustomEditor() {
  if (editor == null) {
    editor = new ShapeCustomEditor(this);
  }
  return editor;
}
```

The remaining piece of the ShapeEditor involves getting and setting the
shape setting from the custom editor. You'll assume that there is a shape property
in the editor that will contain the current shape and use the property to set its
current shape. You'll add that shortly when you work on the CustomShapeEditor.

To get and set the property setting from the custom editor, you need to add
two special methods to the property editor: setValue() and getValue(). These
are part of the PropertyEditor interface. Essentially, when it's time to use the
editor, the original value is sent in and the setValue() method is called. It's
necessary to keep a copy of the setting locally, too. Never change the object
passed in. When you need to get the property setting from the editor, you call the
getValue() method. There's one trick with working with the two methods: They
only work with objects. So, for the shape property, which you'll store in the editor
as an int, it's necessary to convert back and forth between an Integer.

```java
private int shape;
public void setValue(Object o) {
  shape = ((Integer)o).intValue();
  if (editor != null) {
    editor.setShape(shape);
  }
}
```

```
public Object getValue() {
  if (editor != null) {
    shape = editor.getShape();
  }
  return (new Integer(shape));
}
```

That's all that's necessary for the updated property editor. You should save
the changes, but you can't compile yet because you need to finish the
ShapeCustomEditor. It must have a setShape() and getShape() method. In
Listing 14-8, you'll find the complete source for the property editor.

Listing 14-8. The Final ShapeEditor.java Source

```
package skill14;

import java.awt.*;
import java.beans.*;

/**
 * <p>Title: Editor for shape property of ShapeBox</p>
 * <p>Description: Permit user to pick shape from string or custom editor</p>
 * <p>Copyright: Copyright (c) 2001</p>
 * <p>Company: JZ Ventures, Inc.</p>
 * @author John Zukowski
 * @version 2.0
 */

public class ShapeEditor extends PropertyEditorSupport {
  private static String[] resourceStrings =
    { "Oval", "Circle", "Rectangle", "Square", };
  private static int[] intValues =
    { 0, 1, 2, 3, };
  private static String[] sourceCodeStrings =
    { "ShapeBox.OVAL", "ShapeBox.CIRCLE", "ShapeBox.RECTANGLE",
      "ShapeBox.SQUARE", };

  public ShapeEditor() {
  }
  public String[] getTags() {
    return resourceStrings;
  }
```

```java
    public String getJavaInitializationString() {
      Object value = getValue();
      for (int i = 0; i < intValues.length; i++) {
        if (value.equals(new Integer(intValues[i]))) {
          return sourceCodeStrings[i];
        }
      }
      return null;
    }
    public String getAsText() {
      Object value = getValue();
      for (int i = 0; i < intValues.length; i++) {
        if (value.equals(new Integer(intValues[i]))) {
          return resourceStrings[i];
        }
      }
      return null;
    }
    public void setAsText(String text) throws IllegalArgumentException {
      for (int i = 0; i < resourceStrings.length; i++) {
        if (text.equals(resourceStrings[i])) {
          setValue(new Integer(intValues[i]));
          return;
        }
      }
      throw new IllegalArgumentException();
    }

    private ShapeCustomEditor editor;
    public boolean supportsCustomEditor() {
      return true;
    }
    public Component getCustomEditor() {
      if (editor == null) {
        editor = new ShapeCustomEditor(this);
      }
      return editor;
```

```
  private int shape;
  public void setValue(Object o) {
    shape = ((Integer)o).intValue();
    if (editor != null) {
      editor.setShape(shape);
    }
  }

  public Object getValue() {
    if (editor != null) {
      shape = editor.getShape();
    }
    return (new Integer(shape));
  }
}
```

Finishing the ShapeCustomEditor

The initial ShapeCustomEditor was created by JBuilder. To finish it off, you'll start in the UI Designer. You want the custom editor to show four ShapeBox components, one for each shape. So, have the editor use a 2×2 GridLayout and drop in four ShapeBox controls. Set the shape property so that one of each is present.

Now, before you do anything else, you have to fix something. The ShapeCustomEditor class first generated by JBuilder included a constructor. When you used the UI Designer, a new, no-argument constructor was created. You need to pull the newly generated code out of the no-argument constructor and put it in the generated one. Then delete the no-argument constructor.

```
public ShapeCustomEditor(PropertyEditor editor) {
  this.editor = editor;
  try {
    jbInit();
  }
  catch(Exception e) {
    e.printStackTrace();
  }
}
```

Next, click the Bean tab, select the Properties tab, and add a shape property of type int. This will give you the necessary setShape() and getShape() methods.

You should also give your component some size, so the user can pick more easily. If you override getPreferredSize(), this will size the component to the Dimension you return. Instead of creating a new Dimension object with each call, it's best to just create the object once and keep it around.

```
Dimension dim = new Dimension(200, 100);
public Dimension getPreferredSize() {
  return dim;
}
```

The final task of the custom editor is to listen for selection of one of the shapes. You'll do this by reacting to the mouse release event and attaching the same behavior to each component's mouseReleased() event in the Inspector.

For the first shape, select the Event tab and double-click next to mouseReleased. In this event handler, what you want to do is get the shape setting from the selected ShapeBox. You also want to mark that particular shape as filled, as the user will be able to see what he or she just selected. To ensure none of the other shape boxes are filled, you'll clear them all first, and then fill the specific one. Then you'll add a call to repaint() to update the display.

```
ShapeBox shapeBox = (ShapeBox)e.getComponent();
shape = shapeBox.getShape();
shapeBox1.setFilled(false);
shapeBox2.setFilled(false);
shapeBox3.setFilled(false);
shapeBox4.setFilled(false);
shapeBox.setFilled(true);
repaint();
```

Next, copy the method name from the Source pane that this code belongs to. What you're going to do is copy the name to the mouseReleased handler for the other three ShapeBox controls.

Return to the UI Designer and select another shape. Click once in the mouseReleased handler for the component, delete the automatically generated name, and paste (Ctrl-V) the one you just copied. Press Enter to make sure it sticks.

Do the same for the other two components to finish off the custom editor (see Listing 14-9). One thing worth noting, which you may or may not have noticed, is that there's no OK or Cancel button here. The system automatically adds these buttons, with a Help button too. Now you can save your program and rebuild the entire project to make sure everything is compiled.

Listing 14-9. The Final ShapeCustomEditor.java Source

```java
package skill14;

import java.awt.*;
import java.beans.*;
import java.awt.event.*;

/**
 * <p>Title: Custom editor for shape property of ShapeBox</p>
 * <p>Description: Display each ShapeBox shape and let user pick</p>
 * <p>Copyright: Copyright (c) 2001</p>
 * <p>Company: JZ Ventures, Inc.</p>
 * @author John Zukowski
 * @version 1.0
 */

public class ShapeCustomEditor extends Panel {
  private PropertyEditor editor;
  GridLayout gridLayout1 = new GridLayout();
  ShapeBox shapeBox1 = new ShapeBox();
  ShapeBox shapeBox2 = new ShapeBox();
  ShapeBox shapeBox3 = new ShapeBox();
  ShapeBox shapeBox4 = new ShapeBox();
  private int shape;

  public ShapeCustomEditor(PropertyEditor editor) {
    this.editor = editor;
    try {
      jbInit();
    }
    catch(Exception e) {
      e.printStackTrace();
    }
  }

  private void jbInit() throws Exception {
    gridLayout1.setRows(2);
    gridLayout1.setColumns(2);
    this.setLayout(gridLayout1);
    shapeBox2.setShape(ShapeBox.CIRCLE);
    shapeBox2.addMouseListener(new java.awt.event.MouseAdapter() {
      public void mouseReleased(MouseEvent e) {
        shapeBox1_mouseReleased(e);
      }
    });
```

```
                    shapeBox3.setShape(ShapeBox.RECTANGLE);
                    shapeBox3.addMouseListener(new java.awt.event.MouseAdapter() {
                      public void mouseReleased(MouseEvent e) {
                        shapeBox1_mouseReleased(e);
                      }
                    });
                    shapeBox4.setShape(ShapeBox.SQUARE);
                    shapeBox4.addMouseListener(new java.awt.event.MouseAdapter() {
                      public void mouseReleased(MouseEvent e) {
                        shapeBox1_mouseReleased(e);
                      }
                    });
                    shapeBox1.addMouseListener(new java.awt.event.MouseAdapter() {
                      public void mouseReleased(MouseEvent e) {
                        shapeBox1_mouseReleased(e);
                      }
                    });
                  this.add(shapeBox1, null);
                  this.add(shapeBox2, null);
                  this.add(shapeBox3, null);
                  this.add(shapeBox4, null);
                }
                public void setShape(int shape) {
                  this.shape = shape;
                }
                public int getShape() {
                  return shape;
                }
                Dimension dim = new Dimension(200, 100);
                public Dimension getPreferredSize() {
                  return dim;
                }

                void shapeBox1_mouseReleased(MouseEvent e) {
                  ShapeBox shapeBox = (ShapeBox)e.getComponent();
                  shape = shapeBox.getShape();
                  shapeBox1.setFilled(false);
                  shapeBox2.setFilled(false);
                  shapeBox3.setFilled(false);
                  shapeBox4.setFilled(false);
                  shapeBox.setFilled(true);
                  repaint();
                }
              }
```

Using the Custom Property Editor

At this point, return to the Skill14b project and try to set the shape property in the Inspector. In addition to being able to pull down the original list of options, you can select the " . . . " button to get your custom editor, as shown in Figure 14-12.

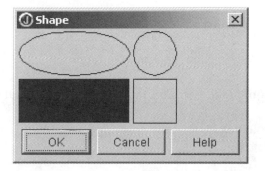

Figure 14-12. The custom editor dialog box for the shape property

Here, if you click a shape it will become filled. If you click OK, the ShapeBox in the ShapeFrame will change to the selection. If you click a shape and click Cancel, nothing happens, besides the editor's selected shape being filled.

Looking beyond Property Editors

Customization isn't just for property editors. If you need to set multiple properties simultaneously, a property editor isn't the way to go. It only permits you to set a single property, and you cannot look at any other bean properties in the process. To alleviate this situation, a bean can have something called a *customizer.* Once you create a customizer, by implementing the Customizer interface, the bean user can use it to configure multiple properties within the bean. If a bean supports a customizer, you can right-click over a component in the Component tree pane and select the Customizer option. An example of a Customizer is in the JavaBeans short course at the Java Developer Connection (http://java.sun.com/jdc/onlineTraining/Beans/JBShortCourse/). The course is a little dated, but most of the information, especially the material related to customizers, is still correct.

ARE YOU EXPERIENCED?

Now that you've made your way through customizing beans, the next skill describes serialization and what you need to know about it when creating beans. It's the last section of the book strictly covering the bean-development arena.

Now you can

- Create property editors

- Display pick lists to choose property settings

- Create custom property editors for more complex operations

- Draw filled shapes

- Draw arcs

Creating Beans: Serialization

- Learning about persistence

- Creating a `Timer`

- Working with transient data

- Saving the transient data's state

- Restoring program state

Learning about Persistence

There is one important aspect of JavaBean components that has been ignored so far. By definition, beans need the capability to save their current state. This means that if a program exits, when it restarts, all the characteristics, or properties, of the beans used will be restored to the state they were in when the program exited. This does not mean calling the individual setProperty() methods again, but instead restoring the bean state from a special format. This skill goes through the steps necessary to save and restore a bean's state. This characteristic is called *persistence,* as it allows a bean to persist beyond the lifetime of the bean.

In this skill, you'll learn what you need to do to make sure your beans can persist. Persistence uses the Serialization API, which allows any Java object, not just beans, to be converted to a stream of bytes that can be saved to disk, transferred over the Internet, or just saved as session data for a Java servlet. You'll start by creating a program that displays a counter. Using multithreading, you'll let the user start and stop the counter's operation, as well as enable the saving and restoring of the counter to disk. Saving basically stores the current value of the counter whether or not the counter is enabled, while restoring does the obvious and restores the saved state.

Creating the Interface

To create the program, close any open projects and run the Application Wizard. Set the Name to **Skill15** and set the Directory to **C:\skills\Skill15**. On the second page of the Application Wizard, name the Frame class **Counter**, and click Finish. The program to create will have a label in the Center area and five buttons along the South area. The buttons will be Start, Stop, Reset, Load, and Save. Perform the following steps:

1. Select Counter.java in the Navigation pane.

2. Select the Design tab in the Content pane so you can drop the components onto the screen.

3. Select the Swing Containers tab on the Component palette.

4. Select the JPanel bean and drop it into the Content pane. Set its constraints property to **South** in the Inspector.

5. Select the Swing tab on the Component palette.

6. Select the JLabel bean from the palette and drop it into the Content pane. Set its constraints property to **Center**, its horizontalAlignment property to **CENTER**, and its text property to **0**. Also, change the font property to a **24-point**, **Bold**, **Serif** font so it appears larger.

7. Select the JButton bean from the Component palette and drop five buttons into the JPanel at the bottom of the screen. Initially, one of them will not be visible until you change the labels.

8. Change the text property of each button. From left to right they should be **Start**, **Stop**, **Reset**, **Load**, and **Save**, although the actual order doesn't really matter.

At this point, save everything and run your program. Running your program will bring up the screen shown in Figure 15-1.

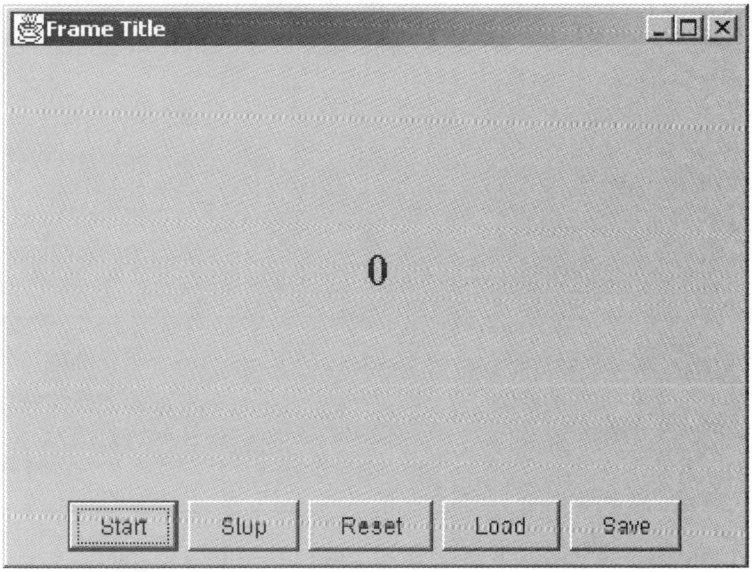

Figure 15-1. The initial screen for the Counter program

Making the Counter Count

To get your counter going, you need to define the functionality of three of the buttons: Start, Stop, and Reset.

Defining the Start Button

The way the Start button will work is it will use a Timer object to periodically perform a task. The task to perform will increment the counter. You'll need to use a thread to increment the counter. A different thread needs to do the incrementing so the screen is still responsive to someone selecting a button. Instead of creating a Thread object yourself, though, you'll rely on the Timer object in the javax.swing package.

> **NOTE**   *There is a second* Timer *object in the* java.util *package. Essentially, both do the same thing, though the Swing version supports stopping and restarting.*

Go into the UI Designer and double-click the Start button. JBuilder will add the adapter to handle the button selection event. You'll just need to add the behavior—the following five lines—into the method JBuilder just created:

```
System.out.println("Start");
if (timer == null) {
  timer = createTimer();
}
timer.start();
```

> **NOTE**   *If the* Timer *is already running, the* start() *call does nothing.*

This in turn requires you to declare a Timer instance variable:

```
Timer timer;
```

And you'll need to define the createTimer() method. Pull this code out of the event-handling method, as you'll need it elsewhere later. The way the Swing Timer object works is you need to provide an ActionListener that does the periodic behavior, in your case incrementing the counter and changing the label. The Timer constructor then takes two arguments: the delay between runs in milliseconds (you'll use 50) and the ActionListener. If 50 milliseconds doesn't work for you, increase the value for the looping speed to decrease, or decrease the value for the task repetition to increase.

```
private Timer createTimer() {
  ActionListener listener = new ActionListener() {
    public void actionPerformed(ActionEvent e) {
      incrementCounter();
    }
  };
  return new Timer(50, listener);
}
```

This leaves you with the incrementCounter() method to define. You've separated that method out as it requires a two-step operation and you need to ensure both operations happen together. You have to change a counter value and update the label. If you're not careful, the value could be changed between operations, as the Reset button will reset the counter and need its own resetCounter() method. All access to the counter setting should be protected.

To protect the counter variable, you'll create the incrementCounter() and resetCounter() methods as synchronized. If you remember from Skill 4, when you have a synchronized block, only one thread can be executing within the block at a time. Here, by making two methods synchronized, only one of them can execute at a time. As with the Timer, you'll need an instance variable to keep track of the count, too.

```
int count;
private synchronized void incrementCounter() {
  count++;
  jLabel1.setText(""+count);
}

private synchronized void resetCounter() {
  count=0;
  jLabel1.setText(""+count);
}
```

Defining the Reset and Stop Buttons

Because you did so much work for the Start button, you can reuse some of it for the Reset and Stop buttons. For the Reset button, you need to reset the counter to zero. After you double-click the button in the UI Designer, add the following source to the new method where JBuilder placed you:

```
System.out.println("Reset");
resetCounter();
```

For the Stop button, the process is just as easy. The `Timer` class has a `stop()` method that will suspend the notification of the `ActionListener`.

```
System.out.println("Stop");
timer.stop();
```

At this point, the `Counter` program is fully functional—from a counting standpoint. If you save everything and run the program, you can select Start, Stop, and Reset to see the program at work. The screen in Figure 15-2 looks the same as the one in Figure 15-1, except that it has a different count in the label.

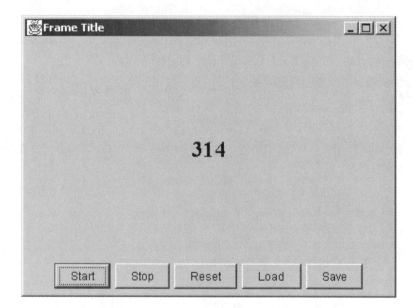

Figure 15-2. The working screen in the Counter program

Enabling Save and Load

Now that the basic program is working, you'd like to save the program state such that when you read it back, the counter value is where it was when saved, and the timer is running if it was running when saved. Two steps are involved in supporting saving.

First, in order for a class' state to be savable, the class must implement the `java.io.Serializable` interface. There are no methods in the interface. It just serves as a flag that says the class can be saved, or *serialized*. Technically speaking, the `Counter` class is already serializable because it subclasses `JFrame`. `JFrame` is a subclass of `Frame`, which is a subclass of `Window`, which is a subclass of

`Container`, which is a subclass of `Component`. `Component` already implements the `Serializable` interface so you don't have to do anything.

Had you not subclassed a component that implements the `Serializable` interface already, you could have used the Implement Interface Wizard to flag your class with the appropriate interface. There are no methods in the interface, so only adding the `implements java.io.Serializable` line to the class definition would have been sufficient. According to the JavaBeans Specification, being `Serializable` is a requirement for something to be considered a JavaBean component.

Then there is the second step. For the actual serialization to occur, just implementing the interface isn't sufficient. Because serialization saves state, every instance variable of the class must also implement the `Serializable` interface. If, however, your class has any class variables defined with the `static` keyword, they aren't saved, as they don't define the state of a specific instance of the class, only the class as a whole.

TIP *Because methods aren't state, they aren't saved. This means that when a saved class needs to be restored, you still need the `.class` file associated with it to be available.*

The process of determining if each variable is serializable gets easier with practice. You learn about the problem cases fairly quickly, and the rest just falls into place. The variable types tend to fall into three groups.

- Primitive variables (such as `int`, `float`, and `boolean`) are automatically serializable. There is nothing special that needs to be done. If all your instance variables are primitives or are classes that have only primitive instance variables, just implementing the interface is sufficient.

- Classes that describe non-platform-specific information are automatically serializable. Because the classes don't depend on the runtime environment specifics, they tend to depend only on primitive variables. These classes may include data structures, AWT components, and lots of things in between. For instance, an AWT `Label` component is defined by its text label and alignment, plus some inherited things, such as foreground color from `Component`. Although the `Label` component may appear and behave differently on different platforms, it's still defined by a set of primitive variables and by classes that are defined by primitive variables.

- The third set of variables is the problem child of the group. These are instance variables for classes that describe platform-specific information.

For instance, java.io.FileDescriptor is not serializable. It describes a specific open file on the running system. Saving this information doesn't make sense because when you restore a class that has a FileDescriptor instance variable, the original value has possibly changed or, even worse, may not exist on the new system. You can save a java.io.File object, which when used with a java.io.FileInputStream creates the current descriptor. However, on its own, a FileDescriptor is not serializable.

 NOTE *The two classes used most frequently that aren't* Serializable *are* Image *and* Thread. *For an* Image, *you can save the URL or filename of the image and reread it. For a* Thread, *you just save the thread state and recreate it.*

Now that you know about the Serializable interface, you can fix up your class so that it can be saved and restored. The problem is the Timer class. Even though the Timer class is Serializable, what it saves isn't of any use, as the action to perform doesn't get saved. You're better off just saving if it's running and recreating the Timer when the class gets restored. Now you know why you created the createTimer() method earlier. To mark an instance variable as something that shouldn't be saved, you need to add the transient keyword to its declaration.

```
transient Timer timer;
```

Now that Timer is transient, you can move on to the writing and reading parts. It's always easier to do the writing part first so you know what to read when it's time to restore. You're not connecting the process to the buttons yet; you're only doing the writing and reading of the state information.

Saving and Restoring the Counter State

When a class is saved, or serialized, the saving process looks for a writeObject() method within any class it serializes. On the *deserializing,* or reading, side, the method the system looks for is readObject(). These two methods offer the opportunity to customize the saving and restoring process. The methods are optional, and when not present they perform some default behavior.

When you save the Counter state, you need to save the Timer state in addition to the rest of the Counter. The writeObject() method passes in an ObjectOutputStream to save the object state to. The default object information is saved by calling the stream's defaultWriteObject() method. In addition to that, you need to save the Timer state. The Timer class has an isRunning() method that reports that state, so you just have to write that to the stream.

The following is the complete definition for the writeObject() method. You'll need to import the java.io package, too.

```
import java.io.*;
  . . .
private void writeObject(ObjectOutputStream oos)
    throws IOException {
  System.out.println("Write object");
  oos.defaultWriteObject();
  oos.writeBoolean(timer.isRunning());
}
```

Reading is a little more complicated. In order for the Timer to be restored, a new Timer needs to be created. Then, if isRunning() reported true when saved, the timer needs to be restarted when restored. The readObject() method passes in an ObjectInputStream to read the state from. You get the default state back by calling its defaultReadObject() method. Then, you need to get the running state back by reading in a boolean with readBoolean(). Finally, if the state is true, start the timer.

```
private void readObject(ObjectInputStream ois)
    throws ClassNotFoundException, IOException {
  System.out.println("Read object");
  ois.defaultReadObject();
  boolean timerRunning = ois.readBoolean();
  timer = createTimer();
  if (timerRunning) {
    timer.start();
  }
}
```

NOTE *The* readObject() *and* writeObject() *methods can throw exceptions during the serialization process for various reasons, such as if the class definition cannot be found, instance variables cannot be serialized, or disk space is an issue. These methods should not worry about the exceptions and should just pass them along to the caller that's doing the saving or restoring. Then, the callers can handle the exceptions as they see fit.*

This same restoration pattern can be used for other classes that have instance variables that aren't serializable. Save the state in something that is serializable, and then restore it based on that setting.

Restoring the Adapters

You might think that everything to restore is done at this point; however, there is one minor problem. All the Swing (and AWT) components flag their event listener lists as transient and don't save them at all. Because it isn't known beforehand if the listeners are themselves serializable, a conservative approach was taken to not save any of them. This means you have to manually recreate the internal listeners when you restore the bean. This just adds another step to the restore process. If you move all the addActionListener() method calls out of the jbInit() method and into their own procedure, you can call this procedure both in jbInit() and within readObject(), after the defaultReadObject() call but before the Timer is started. Listing 15-1 includes the new helper procedure. Be sure not to copy out the button label settings.

Listing 15-1. A Helper Method to Assist in Setting and Restoring the Button Adapters

```
private void setupAdapters() {
  jButton1.addActionListener(new java.awt.event.ActionListener() {
    public void actionPerformed(ActionEvent e) {
      jButton1_actionPerformed(e);
    }
  });
  jButton2.addActionListener(new java.awt.event.ActionListener() {
    public void actionPerformed(ActionEvent e) {
      jButton2_actionPerformed(e);
    }
  });
  jButton3.addActionListener(new java.awt.event.ActionListener() {
    public void actionPerformed(ActionEvent e) {
      jButton3_actionPerformed(e);
    }
  });
}
```

NOTE *Your buttons might be numbered in a different order, so make sure you save the right three adapters. Eventually, you'll have all five saved in this method, but you've only connected three buttons so far.*

Once you have the writeObject() and readObject() methods done, you can move on to actually saving and restoring the Counter. Normally, the saving and restoring is done outside the class definition by whoever is reusing the bean. In this particular case, you want Counter to save itself.

Setting Up the Save Button

Because of all the work you've already done, the saving process is going to be really easy. The only thing new to introduce is the ObjectOutputStream class that you saw briefly. It works similarly to the FileReader and StringWriter classes in Skill 8, but it works with objects instead of characters. When you create an ObjectOutputStream, you need to give it another stream to actually save things in. Then, for any object you want to write to the stream, you call the writeObject() method of ObjectOutputStream. In turn, the ObjectOutputStream writes all the nontransient instance variables of the class you told it to write. If any of those instance variables is itself a class, the stream will recursively save it too, until the only things left are primitive variables.

 **NOTE** ObjectOutputStream *is smart enough to know if it has already written a class out to the stream. So, if there is a circular reference to something already written, it will not rewrite the class data—it will only add a reference to the previously written object.*

If you double-click the Save button, you can add the following source to that event handler:

```
System.out.println("Save");
try {
  FileOutputStream fos = new FileOutputStream("Counter.ser");
  ObjectOutputStream oos = new ObjectOutputStream(fos);
  oos.writeObject(this);
  oos.close();
} catch (IOException exception) {
  System.err.println("Unable to save");
  exception.printStackTrace();
}
```

Also, move the code to connect the new adapter out of jbInit() and put it in setupAdapters():

```
jButton4.addActionListener(new java.awt.event.ActionListener() {
  public void actionPerformed(ActionEvent e) {
    jButton4_actionPerformed(e);
  }
});
```

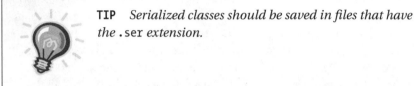

TIP   *Serialized classes should be saved in files that have the .ser extension.*

Enabling Restoration

The final step is to fill in the event-handling code for the Restore button. Reading involves an ObjectInputStream, which is the opposite of an ObjectOutputStream—you read objects from it.

Double-clicking the Restore button in the UI Designer allows you to add the following event-handling code. After you restore the Counter from the file, just call the show() method so the new Counter frame will be visible. You always save to the same file, so you can only remember one at a time.

```
System.out.println("Load");
try {
  FileInputStream fis = new FileInputStream("Counter.ser");
  ObjectInputStream ois = new ObjectInputStream(fis);
  Counter counter = (Counter)ois.readObject();
  ois.close();
  counter.show();
} catch (Exception exception) {
  System.err.println("Unable to load");
  exception.printStackTrace();
}
```

Again, you'll need to move the code to connect the new adapter out of jbInit() and place it in the setupAdapters() method. You'll now have five addActionListener() calls in setupAdapters().

At this point, you can finally save and compile everything. Assuming you've typed everything in correctly, you can try out all the buttons when you run the program. After running the program, then saving and restoring several counters, your screen will look something like the one shown in Figure 15-3. You can also save a counter, exit the program, restart the program, and load the saved version to demonstrate persistence. If you look in the JBuilder Message window, you'll see the different `println()` messages showing when each action occurred.

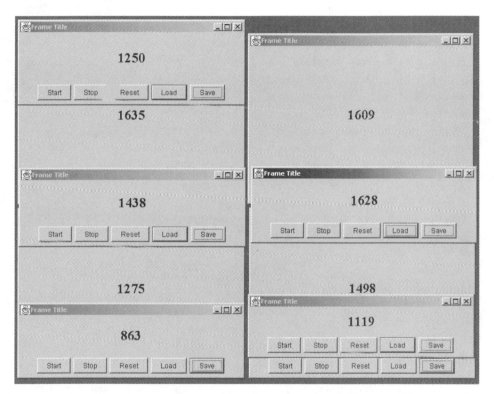

Figure 15-3. Multiple running counters after saving and restoring

 TIP *When you restore the saved screen, it's placed at the same position as when it was saved. If you haven't moved the original screen, it will go right on top of the existing screen. You'll need to move it to see both screens.*

Listing 15-2 shows the complete source code for the Counter class.

Listing 15-2. The Complete Counter.java Application Source

```
package skill15;

import java.awt.*;
import java.awt.event.*;
import javax.swing.*;
import java.io.*;

public class Counter extends JFrame {
  JPanel contentPane;
  BorderLayout borderLayout1 = new BorderLayout();
  JPanel jPanel1 = new JPanel();
  JLabel jLabel1 = new JLabel();
  JButton jButton1 = new JButton();
  JButton jButton2 = new JButton();
  JButton jButton3 = new JButton();
  JButton jButton4 = new JButton();
  JButton jButton5 = new JButton();

  //Construct the frame
  public Counter() {
    enableEvents(AWTEvent.WINDOW_EVENT_MASK);
    try {
      jbInit();
    }
    catch(Exception e) {
      e.printStackTrace();
    }
  }
  //Component initialization
  private void jbInit() throws Exception  {
    contentPane = (JPanel) this.getContentPane();
    contentPane.setLayout(borderLayout1);
    this.setSize(new Dimension(400, 300));
    this.setTitle("Frame Title");
    jLabel1.setFont(new java.awt.Font("Serif", 1, 24));
    jLabel1.setHorizontalAlignment(SwingConstants.CENTER);
    jLabel1.setText("0");
    jButton1.setText("Start");
    jButton2.setText("Stop");
    jButton3.setText("Reset");
    jButton4.setText("Load");
    jButton5.setText("Save");
```

```
  setupAdapters();
  contentPane.add(jPanel1, BorderLayout.SOUTH);
  jPanel1.add(jButton1, null);
  jPanel1.add(jButton2, null);
  jPanel1.add(jButton3, null);
  jPanel1.add(jButton4, null);
  jPanel1.add(jButton5, null);
  contentPane.add(jLabel1, BorderLayout.CENTER);
}
//Overridden so we can exit when window is closed
protected void processWindowEvent(WindowEvent e) {
  super.processWindowEvent(e);
  if (e.getID() == WindowEvent.WINDOW_CLOSING) {
    System.exit(0);
  }
}


transient Timer timer;
void jButton1_actionPerformed(ActionEvent e) {
  System.out.println("Start");
  if (timer == null) {
    timer = createTimer();
  }
  timer.start();
}


void jButton2_actionPerformed(ActionEvent e) {
  System.out.println("Stop");
  timer.stop();
}


void jButton3_actionPerformed(ActionEvent e) {
  System.out.println("Reset");
  resetCounter();
}


void jButton4_actionPerformed(ActionEvent e) {
  System.out.println("Load");
  try {
    FileInputStream fis = new FileInputStream("Counter.ser");
    ObjectInputStream ois = new ObjectInputStream(fis);
    Counter counter = (Counter)ois.readObject();
    ois.close();
```

```
        counter.show();
    } catch (Exception exception) {
      System.err.println("Unable to load");
      exception.printStackTrace();
    }
  }

  void jButton5_actionPerformed(ActionEvent e) {
    System.out.println("Save");
    try {
      FileOutputStream fos = new FileOutputStream("Counter.ser");
      ObjectOutputStream oos = new ObjectOutputStream(fos);
      oos.writeObject(this);
      oos.close();
    } catch (IOException exception) {
      System.err.println("Unable to save");
      exception.printStackTrace();
    }
  }

  int count;
  private synchronized void incrementCounter() {
    count++;
    jLabel1.setText(""+count);
  }

  private synchronized void resetCounter() {
    count=0;
    jLabel1.setText(""+count);
  }

  private void setupAdapters() {
    jButton1.addActionListener(new java.awt.event.ActionListener() {
      public void actionPerformed(ActionEvent e) {
        jButton1_actionPerformed(e);
      }
    });
    jButton2.addActionListener(new java.awt.event.ActionListener() {
      public void actionPerformed(ActionEvent e) {
        jButton2_actionPerformed(e);
      }
    });
```

```
  jButton3.addActionListener(new java.awt.event.ActionListener() {
    public void actionPerformed(ActionEvent e) {
      jButton3_actionPerformed(e);
    }
  });
  jButton4.addActionListener(new java.awt.event.ActionListener() {
    public void actionPerformed(ActionEvent e) {
      jButton4_actionPerformed(e);
    }
  });
  jButton5.addActionListener(new java.awt.event.ActionListener() {
    public void actionPerformed(ActionEvent e) {
      jButton5_actionPerformed(e);
    }
  });
}

private void writeObject(ObjectOutputStream oos)
    throws IOException {
  System.out.println("Write object");
  oos.defaultWriteObject();
  oos.writeBoolean(timer.isRunning());
}

private void readObject(ObjectInputStream ois)
    throws ClassNotFoundException, IOException {
  System.out.println("Read object");
  ois.defaultReadObject();
  boolean timerRunning = ois.readBoolean();
  setupAdapters();
  timer = createTimer();
  if (timerRunning) {
    timer.start();
  }
}

private Timer createTimer() {
  ActionListener listener = new ActionListener() {
    public void actionPerformed(ActionEvent e) {
      incrementCounter();
    }
  };
  return new Timer(50, listener);
}
}
```

 **TIP** *JBuilder allows you to add serialized beans to the Component palette. Add the* Counter.ser *file to the palette to make the last saved version available from the UI Designer. Or, you can right-click over a component in the Component tree and select Serialize there. Then, you can add that object to the Component palette. It will be preinitialized to your desired state.*

ARE YOU EXPERIENCED?

This skill only scratched the surface of what is possible with serialization in Java. It's an important skill to grasp when creating beans. With this skill, you have sufficient knowledge to perform most tasks when working with JavaBeans. However, if you need to know more, such as how to perform validation of what was read, check out the serialization documentation under the JBuilder Help topics.

Now you can

- Describe the serialization process

- Work with the Swing Timer

- Flag instance variables to not be saved

- Save and restore classes, retaining state information beyond the user interface

- Work with ObjectOutputStream and ObjectInputStream

- Override the default object saving and restoring behavior

Together with the last four skills, you should now be able to create some pretty nifty beans with lots of properties and events that can be customized and serialized. Now that you can create all these beans, let's find out how to deploy programs created with them.

Part Three

Advanced Skills

Delivering Programs

- Creating the program to deliver

- Using the Archive Builder

- Working with Java Web Start

- Running from an archive

Scooping Ice Cream

In this skill, you're going to put together some of the concepts you learned in earlier skills to create an applet that you can give away or just post on your Web site. The program you'll create is an ice-cream order form that serves up one, two, or three scoops of vanilla, chocolate, or strawberry ice cream. (For the health conscious, make believe it's yogurt instead.) You'll create the program as an applet, package it up with the JBuilder Deployment Wizard, and then run it through your browser with the Java Plug-in or Java Web Start. The end result will look like the screen shown in Figure 16-1.

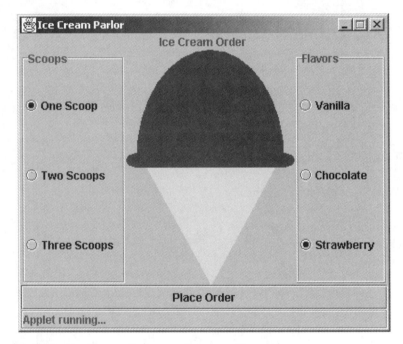

Figure 16-1. The Ice Cream Order program you'll create

Creating the Applet

You'll use the Applet Wizard to create the applet with two parameters.
One parameter, scoops, will be the default number of scoops selected. The other
parameter, flavor, will be the default flavor selected. At this point, close any
open projects and run the Applet Wizard. Name the project **Skill16** and save it to
C:\skills\Skill16. In the first dialog box of the Applet Wizard, name the class
IceCreamOrder, change the base class to **javax.swing.JApplet**, and then click
Next. In the second dialog box, create the two parameters, as shown in Table 16-1
and Figure 16-2, and then click Finish.

> **NOTE** *Since this applet subclasses Swing's* JApplet
> *class, you can't run this applet in a browser without
> doing something special. In most cases, that "something
> special" is using the Java Plug-in, which you can get at*
> http://java.sun.com/products/plugin/. *(It also comes with
> Sun's Java Software Development Kit (SDK).) However, you
> could deliver the Swing classes with the applet. There is one
> major drawback, though. Each time a user wants to run the
> applet, that user would have to download the Swing classes
> again. Not only are the Swing classes several megabytes in
> size, but also the version of the Swing classes that runs in the
> browser is the version of the Swing classes as they existed in
> the 1.2.x release of Java, not the later releases. In other words,
> if you're going to use the Swing classes in an applet, you'll
> need the Java Plug-in (or Java Web Start).*

Table 16-1. IceCreamOrder Parameter Settings

NAME	TYPE	DESCRIPTION	VARIABLE	DEFAULT
scoops	int	Scoop Count	scoops	3
flavor	String	Default Flavor	flavor	Vanilla

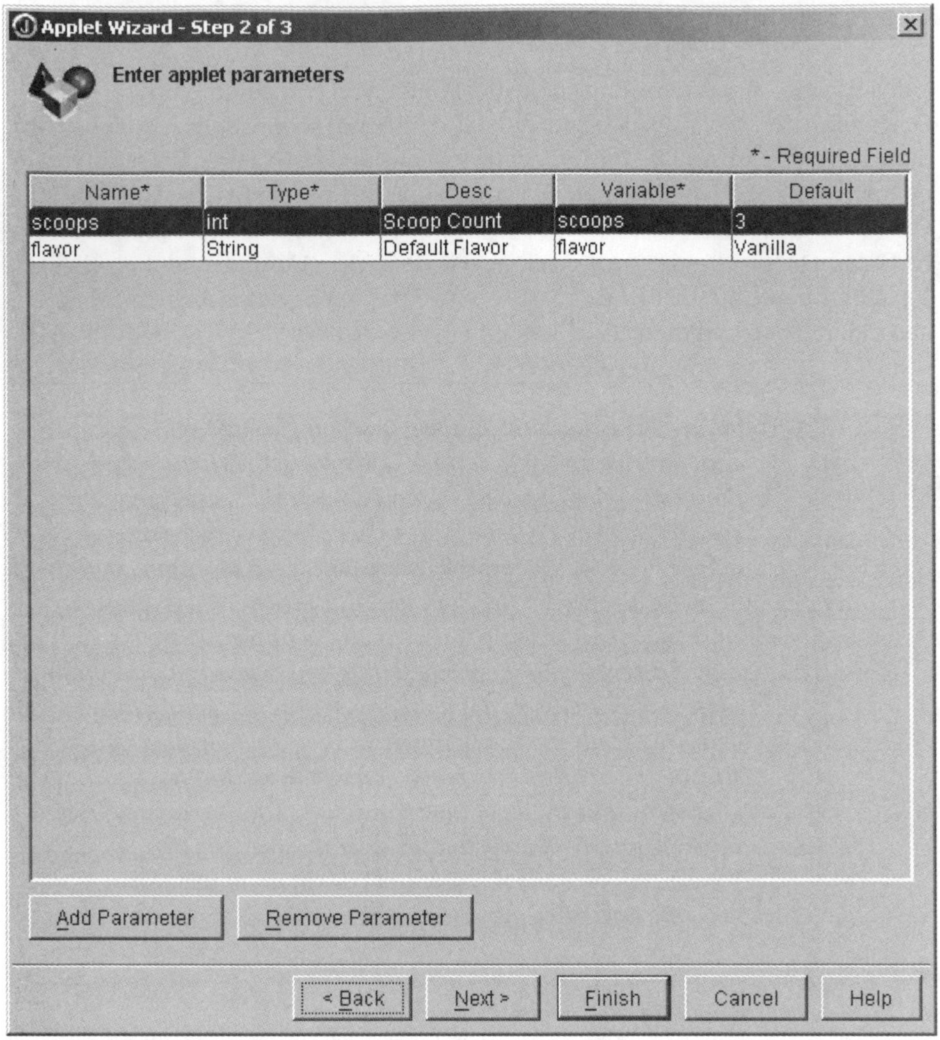
Applet Wizard - Step 2 of 3
Enter applet parameters
* - Required Field
Name*
Type*
Desc
Variable*
Default
scoops
int
Scoop Count
scoops
3
flavor
String
Default Flavor
flavor
Vanilla
Add Parameter
Remove Parameter
< Back
Next >
Finish
Cancel
Help

Figure 16-2. Setting the IceCreamOrder parameter settings in the Applet Wizard

Once JBuilder generates the initial program, go into the UI Designer for `IceCreamOrder.java`. From here, you'll need to set up the screen.

1. Place and center a JLabel in the north area. The text label of the JLabel should be **Ice Cream Order**. Here are the steps to follow:

    a. Select the Swing tab on the Component palette.

    b. Select the JLabel bean from the palette.

    c. Drop the JLabel bean into the top of the screen.

    d. Make sure the constraints property is **North**.

> **TIP**   *If you happen to drop the component into the proper area of the screen, you won't have to reset the* constraints *property.*

    e. Change the text property to **Ice Cream Order**.

    f. Change the horizontalAlignment from LEADING to **CENTER**.

2. Place a JButton in the south area with a text label of **Place Order**.

    a. Select the JButton bean from the palette.

    b. Drop the JButton bean onto the bottom of the screen.

    c. Change the constraints property to **South**.

    d. Change the text property to **Place Order**.

3. Place a JPanel full of JRadioButton components in the west area. Group them with a ButtonGroup and give them labels of **One Scoop**, **Two Scoops**, and **Three Scoops**. Place an etched border around the panel with a title of **Scoops**.

    a. Select the Swing Containers tab on the Component palette.

    b. Select the JPanel bean from the palette.

    c. Drop the JPanel bean onto the left side of the screen.

    d. Change the constraints property to **West**.

    e. Change the name property to **scoopsPanel**.

    f. Change the border property to an **Etched** border with a title of **Scoops**.

    g. Change the layout property to **GridLayout**, and have the grid be **1** column by **3** rows.

    h. Select the Swing tab on the Component palette.

    i. Drop three JRadioButton components into the panel.

    j. Change the text property of the components to **One Scoop**, **Two Scoops**, and **Three Scoops**.

    k. Change the name property of the components to **oneScoop**, **twoScoops**, and **threeScoops**, respectively.

    l. Select the ButtonGroup object from the palette.

    m. Drop the ButtonGroup object onto the screen. This isn't a graphical component, so anywhere will do.

    n. Change the name property of buttonGroup1 to **scoopGroup**.

    o. Change the buttonGroup property of each radio button to **scoopGroup**. This means that only one of the three radio buttons can be selected at once.

4. Place a JPanel full of JRadioButton components in the east area. Group them with a ButtonGroup and give them labels of **Vanilla**, **Chocolate**, and **Strawberry**. Place an etched border around the panel with a title of **Flavors**.

    a. Select the Swing Containers tab on the Component palette.

    b. Select the JPanel bean from the palette.

    c. Drop the JPanel bean onto the right side of the screen.

    d. Change the constraints property to **East**.

    e. Change the name property to **flavorsPanel**.

    f. Change the border property to an **Etched** border with a title of **Flavors**.

    g. Change the layout property to **GridLayout**, and have the grid be **1** column by **3** rows.

    h. Select the Swing tab on the Component palette.

    i. Drop three JRadioButton components into the panel.

    j. Change the text property of the components to **Vanilla**, **Chocolate**, and **Strawberry**.

    k. Change the name property of the components to **vanilla**, **chocolate**, and **strawberry**, respectively.

    l. Select the ButtonGroup object from the palette.

    m. Drop the ButtonGroup object onto the screen.

    n. Change the name property of buttonGroup1 to **flavorGroup**.

    o. Change the buttonGroup property of each radio button to **flavorGroup**.

At this point, if you save everything and run the program, you'll see the screen shown in Figure 16-3.

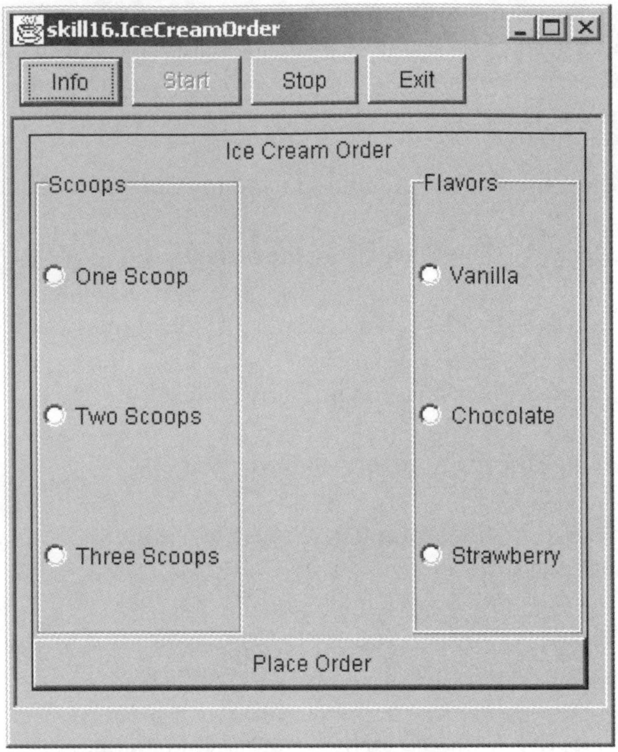

Figure 16-3. The initial IceCreamOrder program screen

Using the Parameters

Now that you've done the general screen setup, you should check the parameter settings to initialize the selections in the onscreen lists. The scoopsPanel needs to be set up with the scoops variable, and the flavorPanel needs to be set up with the flavor variable. If you look in the init() method (see Listing 16-1), you'll remember that JBuilder automatically adds the code to initialize the variables from the HTML parameters.

Listing 16-1. The Automatically Generated init() Method with the Applet Parameters Read In

```java
public void init() {
  try {
    scoops = Integer.parseInt(this.getParameter("scoops", "3"));
  }
  catch(Exception e) {
    e.printStackTrace();
  }
  try {
    flavor = this.getParameter("flavor", "Vanilla");
  }
  catch(Exception e) {
    e.printStackTrace();
  }
  try {
    jbInit();
  }
  catch(Exception e) {
    e.printStackTrace();
  }
}
```

To initialize the appropriate scoop setting, create a method to just select the appropriate radio button based on the number of scoops. A `switch` statement will do—just remember to default to 3 in case the setting is invalid.

```java
private void setScoop(int scoops) {
  switch (scoops) {
    case 1:
      oneScoop.setSelected(true);
      break;
    case 2:
      twoScoops.setSelected(true);
      break;
    case 3:
    default:
      threeScoops.setSelected(true);
      break;
  }
}
```

To initialize the flavor setting, you'll need to compare strings. It's a good idea to convert the input to all lowercase (or uppercase) to deal with different input cases. And default to Vanilla (or your favorite flavor) if the input isn't valid.

```
private void setFlavor(String flavor) {
  String lowercase = flavor.toLowerCase();
  if (lowercase.equals("chocolate")) {
    chocolate.setSelected(true);
  } else if (lowercase.equals("strawberry")) {
    strawberry.setSelected(true);
  } else {
    vanilla.setSelected(true);
  }
}
```

Then just add a call to the two methods at the end of jbInit():

```
setScoop(scoops);
setFlavor(flavor);
```

The complete jbInit() method follows in Listing 16-2. JBuilder generated this entire method except for the two method calls you just added. The setSize() method is highlighted (in bold) in the listing. This line should be deleted as the HTML file controls the applet size. If you were to change the applet size in the HTML file, you would need to change the size here, too. The line isn't necessary.

Listing 16-2. Component Initialization Code
```
private void jbInit() throws Exception {
  border1 = BorderFactory.createEtchedBorder(Color.white,new Color(148, 145,
140));
  titledBorder1 = new TitledBorder(border1,"Scoops");
  border2 = new EtchedBorder(
    EtchedBorder.RAISED, Color.white, new Color(148, 145, 140));
  titledBorder2 = new TitledBorder(border2,"Flavors");
  jLabel1.setHorizontalAlignment(SwingConstants.CENTER);
  jLabel1.setText("Ice Cream Order");
  this.setSize(new Dimension(400,300));
  jButton1.setText("Place Order");
  scoopsPanel.setBorder(titledBorder1);
  scoopsPanel.setLayout(gridLayout1);
  gridLayout1.setColumns(1);
  gridLayout1.setRows(3);
```

```
oneScoop.setText("One Scoop");
twoScoops.setText("Two Scoops");
threeScoops.setText("Three Scoops");
flavorsPanel.setBorder(titledBorder2);
flavorsPanel.setLayout(gridLayout2);
gridLayout2.setColumns(1);
gridLayout2.setRows(3);
vanilla.setText("Vanilla");
chocolate.setText("Chocolate");
strawberry.setText("Strawberry");
this.getContentPane().add(jLabel1, BorderLayout.NORTH);
this.getContentPane().add(jButton1, BorderLayout.SOUTH);
this.getContentPane().add(scoopsPanel, BorderLayout.WEST);
scoopsPanel.add(oneScoop, null);
scoopsPanel.add(twoScoops, null);
scoopsPanel.add(threeScoops, null);
this.getContentPane().add(flavorsPanel, BorderLayout.EAST);
flavorsPanel.add(vanilla, null);
flavorsPanel.add(chocolate, null);
flavorsPanel.add(strawberry, null);
scoopGroup.add(oneScoop);
scoopGroup.add(twoScoops);
scoopGroup.add(threeScoops);
flavorGroup.add(vanilla);
flavorGroup.add(chocolate);
flavorGroup.add(strawberry);
setScoop(scoops);
setFlavor(flavor);
}
```

At this point, open the Source tab for the IceCreamOrder.html file. Change the scoops and flavor parameters to different settings, such as **2** and **Chocolate**. If you then right-click over the IceCreamOrder.html filename and select Run, JBuilder will run the applet from the HTML file. This starts up the appletviewer tool, which is external to JBuilder. Once appletviewer reads in the parameters, it will initialize the two panels and then display them, as shown in Figure 16-4. (You can also start the applet by saving the changes and switching back to the View tab.)

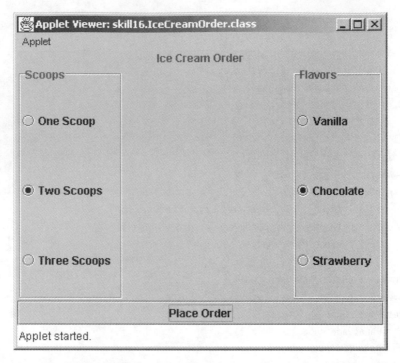

Figure 16-4. The IceCreamOrder program screen under appletviewer, reading in the default settings

> **TIP** *If you want this* `appletviewer` *to run when you press F9 or select Run ➤ Run Project, you need to go to Project ➤ Project Properties, choose the Run tab, choose the Applet subtab, and select the HTML file option. Then, click the "..." button and find* `IceCreamOrder.html` *in* `C:\skills\Skill16\classes`.

Creating the Scoop

Before you can add the action for selecting the ordering button, you need to create the ice cream scoop and cone. Instead of just drawing them directly to the screen, you'll create them to be components, just like any other Swing component.

Using the New Class Wizard, create a class called **Scoop** that subclasses **javax.swing.JPanel**. Uncheck everything, as the class will only be used within this package once the program is published. After you click OK, your source file should look pretty empty:

```
package skill16;

import javax.swing.JPanel;

class Scoop extends JPanel {
}
```

Before the scoop of ice cream can be drawn, you need to know the color and shape to draw. You can add a constructor to get the color and override the paintComponent() method to define the shape.

There are three steps involved in drawing the scoop:

1. Draw the main scoop, leaving room on the sides and below to "crunch up" some ice cream near the next scoop or the cone.

2. On each side, draw a half circle off to the side to provide the edges of the "crunch zone."

3. Fill in the area between the crunch edges with a rectangle.

The completed source for the Scoop class follows in Listing 16-3.

Listing 16-3. The Complete Scoop.java Source

```
package skill16;

import java.awt.*;
import javax.swing.JPanel;

class Scoop extends JPanel {
  public Scoop(Color c) {
    setForeground(c);
  }
  public void paintComponent(Graphics g) {
    super.paintComponent(g);
    Dimension dim = getSize();
    int heightEdge = dim.height/8;
    int widthEdge = dim.width/8;
    // Top
    g.fillArc(widthEdge/2, 0,
      dim.width-widthEdge, dim.height*2-heightEdge, 0, 180);
    // Left edge
    g.fillArc(0, dim.height-heightEdge,
      widthEdge, heightEdge, 90, 180);
```

```
      // Right edge
      g.fillArc(dim.width-widthEdge, dim.height-heightEdge,
        widthEdge, heightEdge, 90, -180);
      // Bottom
      g.fillRect(widthEdge/2, dim.height-heightEdge,
        dim.width-widthEdge, heightEdge);
    }
}
```

> **TIP** *Don't forget the call to* `super.paintComponent(g)` *in* `paintComponent()` *to make sure the component's background gets drawn correctly.*

Creating the Cone

Creating the ice cream cone is even easier than creating the scoop. Here, you use the Class Wizard to create a class named **Cone** that subclasses **javax.swing.JPanel**. Again, uncheck everything and click OK. Just override the `paintComponent()` method to draw the cone in the allotted area. You'll draw the cone as a filled triangle. The complete source for the Cone class follows in Listing 16-4.

Listing 16-4. The Complete Cone.java Source

```
package skill16;

import java.awt.*;
import javax.swing.JPanel;

class Cone extends JPanel {
  public void paintComponent(Graphics g) {
    super.paintComponent(g);
    g.setColor(Color.yellow);
    Dimension dim = getSize();
    int halfWidth=dim.width/2;
    int heightEdge = dim.height/8;
    int widthEdge = dim.width/8;
    Polygon poly = new Polygon();
    poly.addPoint(widthEdge, 0);
```

```
    poly.addPoint(halfWidth, dim.height);
    poly.addPoint(dim.width-widthEdge, 0);
    g.fillPolygon(poly);
  }
}
```

Adding Action

Now that you've defined the ice cream pieces, you can add the source for
how to use them. Some people may find it better to do this step first, and then
define the scoop and cone. Which way you do it is entirely up to you. To add
the button's action handler, select IceCreamOrder.java and return to the UI
Designer. From there, if you double-click the Place Order button, JBuilder
adds an event adapter and places you back into the source code of the new
jButton1_actionPerformed() method.

In this button, you need to find out what flavor of ice cream the patron
wants, determine what color that flavor is, find out how many scoops the
patron wants, create a scoop for each, add a cone, and place it on the screen.
Here are the specifics:

1. Find out how many scoops the patron wants. There is no magical
    method of ButtonGroup to find out the selected button. You have to loop
    through all the components. Don't forget the import statement
    for Enumeration.

    ```
    // With other imports at top of class definition
    import java.util.*;
     . . .
    // In jButton1_actionPerformed ()
    Enumeration scoopEnum = scoopGroup.getElements();
    int scoopCounter = 1;
    while (scoopEnum.hasMoreElements()) {
      AbstractButton button = (AbstractButton)scoopEnum.nextElement();
      if (button.isSelected()) {
        scoops = scoopCounter;
        break;
      } else {
        scoopCounter++;
      }
    }
    ```

2. Find out what flavor was selected:

```
// In jButton1_actionPerformed ()
Enumeration flavorEnum = flavorGroup.getElements();
while (flavorEnum.hasMoreElements()) {
  AbstractButton button = (AbstractButton)flavorEnum.nextElement();
  if (button.isSelected()) {
    flavor = button.getText();
    break;
  }
}
```

3. In the constructor, create a Map as a lookup table, mapping flavors to colors. You'll also need an instance variable.

```
// instance variable
Map colorMap;
. . .
public IceCreamOrder() {
  colorMap = new HashMap();
  colorMap.put("Vanilla", new Color(250, 235, 215));
  colorMap.put("Chocolate", new Color(210, 105,30));
  colorMap.put("Strawberry", new Color(255, 20, 147));
}
```

4. Look up the flavor in the map to get a Color:

```
// In jButton1_actionPerformed ()
Color c = (Color)colorMap.get(flavor);
```

5. Before you create the new scoop(s) and cone, any old ones should have been removed from the display. Keep a Box instance variable around for the old ones:

```
// instance variable
Box centerGroup;
 . . .
// In jButton1_actionPerformed ()
if (centerGroup != null) {
  this.getContentPane().remove(centerGroup);
}
```

6. Create the scoop(s) and cone in their own container. Use a vertical box for the container.

```
// In jButton1_actionPerformed ()
centerGroup = Box.createVerticalBox();
for (int i=0; i < scoops; i++) {
  Scoop scoop = new Scoop(c);
  centerGroup.add(scoop);
}
Cone cone = new Cone();
centerGroup.add(cone);
```

7. Place the scoop(s) and cone on the screen and update the display:

```
// In jButton1_actionPerformed ()
this.getContentPane().add(centerGroup, BorderLayout.CENTER);
this.getContentPane().validate();
```

Once all this is put together, it gives the action handler in Listing 16-5.

Listing 16-5. The Completed Action Handler for the Place Order Button
```
// instance variables
Map colorMap;
Box centerGroup;
 . . .
void jButton1_actionPerformed(ActionEvent e) {
  // Get selected scoop
  Enumeration scoopEnum = scoopGroup.getElements();
  int scoopCounter = 1;
  while (scoopEnum.hasMoreElements()) {
    AbstractButton button = (AbstractButton)scoopEnum.nextElement();
    if (button.isSelected()) {
      scoops = scoopCounter;
      break;
    } else {
      scoopCounter++;
    }
  }
}
```

```
// Get selected flavor
Enumeration flavorEnum = flavorGroup.getElements();
while (flavorEnum.hasMoreElements()) {
  AbstractButton button = (AbstractButton)flavorEnum.nextElement();
  if (button.isSelected()) {
    flavor = button.getText();
    break;
  }
}
Color c = (Color)colorMap.get(flavor);
if (centerGroup != null) {
  this.getContentPane().remove(centerGroup);
}
centerGroup = Box.createVerticalBox();
for (int i=0; i < scoops; i++) {
  Scoop scoop = new Scoop(c);
  centerGroup.add(scoop);
}
Cone cone = new Cone();
centerGroup.add(cone);
this.getContentPane().add(centerGroup, BorderLayout.CENTER);
this.getContentPane().validate();
}
```

Saving, compiling, and running the HTML file at this point will bring up the applet shown in Figure 16-5.

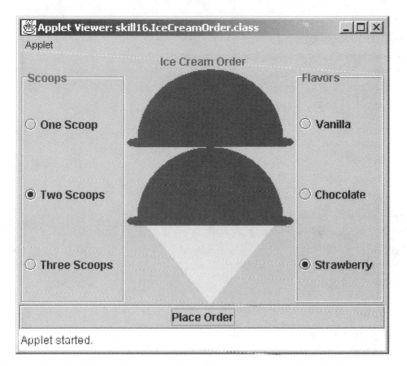

Figure 16-5. The IceCreamOrder applet with two scoops of strawberry

Run the program through the ropes and don't forget to alter the HTML file to change the defaults. The complete source for the applet follows in Listing 16-6.

Listing 16-6. The Complete IceCreamOrder.java Source

```
package skill16;

import java.awt.*;
import java.awt.event.*;
import java.applet.*;
import javax.swing.*;
import javax.swing.border.*;
import java.util.*;

public class IceCreamOrder extends JApplet {
  boolean isStandalone = false;
  int scoops;
  String flavor;
  JLabel jLabel1 = new JLabel();
  JButton jButton1 = new JButton();
  JPanel scoopsPanel = new JPanel();
```

```
Border border1;
TitledBorder titledBorder1;
GridLayout gridLayout1 = new GridLayout();
JRadioButton oneScoop = new JRadioButton();
JRadioButton twoScoops = new JRadioButton();
JRadioButton threeScoops = new JRadioButton();
ButtonGroup scoopGroup = new ButtonGroup();
JPanel flavorsPanel = new JPanel();
Border border2;
TitledBorder titledBorder2;
GridLayout gridLayout2 = new GridLayout();
JRadioButton vanilla = new JRadioButton();
JRadioButton chocolate = new JRadioButton();
JRadioButton strawberry = new JRadioButton();
ButtonGroup flavorGroup = new ButtonGroup();
Box centerGroup;
Map colorMap;

//Get a parameter value
public String getParameter(String key, String def) {
  return isStandalone ? System.getProperty(key, def) :
    (getParameter(key) != null ? getParameter(key) : def);
}

//Construct the applet
public IceCreamOrder() {
  colorMap = new HashMap();
  colorMap.put("Vanilla", new Color(250, 235, 215));
  colorMap.put("Chocolate", new Color(210, 105,30));
  colorMap.put("Strawberry", new Color(255, 20, 147));
}
//Initialize the applet
public void init() {
  try {
    scoops = Integer.parseInt(this.getParameter("scoops", "3"));
  }
  catch(Exception e) {
    e.printStackTrace();
  }
  try {
    flavor = this.getParameter("flavor", "Vanilla");
  }
```

```java
    catch(Exception e) {
      e.printStackTrace();
    }
    try {
      jbInit();
    }
    catch(Exception e) {
      e.printStackTrace();
    }
}
//Component initialization
private void jbInit() throws Exception {
  border1 = BorderFactory.createEtchedBorder(
    Color.white, new Color(148, 145, 140));
  titledBorder1 = new TitledBorder(border1,"Scoops");
  border2 = new EtchedBorder(
    EtchedBorder.RAISED, Color.white, new Color(148, 145, 140));
  titledBorder2 = new TitledBorder(border2,"Flavors");
  jLabel1.setHorizontalAlignment(SwingConstants.CENTER);
  jLabel1.setText("Ice Cream Order");
  jButton1.setText("Place Order");
  jButton1.addActionListener(new java.awt.event.ActionListener() {
    public void actionPerformed(ActionEvent e) {
      jButton1_actionPerformed(e);
    }
  });
  scoopsPanel.setBorder(titledBorder1);
  scoopsPanel.setLayout(gridLayout1);
  gridLayout1.setColumns(1);
  gridLayout1.setRows(3);
  oneScoop.setText("One Scoop");
  twoScoops.setText("Two Scoops");
  threeScoops.setText("Three Scoops");
  flavorsPanel.setBorder(titledBorder2);
  flavorsPanel.setLayout(gridLayout2);
  gridLayout2.setColumns(1);
  gridLayout2.setRows(3);
  vanilla.setText("Vanilla");
  chocolate.setText("Chocolate");
  strawberry.setText("Strawberry");
  this.getContentPane().add(jLabel1, BorderLayout.NORTH);
  this.getContentPane().add(jButton1, BorderLayout.SOUTH);
  this.getContentPane().add(scoopsPanel, BorderLayout.WEST);
```

```
                    scoopsPanel.add(oneScoop, null);
                    scoopsPanel.add(twoScoops, null);
                    scoopsPanel.add(threeScoops, null);
                    this.getContentPane().add(flavorsPanel, BorderLayout.EAST);
                    flavorsPanel.add(vanilla, null);
                    flavorsPanel.add(chocolate, null);
                    flavorsPanel.add(strawberry, null);
                    scoopGroup.add(oneScoop);
                    scoopGroup.add(twoScoops);
                    scoopGroup.add(threeScoops);
                    flavorGroup.add(vanilla);
                    flavorGroup.add(chocolate);
                    flavorGroup.add(strawberry);
                    setScoop(scoops);
                    setFlavor(flavor);
                }
                //Get Applet information
                public String getAppletInfo() {
                    return "Applet Information";
                }
                //Get parameter info
                public String[][] getParameterInfo() {
                    String[][] pinfo =
                        {
                        {"scoops", "int", "Scoop Count"},
                        {"flavor", "String", "Default Flavor"},
                        };
                    return pinfo;
                }

                //static initializer for setting look & feel
                static {
                    try {

//UIManager.setLookAndFeel(UIManager.getSystemLookAndFeelClassName());
//UIManager.setLookAndFeel(UIManager.getCrossPlatformLookAndFeelClassName());
                    }
                    catch(Exception e) {
                    }
                }
```

```
private void setScoop(int scoops) {
  switch (scoops) {
    case 1:
      oneScoop.setSelected(true);
      break;
    case 2:
      twoScoops.setSelected(true);
      break;
    case 3:
    default:
      threeScoops.setSelected(true);
      break;
  }
}


private void setFlavor(String flavor) {
  String lowercase = flavor.toLowerCase();
  if (lowercase.equals("chocolate")) {
    chocolate.setSelected(true);
  } else if (lowercase.equals("strawberry")) {
    strawberry.setSelected(true);
  } else {
    vanilla.setSelected(true);
  }
}


void jButton1_actionPerformed(ActionEvent e) {
  // Get selected scoop
  Enumeration scoopEnum = scoopGroup.getElements();
  int scoopCounter = 1;
  while (scoopEnum.hasMoreElements()) {
    AbstractButton button = (AbstractButton)scoopEnum.nextElement();
    if (button.isSelected()) {
      scoops = scoopCounter;
      break;
    } else {
      scoopCounter++;
    }
  }
```

```
      // Get selected flavor
      Enumeration flavorEnum = flavorGroup.getElements();
      while (flavorEnum.hasMoreElements()) {
        AbstractButton button = (AbstractButton)flavorEnum.nextElement();
        if (button.isSelected()) {
          flavor = button.getText();
          break;
        }
      }
      Color c = (Color)colorMap.get(flavor);
      if (centerGroup != null) {
        this.getContentPane().remove(centerGroup);
      }
      centerGroup = Box.createVerticalBox();
      for (int i=0; i < scoops; i++) {
        Scoop scoop = new Scoop(c);
        centerGroup.add(scoop);
      }
      Cone cone = new Cone();
      centerGroup.add(cone);
      this.getContentPane().add(centerGroup, BorderLayout.CENTER);
      this.getContentPane().validate();
    }
}
```

Creating an Archive

Once you've completed your applet, it's time to package it up to run in a browser outside of JBuilder. JBuilder's Archive Builder is responsible for packaging up the applet. The wizard is only available in JBuilder Professional and Enterprise. Using this wizard, you select what you want to deploy, and the wizard finds any dependencies to make sure you deliver a complete package. If you select Wizards ➢ Archive Builder, you'll see the dialog box shown in Figure 16-6.

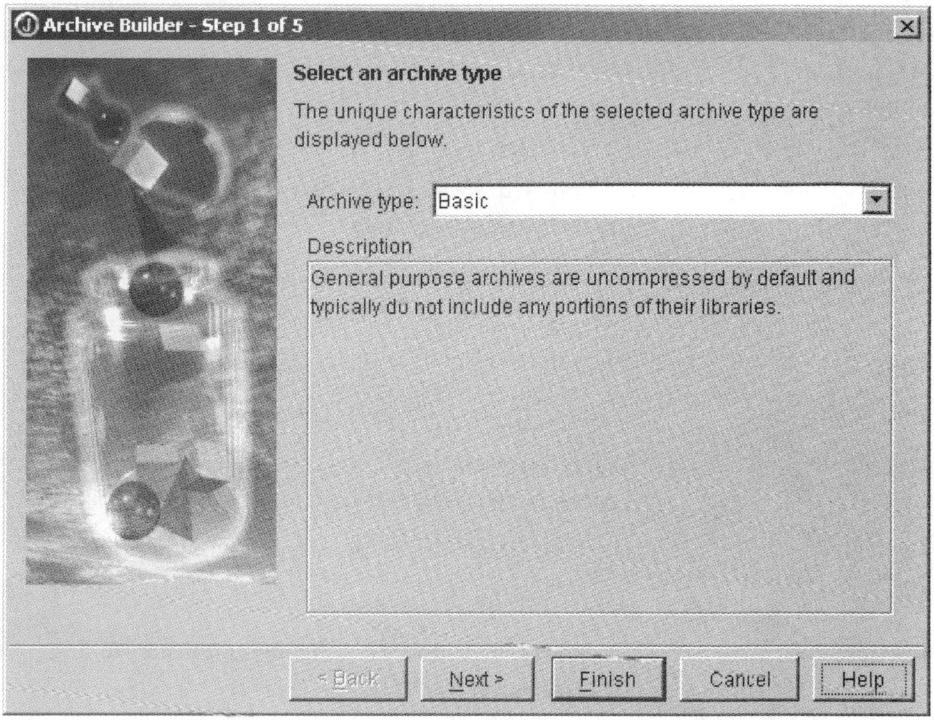

Figure 16-6. The Archive Builder dialog box. From here you pick which files you want to send out, along with a structure to store them.

There are 11 different ways to package your JBuilder program. Table 16-2 highlights the features of each.

Table 16-2. JBuilder Deployment Options

TYPE	DESCRIPTION
Applet JAR	Compressed archive file. Allows a browser to download all classes for the applet at once.
Applet ZIP	Compressed ZIP file. Older browsers (pre-4.*x*) don't understand the JAR format.
Application	Uncompressed archive file. Allows you to run the application with `java -jar filename.jar`.
Basic	Uncompressed archive file. For bundling a single library.
Documentation	Documentation archive for the project.
J2EE Application Client	Contains enterprise beans and resources with the necessary deployment descriptor.
Open Tool	Uncompressed archive for extending JBuilder.
Source	Source files for the project.
Resource Adapter (RAR)	Contains J2EE connector implementations, including platform-specific libraries.
Web Start Applet	Compressed archive format for deploying applets through the Web.
Web Start Application	Compressed archive format for deploying applications through the Web.

Each archive type has its own set of dialog boxes (anywhere from two to seven) to go through. You're going to deploy the applet as a Web Start Applet, so select that option and click Next to get the second dialog box of five (shown in Figure 16-7).

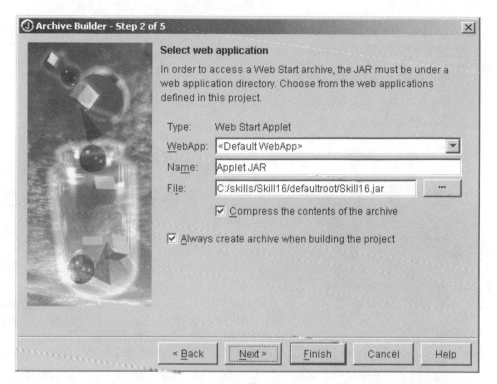

Figure 16-7. The Archive Builder (2 of 5) dialog box. Here you select the Web application to deploy.

On the second screen, you can select the Web application to connect to. Since you didn't create one for the project, it just lists a default. If you want to create one, there's a wizard in the Object Gallery. Just leave the defaults and click Next to move on to the dialog box shown in Figure 16-8.

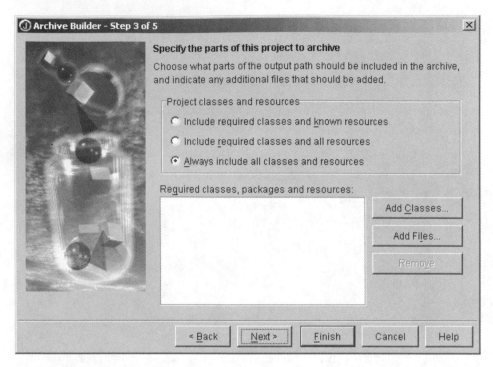

Figure 16-8. The Archive Builder (3 of 5) dialog box. Here you specify what to include from your project in the archive.

The third screen allows you to pick what classes get put in the JAR. You can manually add classes, have JBuilder pick them, and also add support files, such as image files, audio files, or other resources. Leaving the "Always include all classes and resources" option selected adds everything in your project. Click Next to move on to the dialog box shown in Figure 16-9.

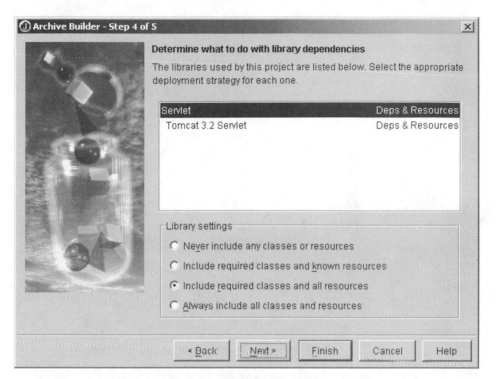

Figure 16-9. The Archive Builder (4 of 5) dialog box. Here you specify what to include from outside your project in the archive.

You select third-party library dependencies from the fourth screen. These would be already configured for your project. You just need to tell the Archive Builder whether or not to include them in the JAR file for your project. Usually, you would include everything necessary to run the applet/application, but if you know users already have something installed locally, possibly because the library is accessible from a network drive, you don't need to include the library with the archive. Click Next one last time to move on to the dialog box shown in Figure 16-10.

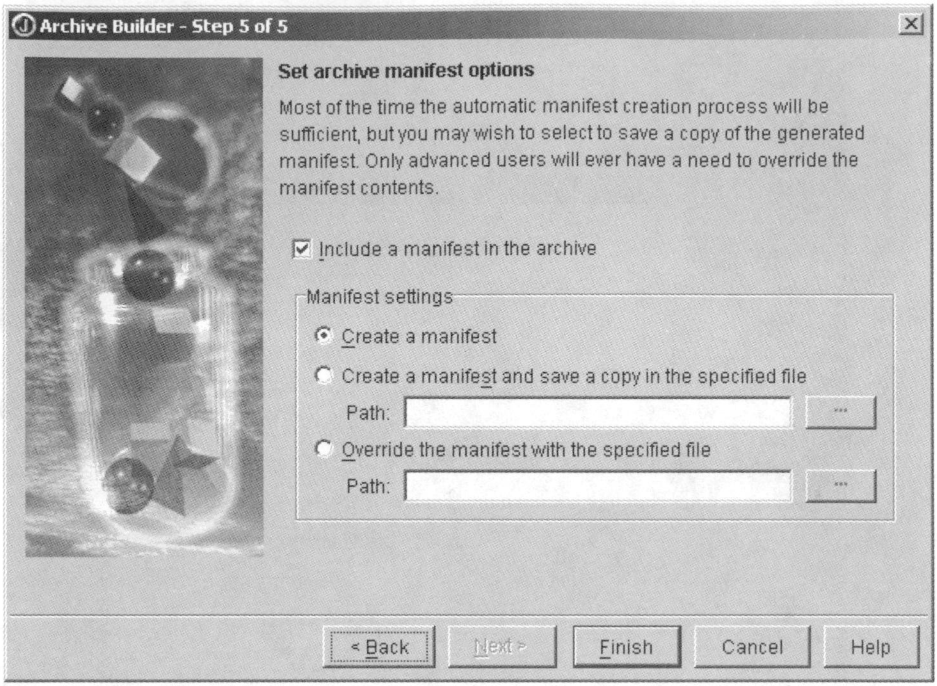

Figure 16-10. The Archive Builder (5 of 5) dialog box. Here you specify manifest options.

A manifest file is a descriptor for the archive. Under normal circumstances, the default one generated based upon the type of archive selected is sufficient. You can even save a copy of the generated file. In cases where the default settings aren't sufficient, you can opt to specify your own. Clicking Finish on this screen finishes up the Archive Builder wizard, but it doesn't create the archive. The archive is built when you Make or Rebuild your current project.

Running IceCreamOrder from the JAR File

To run the applet from the JAR file, you need to tell the HTML loader about the JAR file. Select the Source tab for `IceCreamOrder.html` and add the following within the `<applet>` tag:

```
archive="Skill16.jar"
```

This tells the browser to copy the entire JAR file from the server to the local cache, and then run the applet. Had the applet included many more different classes, users would notice a performance increase, because individual class files don't have to be downloaded separately. There is a slight start-up cost to download everything first, but execution is faster once the applet starts up.

Because this applet uses Swing, though, you can't try it in Internet Explorer or Netscape Navigator/Communicator (unless you have the Plug-in installed). Those browsers don't come with support for the Swing classes. Because they weren't added to the archive, the applet won't run there. That's where Java Web Start comes in.

Setting Up IceCreamOrder for Java Web Start

To configure your applet to run through Java Web Start, so that it can be launched from any browser, you need to create a Web Start Launcher and make sure your Web server has an appropriate MIME-type setup (most don't).

To create a Web Start Launcher, open the Object Gallery (select File ➤ New), choose the Web tab, and then select Web Start Launcher to get the screen shown in Figure 16-11.

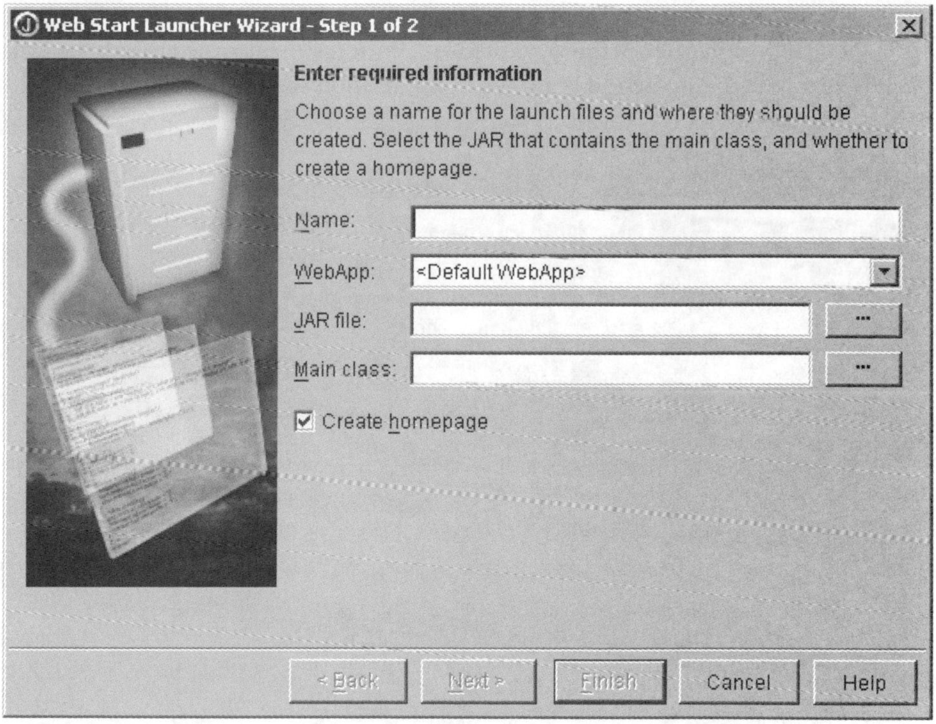

Figure 16-11. The Web Start Launcher Wizard. You'll need to name the program, specify the JAR file, and point to the main applet class.

Figure 16-11 is the first of three screens you need to configure for the launcher. You can't just select the defaults. Name the launcher **BenAndJerrys**.

Click the " . . . " button next to JAR file to find the JAR file for the skill. This should be **C:/skills/Skill16/defaultroot/Skill16.jar**. The defaultroot directory is the directory for the Web server. JBuilder comes with a Web server called Tomcat for you to use. Once you've selected it, click OK to return to Figure 16-11. Then select the "..." button next to the Main class text field to locate the IceCreamOrder class in the skill16 package. Make sure the text field has **skill16.IceCreamOrder** in it.

NOTE *Tomcat is a freely available, open source Web server that supports servlets and JavaServer Pages (JSP). In fact, Tomcat is the reference implementation of the Java Servlets and JSP specifications. It will not stop running after the 30-day trial for the JBuilder Enterprise release. If you find Tomcat useful, you can check to see if a new version of the software is available from* http://jakarta.apache.org/tomcat/.

Once all the options are filled in, the Next button will become clickable. Click Next to move on to the second launcher configuration screen (see Figure 16-12).

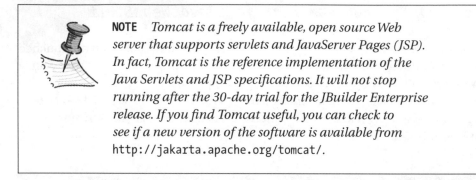

Figure 16-12. The Web Start Launcher Wizard (2 of 3). You'll need to name the applet and specify the document root.

There are four options to configure on the second screen. Two actually have defaults for the applet size. What's left are the Applet name and Document base. Essentially, the Applet name is what the loader will call the applet, similar to the name attribute of <APPLET> tag in the HTML file. The Document base is where the browser will get the applet classes from. Name the applet **IceCreamOrder** and specify a Document base of **http://localhost:8080**. The name *localhost* refers to your own machine. This could also be 127.0.0.1. The port 8080 is where the Tomcat Web server that comes with JBuilder listens for connections. Had this been running from my company's Web server, the Document base would have been **http://www.jzventures.com**, with no port number, since by default HTTP requests listen on port 80. Click Next to move on to the screen shown in Figure 16-13.

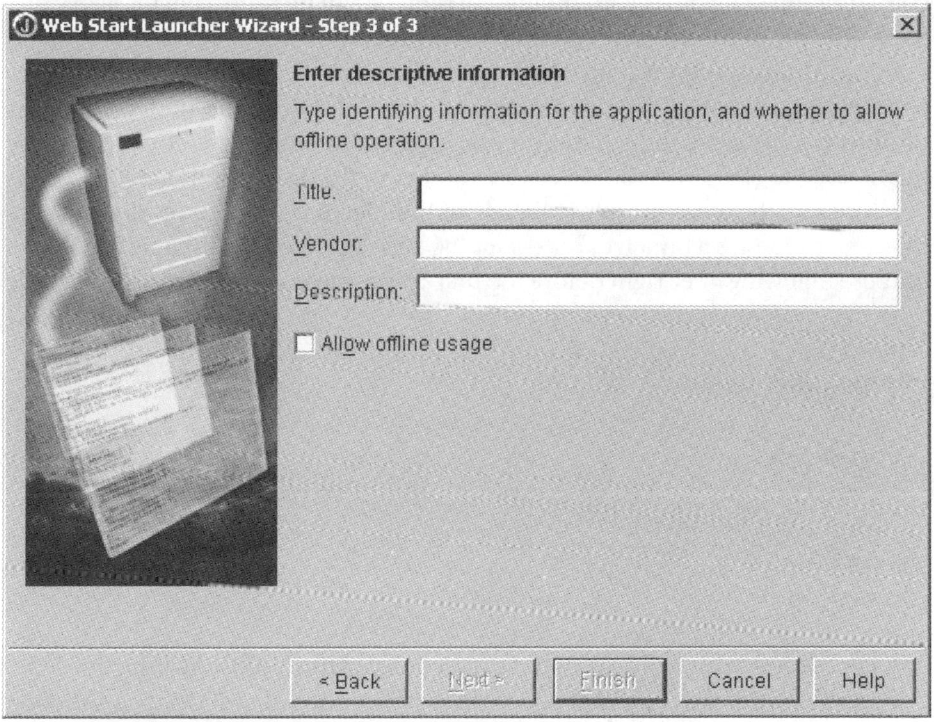

Figure 16-13. The Web Start Launcher Wizard (3 of 3). You'll need to name the applet frame and vendor, as well as provide a description.

On the final screen for the Web Start Launcher Wizard, you provide four pieces of information. First is the title. The title represents the frame title for the window the applet will run in. With Java Web Start, the applet doesn't run within the browser. Instead, it gets its own window outside the browser. Use **Ice Cream Parlor** for the window title. Next fill in the Vendor, **JZ Ventures, Inc.**, and

Description, **Ice Cream Applet**. The last option allows you to install an applet so that it can be launched from the desktop, while offline. Leave this option unchecked.

After you click Finish, you'll find two more files added to your project: BenAndJerrys.html and BenAndJerrys.jnlp. The .jnlp file is just an XML file, while the .html file is the *launcher* that will start up your applet through Java Web Start. If Java Web Start isn't installed, you'll be told where to download it (http://java.sun.com/products/javawebstart/) before you can run the program.

Running IceCreamOrder with Java Web Start

In order to run the Java Web Start–enabled applet, you need to fix up the Tomcat configuration that comes with JBuilder to understand the .jnlp file for Java Web Start. One of the Tomcat configuration files is web.xml. This is located in the conf directory under the Tomcat installation directory. For the one that comes with JBuilder, that would be the jakarta-tomcat-3.2.3 directory under where JBuilder 6 is installed, though this may be different in future versions so you might need to change the 3.2.3 version number in the directory name.

Open up the file in an editor outside of JBuilder. Around 75 lines down into the web.xml file are a bunch of mime-mapping tags. You need to add one more. Add the following lines right before the first <mime-mapping> line:

```
<mime-mapping>
  <extension>
    jnlp
  </extension>
  <mime-type>
    application/x-java-jnlp-file
  </mime-type>
</mime-mapping>
```

These lines essentially say that if a filename has the extension jnlp, the browser should treat it as an application/x-java-jnlp-file MIME type—thus, Java Web Start will run it. If this line isn't added, the browser will treat the launcher program as raw text.

Once you've added these lines, return to the JBuilder window.

Now you need to tell JBuilder to load the BenAndJerrys.html file that launches the Java Web Start–enabled applet. To do this, select Project ➤ Project Properties. Choose the Run tab and then the JSP/Servlet tab to get to the screen shown in Figure 16-14. You need to pick the HTML file from this tab because the HTML file needs to be loaded through the Tomcat Web server, not as a file from your local file system.

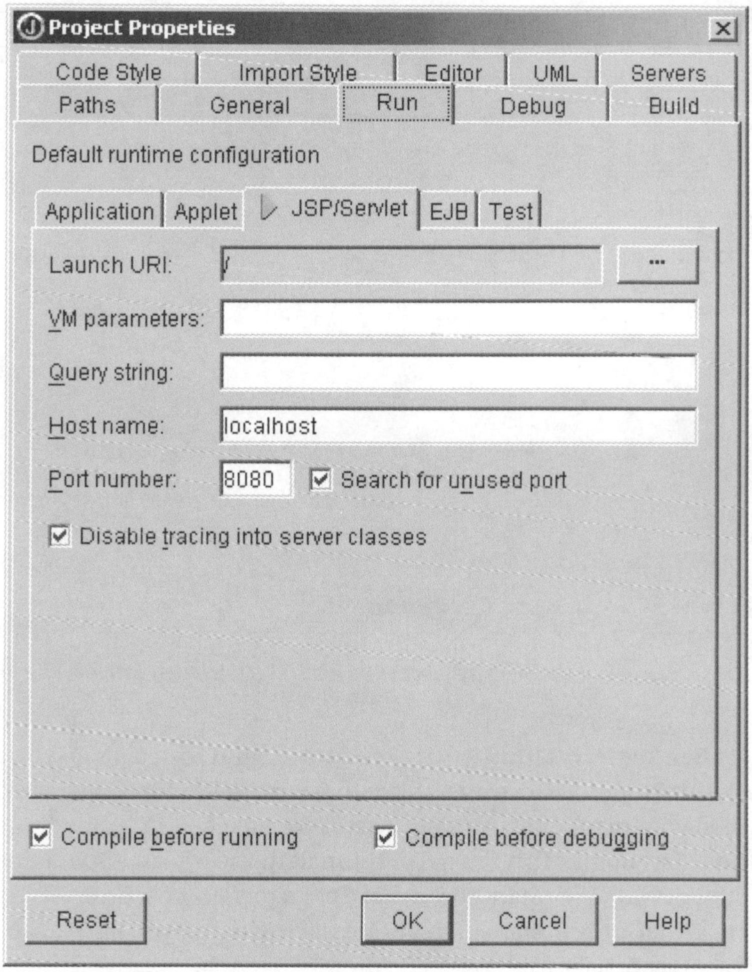

Figure 16-14. Configuring JBuilder to launch the Java Web Start Web page

From the JSP/Servlet tab, click the " . . . " button next to Launch URI to get to the screen in Figure 16-15.

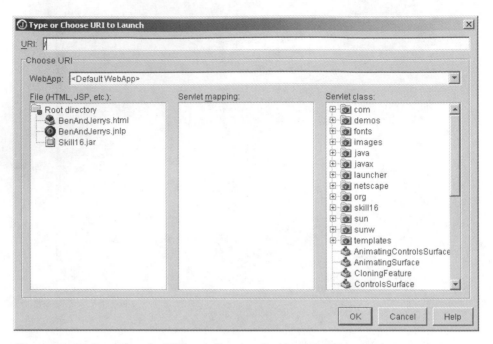

Figure 16-15. Locating the Web application for the Ice Cream Parlor

Select **BenAndJerrys.html** in the first column, and then click OK. Click OK on the Project Properties screen to return to the main JBuilder window. At this point, when you try to run the project (press F9 or select Run ➤ Run Project), Tomcat will start up (the first time). Unfortunately, the browser built into JBuilder doesn't support Java Web Start, so you have to go to your own browser. The key point here is that Tomcat started. In the Message window, you'll see a tab for http://localhost:8080, as shown in Figure 16-16.

Figure 16-16. Message window tab indicating that Tomcat is running

Because you can't run Java Web Start pages in JBuilder, open up your favorite browser and go to http://localhost:8080/BenAndJerrys.html. If Java Web Start isn't installed yet, you'll be prompted to install it. After installation, you'll find that the launcher page is pretty basic, as shown in Figure 16-17. Once you click the link, the applet will launch through Java Web Start. You'll first see an initialization message as the applet downloads (see Figure 16-18) before you see the familiar applet again (see Figure 16-19). This time, the applet is in its own frame, without all the decorations that the `appletviewer` provided to start and stop the program.

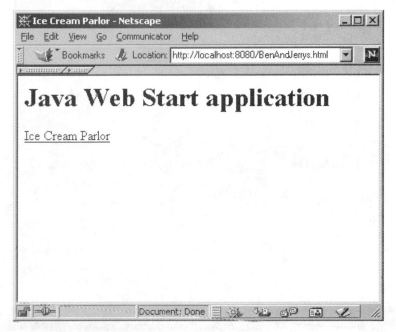

Figure 16-17. The Java Web Start applet launcher page

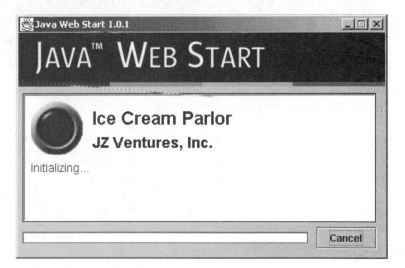

Figure 16-18. The Java Web Start initialization message for the Ice Cream Parlor

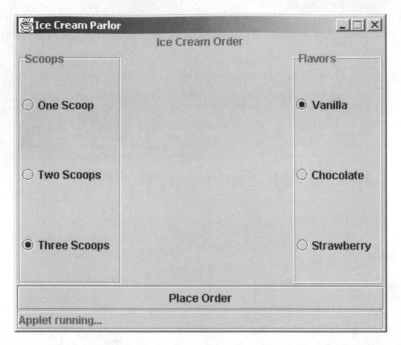

Figure 16-19. The IceCreamOrder applet running through Java Web Start

ARE YOU EXPERIENCED?

Congratulations! You've now successfully created a Swing applet, packaged it up in an archive, and deployed it with Java Web Start. Put it on your Web site to show the world what you've done. Between the launcher and the class files, there's only about 10–20K worth of files you need on your Web server. If you place the files on another server, you'll need to rerun the Web Start Launcher Wizard.

Now you can

- Create new components

- Work with the JRadioButton component

- Package programs in archives with the Archive Builder

- Deploy programs with Java Web Start

- Run Swing applets through standard Web browsers

In the next skill, you'll learn about using menus within your Java programs.

Working with Menus

- Working with an About box

- Working with the Menu Designer to create menus

- Using the JOptionPane

- Changing colors with the JColorChooser

- Changing fonts with the FontChooser

Getting Started

No doubt, you've used menus in normal application programs. With JBuilder, creating menus is a snap with the help of the Menu Designer. In this skill, you'll create a program that allows you to change the font and color of some displayed text, as well as the actual text. You'll also have a pop-up window appear to display information about your program.

To start the skill, select File ➢ Close Projects to close any open projects. Next, use the Application Wizard to create a new project and set up the application framework. In the Project Wizard, enter **Skill17** as a Project name and **C:\skills\Skill17** as the Directory, and then click Next twice. On the final screen of the Project Wizard, fill in the Title, Author, Company, and Description fields with appropriate information, and then click Finish. You'll see where some of these pieces of information are used shortly.

With the Application Wizard, you're going to do a little more than you usually do, too. On the first screen of the Application Wizard, click Next. On the second screen, enter **MenuTester** in the Class name, and then select Generate menu bar and Generate About dialog in the Options area. Click Finish to let JBuilder do its thing. At this point, if you save and run everything, you'll see the screen shown in Figure 17-1.

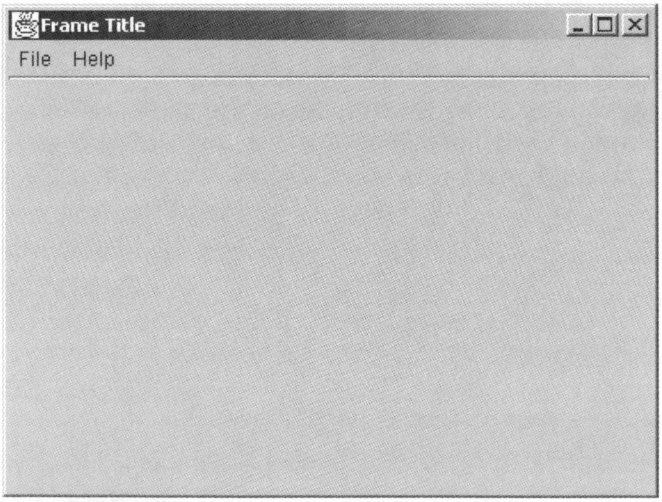

Figure 17-1. The initial screen with the default menu setup. You'll find Exit under the File menu and About under the Help menu.

Before you do anything with the menus, add a `JLabel` to the screen. You'll use this label later with the menus to change the font and color of the text displayed. Drop a `JLabel` (from the Swing tab of the Component palette) into the center of `MenuTester` and change the text property to **Welcome to JBuilder**. Also change the `horizontalAlignment` to **CENTER** so that the text is centered horizontally.

After you add the label to the screen and rerun the application, your program will look like the screen in Figure 17-2. The reason you added the label to the middle of the screen is the height of the component changes when you change the font later and it looks nicer centered.

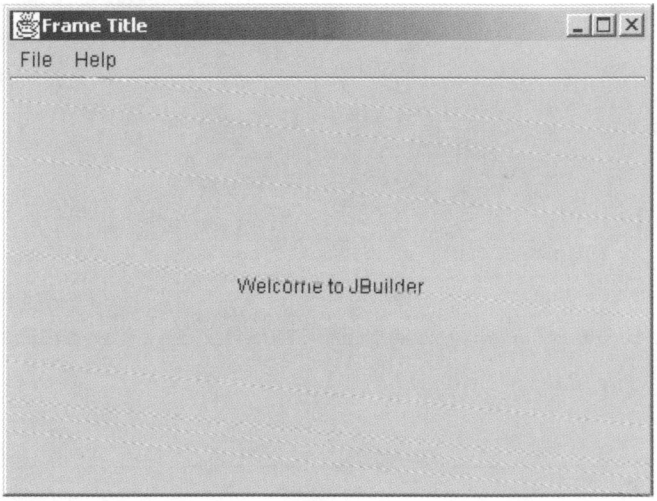

Figure 17-2. The screen with the new label

Working with an About Box

An About box is a pop-up window that usually displays information about the name and version of the current program. In JBuilder, for instance, if you select Help ➢ About, the screen shown in Figure 17-3 appears.

Figure 17-3. The JBuilder 6 About box

TIP *If you type in a special saying in the About box, you'll find one of JBuilder 6's Easter eggs. (Hint: If you type in all the letters of the alphabet, you'll find the first letter of the saying. You can also click each letter as it appears to see a bull's-eye symbol, though the bull's-eye has nothing to do with the Easter egg.)*

For your program, the Application Wizard already added the Help and About menu items, as well as the initial About box. It isn't anywhere near as fancy as JBuilder's, though. You just have to configure the autogenerated one to have your own information. To see the initial About box, as shown in Figure 17-4, run the program and select Help ➢ About.

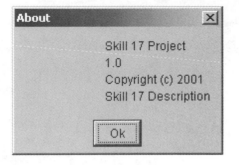

Figure 17-4. The initial About box configuration

You should notice that the Title and Description from the Project Wizard are displayed here. The empty gray area to the left is reserved for an image. This is usually a logo specific to the product or company. There is no way to enter an image filename in the Project Wizard or Application Wizard screen. The right side includes the title from the Project Wizard followed by a version number, a copyright statement with the current year, and the description—again from the Project Wizard. All of this is in the generated MenuTester_AboutBox class.

> **TIP** *If you'd like to add an image to the About box, uncomment the* imageLabel.setIcon(new ImageIcon(MenuTester_AboutBox.class.getResource("[Your Image]")))*; line in the* jbInit() *method. Change the quoted string to the name of the image file. Then place the image file in the same directory as the* MenuTester_AboutBox.class *file, where* Class.getResource() *will look.*

Using the Menu Designer

Now that your program displays a message on the screen, you, the developer, can change the font and color of the displayed text through the Inspector or directly in the source code. In order to change the font and color at runtime, you need to provide some programmatic way for the user to change things. You can do this by adding menu options.

JBuilder has a nice and easy way to create menus graphically; it's called the Menu Designer. To access the Menu Designer for MenuTester, select MenuTester.java in the Navigation pane and the Design tab at the bottom of the Content pane. Then double-click the Menu entry in the Structure pane. The Menu Designer appears in the Content pane, as shown in Figure 17-5.

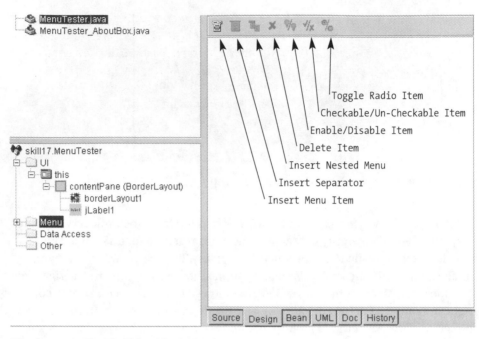

Figure 17-5. The JBuilder Menu Designer

Once the Menu Designer appears, you need to select the menu bar to work with. If you open the Menu folder, you'll see a jMenuBar1. Single-click jMenuBar1 to move that menu bar into the Menu Designer. Once it's in the Menu Designer, you can click File or Help to see the entries under each menu. For the functionality you want to add—changing the text, color, or font of the label—you'll create another pull-down menu instead of adding to the existing ones. To create another pull-down menu, click in the gray box to the right of the Help menu. Here, you enter in a label for your menu—you'll use **Edit**—and then press Enter.

Once the Edit menu appears, you can select it and drag it between the File and Help menus. At any point in time, you can just rearrange the order of entries by dragging and dropping.

TIP   *Usually, Help is the last pull-down menu on a menu bar.*

Now that you have the pull-down menu, you need to add items to it. You want to add one to support each task of changing text, color, and font. You'll also add a separator to the menu to partition the options. A *separator* is an unselectable line that appears on menus for decorative purposes. You'll place the text changing menu item above the separator and the color/font changing item below.

To add the four entries, follow these steps:

1. Click within the box below Edit, type **Text**, and press Enter. (If the area is already blue, you don't even have to click—just type.)

2. To add the separator, use the Insert Separator icon on the Menu Designer toolbar. Click the toolbar icon and the separator will be added below the Text item.

3. In the next box, enter **Color** as the label and press Enter.

4. For the final menu item, type **Font** and press Enter.

 TIP *If you don't like the order of your menu choices, just drag them to a new spot.*

After you save everything and rerun the program, you'll have the Edit menu shown in Figure 17-6.

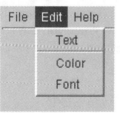

Figure 17-6. The newly created Edit menu

Using the JOptionPane

Just having the Edit menu doesn't do much for your program functionality-wise. In order for a menu to do anything, you have to add an event-handler routine. There are four steps involved here, where the only difference is the last step for each item.

1. From the Menu Designer, select the menu item (Text for the first one).

2. In the Inspector window for the item, select the Events tab.

3. When a menu item is selected, any registered `ActionListener` items are notified. The listener method is `actionPerformed()`, so if you double-click in the `actionPerfomed` line, the framework for responding to selection will be added.

   ```
   void jMenuItem1_actionPerformed(ActionEvent e) {

   }
   ```

4. Define the specific action to be performed when the user selects *that* menu item.

In the case of the Text item, Swing provides you with a `JOptionPane` for support. It actually provides many variations for pop-up windows, of which you're only using one, getting a single line of input. You can also use it to display plain messages, choose input from a pick list, or create some custom pop-up window that has many different display options.

You're going to code an option pane for your program yourself instead of using the Designer. The class has a series of static methods that allow you to create preconfigured option panes. While you can create these all by hand visually, you're not going to, because it's too easy to do it with the static methods shown in Table 17-1.

Table 17-1. Static Methods of JOptionPane

Method	Behavior
showMessageDialog()	For displaying a message, with no input
showConfirmDialog()	For answering a Yes/No-type question
showInputDialog()	For getting input from a `JTextField`, `JComboBox`, or `JList`
showOptionDialog()	For creating custom pop-up windows

NOTE *There are additional methods to create the same set of pop-up windows for* internal frames. *Internal frames are not covered in this book. They are basically frames that stay within a desktop and don't pop up in front of a frame, but instead stay within that frame. For more information on internal frames and the many different options with* JOptionPane, *see my book* Definitive Guide to Swing for Java 2, Second Edition *(Apress, 2000).*

Getting input is as simple as passing in the prompt to the showInputDialog() method. Then, the string returned would be what the user entered. As shown in Figure 17-7, the pop-up window has OK and Cancel buttons.

```
String text = JOptionPane.showInputDialog("Enter new text:");
```

To finish off the jMenuItem1_actionPerformed() method, just check the return value and change the text of the label when appropriate. If the user doesn't enter anything, an empty string is returned. If the user clicks Cancel, null is returned. Here's the completed version of the method:

```
void jMenuItem1_actionPerformed(ActionEvent e) {
  String text = JOptionPane.showInputDialog("Enter new text:");
  if ((text != null) && (!text.equals(""))) {
    jLabel1.setText(text);
  }
}
```

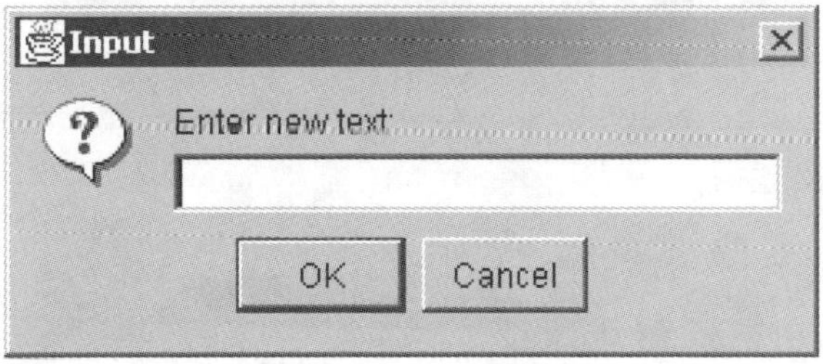

Figure 17-7. The JOptionPane prompting to change the text label

Changing Colors with the JColorChooser

To change colors when the Color button is clicked, you'll use Swing's JColorChooser component. It works like a JOptionPane. You can pick it off the Component palette and configure it yourself, or you can use its static methods to do it for you. Like JOptionPane, you won't configure it yourself.

Now return to the Menu Designer and double-click in the actionPerformed field of the Inspector for the Color menu component. You'll get a jMenuItem2_actionPerformed() for the Color option.

The JColorChooser has a showDialog() method to prompt for changing a color. You need to pass it three parameters: a component to center the pop-up window over (or null to center it in the middle of the screen), a text message, and the initial value of the color being changed. When called, you'll get the screen in Figure 17-8.

```
Color initial = ...
Color newValue = JColorChooser.showDialog(null, "Change text color", initial);
```

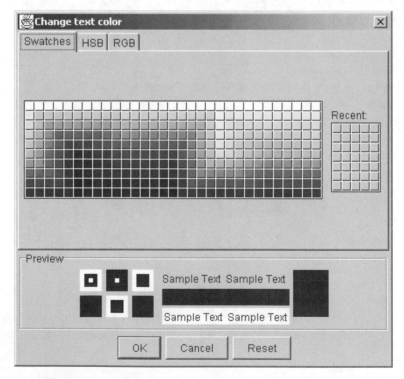

Figure 17-8. The JColorChooser prompting to change the text color

Plugging this method call into the `jMenuItem2_actionPerformed()` method allows you to change the foreground of the text in the label. Just get the initial value from the label and check for null in case the user clicked Cancel in the pop-up window.

```
void jMenuItem2_actionPerformed(ActionEvent e) {
  Color initial = jLabel1.getForeground();
  Color foreground = JColorChooser.showDialog(null, "Change text color",
    initial);
  if (foreground != null) {
    jLabel1.setForeground(foreground);
  }
}
```

Changing Fonts with the FontChooser

The final piece to add to your program is a way to change the font of the message. There is no standard way to change fonts in Java. However, JBuilder comes with a couple of different FontChooser components. One is on the More dbSwing tab of the Component palette (see Figure 17-9) and found in com.borland.dbswing. It includes a list of System fonts to choose from. The other is not on the Component palette and is found in the com.borland.jbcl.control package (see Figure 17-10). This one shows the five internal font names that Java uses and enables Bold and Italic font options.

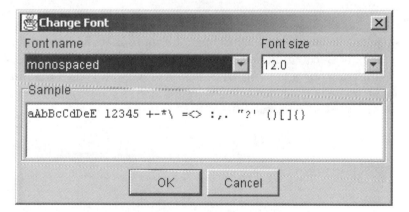

Figure 17-9. The dbSwing FontChooser with System font names

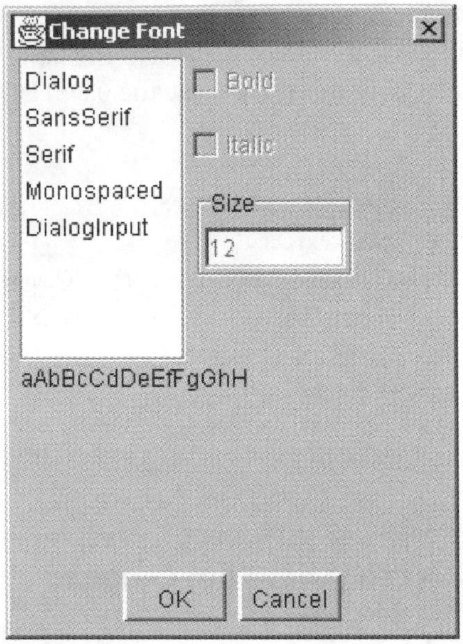

Figure 17-10. The JBCL FontChooser with Bold and Italic options

You're going to add the JavaBeans Component Library (JBCL) version to the program, but you could use either. First, you'll need to add the JBCL library to your project settings. Open the Project Properties dialog box with Project ➤ Project Properties, and then select the Required Libraries subtab on the bottom. Click Add, and then find and select the JBCL entry under the JBuilder folder. Once you click OK, your program will know about the library. Now you can add the component.

By selecting the Bean Chooser icon on the Component palette, you can add the FontChooser to your program. Just open the appropriate folders for the com.borland.jbcl.control package and pick the FontChooser component. When you drop the component onto the UI Designer, JBuilder will add the component to the Other folder in the Component tree pane (see Figure 17-11).

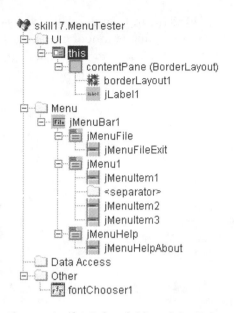

Figure 17-11. The FontChooser in the Other folder of the Component tree

To initialize the component, you need to set its `frame` and `title` attributes. The frame is like the first argument to the `JColorChooser.showDialog()` call, but it doesn't support null as an option. The title is the frame title. These two properties won't change when you use the `FontChooser`. Using the pull-down list in the Inspector, change the frame to **this**. The "this" is a reference to `MenuTester`, which is your program. Set the frame title to **Change Font**.

The only thing left to do now is connect the chooser to the selection of the Font menu option. As you did with the others, double-click in the `actionPerformed` routine on the Events tab for the menu item. This will give you a `jMenuItem3_actionPerformed()` method.

The way to show this `FontChooser` is to call the `show()` method. However, like the `JColorChooser`, you need to tell the chooser what the original value was. The `FontChooser` does it by setting the `value` property, instead of passing an extra parameter to the method to show the component. Then, to get the new setting, you get the value property—again, it being null on a cancel. The whole method is as follows:

```
void jMenuItem3_actionPerformed(ActionEvent e) {
  Font initial = jLabel1.getFont();
  fontChooser1.setValue(initial);
  fontChooser1.show();
  Font font = fontChooser1.getValue();
  if (font != null) {
    jLabel1.setFont(font);
  }
}
```

You've now completed all the tasks in the skill. If you save and run the program, you can change the text, color, or font of the label, as well as display an About box under the Help menu. Also, notice that JBuilder automatically placed code to handle the File ➤ Exit menu. Figure 17-12 shows the program in action, after changing all the settings.

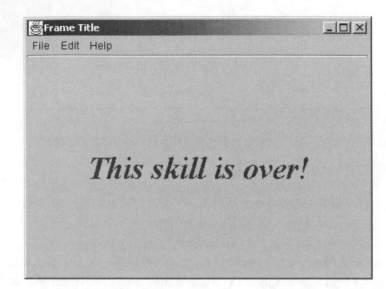

Figure 17-12. Fully functional program, after changing the font, color, and text

The source for the entire program appears in Listing 17-1. Notice how little source you actually typed in yourself.

Listing 17-1. The Complete MenuTester Application Source

```
package skill17;

import java.awt.*;
import java.awt.event.*;
import javax.swing.*;
import com.borland.jbcl.control.*;

/**
 * <p>Title: Skill17 Project</p>
 * <p>Description: Skill 17 Descriptoin</p>
 * <p>Copyright: Copyright (c) 2001</p>
 * <p>Company: JZ Ventures, Inc.</p>
 * @author John Zukowski
 * @version 1.0
 */
```

```java
public class MenuTester extends JFrame {
  JPanel contentPane;
  JMenuBar jMenuBar1 = new JMenuBar();
  JMenu jMenuFile = new JMenu();
  JMenuItem jMenuFileExit = new JMenuItem();
  JMenu jMenuHelp = new JMenu();
  JMenuItem jMenuHelpAbout = new JMenuItem();
  BorderLayout borderLayout1 = new BorderLayout();
  JLabel jLabel1 = new JLabel();
  JMenu jMenu1 = new JMenu();
  JMenuItem jMenuItem1 = new JMenuItem();
  JMenuItem jMenuItem2 = new JMenuItem();
  JMenuItem jMenuItem3 = new JMenuItem();
  FontChooser fontChooser1 = new FontChooser();

  //Construct the frame
  public MenuTester() {
    enableEvents(AWTEvent.WINDOW_EVENT_MASK);
    try {
      jbInit();
    }
    catch(Exception e) {
      e.printStackTrace();
    }
  }
  //Component initialization
  private void jbInit() throws Exception  {
    contentPane = (JPanel) this.getContentPane();
    contentPane.setLayout(borderLayout1);
    this.setSize(new Dimension(400, 300));
    this.setTitle("Frame Title");
    jMenuFile.setText("File");
    jMenuFileExit.setText("Exit");
    jMenuFileExit.addActionListener(new ActionListener()  {
      public void actionPerformed(ActionEvent e) {
        jMenuFileExit_actionPerformed(e);
      }
    });
    jMenuHelp.setText("Help");
    jMenuHelpAbout.setText("About");
    jMenuHelpAbout.addActionListener(new ActionListener()  {
      public void actionPerformed(ActionEvent e) {
        jMenuHelpAbout_actionPerformed(e);
      }
```

```java
    });
    jLabel1.setHorizontalAlignment(SwingConstants.CENTER);
    jLabel1.setText("Welcome to JBuilder");
    jMenu1.setText("Edit");
    jMenuItem1.setText("Text");
    jMenuItem1.addActionListener(new java.awt.event.ActionListener() {
      public void actionPerformed(ActionEvent e) {
        jMenuItem1_actionPerformed(e);
      }
    });
    jMenuItem2.setText("Color");
    jMenuItem2.addActionListener(new java.awt.event.ActionListener() {
      public void actionPerformed(ActionEvent e) {
        jMenuItem2_actionPerformed(e);
      }
    });
    jMenuItem3.setText("Font");
    jMenuItem3.addActionListener(new java.awt.event.ActionListener() {
      public void actionPerformed(ActionEvent e) {
        jMenuItem3_actionPerformed(e);
      }
    });
    fontChooser1.setFrame(this);
    fontChooser1.setTitle("Change Font");
    jMenuFile.add(jMenuFileExit);
    jMenuHelp.add(jMenuHelpAbout);
    jMenuBar1.add(jMenuFile);
    jMenuBar1.add(jMenu1);
    jMenuBar1.add(jMenuHelp);
    contentPane.add(jLabel1, BorderLayout.CENTER);
    jMenu1.add(jMenuItem1);
    jMenu1.addSeparator();
    jMenu1.add(jMenuItem2);
    jMenu1.add(jMenuItem3);
    this.setJMenuBar(jMenuBar1);
  }
  //File | Exit action performed
  public void jMenuFileExit_actionPerformed(ActionEvent e) {
    System.exit(0);
  }
  //Help | About action performed
  public void jMenuHelpAbout_actionPerformed(ActionEvent e) {
    MenuTester_AboutBox dlg = new MenuTester_AboutBox(this);
```

```java
    Dimension dlgSize = dlg.getPreferredSize();
    Dimension frmSize = getSize();
    Point loc = getLocation();
    dlg.setLocation((frmSize.width - dlgSize.width) / 2 + loc.x,
                           (frmSize.height - dlgSize.height) / 2 + loc.y);
    dlg.setModal(true);
    dlg.show();
  }
  //Overridden so we can exit when window is closed
  protected void processWindowEvent(WindowEvent e) {
    super.processWindowEvent(e);
    if (e.getID() == WindowEvent.WINDOW_CLOSING) {
      jMenuFileExit_actionPerformed(null);
    }
  }

  void jMenuItem1_actionPerformed(ActionEvent e) {
    String text = JOptionPane.showInputDialog("Enter new text:");
    if ((text != null) && (!text.equals(""))) {
      jLabel1.setText(text);
    }
  }

  void jMenuItem2_actionPerformed(ActionEvent e) {
    Color initial = jLabel1.getForeground();
    Color foreground = JColorChooser.showDialog(null,
      "Change text color", initial);
    if (foreground != null) {
      jLabel1.setForeground(foreground);
    }
  }

  void jMenuItem3_actionPerformed(ActionEvent e) {
    Font initial = jLabel1.getFont();
    fontChooser1.setValue(initial);
    fontChooser1.show();
    Font font = fontChooser1.getValue();
    if (font != null) {
      jLabel1.setFont(font);
    }
  }
}
```

NOTE *Besides the application driver program, JBuilder also generated the* MenuTester_AboutBox *class. Other than the text entered in the Project Wizard, all the source of that class was automatically generated.*

ARE YOU EXPERIENCED?

Congratulations! You should now have a good feel for how to set up menus within your Java programs with JBuilder.

Now you can

- Create menus

- Create an About box

- Handle menu item events

- Use the JOptionPane

- Use the JColorChooser

- Use the JBCL FontChooser

In the next skill, you'll learn how to add toolbars to your Java programs to make them even more user-friendly.

Creating a JToolBar

- Creating toolbars

- Using a TitledBorder to label an area

- Using an EtchedBorder to highlight an area

- Getting filenames as input from the JFileChooser

- Displaying an image on a label

- Using a status line for messages

- Displaying messages with tool tips

Working with Toolbars

Now that your Java applications can have menus, it's time to add the toolbars. It's not that your applications are incomplete without them, it's just that most current applications have them—just look at JBuilder.

In this skill, you'll create a program that prompts the user for a filename and, if it's an image, displays the file within a label. Any messages to the user will appear along a status bar and as tool tips over the label, while the prompting is done with Open File and Close File buttons from the toolbar. To make things a little prettier, you'll place a titled border around the label that displays the filename selected.

As with the other skills, you'll start by closing any open projects and running through the Application Wizard. Name the project **Skill18**, save the project in **C:\skills\Skill18**, and click Finish. In the first Application Wizard dialog box, click Next to leave the default settings. On the second screen, name the class **ToolbarTester** and then select the Generate toolbar and Generate status bar options. Click Finish to have the Application Wizard generate the code framework. To see what you've generated this time, save everything and run it; you'll see the screen shown in Figure 18-1.

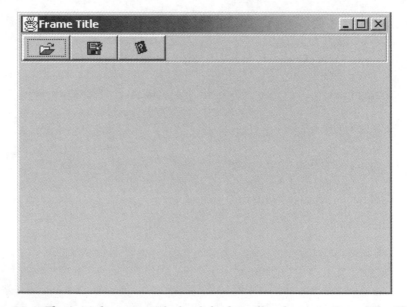

Figure 18-1. The initial screen with the default toolbar buttons: Open File, Close File, and Help. The status bar is at the bottom of the screen.

As in the last skill, you'll do some general housekeeping first, before you add any functionality. You're not going to use the Help button, so you should remove it from the toolbar. Also, you're going to drop a label in the center to receive the image to load. Around both the label and the status bar you're going to change the border to better highlight the areas.

The third button on the toolbar is the Help button. To remove it, select the button within the toolbar and press Delete. You'll also need to delete the image file that was loaded to display on the toolbar. In the Component tree, select image3 and delete that, too. All remnants of the Help button are now gone.

Next, drop a JLabel into the center of the frame. Make sure its constraints property is **Center**. Since you're going to show an image inside the label, you should clear out its text property, so select the text property in the Inspector and delete the contents. The final property to initialize is the border property. A *border* is an object rendered around the edges of a component. If you click in the right column for the border property, you'll see both a pull-down menu and a "..." button to set the label's border. Clicking the "..." button will bring up the property editor for the border (see Figure 18-2).

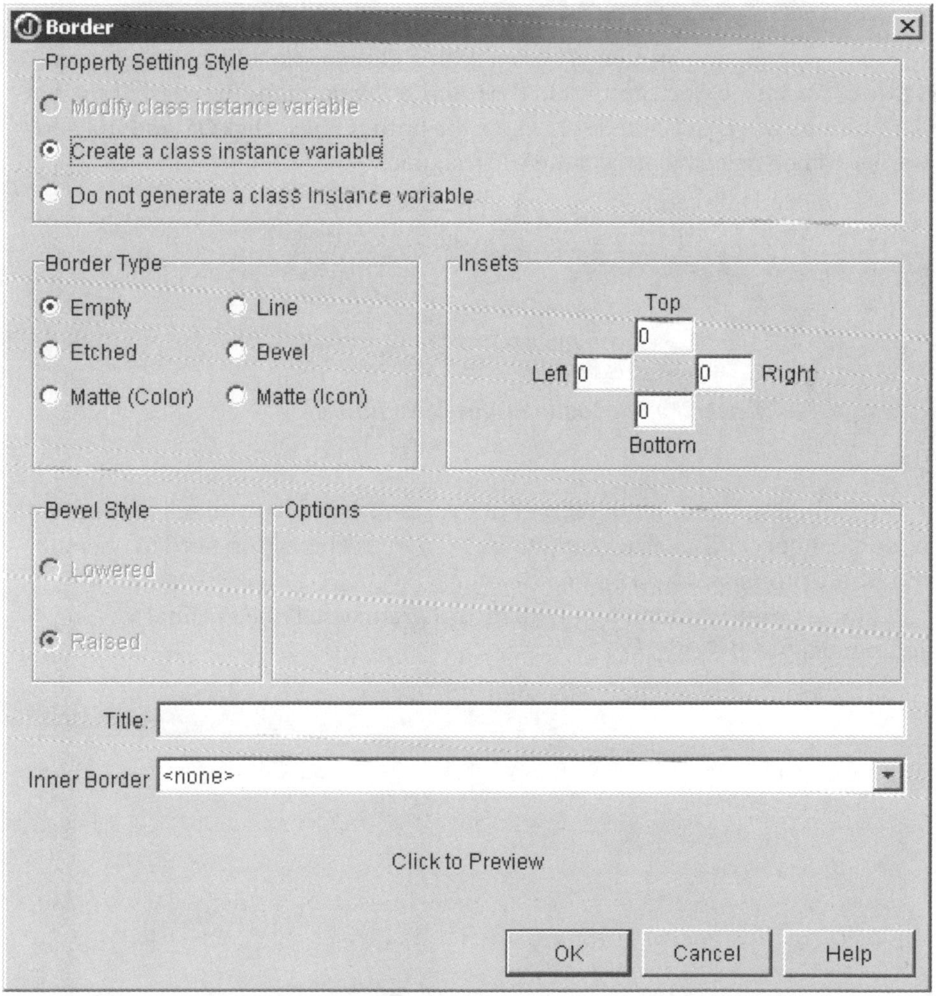

Figure 18-2. The property editor for the border property

In the Border Type area, you can select six different types of borders, with the Title option at the bottom of the dialog box offering a seventh. To see what a current border setting would look like, click in the Click to Preview area at the bottom. For some types, you get to change various options or styles. For instance, the Matte style allows you to repeat an image around the whole border, as shown in Figure 18-3.

Figure 18-3. A matte border with the Open File icon repeated

You want to have an etched border with a title, so select Etched and enter a title of **No Image**. You can click in the Click to Preview area to see what the border will look like (see Figure 18-4). Once the border is set, click OK and the new border will be reflected back in the UI Designer.

> No Image
>
> Click to Preview

Figure 18-4. An etched border with a title of "No Image"

The final step is to set the border of the status bar. After you select the component, choose Etched from the pull-down menu. There is no need to open up the whole property sheet.

At this point, if you save and run the program, you'll see the final screen setup in Figure 18-5.

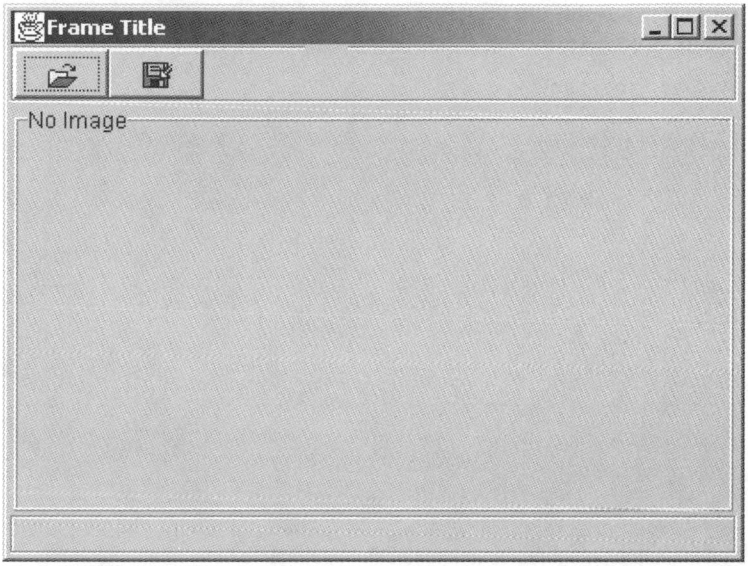

Figure 18-5. The new screen with all the general housekeeping tasks performed

Docking Toolbars

Before you move on to add behavior behind the buttons in the toolbar, there is one aspect of JToolBar that should be mentioned. By default, toolbars are floatable. If you click in an open area of a toolbar and drag the toolbar, the toolbar will appear to float above the application's window, as shown in Figure 18-6.

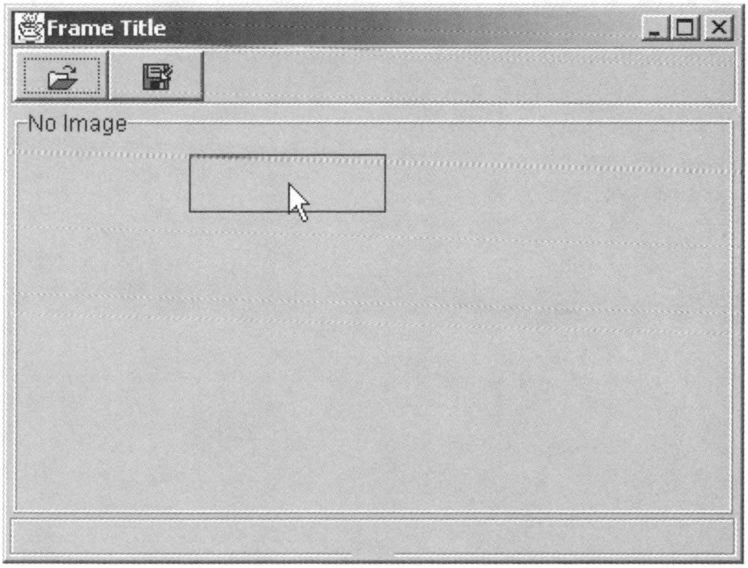

Figure 18-6. A toolbar being dragged away

When dragged along the edges of the frame, the box around the toolbar you're dragging will appear red, as shown in Figure 18-7.

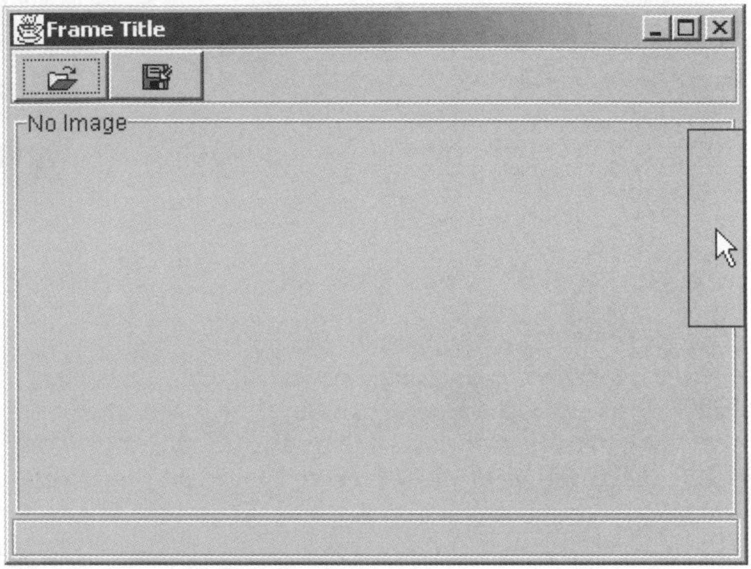

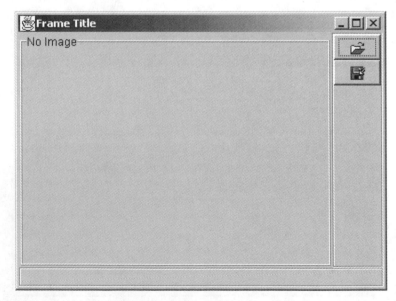

Figure 18-7. The red outline shows that the toolbar can be redocked.

This means you can drop it back into the frame, possibly in a different border layout area, as you can see in Figure 18-8.

Figure 18-8. A redocked toolbar in the east area of a border layout

If you drop it when the border is not red, the toolbar will float above the frame in its own window, as shown in Figure 18-9.

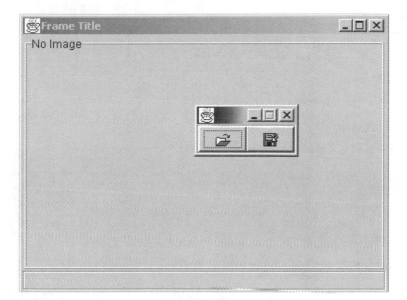

Figure 18-9. A toolbar floating above a frame

To turn off the capability for a toolbar to be dragged away, set the floatable property to **False**.

Picking Files

At this point, it's time to add action to the program. The JToolBar is just a container for components. In order to add behavior to it, you just add behavior to each of the individual components in the toolbar. There is no catchall action handler for a toolbar.

To add an action handler to the Open File button, double-click it in the UI Designer. This will add the method stub to the source for you to fill. What you want this method to do is prompt the user for a filename and then use that filename as the image for the label. You'll also change the title for the border around the label to the filename, display the full path in the status bar, and display some file information in the label's tool tips.

The way to prompt for a file from the user is with the help of the JFileChooser component. This is like the standard file-selection window or Open dialog box, specific to the user's platform. On a Windows platform, the JFileChooser looks like the dialog box in Figure 18-10. The native look and feel for UNIX is Motif. The JFileChooser there looks like Figure 18-11. And, if you choose the native Java look and feel, Metal, you get Figure 18-12.

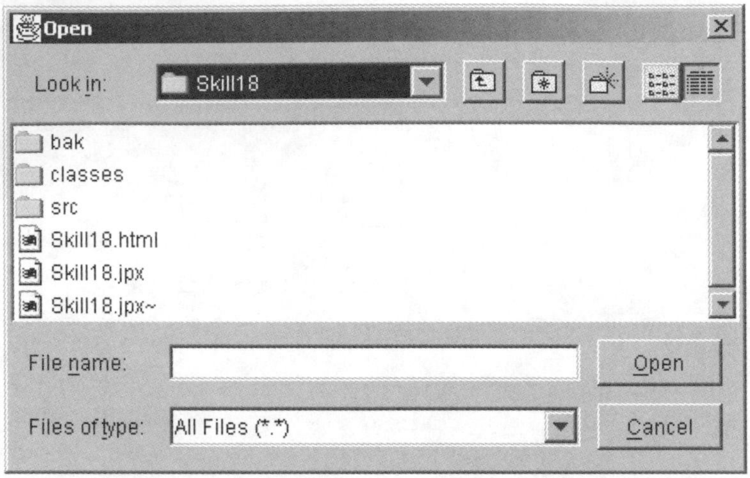

Figure 18-10. The Open dialog box on a Microsoft Windows platform

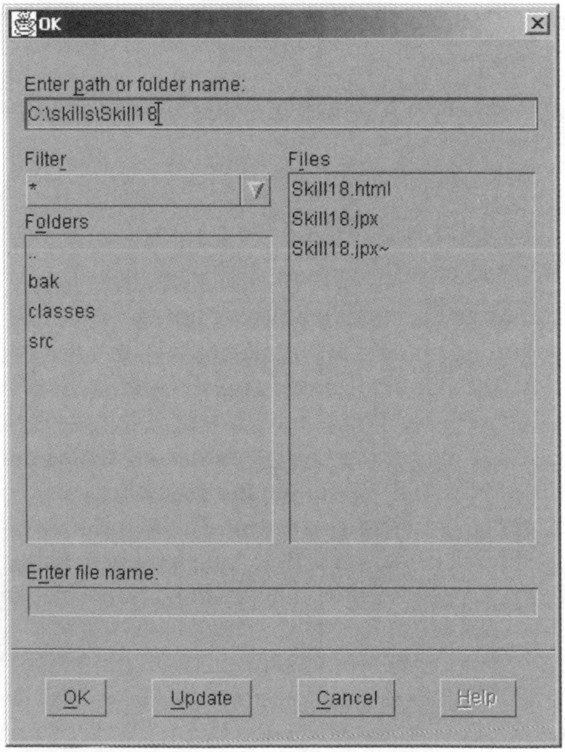

Figure 18-11. The Open dialog box on a Motif platform

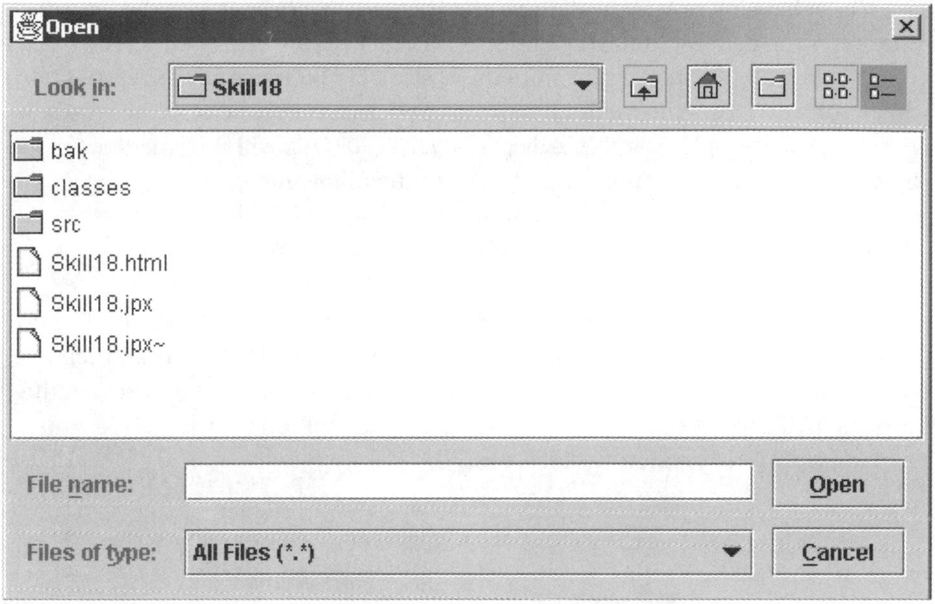

Figure 18-12. The Open dialog box for the Metal look and feel

Like the JColorChooser and JOptionPane shown in the last skill, the JFileChooser doesn't come in its own frame, but it provides methods to create one for you. So, instead of dropping one into your program in the UI Designer, you'll do all the coding yourself.

First, to create the JFileChooser, just call the constructor. By default, the chooser starts in the user's home directory (system property user.home). However, if you'd like to start in another directory, you can pass in a new directory to the constructor. For instance, an argument of "." will start the JFileChooser in the current directory:

```
JFileChooser chooser = new JFileChooser(".");
```

To show the chooser in a pop-up window you have three options: showOpenDialog(), showSaveDialog(), and showDialog(). The first two options have a default string to show on the approval button (Open and Save, respectively), while the last allows you to set the button label yourself. All three require an argument of the parent frame over which to appear. Providing an argument of null has the dialog box appear centered over the whole screen.

```
chooser.showOpenDialog(this);
```

While that single line will allow you to show the chooser, it actually returns a status so you can find out which button was clicked. If the user clicks the approval button (Open, Save, or something else), JFileChooser.APPROVE_OPTION will be returned from the method. If the user clicks Cancel or closes the window without selecting anything, JFileChooser.CANCEL_OPTION will be returned. So, the showing of the dialog box needs to change to the following:

```
int status = chooser.showOpenDialog(this);
```

Then, if the user clicks Open, you get to show the image on the label. To find out the File the user selected, you ask with getSelectedFile(). You can then use that to load the image, change the label's icon, set the label's tool tip text, set the border's title, and set the status message. Since the method returns a File, you'll need to import the java.io package, too.

```
import java.io.*;
...
File file = chooser.getSelectedFile();
```

1. *Load the image:* Use ImageIcon to load the image. It requires a filename string, not a File object, so get the string from the File with getAbsolutePath().

   ```
   String filename = file.getAbsolutePath();
   ImageIcon icon = new ImageIcon(filename);
   ```

NOTE ImageIcon *also will accept a* java.net.URL *for the image location. You could pass the constructor the results of* toURL() *instead of* getAbsolutePath().

2. *Change the label icon:* Use the setIcon() method of JLabel to change the icon.

   ```
   jLabel1.setIcon(icon);
   ```

3. *Get the file length:* Use the length() method of File to get the image size.

   ```
   long length = file.length();
   ```

4. *Set the tool tip text:* Use the `setToolTipText()` method of the label to change the tool tip.

   ```
   jLabel1.setToolTipText(length + " bytes");
   ```

5. *Get the border title:* Use the `getName()` method of the selected file to get just its name, without its whole path.

   ```
   String name = file.getName();
   ```

6. *Set the border title:* Use the `setTitle()` method of the titled border with the name just retrieved.

   ```
   titledBorder1.setTitle(name);
   ```

7. *Set the status message:* Use the full name retrieved for the `ImageIcon` as the message for the status bar.

   ```
   statusBar.setText(filename);
   ```

If you save and run the program now, after you select the Apress logo file from Skill 7, you'll see the screen in Figure 18-13.

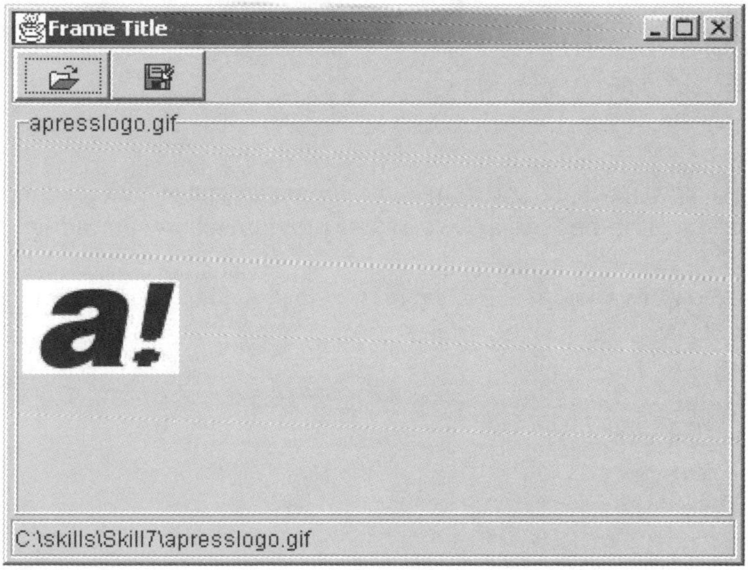

Figure 18-13. Displaying an image in the ToolbarTester program

Standard Java supports the display of GIF (including animated 89A), JPEG, XBM, and PNG formatted images. If you pick another file format to display, no image will be displayed, but the tool tip will be set to the file size. Also, if the image is too tall, the label will display the middle of the image. If the image is too wide, only the left side will display.

 TIP *If you'd like the program to support scrolling to see the rest of the image, add the* JLabel *to a* JScrollPane *and place the titled border around the* JScrollPane.

Closing Up

The only thing left to do is define the behavior for the Close File button on the toolbar. When the user clicks the button, the application needs to remove the image from the button, the title in the border, the text from the tool tip, and the message from the status bar. To remove the icon from the button, just pass in null as the argument to setIcon(). For the labels, just pass in the empty string "", though if you want to give the status bar component some screen space, you'll need to pass in one space instead.

```
jLabel1.setIcon(null);
titledBorder1.setTitle("");
jLabel1.setToolTipText("");
statusBar.setText(" ");
```

Now you can rerun the program and clear out an image after loading. The complete source for the ToolbarTester.java program follows in Listing 18-1.

Listing 18-1. The Complete ToolbarTester.java Application Source

```
package skill18;

import java.awt.*;
import java.awt.event.*;
import javax.swing.*;
import javax.swing.border.*;
import java.io.*;

public class ToolbarTester extends JFrame {
  JPanel contentPane;
```

```java
JToolBar jToolBar = new JToolBar();
JButton jButton1 = new JButton();
JButton jButton2 = new JButton();
ImageIcon image1;
ImageIcon image2;
JLabel statusBar = new JLabel();
BorderLayout borderLayout1 = new BorderLayout();
JLabel jLabel1 = new JLabel();
Border border1;
TitledBorder titledBorder1;

//Construct the frame
public ToolbarTester() {
  enableEvents(AWTEvent.WINDOW_EVENT_MASK);
  try {
    jbInit();
  }
  catch(Exception e) {
    e.printStackTrace();
  }
}
//Component initialization
private void jbInit() throws Exception  {
  image1 = new ImageIcon(skill18.ToolbarTester.class.getResource(
    "openFile.gif"));
  image2 = new ImageIcon(skill18.ToolbarTester.class.getResource(
    "closeFile.gif"));
  contentPane = (JPanel) this.getContentPane();
  border1 = new EtchedBorder(
    EtchedBorder.RAISED, Color.white, new Color(148, 145, 140));
  titledBorder1 = new TitledBorder(border1,"No Image");
  contentPane.setLayout(borderLayout1);
  this.setSize(new Dimension(400, 300));
  this.setTitle("Frame Title");
  statusBar.setBorder(BorderFactory.createEtchedBorder());
  statusBar.setText(" ");
  jButton1.setIcon(image1);
  jButton1.addActionListener(new java.awt.event.ActionListener() {
    public void actionPerformed(ActionEvent e) {
      jButton1_actionPerformed(e);
    }
  });
```

```
                jButton1.setToolTipText("Open File");
                jButton2.setIcon(image2);
                jButton2.addActionListener(new java.awt.event.ActionListener() {
                  public void actionPerformed(ActionEvent e) {
                    jButton2_actionPerformed(e);
                  }
                });
                jButton2.setToolTipText("Close File");
                jLabel1.setBorder(titledBorder1);
                jToolBar.setFloatable(false);
                jToolBar.add(jButton1);
                jToolBar.add(jButton2);
                contentPane.add(jToolBar, BorderLayout.NORTH);
                contentPane.add(statusBar, BorderLayout.SOUTH);
                contentPane.add(jLabel1, BorderLayout.CENTER);
              }
              //File | Exit action performed
              public void jMenuFileExit_actionPerformed(ActionEvent e) {
                System.exit(0);
              }
              //Help | About action performed
              public void jMenuHelpAbout_actionPerformed(ActionEvent e) {
              }
              //Overridden so we can exit when window is closed
              protected void processWindowEvent(WindowEvent e) {
                super.processWindowEvent(e);
                if (e.getID() == WindowEvent.WINDOW_CLOSING) {
                  System.exit(0);
                }
              }


              void jButton1_actionPerformed(ActionEvent e) {
                JFileChooser chooser = new JFileChooser(".");
                int status = chooser.showOpenDialog(this);
                if (status == JFileChooser.APPROVE_OPTION) {
                  File file = chooser.getSelectedFile();
                  String filename = file.getAbsolutePath();
                  ImageIcon icon = new ImageIcon(filename);
                  jLabel1.setIcon(icon);
                  long length = file.length();
                  jLabel1.setToolTipText(length + " bytes");
                  String name = file.getName();
                  titledBorder1.setTitle(name);
```

```
      statusBar.setText(filename);
    }
  }

  void jButton2_actionPerformed(ActionEvent e) {
    jLabel1.setIcon(null);
    titledBorder1.setTitle("");
    jLabel1.setToolTipText("");
    statusBar.setText(" ");
  }
}
```

ARE YOU EXPERIENCED?

In this skill, you worked with toolbars in your programs and loaded images picked from a file chooser.

Now you can

- Use a JToolBar

- Add borders to components

- Label a border with a title

- Manipulate a toolbar's floating capability

- Use a JFileChooser to pick files

- Show messages on a status bar

In the next skill, you'll look at how to prepare your programs for the global marketplace and you'll see a demonstration of JBuilder's internationalization support.

Internationalization

- Understanding the terminology

- Working with locales

- Interacting with the `JComboBox`

- Formatting numbers and dates

- Running the Resource Strings Wizard

- Making localizable property settings

- Creating resource bundles

We Are the World

The Internet has made your area of the world a bigger place. Not only are you able to visit the neighborhood hardware store to buy a tool but also, if some company halfway around the world can sell you the product for less, with shipping of course, what's to stop you from buying it from them? The biggest hindrance, in most cases, is language. The second biggest hindrance is currency.

Price alone isn't the only factor these days, either. Timing is another one. Before the latest J.K. Rowling book on Harry Potter is available in the states, you can hop over to http://www.amazon.co.uk and buy it from the United Kingdom. Even factoring in shipping time, you can still get it sooner in the United States than had you waited until the publisher with the U.S. rights shipped it.

While dealings between the United States and the United Kingdom are fairly easy, given that people in both countries speak English, that isn't always the case when you move to other parts of the world. In Europe, while many countries share a common currency, the euro (€), the native language of each country tends to differ. As soon as you step outside the United States, people are more cognizant of the differences—just seeing the date 01/02/03 in a computer application is ambiguous. Is it January 2, 2003 or February 1, 2003? This, of course, ignores the ambiguity of 1903 versus 2003, which is a Y2K issue in and of itself.

All these issues bring us to the topic at hand: *internationalization.* Internationalization is the concept of developing your applications to be cognizant of the local formatting of things such as dates and numbers as well as using the user's native language, all without delivering separate applications to each area.

NOTE *The word "internationalization" itself tends to be abbreviated as "I18N." This is because there are 18 characters between the first* i *and the last* n *in the word "internationalization."*

Working with Locales

Java programs rely on the Locale class, found in the java.util package, to define the language and country for messages and formatting. Knowing a locale will tell you what 01/02/03 stands for.

The Locale class comes with 21 different predefined locale constants. These are for different language and country combinations and are shown in Table 19-1. Countries are actually more specific than languages, as French in Canada may be different from French in France, just as English is different between the United States and the United Kingdom.

Table 19-1. Predefined Locale Languages and Countries

Name	Language	Country
CANADA	en	CA
CANADA_FRENCH	fr	CA
CHINA	zh	CN
CHINESE	zh	
ENGLISH	en	
FRANCE	fr	FR
FRENCH	fr	
GERMAN	de	
GERMANY	de	DE
ITALIAN	it	
ITALY	it	IT
JAPAN	ja	JP
JAPANESE	ja	
KOREA	ko	KR
KOREAN	ko	
PRC	zh	CN
SIMPLIFIED_CHINESE	zh	CH
TAIWAN	zh	TW
TRADITIONAL_CHINESE	zh	TW
UK	en	GB
US	en	US

The International Standards Organization (ISO) controls the second and third columns shown in Table 19-1. The language abbreviations (column 2) are always listed in lowercase and maintained in the ISO-639 document, which is available from http://www1.ics.uci.edu/pub/ietf/http/related/iso639.txt. There are currently about 150 entries in the list, with some of the more common ones listed in Table 19-2.

Table 19-2. Sampling of Language Codes

Abbreviation	Language
de	German
en	English
fr	French
hi	Hindi
it	Italian
jp	Japanese
jw	Javanese
ko	Korean
zh	Chinese

The country codes are written in uppercase characters and are controlled by their own document, `http://userpage.chemie.fu-berlin.de/diverse/doc/ISO_3166.html`. Table 19-3 presents a sampling of these. Some country codes may look familiar to you, as they are used in the domain name structure of Web sites—for example, `http://www.amazon.de` for a site in Germany. Over 200 country codes are listed in the ISO document.

Table 19-3. Sampling of Country Codes

Abbreviation	Country
AF	Afghanistan
AQ	Antarctica
AU	Australia
CH	China
DE	Germany
FR	France
GB	United Kingdom
ID	Indonesia
IN	India
IT	Italy
JP	Japan
PK	Pakistan
TW	Taiwan
US	United States

In addition to support for languages and countries, there is support for a third configuration called a *variant*. Variants permit you to have different settings for a lower level than country—for example, if you want different messages for New York versus California users. More commonly, variants are used to provide alternatives for use with the euro. For instance, the standard Italy locale is meant for use with its former currency, the lira, while a second locale works with the euro. The locale doesn't do any currency conversion; it just allows you to say that this number represents a value in euros versus in lira.

Creating the Program

Now that you have a basic understanding of locales, let's move on to create this skill's program. The program will have three labeled areas. Areas 1 and 2 are for internationalized numeric and date formatting, respectively, while area 3 will list the names of the months and days of the week for the currently selected language. For a selected subset of supported languages, you'll customize the labels to the appropriate language.

Let's start by closing any open projects in JBuilder and running the Application Wizard. Name the skill **Skill19** and place it in the **C:\skills\Skill19** directory. Click Finish to create the project. On the second page of the Application Wizard, name the frame class **I18N** and set the window title to **Hello, World**. Click Finish to create the application.

Formatting Numbers

Everyone in the world doesn't display currency in the same way. While currency symbols are certainly different, the basic positioning of commas and periods also varies from country to country. For instance, while the floating-point value 1000.50 is written as $1,000.50 in the United States, you'll find it written as € 1.000,50 when in Italy and dealing with euros. Ignoring the value difference ($1,000 is roughly € 1,100), as a programmer, it's your responsibility to display currency in the format appropriate for the user of your program.

You can find support for displaying all kinds of numbers in the NumberFormat class in the java.text package. With NumberFormat, you can say that you want your numbers to be formatted like ##,##.00, where there is a comma every two characters and always exactly two digits after the decimal point. There are some common predefined formats too, for currency, percentages, and basic numbers.

Using the NumberFormat class is a three-step process. You need to first get the number. Essentially, what value are you going to convert to a specific output format? Next, you need to get that specific format. Then, you have to format the number using the format. The basic process looks like this:

```
double input = ...;
NumberFormat nf = NumberFormat.getCurrencyInstance(locale);
String value = nf.format(input);
```

The getCurrencyInstance() method is how you get the specific formatter for formatting numbers to appear as currency. You can also getPercentInstance() or getNumberInstance() for the other two predefined formatters. If you don't like any of the defaults, you can create your own via the DecimalFormat subclass.

To demonstrate the use of number formatting, you'll need to add four items to your application's screen. Go into the UI Designer and drop a JPanel into the top of the frame. Make sure it ends up with a constraints property setting of **North**, change the layout property to **GridLayout**, and set the number of rows in the grid to **2**. The first row needs a JLabel to label the area and a JTextField for input. The second row should have a JComboBox to pick the locale from and a JTextField for output. Drop all four components into the new panel and make sure they're arranged accordingly.

To finish the initial setup of the screen, you'll need to do a few more things. First, the label should actually label the area, so change its text property to **Number**. For the text field on the top row, it would be nice if the input field had a default value. So, change its text property to **1000.50**. For the output text field, you should clear the text property and change the editable property to false to make it read-only.

As far as the screen goes, you're done with setting up its layout, as you can see in Figure 19-1. The remaining two tasks are to initialize the list of locales to choose from and when a new locale is selected, convert the input value to the locale-specific currency formatting.

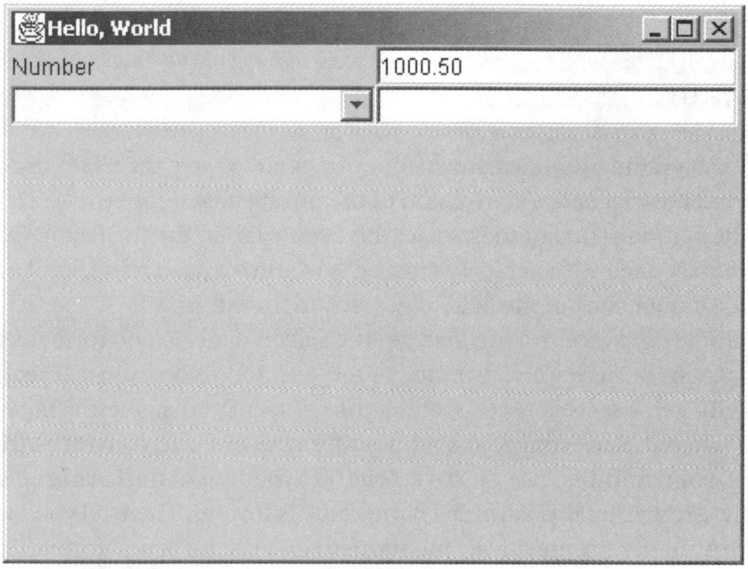

Figure 19-1. The initial numeric conversion screen

To initialize the JComboBox component to a list of locales, you need to figure out which locales you want to work with. While you could manually create this subset yourself from Table 19-2, Table 19-3, and the previously listed URLs, there is a better way. Assuming you want to support the widest possible audience, you can ask the NumberFormat class, via its getAvailableLocales() method, what locales it supports. Assuming you have the right fonts installed, you would then be able to display a numeric value as currency for close to 150 locales.

Once you have the array of Locale objects returned from getAvailableLocales(), you need to get them into the JComboBox. While you could add a locale at a time with the addItem() method, there is a better way. As explained in Skill 8, the Swing components use the Model-View-Controller (MVC) architecture. In the case of the JComboBox component, the model for the component is the ComboBoxModel. So, the easier way is to create a new model for the control from the array of locales and associate that model with the component. The class that implements the ComboBoxModel interface is DefaultComboBoxModel, and its constructor just happens to accept an array.

Adding the following code to the end of the jbInit() method will allow you to preload the combo control:

```
Locale numbers[] = NumberFormat.getAvailableLocales();
ComboBoxModel model = new DefaultComboBoxModel(numbers);
jComboBox1.setModel(model);
```

And of course, don't forget to import the appropriate packages:

```
import java.util.*;
import java.text.*;
```

To finish off the numeric conversion, you need to have the changing of the JComboBox value trigger the conversion of the input value. From the UI Designer, choose the component and then select the Events tab in the Inspector. Here, the event associated with actionPerformed is what you need to respond to for selection. Double-click in the field to go back to the editor.

To handle the event, you need to get the selected locale and format the value for that specific currency instance. To get the selected value from a JComboBox, just ask with getSelectedItem(). Getting the value just means retrieving it from the text field and converting it to a number from a string. To convert a string to a floating-point number, use the parseDouble() method of the Double class. This will throw a NumberFormatException if the value is invalid. Then, all you have to do is get the formatter (as previously mentioned) and do the actual formatting. Here's the entire code block for the event handler:

```
Locale locale = (Locale)jComboBox1.getSelectedItem();
try {
  double input = Double.parseDouble(jTextField1.getText());
  NumberFormat nf = NumberFormat.getCurrencyInstance(locale);
  jTextField2.setText(nf.format(input));
} catch (NumberFormatException nfe) {
  System.err.println("Number Parsing error: " + nfe);
}
```

At this point, the currency formatter piece is complete. Run the program and try converting various numerical values to different currency formats. Notice that only the country-specific locales show a valid currency symbol—language alone does not.

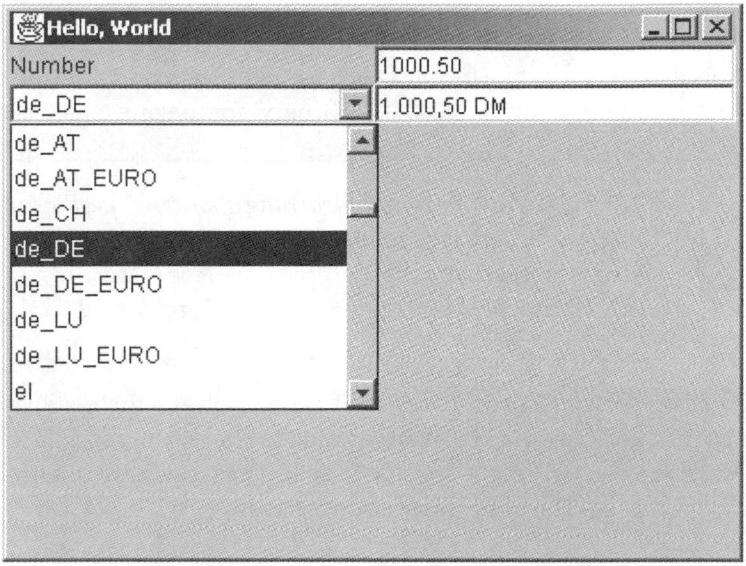

Figure 19-2. A working example of the numeric conversion screen

> **TIP**   *If you ever have a reason to go from a locale string such as "de_AT_EURO" to the appropriate* Locale *for German Austria (with euro support), Borland provides the support class* com.borland.jb.util.LocaleUtil. *Just call its* getLocale() *method to convert a text string to a* Locale.

Formatting Dates

Similar to formatting numbers is formatting dates. Here, the class you work with is DateFormat. Working with this class lets you know what something like 01/02/03 actually means.

Dates come with four different predefined formats, each specified by a constant in the DateFormat class:

- SHORT: Numerical, as in 01/02/03

- MEDIUM: Abbreviated month, as in Feb 1, 2003

- LONG: Full month name, as in February 1, 2003

- FULL: Complete with day of week and era, as in Saturday, February 1, 2003 AD

Besides the four predefined formats, you can create any style of your own. The SimpleDateFormat defines the time format syntax. There are about 20 different symbols that let you define formats such as "EEEE.yyyy.dd.MMMM" to get a custom date format ("Saturday.2003.01.February" for the previously used date).

TIP *If you're interested in learning about the specific formatting strings, look up the javadoc documentation for* SimpleDateFormat *at* http://java.sun.com/j2se /1.3/docs/api/java/text/SimpleDateFormat.html.

Like NumberFormat, using the DateFormat class involves a three-step process. You need to first get a java.util.Date, the value to convert to a specific output format. Next, you need to get the specific format. Then, you have to format the Date using the format. The basic process looks like this:

```
Date input = ...;
DateFormat df = DateFormat.getDateInstance(style, locale);
String value = df.format(input);
```

Because the sample program will get the Date object from a text field, you also need to know how to go from String to Date, and not just the other way around. Not only can you use DateFormat to format() a Date for output as a String, but you can also use it to parse() a String to create a Date.

```
String input = ...;
DateFormat df = DateFormat.getDateInstance(style, locale);
Date value = df.parse(input);
```

Again, you'll need to add four items to the application screen to demonstrate the localized date formatting. However, instead of manually adding four items, you're just going to copy the panel you previously created. First, go to the UI Designer for the frame. In the lower-left corner, you'll find the Component tree. Bring up the context-sensitive menu for the panel by right-clicking the mouse over the component name. Select the Copy option with your mouse. Next, move your mouse over the contentPane, right-click again, and this time select Paste.

After pasting, you'll need to make some cosmetic changes. First, make sure that jPanel1 has a layout constraint of **North** and jPanel2 has a layout constraint of **South**. Next, change the Number label of jPanel2 to be **Date** and clear the initial input value. Also, returning to the Source pane, you'll need to initialize the second combo box to the supported formats of the DateFormat class. There is an existing model changing line for the second combo box that you'll need to modify.

```
Locale dates[] = DateFormat.getAvailableLocales();
ComboBoxModel model2 = new DefaultComboBoxModel(dates);
jComboBox2.setModel(model2);
```

Pasting a set of components not only copies the look and feel aspect of the components, but it also copies the event-handling blocks. You'll find an empty event handler for the selection of the second combo box. Combine the prior code to parse and format the date to get the input from the top text field in the bottom panel and output it into the bottom text field. Be sure to specify a style for the date format, preferably one you like. On the input side, you can also be explicit about the locale of the input string. For instance, if you truly want 01/02/03 to be February 1, 2003, don't use Locale.US as the input format.

```
Locale locale = (Locale)jComboBox2.getSelectedItem();
try {
  String input = jTextField4.getText();
  if (input.length() > 0) {
    DateFormat inputFormat = DateFormat.getDateInstance(
      DateFormat.SHORT, Locale.US);
    Date inputDate = inputFormat.parse(input);
    DateFormat df = DateFormat.getDateInstance(DateFormat.LONG, locale);
    jTextField3.setText(df.format(inputDate));
  }
} catch (ParseException pe) {
  System.err.println("Date parsing error: " + pe);
}
```

> **NOTE** *It may prove helpful to name your text fields instead of relying on the default numbering that JBuilder offers. For instance, notice that the input text field for dates is numbered 4, whereas with the top components, the higher number was in the second row.*

At this point your screen looks like Figure 19-3.

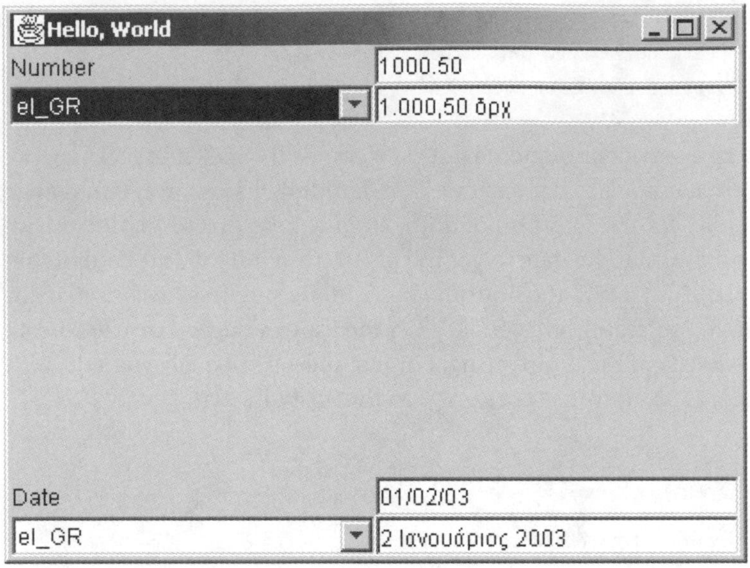

Figure 19-3. An example of the numeric and date conversion screen

For the final interface aspect of the program, you're going to add another label and a JList to the center of the screen. Besides converting dates when changing the bottom JComboBox, you're going to load up the list of month names into the JList control for the selected date Locale.

First, drop a JPanel into the middle of the screen and make sure its constraints are set to **Center**. Next, place a JLabel and a JScrollPane in the panel. Into the JScrollPane, drop a JList component. If you can't get the list to drop into the scroll pane within the UI Designer, drop it into the pane in the Component tree. And, change the label text to **Months**.

To initialize the JList, you'll need to go back to the event handler code for the second combo box. To get the month names, you'll need to find a dictionary that will translate between English and about 40 different languages. Actually, that isn't the case. The DateFormatSymbols class in the java.text package knows about all the supported locales already. All you have to do is ask. Just create a DateFormatSymbols for the locale in question and ask for the month names with getMonths(). (You can also get weekdays with getWeekdays().)

Like the JComboBox component, the JList component maintains its data in its own model, this time a ListModel. The ListModel interface is actually the parent interface of ComboBoxModel, so if you create a ComboBoxModel, you're also creating a ListModel. So, adding the following to the end of the event handler for the second combo box will change the list of months for the JList component in the middle of the screen:

```
DateFormatSymbols symbols = new DateFormatSymbols(locale);
String months[] = symbols.getMonths();
ListModel model = new DefaultComboBoxModel(months);
jList1.setModel(model);
```

Running the program now, and selecting the Russian locale of `ru_RU`, produces the results in Figure 19-4.

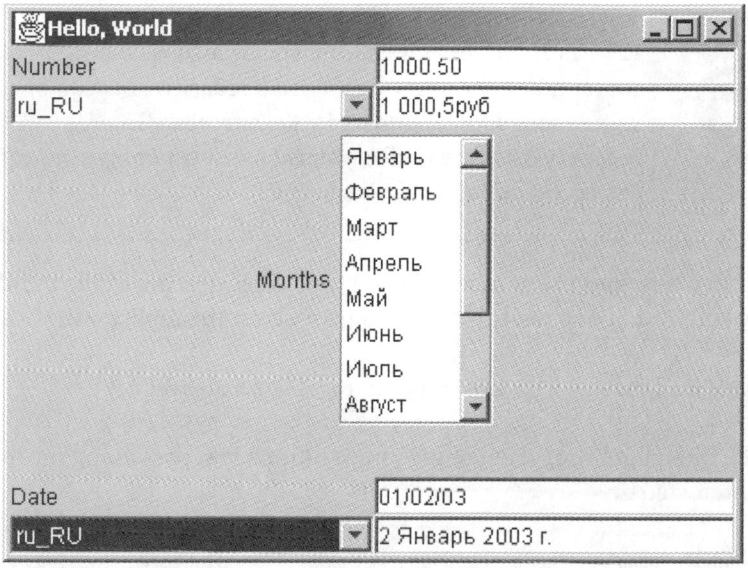

Figure 19-4. Displaying Russian month names with numeric and date conversion

Bundling Resources

Now that you have a fully functional program, it's time to go back and fix it. While the program can properly display currency and dates based upon whatever locale you want, all the text messages in the program are hard-coded. If a French user wanted to run the program, the window title and all the labels next to the different fields would appear in English.

This brings up an important aspect of creating internationalized applications. Essentially, don't hard-code string constants. While moving all the string constants to class-level variables is a good first step, Java provides a better means, called *resource bundles,* and JBuilder offers a way to automate the whole process.

A resource bundle is a way of storing locale-specific resources, whether they are text strings, image files, or any other settings. In Java, the abstract

ResourceBundle class of the java.util package represents these resource bundles. The standard Java libraries provide two concrete subclasses for the mechanism of working with them. First off is the PropertyResourceBundle class. This class permits you to store settings in a text file (called a *properties file*). The settings permit easy manipulation by end users if you want to support users changing settings. More than likely though, you'll use the ListResourceBundle class, which stores these settings in a generated .class file. More often than not, an end user will not change these.

TIP *Borland provides a third resource bundle support class,* com.borland.jb.util.ArrayResourceBundle. *Instead of using string indices into a* ListResourceBundle *or* PropertyResourceBundle, *you get to use an integer index for less overhead (and less flexibility).*

Resource bundles are named, allowing you to request a specific bundle, versus only supporting one really large bundle for an entire application.

```
ResourceBundle bundle = ResourceBundle.getBundle("BundleName");
```

More often then not, when requesting a bundle you pass along the locale you're interested in:

```
ResourceBundle bundle = ResourceBundle.getBundle("BundleName", locale);
```

Now, when you request a bundle, the system will look for the bundle for a specific locale. When no locale is specified, the current locale setting is used, which you can change with Locale.setDefault(*locale*).

The way the searching algorithm works for bundles is it always tries to find the deepest bundle first. If that bundle isn't found, it moves out a level until it eventually has no more levels to move out.

For instance, if a locale were de_DE_EURO and the bundle name were BundleName, the system starts its first bundle hunting for BundleName_de_DE_EURO. If that bundle isn't found, it searches for BundleName_de_DE and then BundleName_de. Assuming both of those aren't found either, the system eventually searches for the base bundle, BundleName, which had better be around.

TIP *When creating resource bundles, you should always remember to define a base bundle to work with, and not just deep, locale-specific bundles.*

To demonstrate, let's see how JBuilder can automate the start of this process. Notice that the title of the frame is "Hello, World." To properly internationalize this application, the frame title should become a resource and stored in a bundle. To do this, bring up the Inspector window in the UI Designer for the frame. If you right-click over the title property, you'll see the screen shown in Figure 19-5.

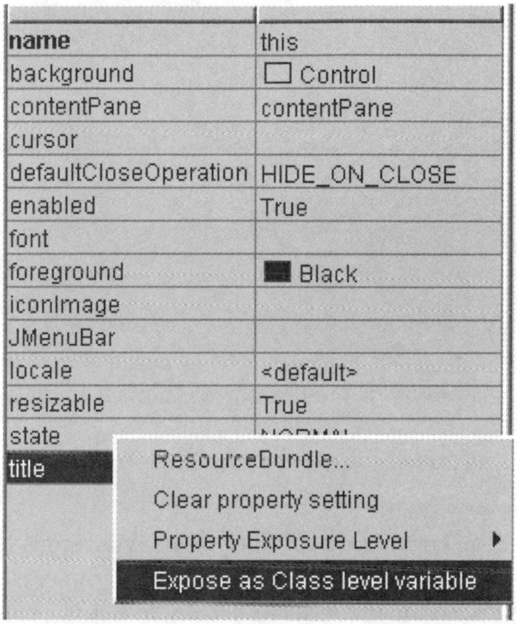

name	this
background	☐ Control
contentPane	contentPane
cursor	
defaultCloseOperation	HIDE_ON_CLOSE
enabled	True
font	
foreground	■ Black
iconImage	
JMenuBar	
locale	<default>
resizable	True
state	
title	

ResourceBundle...

Clear property setting

Property Exposure Level ▶

Expose as Class level variable

Figure 19-5. Starting the Localizable Property Setting Wizard

Selecting the Resource Bundle option opens the Localizable Property Setting Wizard shown in Figure 19-6.

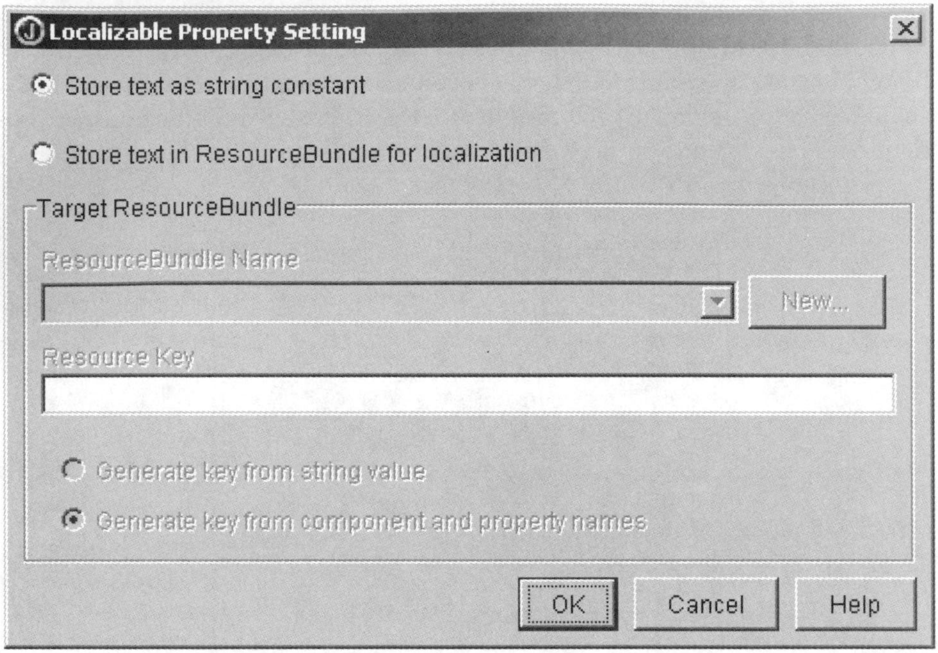

Figure 19-6. The Localizable Property Setting Wizard

The purpose of the Localizable Property Setting Wizard is to create a bundle for the property selected. This wizard is available with the Personal JBuilder version and allows you to move the string setting to a string constant at the class level or to create a bundle.

Instead of creating one bundle for just the frame title, you're going to create one bundle for the frame title, all the text labels, and the error messages. Selecting Wizards ➤ Resource Strings brings up the first screen of the Resource Wizard for just such a task. This screen is shown in Figure 19-7.

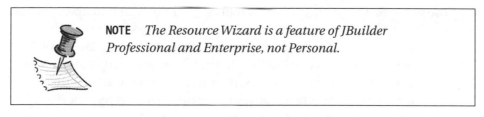

Resource Wizard - Step 1 of 3   ✕

Specify the resource bundle to use

Resource bundles may be a property file or extend ListResourceBundle.
Choose whether only the current file is resourced, or files in the same package

┌─ Target ResourceBundle ────────────────────────────────────┐
│ ResourceBundle Name: │
│ ┌──┐   ┌────────┐ │
│ │ skill19.Res   │   │ New... │ │
│ └──┘   └────────┘ │
│   ● Current source file only   │
│   ○ Source files in current package   │
└───┘

[‹ Back] [Next ›] [Finish] [Cancel] [Help]

Figure 19-7. JBuilder's Resource Wizard, step 1 of 3

> **NOTE** *The Resource Wizard is a feature of JBuilder*
> *Professional and Enterprise, not Personal.*

The wizard first asks you what name to use for the bundle. By default, the
name is the package name you are working in with Res as the specific bundle
name, or skill19.Res in this case. The bundle is also going to be
a ListResourceBundle, unless you click New to choose otherwise.

While you could have the wizard go through all the project source files, you
only need to work with one. So, all you have to do is click Next to bring up the
second screen, as shown in Figure 19-8.

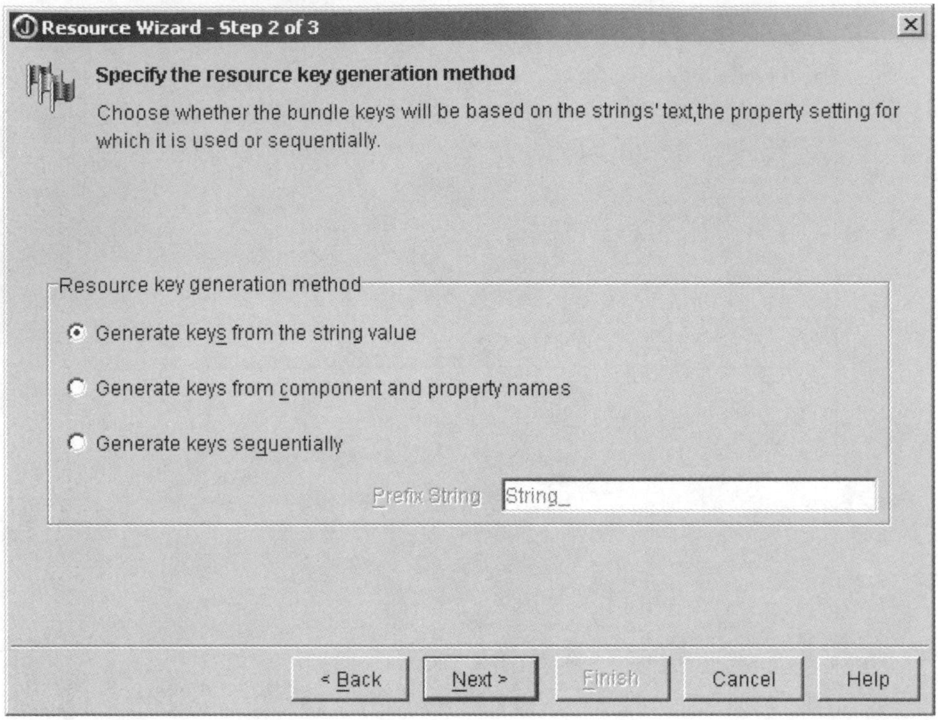

Figure 19-8. JBuilder's Resource Wizard, step 2 of 3

The second screen of the wizard prompts you for how you want the bundles named. The initial selection is a common way and allows you to look up the labels in other languages by using the current language as the key. The second option would generate keys that look like jLabel1_Text, to look up the text property of the first label component. The last option just uses sequential numbering to name the keys. In all cases here, the keys are strings. Leaving the defaults, click Next to move to the final wizard screen (see Figure 19-9).

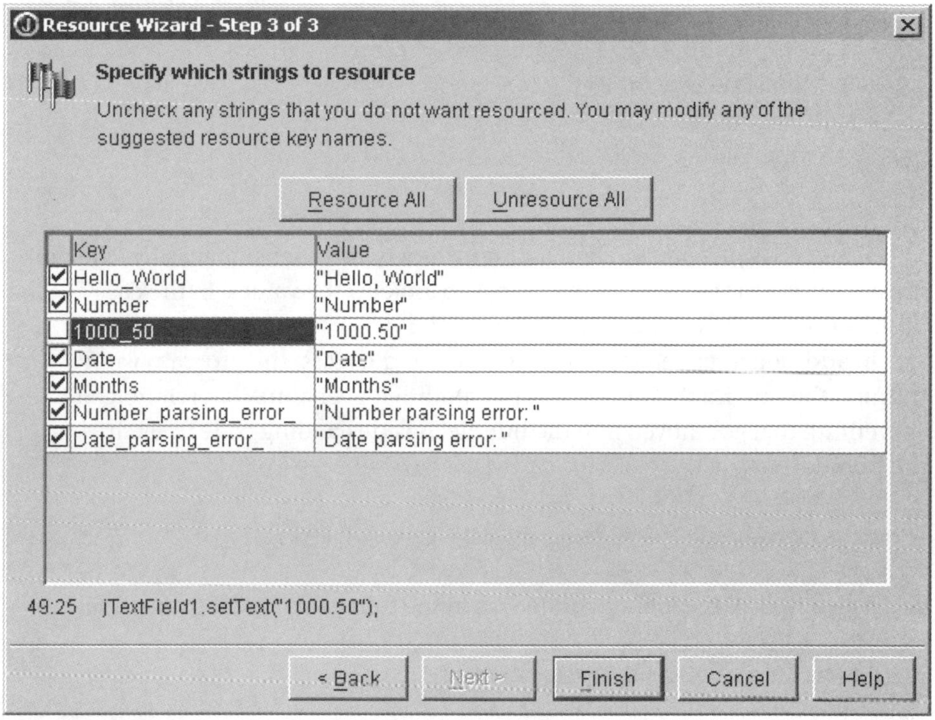

Figure 19-9. JBuilder's Resource Wizard, step 3 of 3

In Figure 19-9, you have a list of all string constants in the class. JBuilder decides which ones it thinks you should move into a resource bundle by checking them off in the first column. Notice that the initial value of a component is not selected, but everything else is. If you don't like a key name (the first column), you can change the value.

When you click Finish, you get the base resource bundle created for your program. Listing 19-1 shows the class that was generated.

Listing 19-1. The Base Generated Resource Bundle Class, Res

```java
package skill19;

import java.util.*;

public class Res extends java.util.ListResourceBundle {
  static final Object[][] contents = new String[][]{
      { "Hello_World", "Hello, World" },
      { "Number", "Number" },
      { "Date", "Date" },
      { "Months", "Months" },
```

```
                    { "Number_parsing_error_", "Number parsing error: " },
                    { "Date_parsing_error_", "Date parsing error: " }};
        public Object[][] getContents() {
          return contents;
        }
      }
```

The class is just one method that returns a two-dimensional array. The bundle handling will then rely on the strings to look up the values. In the case of the base bundle, the two are essentially the same.

In addition to generating the resource bundle class, the program went through the program's source code and modified every line that referenced something that got moved into the bundle. Besides adding code to fetch the bundle:

```
static ResourceBundle res = ResourceBundle.getBundle("skill19.Res");
```

you'll also find all the lookups added, as in the following for the frame title:

```
this.setTitle(res.getString("Hello_World"));
```

Now comes the interesting part. If you want your program to display different labels or a different frame title, you must create more bundles. These bundles have special naming conventions that you must follow so when a bundle is fetched it knows how to follow the trail from specific (e.g., BundleName_de_DE_EURO) to generic (e.g., BundleName, or skill19.Res for this example).

To create a new bundle, you need to create a new class. Bring up the Class Wizard and fill it in as shown in Figure 19-10. If you want a language other than French, change the "_fr" to whatever language you're after. Make sure the Public toggle is selected, or else the bundling won't work. Also be sure to set the base class to a ListResourceBundle. Once you've filled in the form, click OK to generate the class.

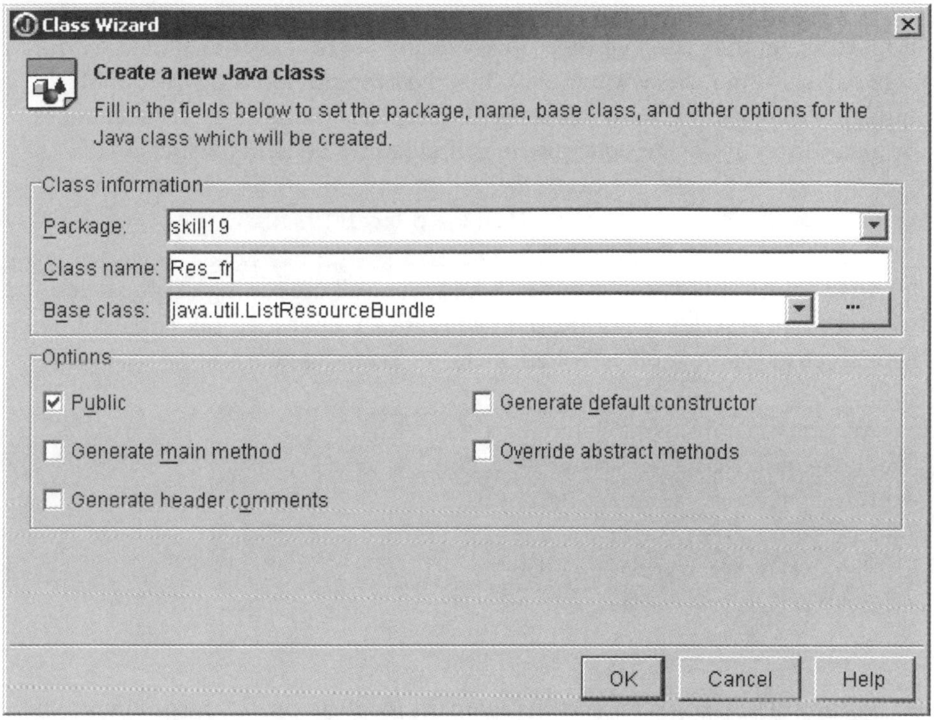

Figure 19-10. Creating a French resource bundle

You must now provide a getContents() method that returns the bundle settings you want to modify from the default. If you don't provide a bundle key, the base setting is retained. For instance, Date is still Date in French so you don't have to provide a setting for that one.

Listing 19-2. The French Resource Bundle Class

```java
package skill19;

import java.util.ListResourceBundle;

public class Res_fr extends ListResourceBundle {
  static final Object[][] contents = new String[][]{
      { "Hello_World", "Bonjour, Monde" },
      { "Number", "Nombre" },
      { "Months", "Mois" },
      { "Number_parsing_error_", "Erreur d'analyse de nombre: " },
      { "Date_parsing_error_", "Erreur d'analyse de date: " }};
  public Object[][] getContents() {
    return contents;
  }
}
```

You would need to create separate bundles for every locale you wanted to support. To get the lesson across, it's only necessary to show one. But, the program still won't use the new bundle. While the program looks up the bundle at start-up, this program needs to change the settings whenever the user changes the locale for numbers or dates and look up the bundle *with* the locale.

```
res = ResourceBundle.getBundle("skill19.Res", locale);
```

To use the bundle properly, you should move all the setting of properties from resource bundles out of jbInit() and into a helper method. Then, call the helper method from jbInit() when the locale is changed.

```
private void initProps(Locale locale) {
  res = ResourceBundle.getBundle("skill19.Res", locale);
  this.setTitle(res.getString("Hello_World"));
  jLabel1.setText(res.getString("Number"));
  jLabel2.setText(res.getString("Date"));
  jLabel3.setText(res.getString("Months"));
}
```

Putting all this together and changing the locale to one of the different "_fr" locales produces Figure 19-11.

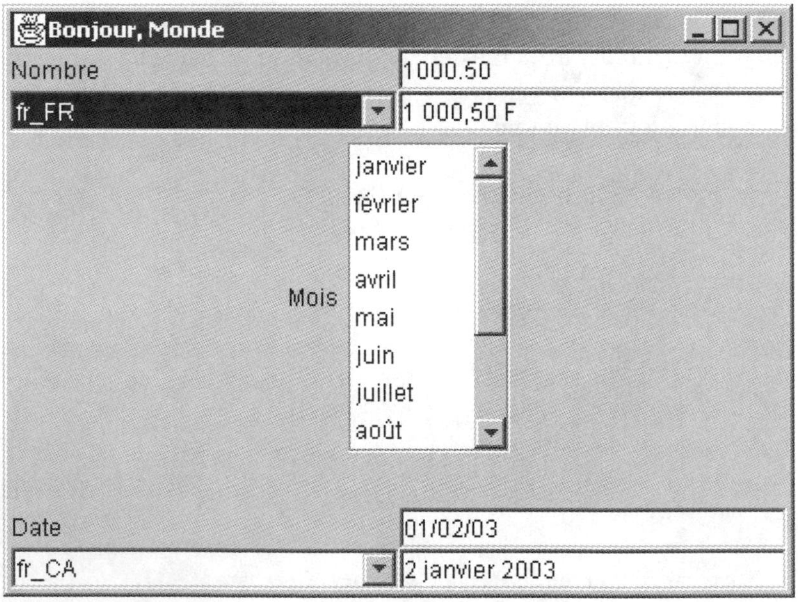

Figure 19-11. The French conversions

Putting everything together provides you with the complete source in Listing 19-3.

Listing 19-3. The Complete I18N.java Source

```java
package skill19;

import java.awt.*;
import java.awt.event.*;
import javax.swing.*;
import java.util.*;
import java.text.*;

public class I18N extends JFrame {
  static ResourceBundle res = ResourceBundle.getBundle("skill19.Res");
  JPanel contentPane;
  BorderLayout borderLayout1 = new BorderLayout();
  JPanel jPanel1 = new JPanel();
  GridLayout gridLayout1 = new GridLayout();
  JLabel jLabel1 = new JLabel();
  JTextField jTextField1 = new JTextField();
  JComboBox jComboBox1 = new JComboBox();
  JTextField jTextField2 = new JTextField();
  GridLayout gridLayout2 = new GridLayout();
  JPanel jPanel2 = new JPanel();
  JTextField jTextField3 = new JTextField();
  JTextField jTextField4 = new JTextField();
  JComboBox jComboBox2 = new JComboBox();
  JLabel jLabel2 = new JLabel();
  JPanel jPanel3 = new JPanel();
  JLabel jLabel3 = new JLabel();
  JScrollPane jScrollPane1 = new JScrollPane();
  JList jList1 = new JList();

  //Construct the frame
  public I18N() {
    enableEvents(AWTEvent.WINDOW_EVENT_MASK);
    try {
      jbInit();
    }
    catch(Exception e) {
      e.printStackTrace();
    }
  }
```

```java
//Component initialization
private void jbInit() throws Exception   {
  contentPane = (JPanel) this.getContentPane();
  contentPane.setLayout(borderLayout1);
  this.setSize(new Dimension(400, 300));
  jPanel1.setLayout(gridLayout1);
  gridLayout1.setRows(2);
  jTextField1.setText("1000.50");
  jTextField2.setEditable(false);
  jComboBox1.addActionListener(new java.awt.event.ActionListener() {
    public void actionPerformed(ActionEvent e) {
      jComboBox1_actionPerformed(e);
    }
  });
  gridLayout2.setRows(2);
  jPanel2.setLayout(gridLayout2);
  jTextField3.setEditable(false);
  jComboBox2.addActionListener(new java.awt.event.ActionListener() {
    public void actionPerformed(ActionEvent e) {
      jComboBox2_actionPerformed(e);
    }
  });
  contentPane.add(jPanel1,  BorderLayout.NORTH);
  jPanel1.add(jLabel1, null);
  jPanel1.add(jTextField1, null);
  jPanel1.add(jComboBox1, null);
  jPanel1.add(jTextField2, null);
  contentPane.add(jPanel2,  BorderLayout.SOUTH);
  jPanel2.add(jLabel2, null);
  jPanel2.add(jTextField4, null);
  jPanel2.add(jComboBox2, null);
  jPanel2.add(jTextField3, null);
  contentPane.add(jPanel3, BorderLayout.CENTER);
  jPanel3.add(jLabel3, null);
  jPanel3.add(jScrollPane1, null);
  jScrollPane1.getViewport().add(jList1, null);
  Locale numbers[] = NumberFormat.getAvailableLocales();
  ComboBoxModel model = new DefaultComboBoxModel(numbers);
  jComboBox1.setModel(model);
  Locale dates[] = DateFormat.getAvailableLocales();
  ComboBoxModel model2 = new DefaultComboBoxModel(dates);
  jComboBox2.setModel(model2);
  initProps(Locale.US);
}
```

```java
//Overridden so we can exit when window is closed
protected void processWindowEvent(WindowEvent e) {
  super.processWindowEvent(e);
  if (e.getID() == WindowEvent.WINDOW_CLOSING) {
    System.exit(0);
  }
}


void jComboBox1_actionPerformed(ActionEvent e) {
  Locale locale = (Locale)jComboBox1.getSelectedItem();
  initProps(locale);
  try {
    double input = Double.parseDouble(jTextField1.getText());
    NumberFormat nf = NumberFormat.getCurrencyInstance(locale);
    jTextField2.setText(nf.format(input));
  } catch (NumberFormatException nfe) {
    System.err.println(res.getString("Number_parsing_error_") + nfe);
  }
}
void jComboBox2_actionPerformed(ActionEvent e) {
  Locale locale = (Locale)jComboBox2.getSelectedItem();
  initProps(locale);
  try {
    String input = jTextField4.getText();
    if (input.length() > 0) {
      DateFormat inputFormat = DateFormat.getDateInstance(
        DateFormat.SHORT, Locale.US);
      Date inputDate = inputFormat.parse(input);
      DateFormat df = DateFormat.getDateInstance(DateFormat.LONG, locale);
      jTextField3.setText(df.format(inputDate));
    }
  } catch (ParseException pe) {
    System.err.println(res.getString("Date_parsing_error_") + pe);
  }
  DateFormatSymbols symbols = new DateFormatSymbols(locale);
  String months[] = symbols.getMonths();
  ListModel model = new DefaultComboBoxModel(months);
  jList1.setModel(model);
}
```

```
private void initProps(Locale locale) {
  res = ResourceBundle.getBundle("skill19.Res", locale);
  this.setTitle(res.getString("Hello_World"));
  jLabel1.setText(res.getString("Number"));
  jLabel2.setText(res.getString("Date"));
  jLabel3.setText(res.getString("Months"));
}
}
```

ARE YOU EXPERIENCED?

You've successfully made your way through the internationalization maze within Java. From formatting numbers and dates to working with locales and resource bundles, you can target your programs for the global market where users will feel comfortable with the application at hand because you've made the extra effort to display elements to their formatting needs. While the coding is relatively easy, you still need to manually translate the text.

Now you can

- Display formatted numbers

- Validate date input

- Work with the JComboBox control

- Use resource bundles

- Internationalize programs

Moving on, it's now time to learn about customizing the JBuilder environment.

Customizing JBuilder

- Setting JBuilder project defaults

- Adding new code templates

- Swapping JDK versions

- Adding tools

- Obfuscating code

Configuring Project Defaults

Well, you're almost done with the book, and by now, you probably have some strong opinions about the JBuilder interface. In case there are some things you'd like to improve, this chapter should help you set up JBuilder to be more user-friendly. Also, even if you just love everything, this skill will show you some pointers for setting up an even better environment.

You've reached Skill 20, and after you've been introduced to the first tip, which covers setting the default project directory, author, and company, you'll probably be very thankful. The first screen of the Project Wizard (see Figure 20-1) is where you've entered **C:\skills** over 20 times so far.

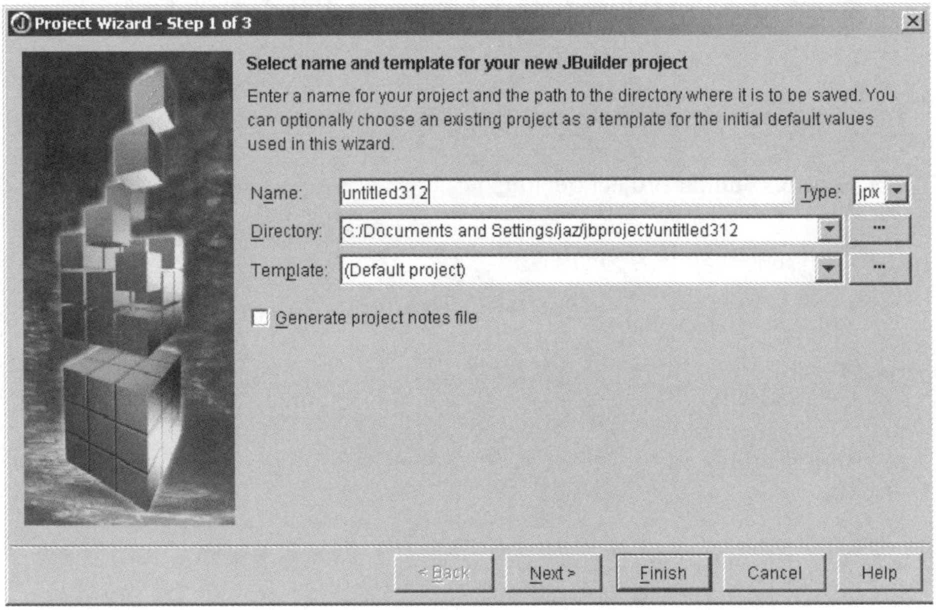

Figure 20-1. The Project Wizard's first screen, where you enter in the default project path

The very first time, you had to enter **C:\skills\Skill***n*, but each additional time you could have just selected the down arrow at the end of the Directory field. This brings up the history of paths entered. From there you could have just selected `C:\skills\Skill`*n* instead of entering it manually. You would have still had to change what the *n* was, though, or go back into the Name field and enter the project name second for the Directory field to be updated.

On the third screen of the Project Wizard (see Figure 20-2) you're prompted for your name and company. This information is displayed in the project file and used for any automatically generated javadoc header comments. While your company may change a little more than you'd like with today's economy, at least your name should stay the same (except for some women who get married and take on their spouse's last name or hyphenate their name).

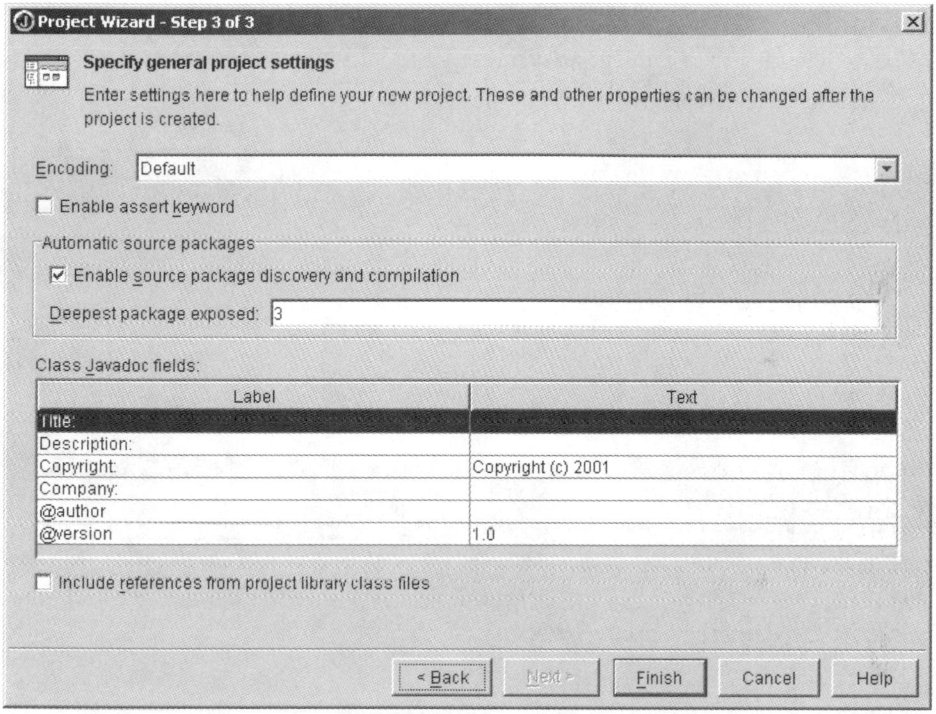

Figure 20-2. The Project Wizard's third screen, where you enter in your name and company

To customize these options, you'll need to open up the Default Project Properties configuration window by selecting Project ➤ Default Project Properties. You configure the project directory under the Paths tab, as shown in Figure 20-3, and you configure the name and company under the General tab, as shown in Figure 20-4.

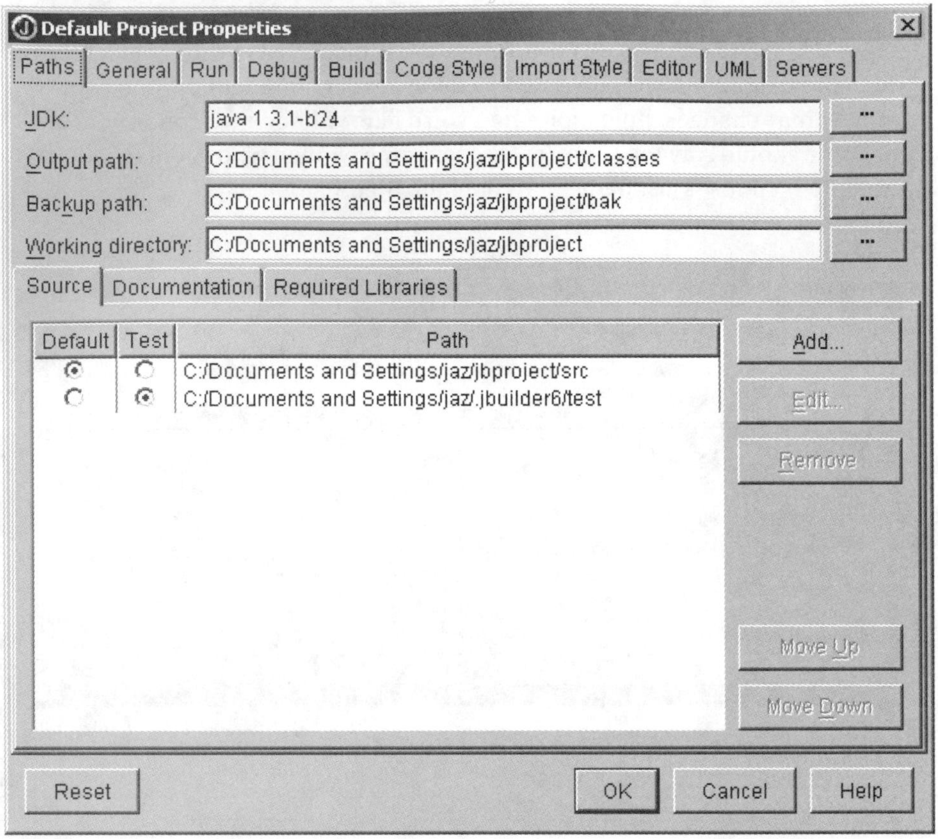

Figure 20-3. The Paths tab of the Default Property Properties window. From here you can configure the working directory.

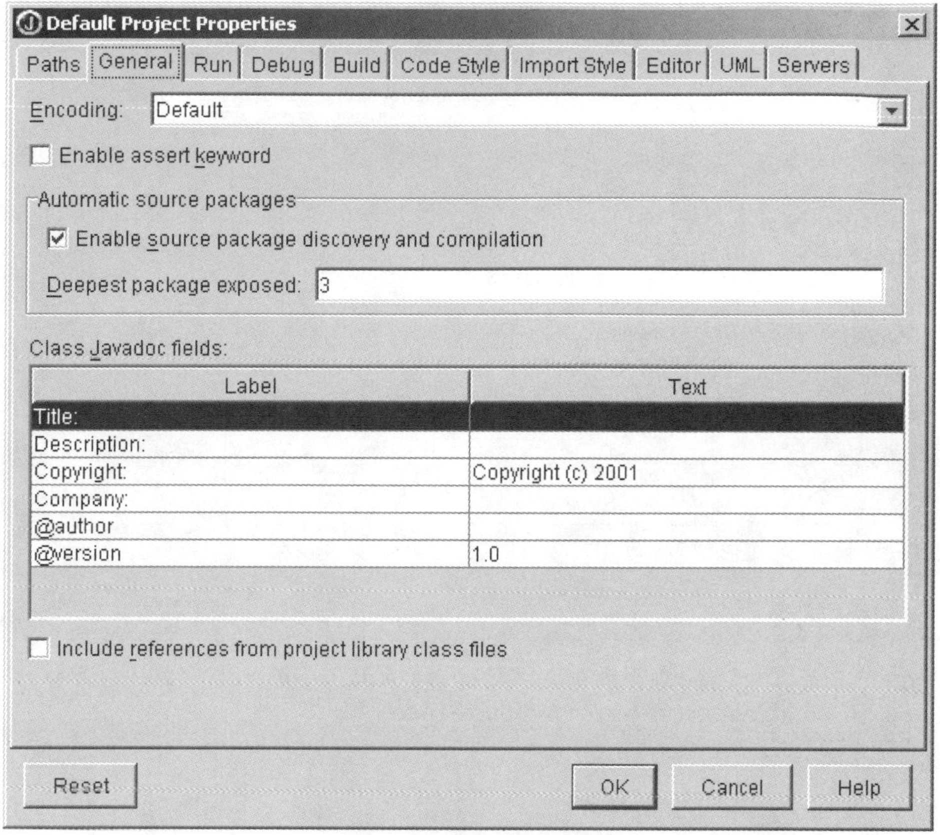

Figure 20-4. The General tab of the Default Property Properties window. From here you can configure the default author and company name.

The default project directory is taken from the default source path; that is, the set of entries at the bottom of the screen, under the Source subtab. Currently, the entry you'll find is your user directory for the operating system, with a jbprojects subdirectory under that, and an src directory under that. For my Windows 2000 box, that translates to C:\Documents and Settings\jaz\jbprojects\src. What this means is the initial default root project directory is C:\Documents and Settings\jaz\jbprojects. The project name is then appended in the Project Wizard, as you can see in Figure 20-1.

To change the default project directory, you need to place a new entry in the list under the Source tab and select it as the default. Click the Add button to get the Select One or More Directories dialog box shown in Figure 20-5. Enter **C:\skills\src** in the directory prompt and click OK. You will be warned that the directory doesn't exist, as shown in Figure 20-6. Click Yes, as the directory will never be needed.

![Select One or More Directories dialog window showing a directory tree with folders labeled Skill10, Skill11, Skill11b, Skill11c, Skill12, Skill13, Skill13b, Skill13c, Skill14, Skill14b, Skill15, Skill16, Skill17, Skill18, Skill2, Skill21 under the skills folder, with Desktop, Home, Project, and Samples sidebar icons, and OK, Cancel, Help buttons]

Figure 20-5. The Select One or More Directories window where you add a new path to the list of directories to search for source code

![No Such Directory warning dialog with the message "The directory 'C:/skills/src' does not exist. Accept it anyway?" and Yes and No buttons]

Figure 20-6. The warning message that you've entered a nonexistent directory. Ignore the warning and click Yes.

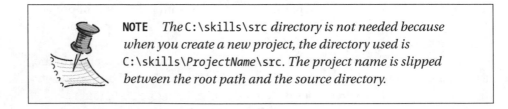

NOTE   *The* C:\skills\src *directory is not needed because when you create a new project, the directory used is* C:\skills\ProjectName\src. *The project name is slipped between the root path and the source directory.*

At this point you have three directories listed under the Source tab. You need to select the Default option for the new C:/skills/src entry. You no longer need to enter or select C:\skills as the project directory, because the wizard will initially display it.

To finish up, select the General tab. On this screen, enter your name in the @author field and your company in the Company field. You can also change the copyright message once the year changes. Once you click OK, all three settings get saved. They'll be used the next time you create a project (see Figure 20-7 and Figure 20-8). Previously generated projects will not be altered.

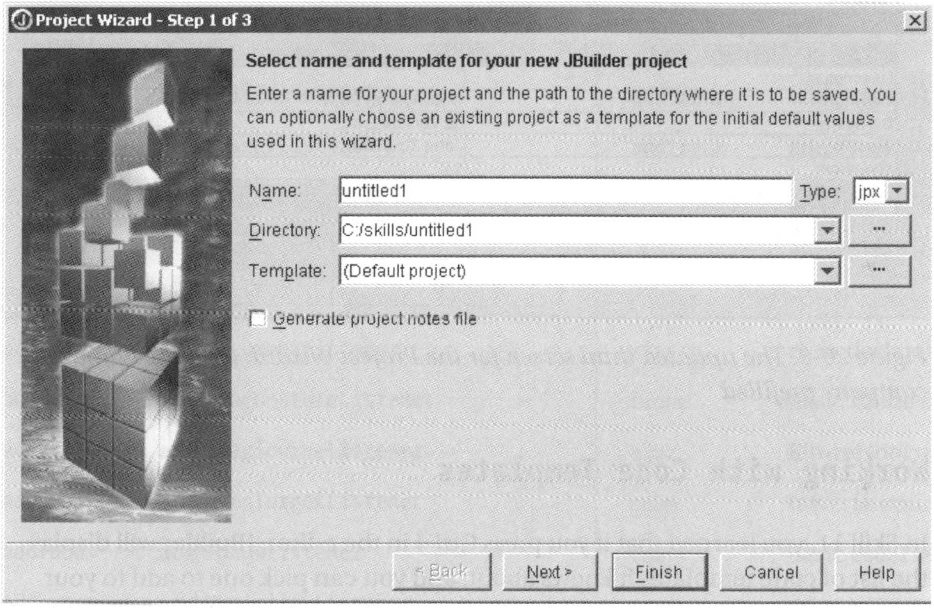

Figure 20-7. The updated first screen for the Project Wizard, with the new default project directory

Table 20-1. JBuilder 6 Template Set (continued)

Name	Description	Name	Description
inito	initOpenTool	syn	synchronized
inst	if instanceof	sys	print to System.err
invoke	invoke later with runnable	timer	new javax.swing Timer
iter	traverse with iterator	todo	todo tag
jdc	JavaDoc comment	tryc	try / catch
jndi	JNDI lookup	tryce	try / catch {throw EJBException}
main	simple main		
mouse	implement Mouse(Motion)Listener	trycf	try / catch / finally
nar	PortableRemoteObject narrow	tryct	try / catch {trace}
out	print to System.out	tryctf	try / catch {trace} / finally
sbpr	SessionBean provider/resolver methods		
sleep	try / thread.sleep	tryf	try / finally
switchd	switch statement (with default)	whileb	while
switchs	switch statement	whiles	while (no braces)

In the Personal Edition of JBuilder, the template set is read-only; you can't change any existing templates or add new ones. With the Professional and Enterprise Editions, you can modify the template set. Assuming you have either the Professional or Enterprise Edition, or at least the 30-day trial version, you might add a new template if you constantly find yourself entering the same block of code, or if you don't use something that frequently and constantly get it wrong when you do.

To demonstrate, add a template that creates a paintComponent() method template for when you create your own custom Swing component. Personally, I always forget the call to super.paintComponent() and then wonder why the component isn't painting properly. Creating a template, and remembering to use it, will ensure that will never happen again.

When you create new templates, there's one special character you need to know about: the pipe (|) character. You can place a pipe character in the template. It tells JBuilder where to position the cursor after the template code is inserted.

TIP *If multiple pipe characters are in the template, the cursor will be placed at the last one. If the pipe character is within a quoted string, the cursor will be placed within the quoted string. If you truly need the pipe character to appear in the code snippet, place a backslash in the template:* \|.

To add a template, select Tools ➤ Editor Options, and choose the Templates tab (see Figure 20-9). Then click the Add button to get the Add Code Template dialog box (see Figure 20-10).

```
Editor Options                                          ×

Editor | Display | Color | CodeInsight | Templates | Java Structure

Templates:

        Name                    Description
addaction              add ActionListener
addadjust              add AdjustmentListener
addanc                 add AncestorListener
addawt                 add AWTEventListener
addbeanm               add BeanContextMembership...
addbeans               add BeanContextServicesList...
addcaret               add CaretListener

  [ Add... ]    [ Edit... ]   [ Delete ]

Code:

addActionListener(new ActionListener() {
  public void actionPerformed(ActionEvent e) {
     |
  }
});


  [ Reset ]              [ OK ]  [ Cancel ]  [ Help ]
```

Figure 20-9. The Templates tab of the Editor Options dialog box, where you add, edit, or delete templates

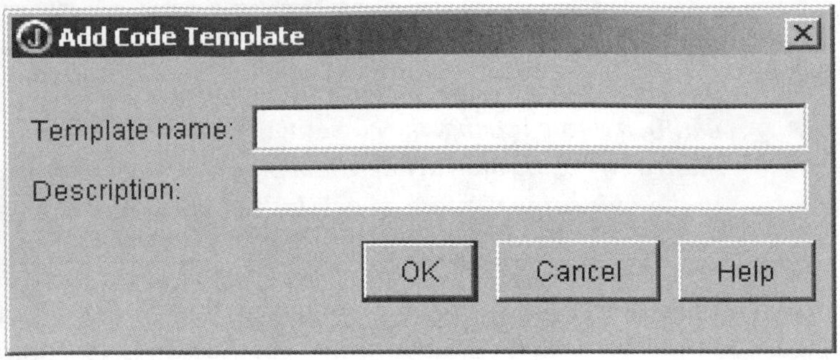

Add Code Template   ☒

Template name: [   ]

Description: [   ]

[OK]   [Cancel]   [Help]

Figure 20-10. The Add Code Template dialog box. Enter a name and description here, and then click OK.

Since you'll be providing a `paintComponent()` template, enter a name of **paintcomp** and a description of **basic paintComponent method**. Once you click OK, you'll be returned to the screen in Figure 20-9, where you provide the code in the Code area of the form. Enter the following source and click OK:

```
public void paintComponent(Graphics g) {
  super.paintComponent(g);
  Graphics2D g2d = (Graphics2D)g;
  |
}
```

Now, in your custom Swing components, you can get started with the drawing aspect of the component by typing **paintcomp** and pressing Ctrl-J. You'll need to manually import the `java.awt` package, as code templates don't support entering source in multiple places. Templates do preserve the indentation level, though, so be sure you're at the right level before entering in the template.

At any point you can modify the code for the template. The Edit button on the screen in Figure 20-9 is to change the name and description, not the code fragment.

 TIP   *Not only do templates work for Java source files, but they work for non-Java files as well. For instance, you may find templates useful if you're creating XML files within the JBuilder environment.*

Changing the JDK Version

When JBuilder 6 first shipped, the Java 2 Standard Edition was at release 1.3.1_b24. Originally, when Java IDEs first came out, if a new version of Java shipped, whether a point release, such as 1.1.8, or a more significant release, such as Java 1.2, the IDE vendor had to release a new version of the tool to support the new Java version. Nowadays, most IDE tools support what is called *JDK swapping*. JDK swapping is the ability to tell the tool to use a different Java runtime for compilation and execution. Since JBuilder is written in Java, you can't tell JBuilder to swap what it uses, but you can still create programs with newer or older releases of the Java Development Kit.

 NOTE *JDK swapping essentially means that you can't use the UI Designer with capabilities introduced in the new release, but you can use the editor and debugger.*

You can swap the JDK version on a project level or for all projects. In this skill, you'll do it for just one. This is best to show with a newer JDK version rather than reverting to an older version, as you can't be too sure the new compiler isn't still compiling the source code for the older release. To do this, you'll need to have the Java 2 SDK, Standard Edition, version 1.4 available on your system, which you can download from `http://java.sun.com/j2se/1.4/`. Once you've downloaded and installed the tool, continue with this skill.

To try out JDK swapping, start the Project Wizard. Change the project name to **Skill20**. You won't need to change the project directory. However, click Next to move on to the second page (shown in Figure 20-11). This is where you swap JDK versions.

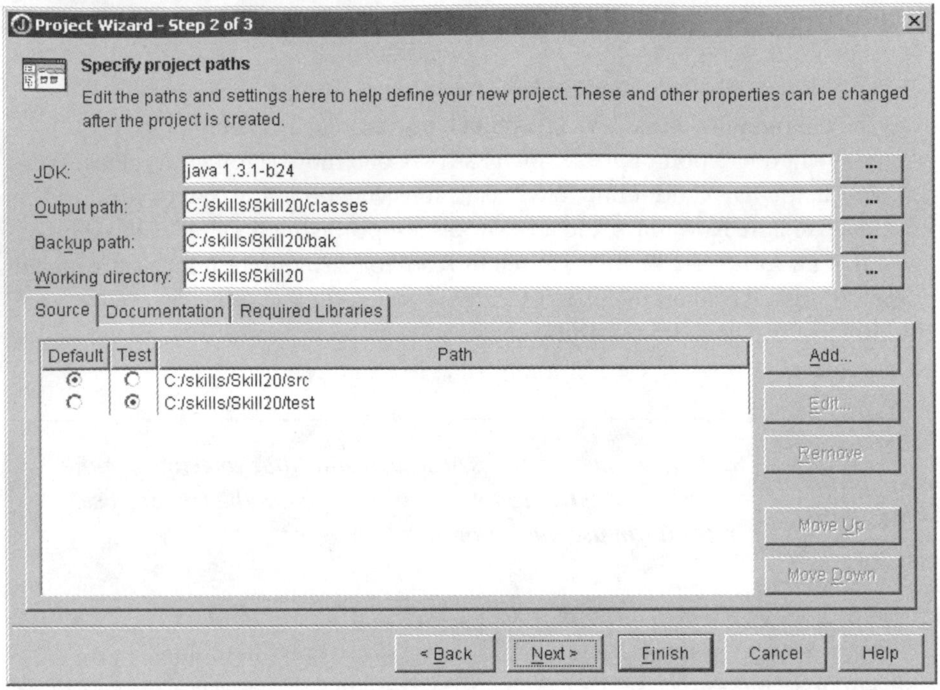

Figure 20-11. The second screen for the Project Wizard, where you can swap JDK releases

You'll notice the first option is JDK, with a current setting of java `1.3.1_b24`. Clicking the " . . . " button to the right of the text box brings up the screen shown in Figure 20-12.

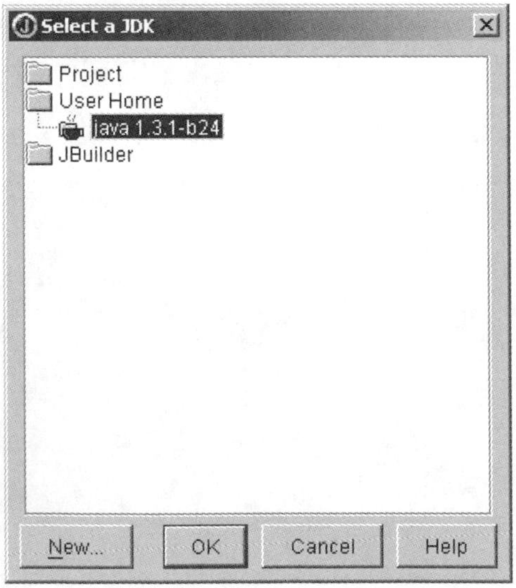

Figure 20-12. The Select a JDK dialog box, where you can swap the JDK version

Since there are no other JDK versions initially configured to swap to, you'll need to create a new one. Click New to bring up the New JDK Wizard (see Figure 20-13). This is where you get to pick the version. Click the " . . . " button to the right of the Existing JDK home path text box to access the Select Directory window (see Figure 20-14). This is the same screen shown in Figure 20-5 with a different screen title. Here is where you find or enter the installation directory for the other JDK release. For the 1.4 release, this would usually be **C:\jdk1.4**, so enter that and click OK. This will fill in the name for the JDK (see Figure 20-15), and then you can click OK.

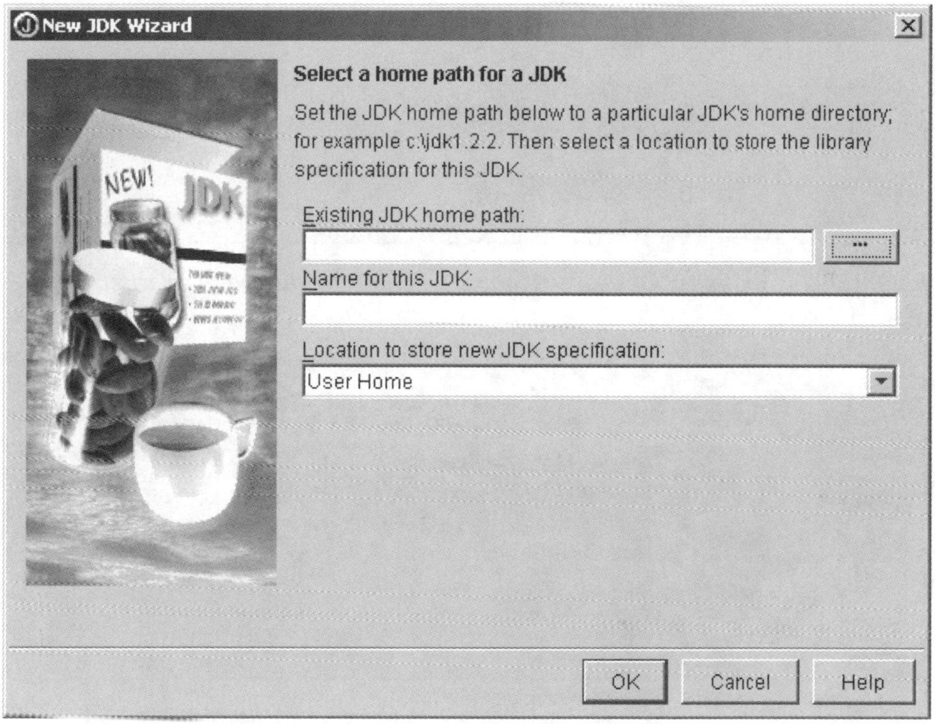

Figure 20-13. The initial New JDK Wizard dialog box. Click the " . . . " button to find the JDK path.

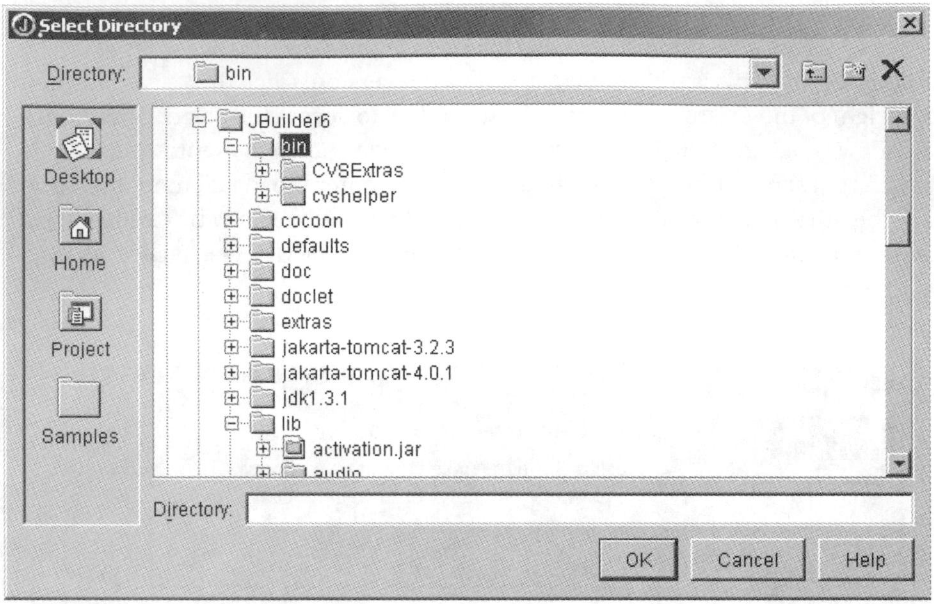

Figure 20-14. The Select Directory window for choosing the root level directory of a different JDK

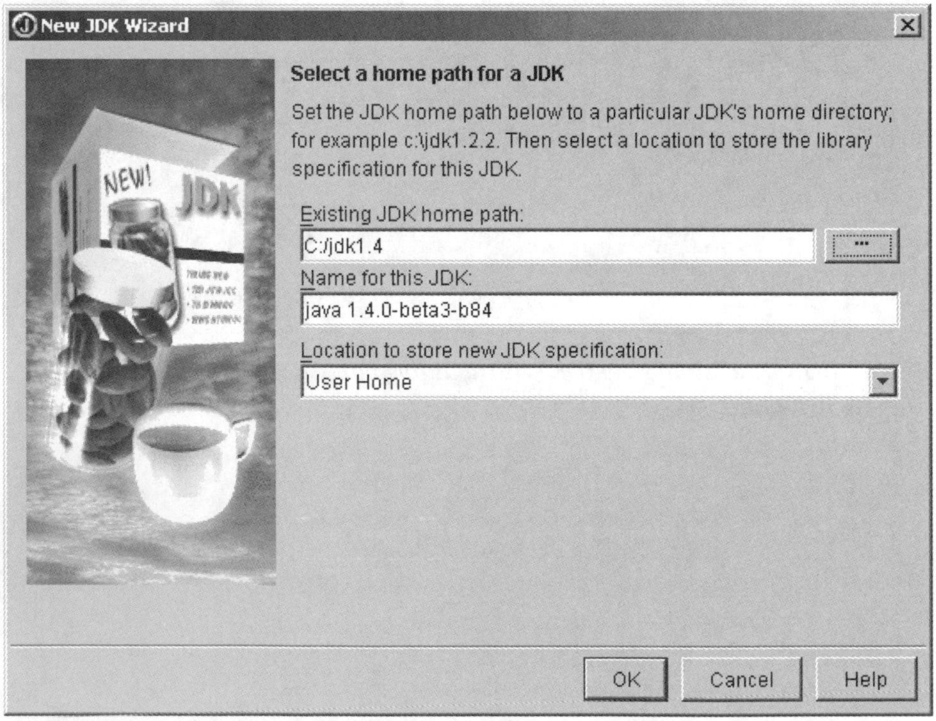

Figure 20-15. The completed New JDK Wizard dialog box. Your version number will more than likely differ.

You'll now be back to the screen shown in Figure 20-12, where you can select the newly installed JDK version and click OK. This returns you to the Project Wizard. Click Finish and your project will be generated.

 NOTE *To change the JDK for all future projects, open the Default Project Properties window (see Figure 20-3) and change the JDK there.*

To test out the new JDK, start the Application Wizard. Name the frame class **OneFour** and click Finish. One of the additions to the 1.4 release is a new Swing control called a *spinner.* Given some list of options, the spinner lets you spin through them by providing an up arrow and a down arrow. So, you can use this new JSpinner control in your program. Since the control isn't available under the 1.3 release, you'll be sure the program uses the new 1.4 version. At the bottom of the jbInit() method, add the following three lines:

```
SpinnerModel model = new SpinnerNumberModel(50, 0, 100, 5);
JSpinner spinner = new JSpinner(model);
contentPane.add(spinner, BorderLayout.NORTH);
```

Running the program will display the frame and the JSpinner control shown in Figure 20-16. That's really all there is to JDK swapping.

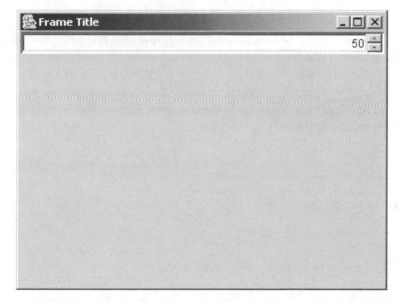

Figure 20-16. Demonstrating JDK swapping by using the new JSpinner control

Adding Tools

The JBuilder Tools menu is full of many interesting options. Besides using all the preconfigured choices, you can add new ones by selecting Tools ➤ Configure Tools, which brings up the dialog box shown in Figure 20-17. New tools then get added to the menu below the Configure Tools menu choice.

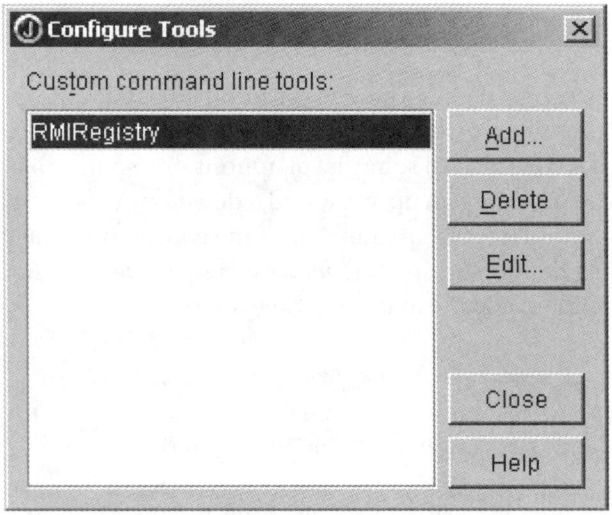

Figure 20-17. The Configure Tools dialog box, where you can install custom command-line tools

To add a new tool, just click the Add button to access the Add Tool dialog box (see Figure 20-18). There are four choices on this screen: Title, Program, Service, and Parameters. The text in the Title option is displayed on the menu. The program is what to execute when the menu is selected. The parameters are any command-line parameters to pass to the program. And service means the tool can be started *and* stopped from the menu.

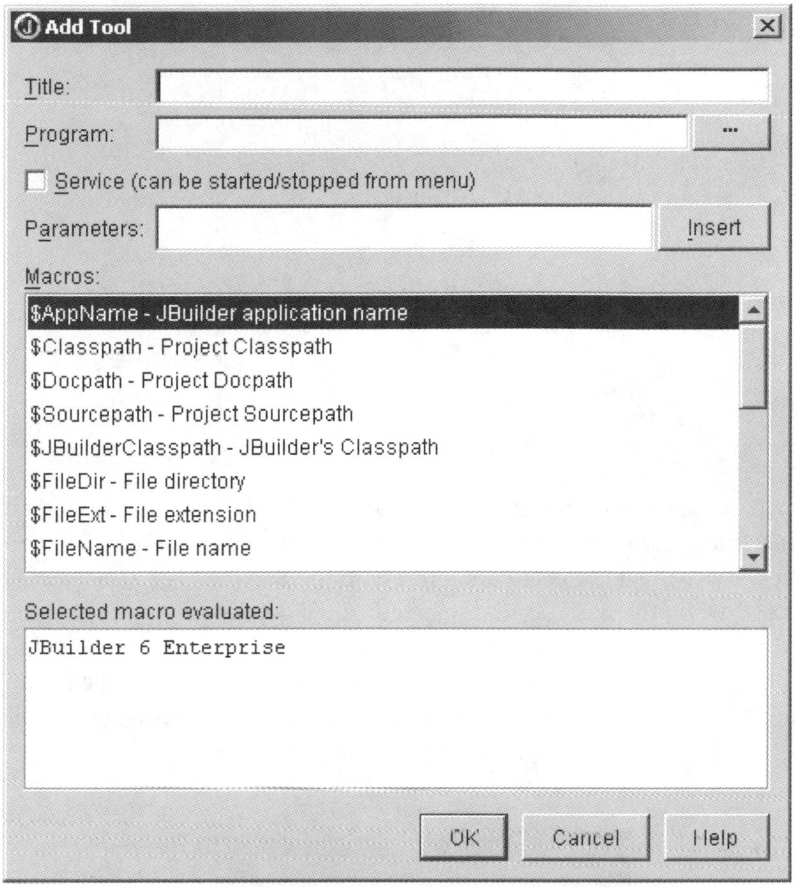

Figure 20-18. The Add Tool dialog box. Here you enter the title to appear on the menu, the program to execute, and any parameters. You also choose whether or not the service can be started/stopped from the menu.

To help with the parameters, several macros are listed in the Macros area. These macros allow you to pass information about the current file or project to the external tool. To use one as a parameter, select it in the Macros area, and then click Insert. You'll notice the macro name entered in the Parameters field, surrounded by parentheses. Table 20-2 lists the different macros available. The Selected macro evaluated area of the screen shows you what each macro would translate to for the current file/project, in case you're not sure. The $Prompt macro is probably the most interesting, as it allows you to prompt for a parameter when the menu is selected.

Table 20-2. Configure Tool Macros

Name		
$AppName	$FileExt	$OutputDir
$Classpath	$FileName	$ProjectDir
$Docpath	$FilePackage	$ProjectPath
$Sourcepath	$FilePath	$Prompt
$JBuilderClasspath	$FileUrl	$RootDir
$FileClass	$HomeDir	$TargetDir
$FileDir	$JDKPath	$TargetPath

To demonstrate, add the standard Windows calculator to the Tools menu. Provide a title of **Calculator**, a program of **calc**, and no parameters. Try it once with the Service toggle selected and once with the Service toggle unselected. In either case, when the menu is first selected, you'll get the calculator to open, as shown in Figure 20-19. When the Service toggle is selected and you select the menu again, the Calculator window will go away. If the service toggle is not selected, when you select the menu again, a second Calculator window will open.

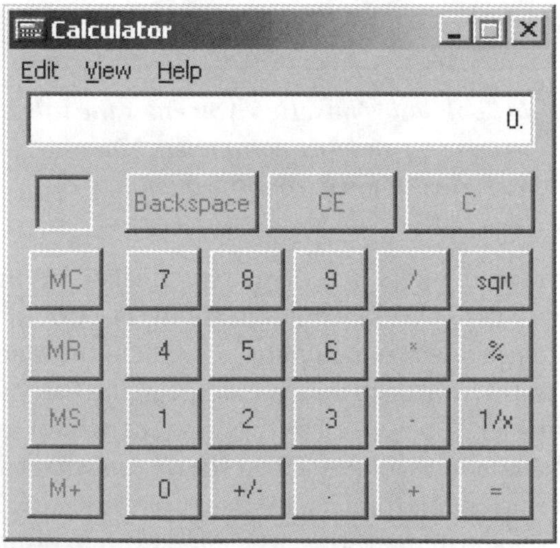

Figure 20-19. The Windows calculator opened from the Tools menu

Adding tools is that easy.

Understanding Obfuscation

The final option to set in this skill is to enable the obfuscator. Because Java is an interpreted language, the class files contain much more information than platform-specific executables. There are decompilers available that can try to recreate source code from the compiled `.class` files. When it comes time to deliver your applications to third parties, you can partially protect yourself by using obfuscation.

> **NOTE** *Just like with delivering executables, there is no way to completely protect yourself from reverse engineering if you're giving the program to the "enemy." If you're that concerned about reverse engineering proprietary algorithms, keep the code within your Web space by using servlets or some other server-side technology that runs within your control.*

Quite simply, *obfuscation* is the mangling of class and variable names so that they're unrecognizable to the human eye. They still must be valid for the byte code verifier and class loader to load them, but decompiling an obfuscated class results in code that loses meaning in the translation. Algorithms are still extractable, but any meaning offered by useful variable names is completely lost.

To enable obfuscation at the project level, select Project ➤ Project Properties, and then choose the Build tab. This brings up the window in Figure 20-20. You'll notice that the Obfuscate option in the middle of the screen is unchecked. Check it and click OK to obfuscate the class files when you build the project.

Project Properties

Paths | General | Run | Debug | Build | Code Style | Import Style | Editor | UML | Servers

Java | IDL | JSP | Resource

Debug options: Source, line, and variable information ▾

Target VM: All Java SDKs ▾

Other compiler options

☑ Show warnings   ☑ Check stable packages

☑ Show deprecations   ☐ Make stable packages

☑ Synchronize output dir ☐ Obfuscate

☐ Exclude class: [   ] [...]

☑ Autosave all files before compiling

☑ Generate source to output path

☐ Autocancel build on error

Reset   OK   Cancel   Help

Figure 20-20. The Project Properties window where you can enable obfuscation

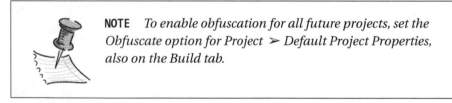

NOTE   *To enable obfuscation for all future projects, set the Obfuscate option for Project ➢ Default Project Properties, also on the Build tab.*

Obfuscated code tends to produce smaller class files, as `private` methods such as `generateKey()` might get renamed to names such as `a1()`. The generated class files will not execute any slower. If anything, you might notice a slight speed improvement due to the smaller class sizes.

ARE YOU EXPERIENCED?

With the customizations you learned in this skill, you should become more productive in the JBuilder environment.

Now you can

- Reset the project author and company

- Change the default project directory

- Create your own code templates

- Swap JDK releases

- Add new tools to the menu

- Obfuscate your class files

Two more skills worth learning are using the debugger and gaining a better understanding of multithreading. Skill 21 explains these two abilities.

Debugging
Multithreaded Programs

- Working with threads

- Executing code in the event-handling thread

- Communicating between threads

- Working with the debugger

- Stepping through the source

- Modifying variables

- Setting breakpoints

Creating the Test Program

Taking the debugger through the ropes is always interesting. You can create a bug-ridden example and use the debugger to squash the bugs, or you can create a working example and use the debugger to examine known pieces of a working program. In this skill, you'll do the latter.

The program you'll create will use multiple threads to show off the debugger's multithreading support. The first thread works as a manufacturer. It produces strings for someone else to use. Call this thread the *producer.* Next is the consumer, which uses up the strings manufactured by the producer. Call this piece the *consumer.* The last thread works as a buffer. Because the producer and consumer work at different speeds, you need a holding group that stores strings and displays what's currently stored on the screen. Call it a *display buffer.* There's one catch in all this: The display buffer has a fixed size. This means that if the producer manufactures strings faster than the consumer uses them, the producer will need to slow down when the buffer is full. This adds interthread communication to the picture. Once you create the program, you'll use the debugger to examine the pieces.

At this point, close all your open projects and create a new application. Call the project **Skill21** and save it in **C:\skills\Skill21**. (You won't have to change the root directory this time.) Click Finish. Then, within the Application Wizard, click Next to name the Frame class **DisplayBuffer**. Click Finish again.

Creating the Producer

The first piece to create is the producer. This class needs to work independently of everything else, as its sole purpose is the production of strings. The way you did this in Skill 4 was by implementing the Runnable interface, creating a Thread, and passing the thread the class that implemented the interface. Once started, the thread did the work within the run() method of the interface implementer. Here's the general framework you used:

```
public class MyClass extends MyOtherClass implements Runnable {
  . . .
  public void run() {
  }
  . . .
  public void aMethod() {
    Thread runner = new Thread(this);
    runner.start();
  }
}
```

You use the `Runnable` interface for those cases where the class you're working with is a subclass of any other class *besides* `Object`. Because Java doesn't permit extending multiple classes, it needs to provide an alternate way to work with multiple threads. In the case where the direct parent is `Object`, you can change your class to subclass `Thread`. Because `Thread` already implements the `Runnable` interface, you can just provide a `run()` method directly within the subclass.

Getting back to the producer, its sole job is production; it doesn't do anything else. Therefore, you can create a `Thread` subclass for the producer to work. To create a new independent class, use the Class Wizard. Select File ➤ New Class to start up the wizard. This brings up the dialog box shown in Figure 21-1.

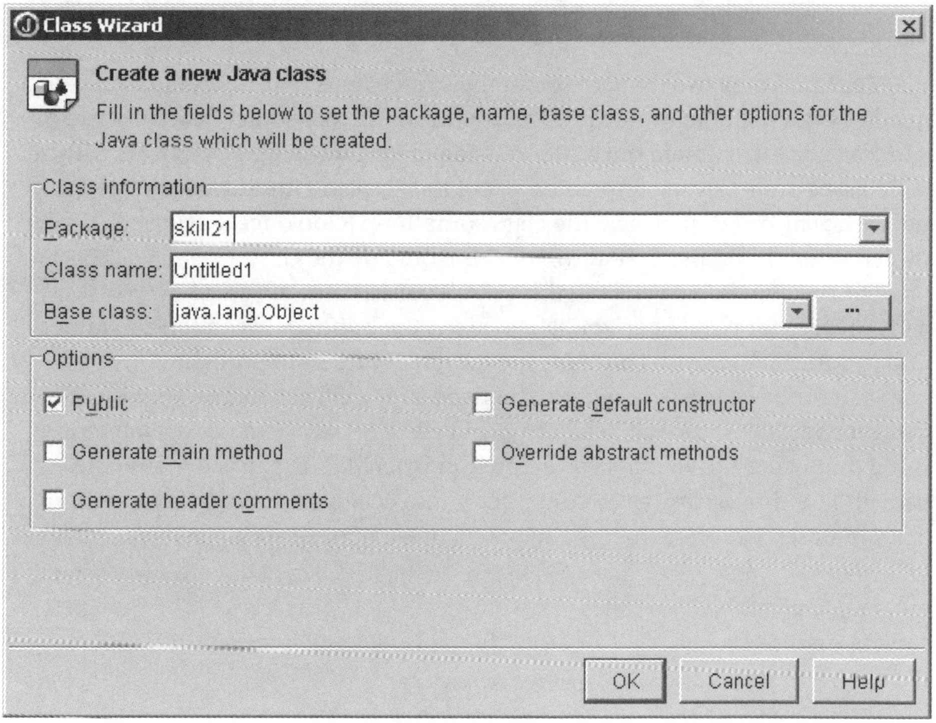

Figure 21-1. The Class Wizard dialog box. Here, you create new classes in separate source files within the project.

In the Class Wizard dialog box, enter a Class name of **Producer** and fill in the Base class field with **java.lang.Thread**. You can either type the class name in yourself or find it by clicking the " . . . " button. Be sure the Public, Generate default constructor, and Generate header comments options are selected and then click OK. This action adds a new file to the project called `Producer.java`.

First, fill in the header comments. You really should do this with all the classes you create. It helps that JBuilder can provide the framework for you to complete. Notice that your own name and company is used since you set this up in Skill 20. Something like the following should suffice:

```
/**
 * <p>Title: Producer</p>
 * <p>Description: Repeatedly generates strings and stores in buffer</p>
 * <p>Copyright:    Copyright (c) 2001</p>
 * <p>Company: JZ Ventures, Inc.</p>
 * @author John Zukowski
 * @version 1.0
 */
```

There are only two things to do in the source here. In the constructor, you need to get a buffer to work with. The producer and consumer need to share a buffer, so you maintain the buffer outside the producer class. Then, as with all subclasses of Thread and implementers of the Runnable interface, you need to define a run() method to give the class something to do once it's started. The thread doesn't start itself. That will be done outside the class.

For the constructor, change the default constructor to accept a DisplayBuffer parameter. You'll use this as the buffer between the consumer and producer. Also, get a count for the number of items to produce. Once the constructor has these parameters, you need to store them somewhere, so add instance variables to save the two to use later, in the run() method. One more thing that will make your life easier later on when debugging is to name the thread. The Thread class has a constructor that accepts a String parameter, so call the superclass' constructor and pass along a name, **Producer**.

```
private DisplayBuffer buffer;
private int runs;

public Producer(DisplayBuffer db, int testRuns) {
   super("Producer");
   buffer = db;
   runs = testRuns;
}
```

Now on to the run() method. Here, just loop for the number of runs requested, generating a new string each time. Instead of complete randomness in the strings, you'll pick them out of an array. Initially, this looks like the following code, with the added println() call to show the choice selected:

```java
public void run() {
  String choices[] = {
    "The", "Quick", "Brown", "Fox",
    "Jumps", "Over", "The", "Lazy", "Dog"};
  String choice;
  for (int i=0; i<runs; i++) {
    choice = choices[(int)(Math.random() * choices.length)];
    System.out.println("Added: " + choice);
  }
}
```

NOTE *For those unfamiliar with the phrase "The quick brown fox jumps over the lazy dog," it's a sentence commonly used in beginning typing classes. It consists of at least one instance of each letter of the alphabet.*

To notify the buffer of the new choice, you'll call an add() method that needs to be defined. You also need to add a delay to the producer, as production usually takes some time, so you'll add a random delay of under a half-second between runs. This completes the Producer class definition. Listing 21-1 provides the final source.

Listing 21-1. The Complete Producer.java Source

```java
package skill21;

/**
 * <p>Title: Producer</p>
 * <p>Description: Repeatedly generates strings and stores in buffer</p>
 * <p>Copyright:    Copyright (c) 2001</p>
 * <p>Company: JZ Ventures, Inc.</p>
 * @author John Zukowski
 * @version 1.0
 */

public class Producer extends Thread {

  private DisplayBuffer buffer;
  private int runs;
  private final static int DELAY = 500;
```

```
        public Producer(DisplayBuffer db, int testRuns) {
          super("Producer");
          buffer = db;
          runs = testRuns;
        }

        public void run() {
          String choices[] = {
            "The", "Quick", "Brown", "Fox",
            "Jumps", "Over", "The", "Lazy", "Dog"};
          String choice;
          for (int i=0; i<runs; i++) {
            choice = choices[(int)(Math.random() * choices.length)];
            buffer.add(choice);
            System.out.println("Added: " + choice);
            try {
              sleep((int)(Math.random() * DELAY));
            } catch (InterruptedException ignored) {
              // Ignored
            }
          }
        }
      }
```

Notice how the producer doesn't care about the size of the buffer, or whether or not the buffer is full. It isn't the producer's job to worry about that.

Creating the Consumer

Next, create the consumer. Use the Class Wizard again to create a new class. Call it **Consumer**, and subclass **java.lang.Thread** again. The Thread class should already be in the Base class field as it was the last class extended. The main differences here are the use of the remove() method to get the string out of the buffer and a different delay speed. The Consumer.java source in Listing 21-2 provides the definition of your consumer.

Listing 21-2. The Complete Consumer.java Source

```java
package skill21;

/**
 * <p>Title: Consumer</p>
 * <p>Description: Repeatedly consume strings from buffer</p>
 * <p>Copyright:    Copyright (c) 2001</p>
 * <p>Company: JZ Ventures, Inc.</p>
 * @author John Zukowski
 * @version 1.0
 */

public class Consumer extends Thread {

  private DisplayBuffer buffer;
  private int runs;
  private final static int DELAY = 2000;

  public Consumer(DisplayBuffer db, int testRuns) {
    super("Consumer");
    buffer = db;
    runs = testRuns;
  }

  public void run() {
    String choice;
    for (int i=0; i<runs; i++) {
      choice = buffer.remove();
      System.out.println("Removed " + choice);
      try {
        sleep((int)(Math.random() * DELAY));
      } catch (InterruptedException ignored) {
        // Ignored
      }
    }
  }
}
```

Creating the Display Buffer

The DisplayBuffer is what makes the whole thing work. In it is a buffer. Strings are added to it with add() and removed with remove(). The buffer also needs to display the current buffer contents to the screen. The simplest way to do this is with components. Because DisplayBuffer is a frame, just add and remove components from it. Use buttons for this. In order for the screen to look somewhat decent, you should change the layout manager of the content pane to GridLayout, with one column and five rows. This keeps the buttons in one column, with space reserved when the number of rows is fewer than five.

To change the layout manager of the content pane, select DisplayBuffer.java in the Navigation pane and the Design tab at the bottom of the Content pane. Selecting contentPane (BorderLayout) in the Structure pane focuses the Inspector's view on that component. Change the layout property to **GridLayout**. The borderLayout1 entry in the Structure pane should now be gridLayout1; select it. In the Inspector, change the columns property to **1** and the rows to **5** to complete the screen setup.

Because you'll be using a fixed-size buffer, you need to reserve the space. You'll use five labels in the screen. Then, you have to maintain your positioning within the so-called buffer. The positioning variable will indicate how many objects are currently in the buffer. The buffer will work as a last-in, first-out structure—the last element added is the next one removed. Add the following instance variable to DisplayBuffer.java:

```
private int position = 0;
```

Add five JLabel objects to the screen with a **CENTER** horizontal alignment and no text label. Also, define a constant LENGTH that you'll need a little later on.

```
private final static int LENGTH = 5;
```

Adding to the Buffer

Adding to the buffer seems like the next most logical thing to do. In the producer, you defined the method to be called add(), which accepts one String parameter.

```
public void add(String s)
```

In order to add to the buffer, you have to make sure the buffer isn't full. The buffer is full when the position setting is the LENGTH constant you just created:

```
while (position == LENGTH);
```

To add the string to the screen, you just get the right JLabel and set its text property, moving the position along for the next element:

```
Container pane = getContentPane();
JLabel label = (JLabel)pane.getComponent(position++);
label.setText(s);
```

Putting all this together gives you the following:

```
public void add(String s) {
    while (position == LENGTH);
    Container pane = getContentPane();
    JLabel label = (JLabel)pane.getComponent(position++);
    label.setText(s);
}
```

While this will work, there are some major flaws with it—the most obvious being the while loop. The while loop is structured as what's called a *busy-wait loop*. While the system is waiting for some condition to be true, it keeps the CPU busy. That is a bad thing. You could use the sleep() method of Thread to pause for a short period, but for how long? Instead of trying to sleep for a random amount of time and trying to discover when things have cleared up, there is a better way: the wait() method from Object that everyone inherits. This allows you to not use the CPU until someone notifies you via a method called notify() or notifyAll().

Also, if there are multiple producers, each may discover that the buffer isn't full and try to place something into it. To remedy this, you need to use the synchronized keyword. You first saw this in Skill 4 when you had the scrolling billboard. Here, you want to synchronize the whole method so that only one producer can run at a time. The wait() method mentioned previously must also be within a try-catch block because wait() can throw an InterruptedException. Inside the catch block you'll print out a stack trace and exit the application as you've been interrupted when you shouldn't have.

There's an additional tricky thing involved here, though. Changes to properties of visible Swing components *must* be done in the events thread. All you have to do is put the method calls to change the component(s) in the run() method of a Runnable object and pass it off to the EventQueue. The EventQueue class has two methods that will execute a Runnable object in the events thread for you: invokeAndWait() and invokeLater(). The first runs synchronously, where the calling routine won't continue until the Runnable returns. The second runs asynchronously, where the calling routine immediately continues. Since you want the screen to be updated immediately, you'll use invokeLater(). The basic framework follows. The invokeLater() version may throw an exception, though.

```java
Runnable runner = new Runnable() {
  public void run() {
    // Code to update Swing component properties
  }
};
try {
  EventQueue.invokeLater(runner);
} catch (Exception exception) {
  // Can throw an InterruptedException or InvocationTargetException
}
```

Putting all this together results in the updated add() method in Listing 21-3 (I'll explain the notifyAll() call shortly). The String parameter to add() was made final because it's accessed from within the inner Runnable object that is created.

Listing 21-3. The Final add() Version of the DisplayBuffer.java Source
```java
public synchronized void add(final String s) {
  while (position == LENGTH) {
    try {
      wait();
    } catch (InterruptedException exception) {
      exception.printStackTrace();
      System.exit(-1);
    }
  }
  Runnable runner = new Runnable() {
    public void run() {
      Container pane = getContentPane();
      JLabel label = (JLabel)pane.getComponent(position++);
      label.setText(s);
    }
  };
  try {
    EventQueue.invokeAndWait(runner);
  } catch (Exception exception) {
    exception.printStackTrace();
    System.exit(-1);
  }
  notifyAll();
}
```

The notifyAll() call at the end is not what notifies the wait() method at the beginning. You need some way to notify the consumer when there is something in a previously empty buffer. It's the consumer (via the remove() method) that notifies the producer when there is free space in a previously full buffer. The remove() method will have corresponding wait() and notifyAll() methods. When remove() frees some space in the buffer, it calls notifyAll(), which signals the wait() method of add(). Then, the notifyAll() method of add() signals the wait() method of remove().

Removing from the Buffer

The Consumer class defined your remove() method signature for you and had it return the element removed. The primary difference within remove() is the while condition: When the position is zero, there is nothing to remove so you have to wait. To remove an element from the screen, just change the text for the label at the right position, saving the original value first, and then notify the producer that there is some free space. Listing 21-4 shows the final remove() method.

Listing 21-4. The Final remove() Version of the DisplayBuffer.java Source

```
String oldLabel;
 . . .
public synchronized String remove() {
  while (position == 0) {
    try {
      wait();
    } catch (InterruptedException exception) {
      exception.printStackTrace();
      System.exit(-1);
    }
  }
  Runnable runner = new Runnable() {
    public void run() {
      Container pane = getContentPane();
      JLabel label = (JLabel)pane.getComponent(-position);
      oldLabel = label.getText();
      label.setText(null);
    }
  };
```

```
    try {
      EventQueue.invokeAndWait(runner);
    } catch (Exception exception) {
      exception.printStackTrace();
      System.exit(-1);
    }
    notifyAll();
    return (oldLabel);
  }
```

 **NOTE** *Having both the* add() *and* remove() *methods synchronized means only one will run at a time. The way the* wait()*-*notifyAll() *locks work is when* add() *or* remove() *goes into a wait state, it gives up its* synchronized *lock. Then, when it's notified, it won't continue until it gets the lock again (the notifier relinquishes the* synchronized *lock first).*

The complete `DisplayBuffer` source follows in Listing 21-5.

Listing 21-5. The Complete DisplayBuffer.java Source

```java
package skill21;

import java.awt.*;
import java.awt.event.*;
import javax.swing.*;

public class DisplayBuffer extends JFrame {
  JPanel contentPane;
  GridLayout gridLayout1 = new GridLayout();
  String oldLabel;
  private final static int LENGTH = 5;
  private int position = 0;
  JLabel jLabel1 = new JLabel();
  JLabel jLabel2 = new JLabel();
  JLabel jLabel3 = new JLabel();
  JLabel jLabel4 = new JLabel();
  JLabel jLabel5 = new JLabel();

  //Construct the frame
  public DisplayBuffer() {
    enableEvents(AWTEvent.WINDOW_EVENT_MASK);
```

```java
    try {
      jbInit();
    }
    catch(Exception e) {
      e.printStackTrace();
    }
  }
  //Component initialization
  private void jbInit() throws Exception  {
    contentPane = (JPanel) this.getContentPane();
    gridLayout1.setRows(5);
    gridLayout1.setColumns(1);
    contentPane.setLayout(gridLayout1);
    this.setSize(new Dimension(400, 300));
    this.setTitle("Frame Title");
    jLabel1.setHorizontalAlignment(SwingConstants.CENTER);
    jLabel2.setHorizontalAlignment(SwingConstants.CENTER);
    jLabel3.setHorizontalAlignment(SwingConstants.CENTER);
    jLabel4.setHorizontalAlignment(SwingConstants.CENTER);
    jLabel5.setHorizontalAlignment(SwingConstants.CENTER);
    contentPane.add(jLabel1, null);
    contentPane.add(jLabel2, null);
    contentPane.add(jLabel3, null);
    contentPane.add(jLabel4, null);
    contentPane.add(jLabel5, null);
  }
  //Overridden so we can exit when window is closed
  protected void processWindowEvent(WindowEvent e) {
    super.processWindowEvent(e);
    if (e.getID() == WindowEvent.WINDOW_CLOSING) {
      System.exit(0);
    }
  }

  public synchronized void add(final String s) {
    while (position == LENGTH) {
      try {
        wait();
      } catch (InterruptedException exception) {
        exception.printStackTrace();
        System.exit(-1);
      }
    }
```

```
        Runnable runner = new Runnable() {
          public void run() {
            Container pane = getContentPane();
            JLabel label = (JLabel)pane.getComponent(position++);
            label.setText(s);
          }
        };
        try {
          EventQueue.invokeAndWait(runner);
        } catch (Exception exception) {
          exception.printStackTrace();
          System.exit(-1);
        }
        notifyAll();
      }

      public synchronized String remove() {
        while (position == 0) {
          try {
            wait();
          } catch (InterruptedException exception) {
            exception.printStackTrace();
            System.exit(-1);
          }
        }
        Runnable runner = new Runnable() {
          public void run() {
            Container pane = getContentPane();
            JLabel label = (JLabel)pane.getComponent(--position);
            oldLabel = label.getText();
            label.setText(null);
          }
        };
        try {
          EventQueue.invokeAndWait(runner);
        } catch (Exception exception) {
          exception.printStackTrace();
          System.exit(-1);
        }
        notifyAll();
        return (oldLabel);
      }
    }
```

Putting It All Together

The last thing you need to do is create the producer and consumer and then send them off on their merry way. You do this in the application's constructor in Application1.java. First, you need to set up how many strings will be generated by the producer and consumed by the consumer. You can declare a final static int to store the number of runs (the final static keywords here tell the compiler that this is a constant literal [like C's #define]) at the class level. The last thing you'll do in the constructor is create the new objects:

```
private final static int TEST_RUNS = 20;
 . . .
Producer p = new Producer(frame, TEST_RUNS);
Consumer c = new Consumer(frame, TEST_RUNS);
```

In Skill 4, you learned that the way to start a Runnable object is with the start() method of the thread. You do not call the run() method directly. Calling start() on a Runnable object or a Thread causes the thread to enter the runnable state. Then, the system's scheduler will look through all the runnable threads and pick one to run.

```
p.start();
c.start();
```

NOTE *The scheduler determines the execution order of multiple runnable threads. With one CPU, it picks one thread at a time to run. With multiple CPUs, it can pick many threads, one per CPU. Which thread is picked and for how long it runs is dependent on the scheduler. Scheduling is specific to the JVM vendor and platform.*

Putting all this together gives you Application1.java, as shown in Listing 21-6.

Listing 21-6. The Complete Application1.java Source
```
package skill21;

import javax.swing.UIManager;
import java.awt.*;
```

```
public class Application1 {
  boolean packFrame = false;
  private final static int TEST_RUNS = 20;

  //Construct the application
  public Application1() {
    DisplayBuffer frame = new DisplayBuffer();
    //Validate frames that have preset sizes
    //Pack frames that have useful preferred size info, e.g. from their layout
    if (packFrame) {
      frame.pack();
    }
    else {
      frame.validate();
    }
    //Center the window
    Dimension screenSize = Toolkit.getDefaultToolkit().getScreenSize();
    Dimension frameSize = frame.getSize();
    if (frameSize.height > screenSize.height) {
      frameSize.height = screenSize.height;
    }
    if (frameSize.width > screenSize.width) {
      frameSize.width = screenSize.width;
    }
    frame.setLocation((screenSize.width - frameSize.width) / 2,
                      (screenSize.height - frameSize.height) / 2);
    frame.setVisible(true);
    Producer p = new Producer(frame, TEST_RUNS);
    Consumer c = new Consumer(frame, TEST_RUNS);
    p.start();
    c.start();
  }
  //Main method
  public static void main(String[] args) {
    try {
      UIManager.setLookAndFeel(UIManager.getSystemLookAndFeelClassName());
    }
    catch(Exception e) {
      e.printStackTrace();
    }
    new Application1();
  }
}
```

At this point, you can save everything and run it. With the initial settings, the buffer should fill quickly before the consumer has time to pick at it much. You can also add more producers or consumers, or change the delay times, to see the effects. Figure 21-2 shows one possible screen display with the buffer partially full. Look in the Message window to see the `println()` output.

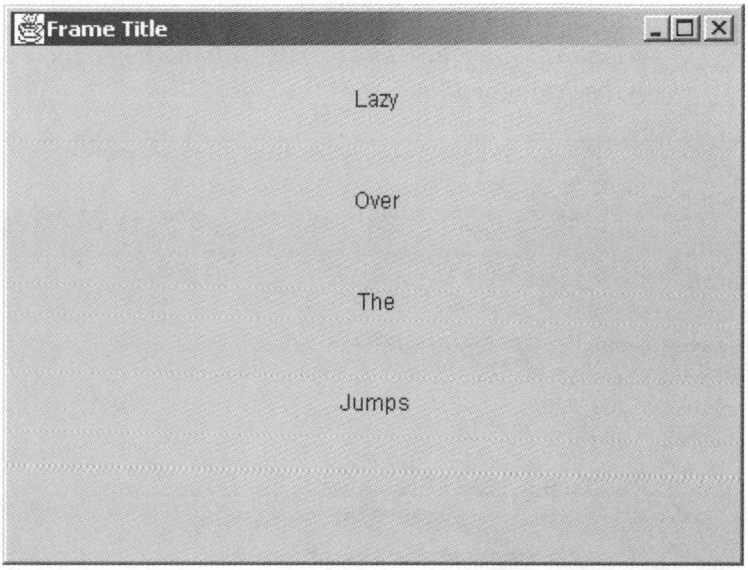

Figure 21-2. The DisplayBuffer program in the middle of executing

Debugging the Program

Now that you have an interesting, multithreaded program to play with, let's jump over to the debugger. A debugger helps you find problems in your source code. The first stage of debugging usually involves adding `System.out.println()` statements throughout your code, to check on the state of the system at certain places. Instead of having to change your source, you can use a debugger and ask it what the system state is.

To start the debugging process, do one of the following:

- Press Shift-F9.

- Select Run ➤ Debug Project.

- Click the Debug icon on the toolbar.

- Right-click Application1.java in the Navigation pane and select Debug.

This action turns the Message pane of the tool into a debugger (see Figure 21-3). When you execute the program in Debugger mode, it runs to completion with the extra options on the bottom.

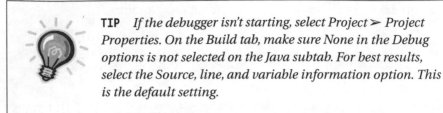

TIP   *If the debugger isn't starting, select Project ➢ Project Properties. On the Build tab, make sure None in the Debug options is not selected on the Java subtab. For best results, select the Source, line, and variable information option. This is the default setting.*

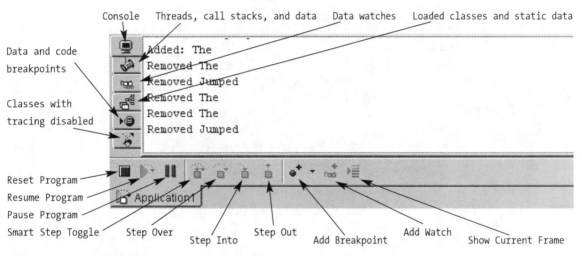

Figure 21-3. The Message pane in Debugger mode

You'll probably find yourself making the Message pane much larger while you debug, as there is a lot of information that can be displayed. For instance, the Thread and Stack pane (the second button from the top on the left side) displays the list of threads running along with what they're running, a *call stack*. The Data pane appears to its right, showing the data variables currently visible.

On the left side of the original Source pane (see Figure 21-4), you'll see a gray vertical bar. In this bar, blue dots indicate source lines and a green arrow indicates the currently executing line, while comment lines are blank. A red dot with a check mark indicates a *breakpoint,* a place where you've told the debugger to stop. To set a breakpoint, just click in the gray bar. The system won't stop you from trying to set a breakpoint on a comment line; it just won't stop anything at runtime.

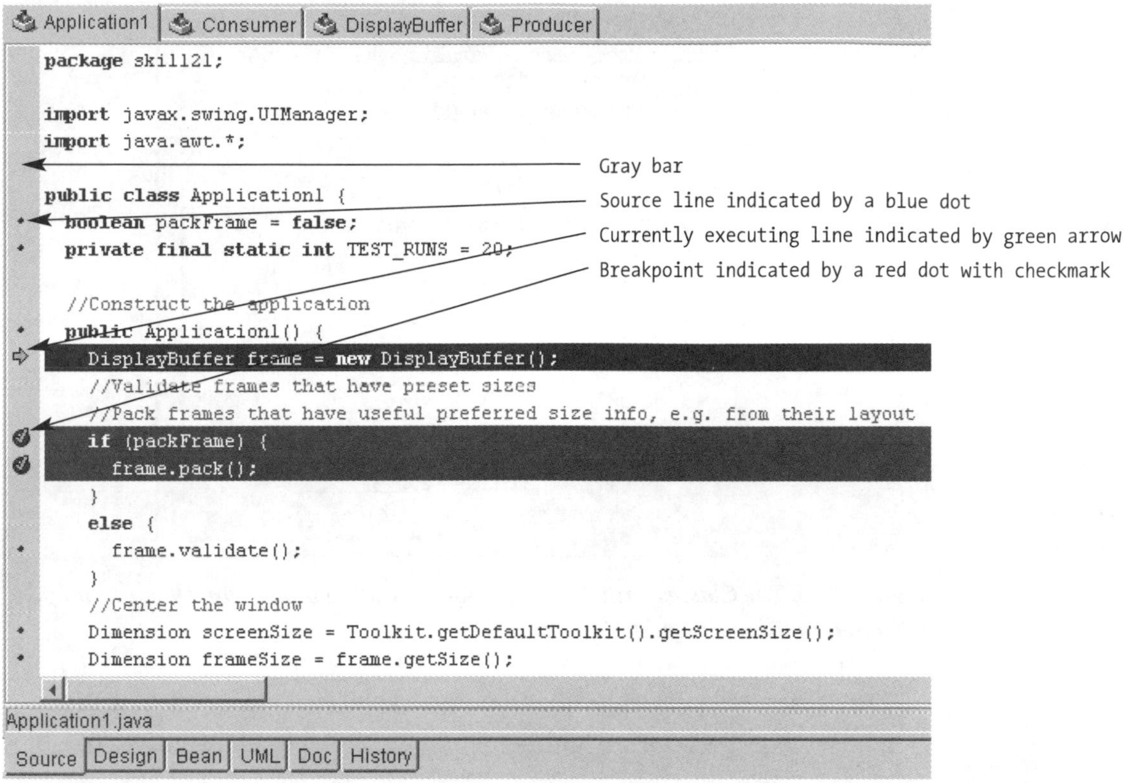

Figure 21-4 shows a screenshot of the Source pane with the following content:

Tabs: Application1 | Consumer | DisplayBuffer | Producer

```
package skill21;

import javax.swing.UIManager;
import java.awt.*;                                    ← Gray bar

public class Application1 {                           Source line indicated by a blue dot
  boolean packFrame = false;                          Currently executing line indicated by green arrow
  private final static int TEST_RUNS = 20;            Breakpoint indicated by a red dot with checkmark

  //Construct the application
  public Application1() {
    DisplayBuffer frame = new DisplayBuffer();
    //Validate frames that have preset sizes
    //Pack frames that have useful preferred size info, e.g. from their layout
    if (packFrame) {
      frame.pack();
    }
    else {
      frame.validate();
    }
    //Center the window
    Dimension screenSize = Toolkit.getDefaultToolkit().getScreenSize();
    Dimension frameSize = frame.getSize();
```

Application1.java

Source | Design | Bean | UML | Doc | History

Figure 21-4. The Source pane in Debugger mode

The four icons in the middle of the bottom of the dialog box shown in Figure 21-3 are the most interesting while debugging. I'll explain the first button, the Smart Step Toggle, shortly. The Step Over icon lets you avoid going through every single line within a method. Step Into allows you to single-step through the source—into every method where the source is available. The Step Out button lets you immediately return from a method, instead of continuing to single-step through the method's source. The Smart Step Toggle button is the most useful, and you usually want to leave it on. When this button is on, you can avoid stepping into some libraries, such as the system classes. You can turn off whole packages by selecting the last tab or choosing the Run ➤ View Classes with Tracing Disabled menu. This brings up the dialog box in Figure 21-5. By right-clicking a package, you can enable stepping into the library when Smart Step is on. By right-clicking in an open area, you can add more packages or classes.

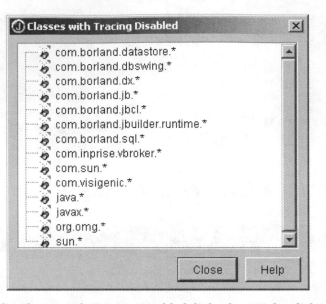

Figure 21-5. The Classes with Tracing Disabled dialog box. Right-click in an open area to add more classes and packages.

To pause a program while it's running, click the Pause icon. Clicking the Reset icon stops the program and allows you to rerun it from the beginning.

Stepping Through the Program

Let's work our way into the program a little and then examine a few pieces of it. In the Application1.java source, click the mouse in the gray bar so a red dot appears on the constructor line for the class. Then press Shift-F9 to start up the debugger. Click the Step Over button 11 times until the current line of code creates a producer (Producer p = new Producer(frame, TEST_RUNS);). Now you can look at the Thread and Stack pane, as shown in Figure 21-6.

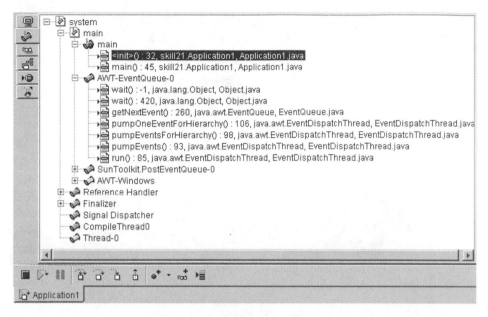

Figure 21-6. The Thread and Stack pane shortly after the program has started

There are four system threads under main listed in this pane for your program and five other threads not under main. You did not create any of these threads explicitly. The first entry is your main program thread; it has a little red dot under the spool to indicate it's the thread you're watching. The next three threads, AWT-EventQueue-0, SunToolkit.PostEventQueue-0, and AWT-Windows, were created when the DisplayBuffer frame was created. This shows that the event handling and window refreshing is done in separate threads. The Finalizer thread is responsible for garbage collection, freeing up memory when you no longer need it. The other four threads are also doing system-related tasks.

Under each thread is a set of call stacks. For instance, under main, the main() method called the <init>() method (the constructor). When you click one of the call stacks, in the Data pane to the right, you can see the visible variables to the stack. For instance, if you select the first JLabel in the frame, you can see that the text label is empty, meaning the current data buffer is empty. This is shown in Figure 21-7.

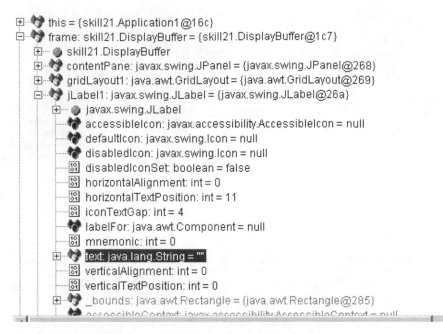

Figure 21-7. The initial Data pane with an empty text property for the first label in the data buffer

The next time you click the Step Into icon, you will be taken into the Producer constructor. If you scroll down a little and select the for loop line, you can press the F5 key to toggle on a breakpoint. Or, you can click the blue dot in the gray bar to do the same thing. The line will turn red. At this point, if you click the Resume Program icon, the program will continue and stop at the for loop.

Examining the Variables

If you click the Step Into icon again, you're in the loop, and the i variable is now defined. Then, if you look in the Data pane, you'll see i: int=0. Another way to examine the variable is with the Evaluate/Modify dialog box. Selecting Run ➤ Evaluate/Modify brings up the dialog box shown in Figure 21-8. Entering **i** in the Expression field and clicking Evaluate shows a 0 in the Result box.

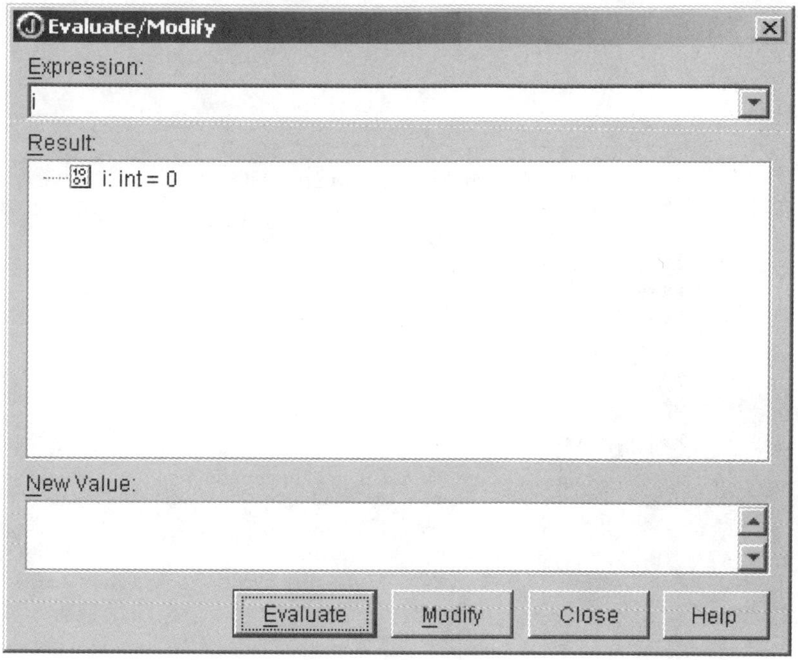

Figure 21-8. The Evaluate/Modify dialog box, where you can examine and change variable settings

You can also right-click over a variable to get the same Evaluate/Modify option. If what you select is an array, you'll see the array declaration and contents (see Figure 21-9). When you right-click over the variable, the name is automatically filled in for you.

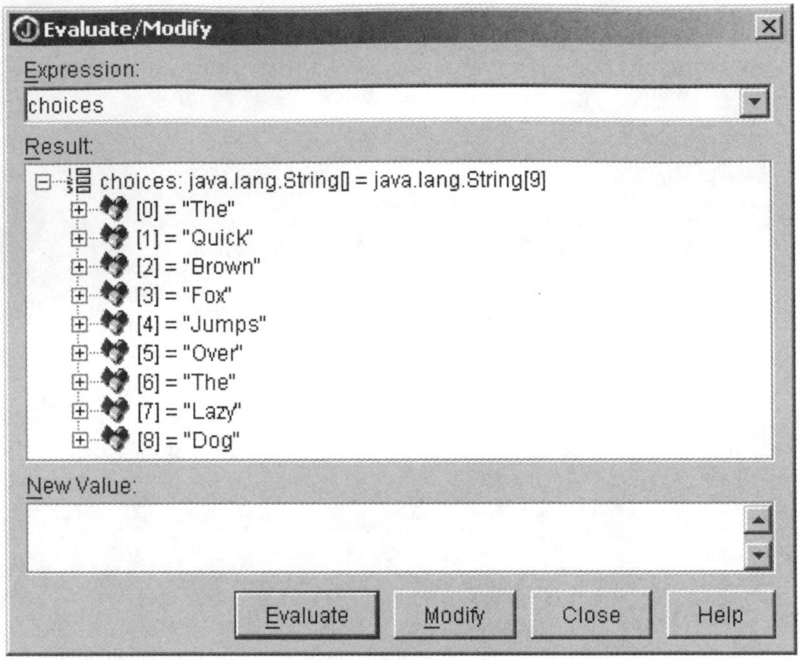

Figure 21-9. Inspecting an array variable

If your array size is large, you can reduce the range of entries shown by right-clicking over the first line in the Result box. Select Adjust Display Range and enter a new range.

If you want to modify the value, enter a new value at the bottom and click Modify. In the case of an array entry, you'll have to right-click over the entry and select Change Value to get the dialog box to enter a new setting. For instance, the dialog box in Figure 21-10 would appear if you tried to change an entry of the choices array. Notice that it tells you what data type you must enter. For strings, you must quote the value.

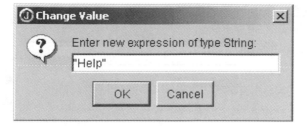

Figure 21-10. Modifying the value of String array while the program is running

Setting Breakpoints

Just using the Step Over and Step Into buttons can create rather long debugging sessions. There are various ways to improve upon this experience. Pressing F5 on a line of source is one way to set the breakpoints already discussed, as is selecting a blue dot in the gray bar to turn the little dot into a big red dot with a green check mark.

Other options of executing within the debugger you might come to like are Run ➢ Run to Cursor (F4) and Run ➢ Run to End of Method. The Run to Cursor option continues the program up to the line the cursor is currently on. You'll typically use the Run to End of Method option when you enter a method you think you want to step through or accidentally step into. If you select Run to End of Method, the program will run until the end of the current method.

The most powerful way to set breakpoints, though, is through the Run ➢ Add Breakpoint menu, which has five suboptions. The same five options are available from the third icon from the end on the bottom of the Message pane in Debugger mode (see Figure 21-3). The options are as follows:

- A line breakpoint (see Figure 21-11)

- An exception breakpoint (see Figure 21-12)

- A class breakpoint (see Figure 21-13)

- A method breakpoint (see Figure 21-14)

- A cross-process breakpoint (see Figure 21-15)

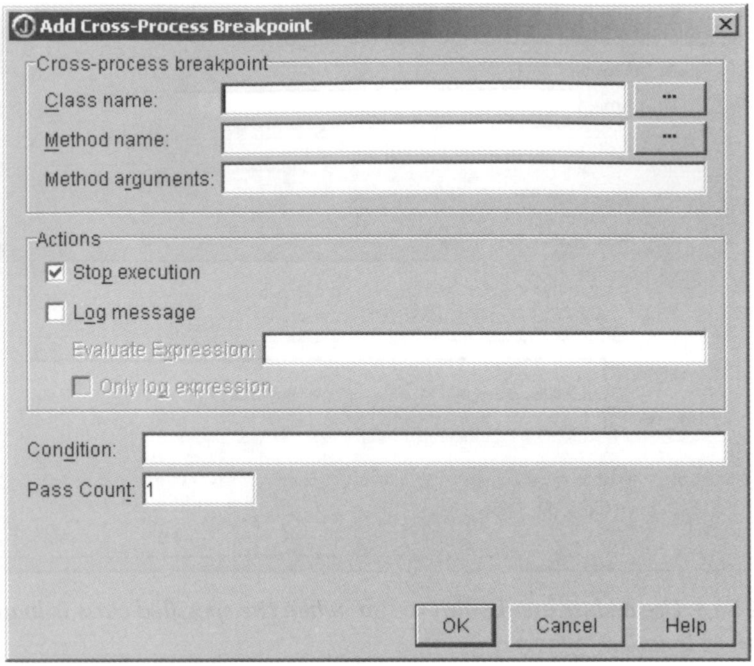

Figure 21-15. Set a process breakpoint by specifying the server-side class and method to break in. Specify arguments for overloaded methods.

When you set a breakpoint, your program doesn't have to stop. You can set up the program to log the breaks or you can set up a condition to break on, where you only stop if a variable is over 5,000 so you don't have to check for the first 5,000 times. If you know the program is failing around pass 5,020, this will leave you with just a few passes to check. Combining pass counts and conditions adds even more flexibility to setting breakpoints. If variable var loops from 0 to 49 and you know the program breaks the hundredth time through the loop when var > 10, you can enter **var > 10** in the Condition field and **100** in the Pass Count field. Then, the hundredth time var is greater than 10, the program stops.

Once you've set all those breakpoints, the last thing you'll do is find them, disable them, or delete them. Select Run ➤ View Breakpoints or right-click in the Data and code breakpoints pane in the Message area. This will bring up the window in Figure 21-16. The windows that appear when you select Run ➤ View Breakpoints or right-click in the Data and code breakpoints pane are slightly different.

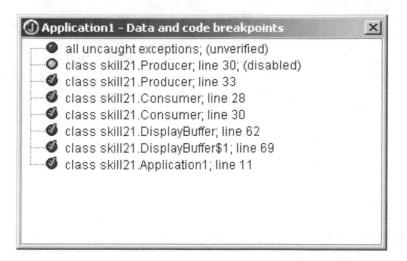

Figure 21-16. Find your breakpoints in the Data and code breakpoints window. Right-click over a breakpoint to modify the settings.

From the Data and code breakpoints window, right-clicking over a break-point brings up a menu full of choices. You can select Go to Breakpoint to locate the specific source line, Enable Breakpoint to toggle the state of the breakpoint, or Remove Breakpoint to completely eliminate the breakpoint from the list. The last option, Breakpoint Properties, will bring up one of the boxes in Figures 21-11 through 21-15, depending upon which was used to create the breakpoint. If you right-click over an area without a breakpoint under the mouse, you can add addi-tional breakpoints or deal with all breakpoints together, rather than separately.

Now you should run the program a few times, stepping all over the place, to get a good feel for the debugger. Instead of adding `System.out.println()` state-ments to your programs, you'll be able to use the debugger to help you find your problems much more easily, and in the end it will make you a better Java programmer.

ARE YOU EXPERIENCED?

Congratulations! You've had a very full tour around the JBuilder debugger, working your way through a multithreaded Java program. You saw not only how to step through the program, but also how to modify and evaluate different settings along the way.

Now you can

- Create threads for multithreaded programs

- Synchronize communications across threads

- Execute tasks in the event thread

- Use the JBuilder debugger

- Step through source

- Inspect data variables

- Modify data variables during program execution

- Set breakpoints

- Brag about your JBuilder proficiency

Now that you've learned many of the core skills necessary to become a productive Java developer with JBuilder, in the next chapter you'll take a quick tour through some of the remaining options available only in the Professional and Enterprise Editions.

Exploring JBuilder Professional and JBuilder Enterprise

- Versioning files

- Visualizing code in UML

- Refactoring

- Unit testing

- Working with the two-way EJB Designer

Beyond JBuilder Basics

Personally, I've been using JBuilder since version 1.0 of the product—actually longer if you include beta (and alpha) releases. Does anyone else remember the early code name Latté for the product? Like the Java platform, with every new release of the JBuilder product more and more capabilities get added into the tool. In this skill, you'll explore tool features that are both new and useful. Many of these features are limited to the Professional and Enterprise versions of the tool, though.

You'll look at five different features of JBuilder 6 in this, the final chapter. First, you'll explore two of the tabs on the bottom of the UI Designer you haven't looked at yet: History and UML. Then you'll delve into JBuilder's refactoring capabilities to improve code design and the integrated JUnit support for testing. Finally, you'll close the chapter with a look at the Enterprise JavaBeans Designer.

Versioning Files

All versions of JBuilder 6 come with built-in support for managing changes to a source file. At the single file level, you can see revisions between versions of a file, see differences between multiple versions of a file, and undo changes made to a file. This isn't a complete version control system—for that you need JBuilder Enterprise. With the regular History function, there is no support for multifile change management or reverting of changes.

 TIP *Users who want to use the built-in version control system of JBuilder Enterprise can select Team ➤ Select Project VCS, and then select ClearCase, CVS, or Visual SourceSafe. This will allow you to revert changes across multiple files.*

To demonstrate the versioning support, create an application where the project is named **Skill22**. On the second screen of the Application Wizard, check everything so you don't have to manually create much original code. This will give you a frame with a toolbar, menu, and status bar with a generated About dialog box. Once everything is generated, select File ➤ Save All. You now have the baseline set of source files for your project.

To create a change, go into the UI Designer and drop a JToggleButton into the center of the screen. Then, select File ➤ Save Frame1.java (or press Ctrl-S). You've now created revision 1 of the file. Change the text property of the component and save again to create revision 2.

At this point, if you select the History tab you'll see the screen in Figure 22-1.

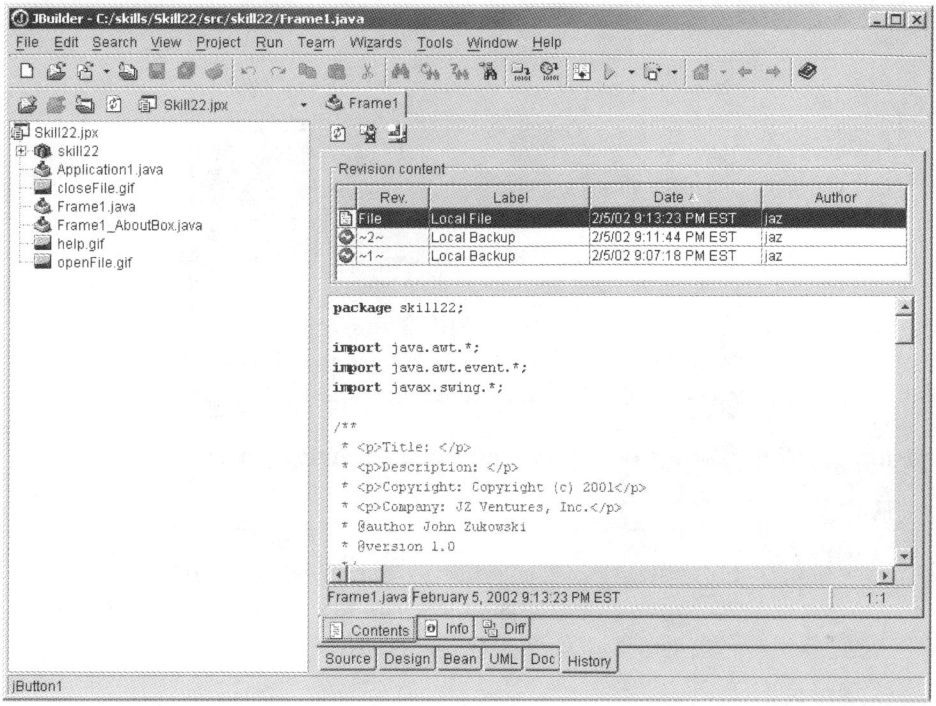

Figure 22-1. The first screen for the Project Wizard. Here, you enter in the default project path.

At the very top of the UI Designer is a tab for the file you're viewing, Frame1 here. Immediately below the tab are three icons that let you refresh the revision information, revert to a previous file version, or synchronize the scrolling.

Immediately below the icons is the Revision content section. This is a numbered list of the revisions of a file. You'll find the most recent version of the file at the top of the list. For instance, clicking revision ~1~ will bring up the source file in the viewer for the older version of the file. (It doesn't change the current version of the file.) If you look carefully, you'll notice that there is no JToggleButton mentioned in the source.

If you'd like to return the current source file to an old version of the file, click the Revert icon above the Revision content section. It's the middle one. You'll then be prompted with a dialog box like the one shown in Figure 22-2 to make sure you want to revert back.

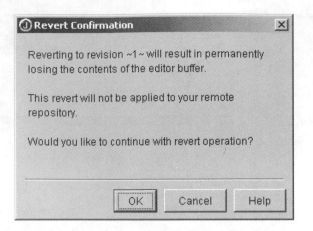

Figure 22-2. The revert to old version confirmation dialog box

> **NOTE**   *When the Synchronized Scrolling button is selected, this option tries to keep the cursor at or near the same source line when you change versions of the file.*

If all you have is the Personal Edition of JBuilder, this is the only feature from the History tab that you can use. Professional users get to select Diff, and Enterprise users get to select Diff and Info.

When you select the Diff button, you're provided with a From and To area to select which file versions you want to compare. The To area also lets you select the current Buffer to compare against.

Once you've selected two different versions, the screen area will highlight the changes. New or changed lines have a plus sign (+) next to them and are in yellow. Old lines that have been deleted (or changed) have a minus sign (-) next to them and are in red. Changes are at the line level so, as Figure 22-3 shows, just changing the text property of the toggle button results in one line deleted and one line added, even though only the value between the quotes changed.

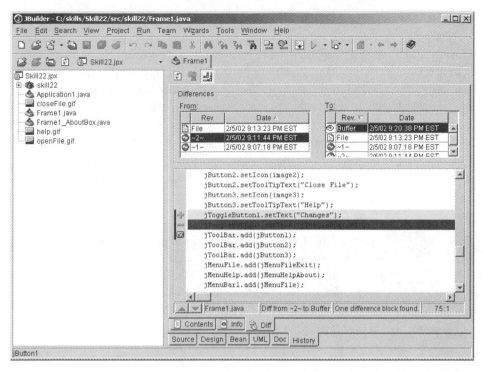

Figure 22-3. Comparing file versions under the Diff subtab

If the destination or To side of the Diff window is the Buffer, below the +/-indicators will be an Undo change button. Selecting this button brings up a pop-up menu (see Figure 22-4) that lets you undo the change. If the Buffer is not selected on the To side, the Undo change button is not available.

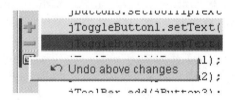

Figure 22-4. Selecting the Undo change button

If you're using the Enterprise version of JBuilder and you enabled a source code management system, selecting the Info tab would provide access to the comments and labels within the revision files.

UML Code Visualization

The Unified Modeling Language (UML) is a standard way of modeling object-oriented systems. Created when Grady Booch, James Rumbaugh, and Ivar Jacobson combined their different modeling processes together, the standard is now kept by Object Management Group (`http://www.omg.org`).

While using the 30-day trial of JBuilder Enterprise, you can try out the UML tab at the bottom of the Source pane/UI Designer window. The UML support in JBuilder Enterprise is not a full-blown diagramming tool. Instead, what you get is a visualization tool that lets you visually examine your class design.

 **NOTE** *If you aren't familiar with UML, consider getting* The Unified Modeling Language User Guide *by Grady Booch, James Rumbaugh, and Ivar Jacobson (Addison-Wesley, 1999) or* UML Distilled *by Martin Fowler and Kendall Scott (Addison-Wesley, 1999). Cetus also maintains a collection of useful Web links at* `http://www.cetus-links.org/oo_uml.html`. *From these resources, you should be able to get a good understanding of at least the diagramming syntax.*

UML is full of many different diagrams, of which JBuilder 6 supports two: the package dependency diagram and the combined class diagram. JBuilder's package dependency diagram shows the packages a given package is dependent on. It is unidirectional. The combined class diagram shows class associations and dependencies.

Before doing anything with UML in JBuilder, you must compile your class files. If you don't, you'll be warned (see Figure 22-5) when you try to view the UML.

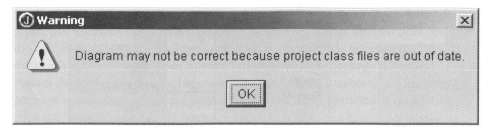

Figure 22-5. The warning you receive when you try to view UML when classes aren't compiled

A package dependency diagram is shown by double-clicking the name of the package (skill22) in the Navigation pane of the AppBrowser (top left). At first, this will just display the automatically generated javadoc documentation for the classes in the package, as shown in Figure 22-6. When you click the UML tab for the package, you get the package dependency diagram, as shown in Figure 22-7.

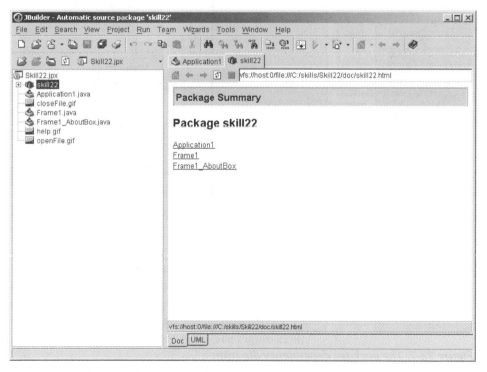

Figure 22-6. The javadoc window for a package

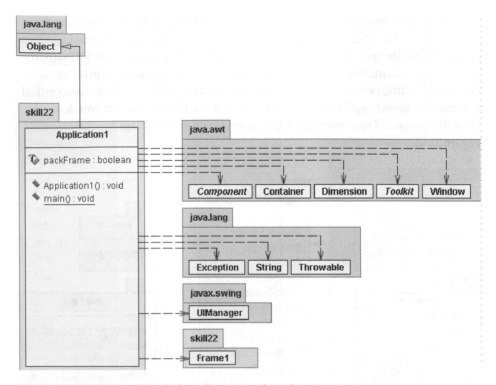

Figure 22-9. The combined class diagram of Application1

In a combined class diagram, dependencies to other packages are still shown, but so are class hierarchy relationships, interface implementations, and the fields, methods, and properties of the central class. For instance, in Figure 22-9, you can see that Application1 is a subclass of the Object class. It has one field, packFrame, of type boolean, and methods, one being a constructor. The underline under the main() method means it is static. The icons next to the fields and methods are the visibility modifiers. These are the same icons shown in the Structure pane when you are viewing/editing source.

In Figure 22-9, there are no properties of the Application1 class. Had they been present, they would have been shown below the list of methods. Figure 22-10 shows the class diagram for the java.awt.Dimension class. Notice that it has height and width properties. Also here, Dimension subclasses the java.awt.geom.Dimension2D class and implements the java.io.Serializable interface.

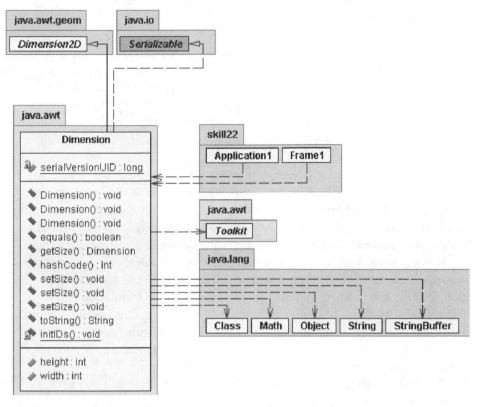

Figure 22-10. The combined class diagram of Dimension

TIP *Right-clicking your mouse over any of the UML diagrams allows you to save them as a PNG-formatted image.*

While you can't move the different pieces of the UML diagrams around, there are some things you do have control over. You can bring up the Project Properties window to select packages and package trees you want excluded from all UML diagrams within that project. Also, from the Tools ➤ IDE Options window you can change fonts, colors, and groupings.

Refactoring

Martin Fowler has a 400+-page book dedicated to refactoring appropriately titled *Refactoring* (Addison-Wesley, 1999). He defines *refactoring* as "the process of changing a software system in such a way that it does not alter the external behavior of the code yet improves its internal structure." The book goes on to describe 72 common ways of refactoring your code, such as replacing constructor calls with the use of factory methods and replacing magic numbers with symbolic constants.

Many of these refactoring tasks are rote skills. Once you've done them a hundred times, you can do them in your sleep—in a way, this is similar to creating JavaBean component properties. Others aren't necessarily rote, but they're more on the tedious side. It's two of this latter type of refactoring tasks that JBuilder Professional and Enterprise provide support for: renaming and moving.

Renaming refactoring is the task of renaming a package, class, method, field, property, or local variable. It sounds easy, but the task isn't just search and replace. You have to worry about scope for variables, the destination name already existing as the new name propagates to subclasses, and even about moving subpackages and correcting all their usage when moving packages.

Moving refactoring only works with classes and interfaces. Its whole purpose is to change the package that a class or interface belongs to.

The only restriction to both forms of refactoring is you must stay within a single project.

To demonstrate refactoring, return to the Source pane for the `Frame1` class. If you wanted to rename the class, what would you have to do? There are actually only four requirements here:

- The declaration line needs to change (`class Frame1`).

- All constructors need to change.

- The filename needs to change.

- All calls to the constructor need to change.

Instead of manually performing the task, let JBuilder do it for you. In the Source pane, right-click the `Frame1` class name. This brings up the menu shown in Figure 22-11.

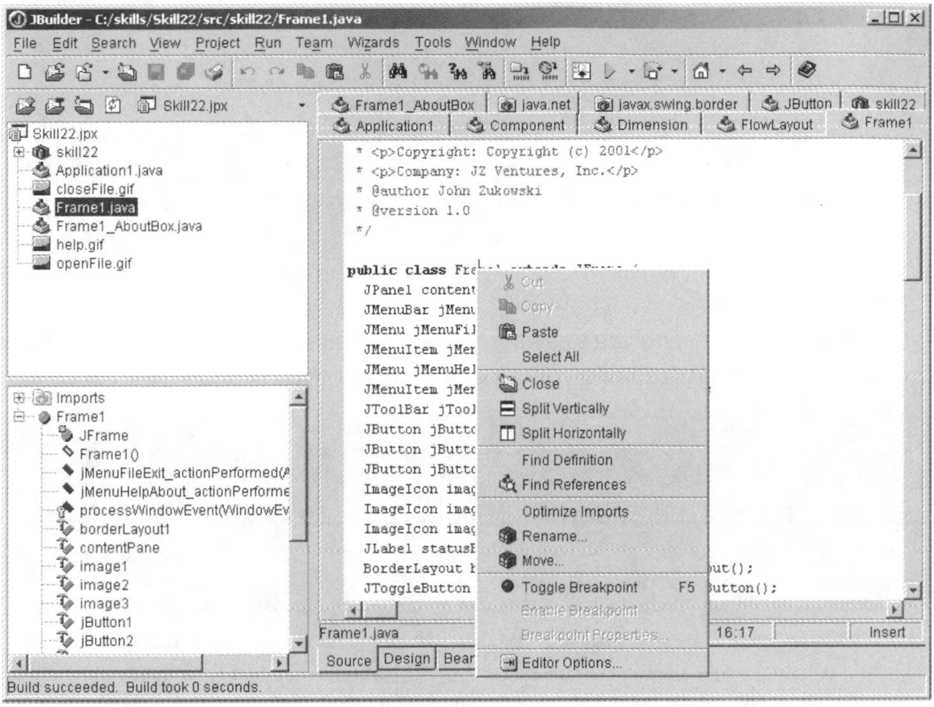

Figure 22-11. Context menu for the Frame1 class

Notice here among all the other choices are Rename and Move options. These are the refactoring triggers. Selecting Rename here allows you to rename the class to **MyFrame**, as shown in Figure 22-12.

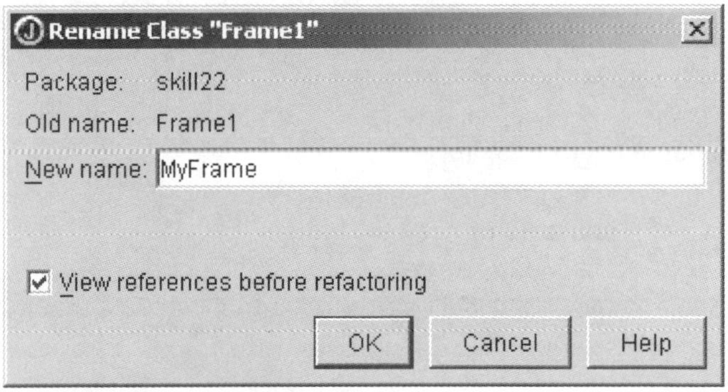

Figure 22-12. Rename Class dialog box

Clicking the OK button triggers the start of the renaming process. When the View references before refactoring option is checked, you'll see what the changes will be before the changes actually happen. These changes are shown in the Message View of the AppBrowser, as displayed in Figure 22-13.

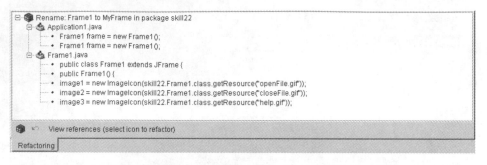

Figure 22-13. A log of the class rename changes that will be done

Oops, the list of changes to be done was incomplete. Because the program displays images on the JToolBar, it uses a reference to the class name to load the images. While a compilation-time error would have indicated that you missed the changes, using the refactoring tool automates the process so the changes won't be missed.

To do the actual refactoring, click the icon in the bottom-left corner. The message next to the icon will change to "Refactoring completed" when the refactoring task is done. Looking in the Navigation pane (see Figure 22-14) and within the source reveals that the change was a success. You can also compile and run the program to make sure.

Figure 22-14. The Navigation pane after the class rename refactoring

Refactoring doesn't have to be started from the editor. In fact, with the Enterprise version of JBuilder, you can start up refactoring from the UML diagrams. To demonstrate, open up the UML diagram for the about box class. Pick a variable and right-click over it. This will bring up the menu shown in Figure 22-15.

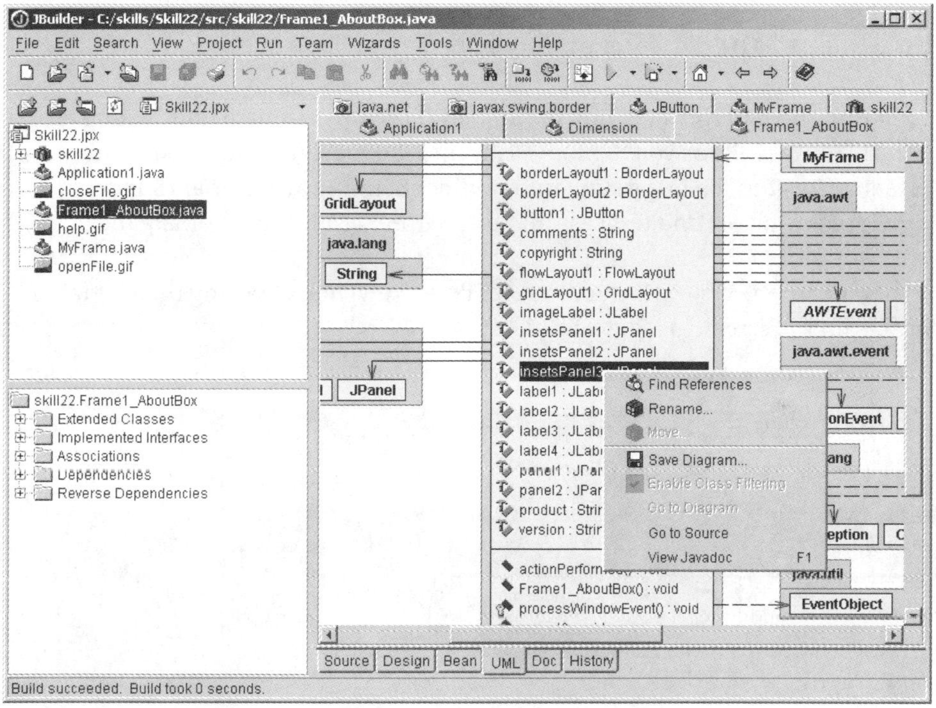

Figure 22-15. Refactoring code from the UML diagram

Selecting Rename from here allows you to rename a field.

As previously mentioned, the refactoring tool makes sure you don't use a name already in use. If you do, you'll get a message in the Message View, as shown in Figure 22-16.

Figure 22-16. Error message from trying to rename a field to one already in use

> **NOTE** *When you do refactoring tasks, files to be refactored do not need to be open. JBuilder checks all files in the current project to see if any of them need to be changed.*

Unit Testing

Built into the Enterprise Edition of JBuilder is the open-source unit-testing tool JUnit. This tool allows you to more easily include repeatable test cases with your projects. Besides the integration into JBuilder 6, the key thing that JBuilder provides is a set of JUnit test case and test fixture wizards to automate the creation process.

Going to the Object Gallery (select File ➤ New) and choosing the Test tab brings up the screen in Figure 22-17.

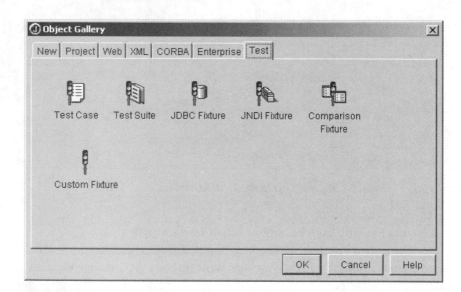

Figure 22-17. The Test Case Wizard Gallery

For additional information on JUnit, visit http://www.junit.org. For a tutorial on using JUnit with JBuilder 6, see Chapter 14 of the *Building Applications* book that comes with the tool.

Two-Way EJB Designer

Enterprise JavaBeans (EJB) technology is foreign to new Java developers. It provides the basis for developing and deploying transactional applications over a distributed architecture. Essentially what this means is that pieces of the application run all over the network. This is unlike the way regular JavaBeans technology works, where the beans are meant to work within the runtime of the executing program, whether that be an applet, an application, a servlet, or otherwise.

The way JBuilder works with JavaBeans components, where you can work in either the UI Designer or the text editor and swap back and forth without losing changes, now holds true for the Enterprise JavaBeans world also, though the back and forth works with the EJB Designer instead of BeansExpress.

To start up the EJB Designer, you need to create an EJB 2.0 module. You'll pick the appropriate wizard from the Object Gallery (see Figure 22-18) to do this.

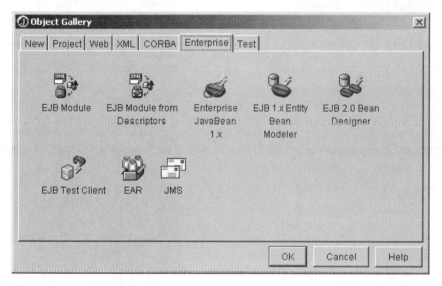

Figure 22-18. The EJB Wizard Gallery

First, select the EJB Module Wizard. Create an EJB 2.0–compliant module and click OK. At this point, you are in the EJB Designer, as shown in Figure 22-19.

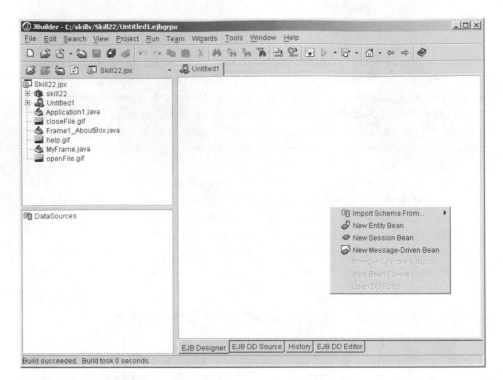

Figure 22-19. The two-way EJB Designer

At this point, you basically need to understand EJB to create and connect the necessary components. Similar to working with JavaBean components, you can create and connect the EJB components by filling in property sheets. For instance, Figure 22-20 shows the creation of a stateless session bean.

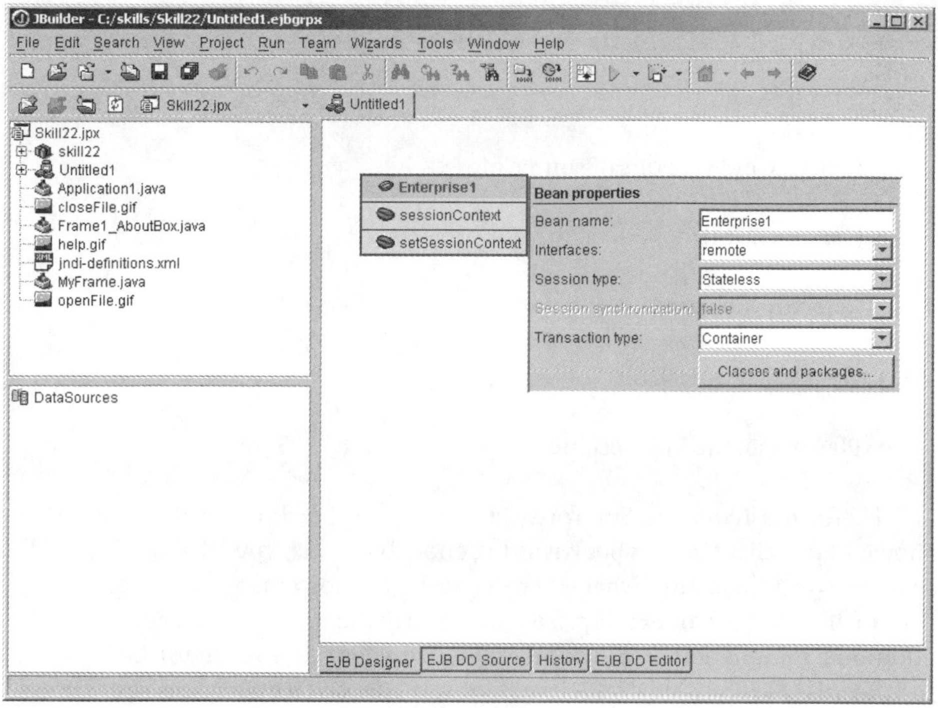

Figure 22-20. Creating a stateless session bean

After you've configured the bean with the wizards and property sheets, you can right-click the bean, select the View Bean Source option shown in Figure 22-21, and edit the source. You can then swap back to the EJB Designer and your source changes are preserved.

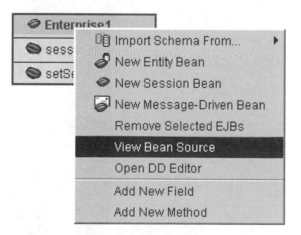

Figure 22-21. Going from the EJB Designer to the text editor

ARE YOU EXPERIENCED?

Now you can

- Revert to old versions of source files

- Generate UML diagrams for your projects

- Refactor your projects

- Get started with JUnit

- Play within the EJB Designer

There's much more to Enterprise JavaBeans (EJB) technology than shown in this chapter. This book isn't big enough to teach you all about EJB. Instead, you got a taste of what you can use the tool for, essentially to see if it's worth paying for that Enterprise Edition once the trial runs out. For additional information on EJB components, consider getting *Enterprise JavaBeans* (O'Reilly, 2001) by Richard Monson-Haefel. The book has free PDF workbooks for WebLogic and WebSphere available as supplemental material from http://www.titan-books.net/download.html.

Glossary

Term	Meaning
A	
abstract	Retaining the essential features of some thing, process, or structure. The opposite of *concrete. See also* **concrete.**
abstract class	A partial class definition that requires additional definition for completion. Abstract classes cannot be instantiated.
abstract method	A method that is declared but not implemented. Abstract methods are used to ensure that subclasses implement the method.
Abstract Window Toolkit (AWT)	The collection of Java classes that allows you to implement platform-independent (hence *abstract*) GUIs. *See also* **Swing.**
accessor methods	A set of methods to get and set a property. You make the accessor methods public and keep the property variable private.
adapter class	A class, possibly generated by JBuilder, that implements an event listener.
anonymous class	A special type of inner class with no name.
Apache	A consortium of open-source developers that manages the Tomcat project. *See also* **Tomcat**.
API	*See* **Application Programming Interface.**
AppBrowser	The primary JBuilder window for developing programs. It consists of three areas: the Navigation pane in the upper left, the Structure pane in the lower left, and the Content pane on the right.

Term	Meaning
applet	A Java program that runs within the context of a browser and is launched from, and appears to be embedded within, a Web document.
`appletviewer`	A Software Development Kit (SDK) utility that displays only Java applets within HTML documents, as opposed to a Web browser, which shows applets embedded within Web documents.
Application Programming Interface (API)	A set of methods, classes, or libraries provided by a language or operating system to help application developers write applications without needing to reinvent low-level functions. All of the standard Java packages combined form the Java Core API. An API can also be an interface to an application that allows other programs to manipulate the application from within the other programs.
application server	A Web server with additional intelligence to handle large-scale, middleware-related tasks, such as user profiling, session tracking, server failover, and more.
Archive Builder	Mechanism in JBuilder to deploy programs.
arguments	The parameters passed into a method.
array	A group of variables of the same type that can be referenced by a common name and an index value. An array is an object with `length` as its public data member holding the size of the array. It can be initialized by a list of comma-separated expressions surrounded by curly braces.
atomic	Indivisible or uninterruptible. In the context of multithreading, an operation (statement, code block, or even an entire method) that cannot be interrupted. Code that accesses composite data structures shared with other threads usually must protect its critical code sections by making them atomic.
AWT	*See* **Abstract Window Toolkit.**

Term	Meaning
B	
base class	The superclass from which other classes can inherit state and behavior.
baseline	The imaginary line text is drawn on.
BDK	*See* **Beans Development Kit.**
bean	A reusable software component created with a specific naming convention for methods to define properties and events. It can be manipulated visually in a builder tool.
`BeanInfo`	A bean support class that defines information about the bean with the same bean name.
Beans Development Kit (BDK)	A Sun tool that helps Java developers create reusable components (beans) through the inclusion of introductory documentation, a tutorial, sample beans, and a test container.
`boolean`	A variable that can assume only two values: true and false. Booleans can be used to represent objects that have a binary state, such as alive/dead, connected/disconnected, same/different, open/closed, and so on.
break statement	One of the flow-breaking statements. Without a label, control will be transferred to the statement just after the innermost enclosing looping or `switch` statement. With a label, control will be transferred to the statement after the enclosing statement or block of statements carrying the same label.
breakpoint	A place where you've told the debugger to stop.
buffer	An amount of storage set aside to temporarily hold and/or accumulate some information, such as write and read (disk) buffers and frame buffers.
byte code verifier	Part of Java's security precautions; the byte code verifier checks that the byte codes can be executed safely by the Java Virtual Machine (JVM).

Term	Meaning
DataExpress	JBuilder Professional and Enterprise Edition JDBC-aware component library.
debugger	A utility that can monitor and suspend execution of a program so that the state of the running program can be examined.
default clause	An optional part of a `switch` statement. It consists of the `default` keyword followed by a colon (:) and one or more statements. Its statements are executed when none of the other case clauses is satisfied. *See also* `switch` **statement.**
default constructor	A constructor that is automatically available to a class that does not define its own constructor. It has no parameters.
deprecated methods	Methods that were supported in previous versions of the Software Development Kit (SDK) but are not preferred ones in the current release. Future releases may drop the methods altogether.
design pattern	A reusable, standard approach to design problems. This approach is different from algorithms in that design patterns address higher-level issues and usually describe solutions in structural/relationship terms.
destructor	A method that is called to delete an object from memory. This method is executed when an object goes out of scope. Java does not support destructors directly. *See also* **finalizer.**
DNS	*See* **Domain Name System.**
do statement	One of the looping statements. The loop body is executed once, and then the conditional expression is evaluated. If it evaluates to true, the loop body is re-executed and the conditional expression is retested. It will be repeated until the conditional expression evaluates to false.
documentation comment	A comment block that will be used by the `javadoc` tool to create documentation.

Term	Meaning
Domain Name System (DNS)	A distributed Internet database that can resolve textual Internet addresses to their real numeric forms. The DNS is organized as a hierarchy with each node responsible for a subset of the Internet host address namespace (hence the distributed database).
double buffering	In general, the use of two buffers to allow one buffer to be constructed in the background while the other is being displayed. Double buffering is used in animation to display one animation frame while the next is being drawn off-screen. Double buffering is also used in the context of I/O logic to decouple an algorithm's performance from the performance limits of an I/O device (called being *I/O bound*).

E

EJB	*See* **Enterprise JavaBeans.**
else clause	An optional clause for an `if` statement. If the conditional expression on an `if` statement is evaluated to false, the statement or block of statements of the `else` clause will be executed.
encapsulation	Embedding both data and code into a single entity.
Enterprise JavaBeans (EJB)	Components for distributed applications that handle transactions, security, and persistence, leaving only the business logic for the developer to focus on. Not JavaBean components.
event	A system-generated object for when something interesting happens. Java components serve as event sources for events such as key presses, mouse clicks, or changes to bean properties.
event-driven programming	Programming that allows the user to control the sequencing of operations that the application executes via a graphical user interface (GUI).
exception	An abnormal condition that disrupts normal program flow.

Term	Meaning
expression	A combination of terms that evaluates to a single data value.
extend	*See* **subclass.**
Extensible Markup Language (XML)	A standard way of representing data in a vendor-neutral format by separating the data's content from its presentation.

F

finalizer	A method that is called immediately before a class is garbage-collected.
flow-breaking statement	A statement for breaking the program's flow. These include the break, continue, and return statements.
flow-control statement	A statement for flow control. These include conditional, looping, and flow-breaking statements.
flushing	Final writing of any output data left in a write buffer. When files and streams are closed, their data buffers are flushed automatically (this is one of the reasons to close files and streams).
FontMetrics	A class that indicates how much space a string takes.
for statement	One of the looping statements. The initialization part is executed, followed by the evaluation of the conditional expression. If the expression evaluates to true, the loop body is executed, followed by the execution of the update expression. This cycle is repeated until the conditional expression evaluates to false.
frame	In the context of graphical user interfaces (GUIs), the graphical outline of a window.

G

garbage collection	A feature of automatic memory management that discards unused blocks of memory, freeing the memory for new storage.
GIF	*See* **Graphics Interchange Format.**

Term	Meaning
graphical user interface (GUI)	The mouse-driven iconic interface to modern computer operating systems. Also called *WIMP* for Windows, Icons, Menus, and Pointer interface.
Graphics Interchange Format (GIF)	A standard format for storing compressed images.
GUI	*See* **graphical user interface.**
H	
Hotspot	An optimized Just-in-Time (JIT) compiler that analyzes program execution to optimize the frequently executed areas, or *hot spots*.
HTML	*See* **Hypertext Markup Language.**
HTTP	*See* **Hypertext Transfer Protocol.**
Hypertext Markup Language (HTML)	The language in which Web documents are written. Java applets appear embedded in HTML documents.
Hypertext Transfer Protocol (HTTP)	The application protocol used by the World Wide Web for requesting, transmitting, and receiving Web documents.
I	
I18n	Shorthand for *internationalization*. (Hint: Count the characters in the word.)
IDE	*See* **Integrated Development Environment.**
identifier	A name you give to a class, variable, or method. Identifiers have restrictions on their leading character.
if statement	One of the two types of conditional statements. It consists of the if keyword followed by a conditional expression enclosed within a pair of parentheses and a statement (or block of statements) to be executed when the conditional expression evaluates to true. It may be followed by an optional else clause, consisting of the else keyword and a statement (or group of statements) to be executed when the conditional expression evaluates to false.

Term	Meaning
immutable	Not changeable. Java `String` objects are immutable.
inheritance	The ability to write a class that inherits the member variables and member methods of another class.
inner class	Classes that are defined within other classes, much in the same way methods are defined within those classes. Inner classes have the same scope and access as other variables and methods defined within the same class. Their existence can be hidden from view behind the enclosing class.
Inprise	Former name of Borland.
Inspector	Part of the JBuilder UI Designer where properties and events are customized for the component selected within the Structure pane.
instance	An instance of a class; in other words, an object.
instance variable	A variable within a class, a new copy of which is available for storage in each instance of that class. Each object of that class has its own copy of the instance variable, as opposed to a class variable where there is one copy for all instances.
instantiation	The process of creating an object instance of a class.
Integrated Development Environment (IDE)	A program that aids in application development by providing a graphical environment that combines all the tools required to edit, compile, and debug code.
interface	A formal set of method and constant declarations that must be defined by classes that implement it.
interpreter	A utility that reads the commands in a file, and then interprets and executes them one at a time.
introspection	A mechanism that allows classes to publish the operations and properties they support, and a mechanism to support the discovery of such mechanisms.
IP*Works!	A set of networking components that comes with JBuilder.

Term	Meaning
J	
J2EE	Abbreviation for Java 2 Enterprise Edition. Standard set of extension APIs for building enterprise-class applications. Includes EJB, servlets, and JSP, among other things.
J2ME	Abbreviation for Java 2 Micro Edition. Subset of J2SE for developing applications for personal digital assistants (PDAs), cell phones, pagers, and other small-scale devices.
J2SE	Abbreviation for Java 2 Standard Edition. Basic Java. The Java Core APIs. What you get with the Java 2 Software Development Kit (SDK).
JAR	*See* **Java Archive (JAR) file.**
Java Archive (JAR) file	Like a TAR or ZIP file, a file that holds an aggregate of files. These may be signed by their creator to permit greater access to the user.
Java Core API	Java standard class libraries. It contains core language features and functions for such tasks as networking, I/O, and graphics.
Java Database Connectivity (JDBC)	Defines a set of Java classes and methods to interface with relational databases.
Java Development Kit (JDK)	Previous name of the Java Software Development Kit (SDK). *See also* **Software Development Kit.**
Java Foundation Classes (JFC)	*See* **Swing.**
Java Plug-in	A browser add-in that updates the Java Virtual Machine (JVM) used within the browser.
Java Virtual Machine (JVM)	The system that loads, verifies, and executes Java byte codes.
Java Web Start	Sun tool for installing Java programs.
JavaBeans API	An API for the creation of reusable components. A JavaBean component is a single reusable software object.
javadoc	Standard Software Development Kit (SDK) tool that takes documentation comments within source files and generates HTML documentation of the classes.

Term	Meaning
JavaScript	A separate programming language loosely related to Java. JavaScript can be coded directly in HTML documents, to be executed within the Web browser.
JavaServer Pages (JSP)	A Web server–neutral mechanism of embedding Java source and custom tag libraries inside HTML files to create servlets to generate dynamic Web pages.
JBCL	*See* **JBuilder Component Library.**
JBuilder Component Library (JBCL)	A package of graphical components included with JBuilder.
JDataStore	Embedded database server available with JBuilder Professional and Enterprise.
JDBC	*See* **Java Database Connectivity.**
JDK	*See* **Java Development Kit.**
JFC	*See* **Java Foundation Classes.**
JIT compiler	*See* **Just-in-Time (JIT) compiler.**
Joint Photographic Experts Group (JPEG)	A compressed graphics file format. JPEG images may be compressed in a *lossy* fashion, which sacrifices image detail for smaller image size, or in a *lossless* method, where information about the image is retained, but the file size increases accordingly.
JPEG	*See* **Joint Photographic Experts Group.**
JSP	*See* **JavaServer Pages.**
Just-in-Time (JIT) compiler	A compiler that converts verified byte codes to native processor instructions before execution and can significantly improve Java program performance.
JVM	*See* **Java Virtual Machine.**
K	
keyword	A word that has a special meaning to the Java compiler, such as a data type name or a program construct name.

Term	Meaning
L	
`LayoutManager`	A Java class that handles programmed layout styles for the graphical user interface (GUI) components.
life-cycle methods	Applet methods, such as `init()`, that you do not call directly—the browser calls them for you.
literal	An actual value, such as 35, true, or "Hello", as opposed to an identifier, which is a symbol for a value.
`Locale`	The language and country that defines the region for a program's content.
looping statement	A statement for the repeated execution of a block or program statements. These include `for`, `while`, and `do` statements.
M	
megabyte (MB)	A megabyte is 1 million characters of information.
member	The generic term for data or code entities within a class.
member function	*See* **method.**
member variable	A variable that is part of a class.
Menu Designer	The JBuilder interface that allows you to visually create menus.
message	A method call.
method	A function or routine in a class. Also called a *member function.*
multidimensional array	An array of arrays. It can be nonrectangular. A multidimensional array can be initialized by grouping comma-separated expressions within nested curly braces.
multiple inheritance	The ability to write a class that inherits the member variables and methods from more than one class. Java does not support multiple inheritance. *See also* **inheritance.**
multithreading	The means to perform multiple tasks independent of each other.

Term	Meaning
N	
native method	Code that is native to a specific processor. On Windows XP, native methods refer to code written specifically for Intel x86 processors.
Navigation pane	The part of the JBuilder AppBrowser interface that allows you to move through the different parts of the current project or highlighted area.
nesting	The "Russian dolls" effect of repeatedly wrapping or layering entities around other entities. In graphical user interface (GUI) design, components are nested in container components, which themselves are nested in bigger containers, and so on.
null	A value that means *no object*; can be held by any object variable.
O	
object	A reusable software bundle that has characteristics (state) and behavior (methods).
Object Gallery	The area in JBuilder for the wizards to create new objects.
object-oriented programming (OOP)	Programming that focuses on independent objects and their relationships to other objects rather than using a top-down, linear approach (as with traditional Pascal or C).
object pointer	In C++ and Delphi, an object variable that points to a specific memory location.
object variable	A name for an object. It may refer to an object or null.
octet	Another term for half a byte. Used only in the data communications world.
OOP	*See* **object-oriented programming.**
overloaded methods	Methods defined multiple times, with each definition having the same name but accepting different parameters, either in number or type. The compiler determines which method to call based upon the parameters passed in.

Term	Meaning
overridden methods	Methods in subclasses that replace methods in superclasses. They must have the same method *signature*.

P

package	A collection of related classes.
pane	A screen area within JBuilder.
parent class	*See* **superclass.**
persistence	The ability of a Java object to record its state so it can be reproduced in the future, perhaps in another environment.
persistent object stores	Database-independent, object-oriented storage systems for storing various types of objects, such as video, audio, and graphics.
pixel	Display unit on a computer screen.
PNG	*See* **Portable Network Graphics.**
polymorphism	The ability of a single object to operate on many different types.
Portable Network Graphics (PNG)	A compressed graphics file format. Created to avoid the commercial usage claims against the LZH compression patent potentially used within GIF images.
project	A grouping of related files within JBuilder, usually to create a specific application, applet, servlet, or bean.
property	Describes an attribute associated with a component in a graphical user interface (GUI), such as color, size, or the string to be used as a label.

R

RAD	*See* **rapid application development.**
rapid application development (RAD)	A development methodology that enables you to create sophisticated programs quickly.
reader	Similar to an input stream (used in I/O programming), but the basic unit of data is a Unicode character.

Term	Meaning
recursive	Self-calling. A recursive method calls itself repeatedly, either directly or indirectly.
rendering	Computer graphics jargon for drawing. Used as both a verb and a noun.
resource bundle	A way of packaging text when internationalizing programs.
return statement	One of the flow-breaking statements. It's used to return control to the caller from within a method. Before the control is passed back to the caller, all `finally` clauses of enclosing `try` statements are executed, from the innermost `finally` clause to the outermost.
root class	In general, any class that acts as the superclass for a subhierarchy. An entire inheritance hierarchy, such as Java's, has a single absolute root class: `Object`.

S

Term	Meaning
SDK	*See* **Software Development Kit.**
SecurityManager	A Java class that restricts access to files, the network, or other parts of the system for security purposes.
separator	An unselectable line that appears on menus and toolbars for decorative purposes.
serialization	The process whereby an object records itself by writing out the values that describe its state. *Deserialization* is the reverse process of restoring serialized objects.
servlet	A Java program that runs within the context of a Web server.
signature	A method's unique profile, consisting of its name, argument list, and return type. If two methods with the same name have the slightest difference in their argument lists, they're considered totally unrelated as far as the compiler is concerned. *See also* **overloaded methods.**

Term	Meaning
Sitraka	Maker of the third-party JClass graphical user interface (GUI) component set that comes with JBuilder.
Software Development Kit (SDK)	The set of Java development tools distributed (for free) from Sun Microsystems. The SDK consists mainly of the Java Core API classes (including their source), a command-line Java compiler (written in Java), and the Java Virtual Machine (JVM).
source file	A text file containing human-readable instructions. A Java source file is a text file containing instructions written in the Java programming language.
state	An unambiguous, nonoverlapping mode of "being"—for example, the binary states *on* and *off.*
stream	An abstract concept used in the context of I/O programming to represent a linear, sequential flow of bytes of input or output data. A program can read from *input streams* (that is, read the data a stream delivers to it) and write to *output streams* (that is, transfer data to a stream).
streaming	Term used to denote audio, video, and other Internet content that is distributed in real time and doesn't need to be downloaded.
Structure pane	The part of the JBuilder AppBrowser interface that displays the objects of the current application or object. The items shown in the Structure pane change whenever a different object is selected in the Navigation pane.
stub	A method with no body. It satisfies the compiler's need for completeness and lets you add real behavior in a subclass.
subclass	A class that descends or inherits (*extends* in Java terminology) from a given class. Subclasses are more specialized than the classes they inherit from.

Term	Meaning
superclass	A class from which a given class inherits. This can be its immediate parent class or more levels away. Superclasses become more and more generic the further you travel up the inheritance hierarchy and, for this reason, can often be abstract.
Swing	The collection of second generation Java classes that allows you to implement platform-independent graphical user interfaces (GUIs). *See also* **Abstract Window Toolkit.**
switch statement	A multiway selection statement. The integer expression is evaluated, and the first case clause whose constant expression is evaluated to the same value is executed. The optional default clause is executed if there is no case clause matching the value. The break statement is usually used as the last statement of a case clause so the control won't continue on to statements of later case clauses.
system property	An attribute defined automatically for the current Java session. For instance, the location of the Java runtime environment is one of the automatic system properties.
T	
thread	A single flow of control within a program, similar to a process (or running program), but easier to create and destroy than a process because less system resource management is involved. Each thread must have its own resources, such as a program counter and execution stack, as the context for execution. However, all threads in a program share many resources, such as heap memory and opened files.
Threads and Stack pane	Within the JBuilder debugger, the screen area where the threads are displayed with each call stack.
Tomcat	Open source Web server; reference implementation of the latest Servlets and JSP specifications.

Term	Meaning
tool tip	A pop-up box that describes an item's purpose. It appears when the mouse cursor dwells (rests) over an area designated with a defined tip.

U

UI Designer	A drag-and-drop visual design tool within JBuilder.
Unicode	An international character-mapping scheme. See `http://www.unicode.org/` for more information.
Uniform Resource Locator (URL)	A string that identifies the location of a resource on the World Wide Web and the protocol used to access it.
untrusted applet	Applets downloaded from a network whose source hasn't been trusted. By default, all applets are untrusted.
URL	*See* **Uniform Resource Locator.**

V

Virtual Machine	*See* **Java Virtual Machine.**

W

Watch pane	A screen area shown while debugging JBuilder programs. Variables placed within the window are dynamically updated during program execution pauses.
Web browser	A viewer program used by the client machine to display Web documents.
while statement	One of the looping statements. The conditional expression is first evaluated. If it evaluates to true, the loop body is executed, and the conditional expression is re-evaluated. It will cycle through the testing of the conditional expression and the execution of the loop body until the conditional expression evaluates to false.
widgets	From "window gadgets," a generic term for graphical user interface (GUI) components, such as buttons, scrollbars, radio buttons, text input fields, and so on.

Term	Meaning
WORA	*See* **Write Once, Run Anywhere.**
Write Once, Run Anywhere (WORA)	The goal of Java's platform independence.
writer	Similar to an output stream (used in I/O programming), but the basic unit of data is a Unicode character.

X

XML	*See* **Extensible Markup Language.**

Index

Apress Titles

ISBN	PRICE	AUTHOR	TITLE
1-893115-73-9	$34.95	Abbott	Voice Enabling Web Applications: VoiceXML and Beyond
1-893115-01-1	$39.95	Appleman	Dan Appleman's Win32 API Puzzle Book and Tutorial for Visual Basic Programmers
1-893115-23-2	$29.95	Appleman	How Computer Programming Works
1-893115-97-6	$39.95	Appleman	Moving to VB. NET: Strategies, Concepts, and Code
1-893115-09-7	$29.95	Baum	Dave Baum's Definitive Guide to LEGO MINDSTORMS
1-893115-84-4	$29.95	Baum, Gasperi, Hempel, and Villa	Extreme MINDSTORMS: An Advanced Guide to LEGO MINDSTORMS
1-893115-82-8	$59.95	Ben-Gan/Moreau	Advanced Transact-SQL for SQL Server 2000
1-893115-91-7	$39.95	Birmingham/Perry	Software Development on a Leash
1-893115-48-8	$29.95	Bischof	The .NET Languages: A Quick Translation Guide
1-893115-67-4	$49.95	Borge	Managing Enterprise Systems with the Windows Script Host
1-893115-28-3	$44.95	Challa/Laksberg	Essential Guide to Managed Extensions for C++
1-893115-44-5	$29.95	Cook	Robot Building for Beginners
1-893115-99-2	$39.95	Cornell/Morrison	Programming VB .NET: A Guide for Experienced Programmers
1-893115-72-0	$39.95	Curtin	Developing Trust: Online Privacy and Security
1-59059-008-2	$29.95	Duncan	The Career Programmer: Guerilla Tactics for an Imperfect World
1-893115-71-2	$39.95	Ferguson	Mobile .NET
1-893115-90-9	$49.95	Finsel	The Handbook for Reluctant Database Administrators
1-893115-42-9	$44.95	Foo/Lee	XML Programming Using the Microsoft XML Parser
1-893115-55-0	$34.95	Frenz	Visual Basic and Visual Basic .NET for Scientists and Engineers
1-893115-85-2	$34.95	Gilmore	A Programmer's Introduction to PHP 4.0
1-893115-36-4	$34.95	Goodwill	Apache Jakarta-Tomcat
1-893115-17-8	$59.95	Gross	A Programmer's Introduction to Windows DNA
1-893115-62-3	$39.95	Gunnerson	A Programmer's Introduction to C#, Second Edition
1-893115-30-5	$49.95	Harkins/Reid	SQL: Access to SQL Server
1-893115-10-0	$34.95	Holub	Taming Java Threads
1-893115-04-6	$34.95	Hyman/Vaddadi	Mike and Phani's Essential C++ Techniques
1-893115-96-8	$59.95	Jorelid	J2EE FrontEnd Technologies: A Programmer's Guide to Servlets, JavaServer Pages, and Enterprise JavaBeans
1-893115-49-6	$39.95	Kilburn	Palm Programming in Basic
1-893115-50-X	$34.95	Knudsen	Wireless Java: Developing with Java 2, Micro Edition
1-893115-79-8	$49.95	Kofler	Definitive Guide to Excel VBA

ISBN	PRICE	AUTHOR	TITLE
1-893115-57-7	$39.95	Kofler	MySQL
1-893115-87-9	$39.95	Kurata	Doing Web Development: Client-Side Techniques
1-893115-75-5	$44.95	Kurniawan	Internet Programming with VB
1-893115-46-1	$36.95	Lathrop	Linux in Small Business: A Practical User's Guide
1-893115-19-4	$49.95	Macdonald	Serious ADO: Universal Data Access with Visual Basic
1-893115-06-2	$39.95	Marquis/Smith	A Visual Basic 6.0 Programmer's Toolkit
1-893115-22-4	$27.95	McCarter	David McCarter's VB Tips and Techniques
1-893115-76-3	$49.95	Morrison	C++ For VB Programmers
1-893115-80-1	$39.95	Newmarch	A Programmer's Guide to Jini Technology
1-893115-58-5	$49.95	Oellermann	Architecting Web Services
1-893115-81-X	$39.95	Pike	SQL Server: Common Problems, Tested Solutions
1-59059-017-1	$34.95	Rainwater	Herding Cats: A Primer for Programmers Who Lead Programmers
1-893115-20-8	$34.95	Rischpater	Wireless Web Development
1-893115-93-3	$34.95	Rischpater	Wireless Web Development with PHP and WAP
1-893115-89-5	$59.95	Shemitz	Kylix: The Professional Developer's Guide and Reference
1-893115-40-2	$39.95	Sill	The qmail Handbook
1-893115-24-0	$49.95	Sinclair	From Access to SQL Server
1-893115-94-1	$29.95	Spolsky	User Interface Design for Programmers
1-893115-53-4	$44.95	Sweeney	Visual Basic for Testers
1-59059-002-3	$44.95	Symmonds	Internationalization and Localization Using Microsoft .NET
1-893115-29-1	$44.95	Thomsen	Database Programming with Visual Basic .NET
1-893115-65-8	$39.95	Tiffany	Pocket PC Database Development with eMbedded Visual Basic
1-893115-59-3	$59.95	Troelsen	C# and the .NET Platform
1-893115-26-7	$59.95	Troelsen	Visual Basic .NET and the .NET Platform
1-893115-54-2	$49.95	Trueblood/Lovett	Data Mining and Statistical Analysis Using SQL
1-893115-16-X	$49.95	Vaughn	ADO Examples and Best Practices
1-893115-68-2	$49.95	Vaughn	ADO.NET and ADO Examples and Best Practices for VB Programmers, Second Edition
1-893115-83-6	$44.95	Wells	Code Centric: T-SQL Programming with Stored Procedures and Triggers
1-893115-95-X	$49.95	Welschenbach	Cryptography in C and C++
1-893115-05-4	$39.95	Williamson	Writing Cross-Browser Dynamic HTML
1-893115-78-X	$49.95	Zukowski	Definitive Guide to Swing for Java 2, Second Edition
1-893115-92-5	$49.95	Zukowski	Java Collections
1-893115-98-4	$54.95	Zukowski	Learn Java with JBuilder 6

Available at bookstores nationwide or from Springer Verlag New York, Inc. at 1-800-777-4643; fax 1-212-533-3503. Contact us for more information at sales@apress.com.

Apress Titles Publishing SOON!

ISBN	AUTHOR	TITLE
1-59059-023-6	Baker	Acrobat 5: A User Guide for Professionals
1-893115-39-9	Chand	A Programmer's Guide to ADO.NET in C#
1-59059-000-7	Cornell	Programming C#
1-59059-024-4	Fraser	Real World ASP.NET: Building a Content Management System
1-59059-009-0	Harris/Macdonald	Moving to ASP.NET
1-59059-016-3	Hubbard	Windows Forms in C#
1-893115-38-0	Lafler	Power AOL: A Survival Guide
1-59059-003-1	Nakhimovsky/Meyers	XML Programming: Web Applications and Web Services with JSP and ASP
1-893115-27-5	Morrill	Tuning and Customizing a Linux System
1-59059-020-1	Patzer	JavaServer Pages: Examples and Best Practices
1-59059-025-2	Rammer	Advanced .NET Remoting
1-893115-43-7	Stephenson	Standard VB: An Enterprise Developer's Reference for VB 6 and VB .NET
1-59059-007-4	Thomsen	Building Web Services with VB .NET
1-59059-010-4	Thomsen	Database Programming with C#
1-59059-011-2	Troelsen	COM and .NET Interoperability
1-59059-004-X	Valiaveedu	SQL Server 2000 and Business Intelligence in an XML/.NET World
1-59059-012-0	Vaughn/Blackburn	ADO.NET Examples and Best Practices for C# Programmers

Available at bookstores nationwide or from Springer Verlag New York, Inc. at 1-800-777-4643; fax 1-212-533-3503. Contact us for more information at sales@apress.com.

books for professionals by professionals™

apress™

About Apress

Apress, located in Berkeley, CA, is a fast-growing, innovative publishing company devoted to meeting the needs of existing and potential programming professionals. Simply put, the "A" in Apress stands for *"The Author's Press*™*"* and its books have *"The Expert's Voice*™*".* Apress' unique approach to publishing grew out of conversations between its founders Gary Cornell and Dan Appleman, authors of numerous best-selling, highly regarded books for programming professionals. In 1998 they set out to create a publishing company that emphasized quality above all else. Gary and Dan's vision has resulted in the publication of over 50 titles by leading software professionals, all of which have *The Expert's Voice*™.

Do You Have What It Takes to Write for Apress?

Apress is rapidly expanding its publishing program. If you can write and refuse to compromise on the quality of your work, if you believe in doing more than rehashing existing documentation, and if you're looking for opportunities and rewards that go far beyond those offered by traditional publishing houses, we want to hear from you!

Consider these innovations that we offer all of our authors:

- **Top royalties with *no* hidden switch statements**
  Authors typically only receive half of their normal royalty rate on foreign sales. In contrast, Apress' royalty rate remains the same for both foreign and domestic sales.

- **A mechanism for authors to obtain equity in Apress**
  Unlike the software industry, where stock options are essential to motivate and retain software professionals, the publishing industry has adhered to an outdated compensation model based on royalties alone. In the spirit of most software companies, Apress reserves a significant portion of its equity for authors.

- **Serious treatment of the technical review process**
  Each Apress book has a technical reviewing team whose remuneration depends in part on the success of the book since they too receive royalties.

Moreover, through a partnership with Springer-Verlag, New York, Inc., one of the world's major publishing houses, Apress has significant venture capital behind it. Thus, we have the resources to produce the highest quality books *and* market them aggressively.

If you fit the model of the Apress author who can write a book that gives the "professional what he or she needs to know™," then please contact one of our Editorial Directors, Gary Cornell (gary_cornell@apress.com), Dan Appleman (dan_appleman@apress.com), Peter Blackburn (peter_blackburn@apress.com), Jason Gilmore (jason_gilmore@apress.com), Karen Watterson (karen_watterson@apress.com), or John Zukowski (john_zukowski@apress.com) for more information.

Apress™

To activate JBuilder 6 Enterprise trial read Chapter 1 and/or visit
`http://www.borland.com/jbuilder/keys/jb6_ent_steps.html`.

License Agreement (Single-User Products)

THIS IS A LEGAL AGREEMENT BETWEEN YOU, THE END USER, AND APRESS. BY OPENING THE SEALED DISK PACKAGE, YOU ARE AGREEING TO BE BOUND BY THE TERMS OF THIS AGREEMENT. IF YOU DO NOT AGREE TO THE TERMS OF THIS AGREEMENT, PROMPTLY RETURN THE UNOPENED DISK PACKAGE AND THE ACCOMPANYING ITEMS (INCLUDING WRITTEN MATERIALS AND BINDERS AND OTHER CONTAINERS) TO THE PLACE YOU OBTAINED THEM FOR A FULL REFUND.

APRESS SOFTWARE LICENSE

1. GRANT OF LICENSE. Apress grants you the right to use one copy of this enclosed Apress software program (the "SOFTWARE") on a single terminal connected to a single computer (e.g., with a single CPU). You may not network the SOFTWARE or otherwise use it on more than one computer or computer terminal at the same time.
2. COPYRIGHT. The SOFTWARE copyright is owned by Apress and is protected by United States copyright laws and international treaty provisions. Therefore, you must treat the SOFTWARE like any other copyrighted material (e.g., a book or musical recording) except that you may either (a) make one copy of the SOFTWARE solely for backup or archival purposes, or (b) transfer the SOFTWARE to a single hard disk, provided you keep the original solely for backup or archival purposes. You may not copy the written material accompanying the SOFTWARE.
3. OTHER RESTRICTIONS. You may not rent or lease the SOFTWARE, but you may transfer the SOFTWARE and accompanying written materials on a permanent basis provided you retain no copies and the recipient agrees to the terms of this Agreement. You may not reverse engineer, decompile, or disassemble the SOFTWARE. If SOFTWARE is an update, any transfer must include the update and all prior versions.
4. By breaking the seal on the disc package, you agree to the terms and conditions printed in the Apress License Agreement. If you do not agree with the terms, simply return this book with the still-sealed CD package to the place of purchase for a refund.

DISCLAIMER OF WARRANTY

NO WARRANTIES. Apress disclaims all warranties, either express or implied, including, but not limited to, implied warranties of merchantability and fitness for a particular purpose, with respect to the SOFTWARE and the accompanying written materials. The software and any related documentation is provided "as is." You may have other rights, which vary from state to state.

NO LIABILITIES FOR CONSEQUENTIAL DAMAGES. In no event shall be liable for any damages whatsoever (including, without limitation, damages from loss of business profits, business interruption, loss of business information, or other pecuniary loss) arising out of the use or inability to use this Apress product, even if Apress has been advised of the possibility of such damages. Because some states do not allow the exclusion or limitation of liability for consequential or incidental damages, the above limitation may not apply to you.

U.S. GOVERNMENT RESTRICTED RIGHTS

The SOFTWARE and documentation are provided with RESTRICTED RIGHTS. Use, duplication, or disclosure by the Government is subject to restriction as set forth in subparagraph (c) (1) (ii) of The Rights in Technical Data and Computer Software clause at 52.227-7013. Contractor/manufacturer is Apress, 901 Grayson Street, Suite 204, Berkeley, California, 94710.

This Agreement is governed by the laws of the State of California.

Should you have any questions concerning this Agreement, or if you wish to contact Apress for any reason, please write to Apress, 901 Grayson Street, Suite 204, Berkeley, California, 94710.